Conflicting Interests

Conflicting Interests

Interests

Readings in Social Problems and Inequality

ROBERT HEINER
Plymouth State University

New York   Oxford

OXFORD UNIVERSITY PRESS

2010

Oxford University Press, Inc., publishes works that further Oxford University's
objective of excellence in research, scholarship, and education.

Oxford   New York
Auckland   Cape Town   Dar es Salaam   Hong Kong   Karachi
Kuala Lumpur   Madrid   Melbourne   Mexico City   Nairobi
New Delhi   Shanghai   Taipei   Toronto

With offices in
Argentina   Austria   Brazil   Chile   Czech Republic   France   Greece
Guatemala   Hungary   Italy   Japan   Poland   Portugal   Singapore
South Korea   Switzerland   Thailand   Turkey   Ukraine   Vietnam

Published by Oxford University Press, Inc.
198 Madison Avenue, New York, New York 10016
http://www.oup.com

Library of Congress Cataloging-in-Publication Data

Heiner, Robert, 1956–
Conflicting interests : readings in social problems and inequality / Robert Heiner.
    p. cm.
Includes bibliographical references.
ISBN 978-0-19-537507-7 (alk. paper)
1. Social problems.   2. Equality.   I. Title.
HN17.5.H412   2009
361—dc22   2009015585

Printing number: 9 8 7 6 5 4 3 2

Printed in the United States of America
on acid-free paper

For Aunt Edith
who decided to become the best and became the best

CONTENTS

PREFACE

It is spring 2009 as this book goes into production. A main theme through-out most of my work over the past decade is that corporations have far too much influence over the workings of government; that the welfare of the lower, working, and middle classes are in jeopardy because of this influence; and that this influence subverts our democracy. Now we are in the midst of an economic "slump"/"downturn"/"crisis." Nobody knows how bad it is going to get: The most optimistic estimates suggest the worst will soon be over; the least say we are headed for the likes of the Great Depression. More and more people are recognizing the influence of corporate greed, but it is hard to say what will come—policy-wise—from this recognition. Most agree that the crisis was brought about by the gov-ernment's failure to regulate financial corporations. Few would be surprised by the amounts of corporate money spent on lobbying government officials and financing their campaigns; but, as this book goes to press, lobbying and cam-paign finance are rarely the subject of the public's or the pundits' ire over the state of the economy.

This volume, in a sense, is a history book. Most of the articles selected were written a few years ago. When I selected them, they had a certain relevance to ongoing events. When the book comes out, when you read it, they will have a different relevance—depending on how deep the current recession goes and how long it lasts, depending on how involved government intervention becomes, depending on the success of conservative and corporate resistance to ongoing efforts to remedy the problem, depending on changes in the financing and deliv-ery of health care services, depending on so many changes—relevant to the selec-tions in this book—that could or could not take place.

One is reminded of the ancient Chinese curse: "May you live in interesting times." Perhaps the curse is so enduring because nothing can be so "interesting" as that which puts our "interests" in such peril. Hopefully, when you read this, the times won't be quite so interesting and some of the problems addressed in this book will have been moderated by public policy. The prevalence of powerful interests holding sway over the political process, however, has been an enduring influence for millennia, and I doubt much will have changed in that regard. Inequality, of course, gives rise to this imbalance of power, and more inequalities are the result. We should note, though, that inequality can also be the cause of sweeping social change. That too could affect the historical relevance of the selections in this book.

I wish to thank Sherith Pankratz, my editor at Oxford University Press, for encouraging me to put this book together. My thanks go also to Whitney Laemmli, Marianne Paul and all the others at OUP who helped me with this project. I wish also to thank the people who have commented on this book while in its earlier stages. They include Nicole J. Grant, Northern Kentucky University; Herbert Ziegler, Chesapeake College; Bryan K. Robinson, University at Albany; Scott Schaffer, University of Western Ontario; Stuart Shafer, Johnson County Community College; G. William Domhoff, University of California—Santa Cruz; Margarethe Kusenbach, University of South Florida—Tampa; Mindy Stombler, Georgia State University. Their suggestions proved very useful. And my special thanks to all of those here in central New Hampshire that have made my life a lot better or a little easier. That list would be too long for a preface I want to keep brief, but at the top of the list go my family and friends.

Conflicting Interests

PART I

Thinking about Social Problems

Social problems are phenomena that concern many, and sometimes most, people in a society. The perspectives employed by the public to make sense of social problems and those employed by sociologists are considerably different. The first three articles in this part try to elucidate some of those differences. These articles by no means represent all sociological perspectives, but what they have in common with all sociological perspectives is that they are, or try to be, more systematic, more circumspect, more theoretical, and more thorough in their examination of social problems than the lay public.

The first selection is a classic by C. Wright Mills in which he identifies the "sociological imagination" as the principle difference between the public and the sociological view of social problems. This "imagination," he argues, is an ability to see our personal experiences within the broader contexts of society and history. Mills does not argue in an elitist way that sociologists have this ability and the average person does not but, rather, that sociologists—especially the great sociologists—have refined this ability and that all of our lives would be enriched by developing this ability. In this context, Mills also introduces the concepts of "private troubles" and "public issues." The distinction between the two has since been the focus of considerable attention in the sociology of social problems. More specifically, it is the transformation of private troubles into public issues that bring a social problem into being. It is the public awareness of the phenomenon, according to many sociologists, that is the defining feature of a social problem.

The next article by Spector and Kitsuse focuses on the activities involved in bringing about this transformation. They, in fact, go so far as to define a social problem solely in terms of those activities. In so doing, they are able to avoid much of the bias that is inherent in most lay perceptions of social problems and direct our attention to the claims-making activities, strategies, and contingencies that contribute to the transformation of private troubles into public issues.

The third article introduces the critical constructionist perspective, which, like the previous article, focuses on the process of problem construction. With

its roots in conflict theory, critical constructionism emphasizes that the transformation of private troubles into public issues is a political process and that the
imbalance of power between the parties involved has a substantial influence over
which troubles are successfully transformed into problems and which are not.
Accordingly, this perspective directs our attention to the conflicting interests
of different groups and the resources these groups have at their disposal that
can influence the public's perceptions of social problems. From this perspective,
social problems and social inequality are inextricably linked.

One very important resource in influencing public perceptions is, of course,
the media, and the fourth selection focuses on the political economy of the media.
In keeping with the sociological imagination, McChesney demonstrates how the
history of the American news media got us to where we are today and how the
concentration of media ownership in fewer and fewer hands and the commercial imperatives of management affect the information that is delivered to us by
the media. McChesney argues that ostensible "balance" in news reporting is not
about providing us with unbiased, objective information, but about alienating
the fewest numbers in the audience so that more advertising can be sold. The
appearance of neutrality is maintained by adhering to the following conventions:
allowing political officials and the business elite to set the news agenda, avoiding
the contextualization of issues, and a pro-corporate bias that favors "digging here
and not there," exposing flaws in the political system, but not in the economic
system. Had it not been for these tendencies, serious flaws in the country's financial system might have been revealed *before* the most recent economic crisis. The
commercial imperative that drives the media to rely on these conventions and
facilitates journalism's masquerading as "balanced" is threatening to our democracy in that the people require sound information to make sound judgments.
A media system that is not so commercially driven would likely expose different
sets of social problems to the public and might even direct our attention to the
role inequality plays in engendering these problems.

CHAPTER 1

The Sociological Imagination: The Promise

C. Wright Mills

Nowadays, men often feel that their private lives are a series of traps. They sense that, within their everyday worlds, they cannot overcome their troubles, and in this feeling, they are often quite correct: What ordinary men are directly aware of and what they try to do are bounded by the private orbits in which they live; their visions and their powers are limited to the close-up scenes of job, family, neighborhood; in other milieux, they move vicariously and remain spectators. And the more aware they become, however vaguely, of ambitions and of threats that transcend their immediate locales, the more trapped they seem to feel.

Underlying this sense of being trapped are seemingly impersonal changes in the very structure of continent-wide societies. The facts of contemporary history are also facts about the success and the failure of individual men and women. When a society is industrialized, a peasant becomes a worker; a feudal lord is liquidated or becomes a businessman. When classes rise or fall, a man is employed or unemployed; when the rate of investment goes up or down, a man takes new heart or goes broke. When wars happen, an insurance salesman becomes a rocket launcher; a store clerk, a radar man; a wife lives alone; a child grows up without a father. Neither the life of an individual nor the history of a society can be understood without understanding both.

Yet, men do not usually define the troubles they endure in terms of historical change and institutional contradiction. The well-being they enjoy, they do not usually impute to the big ups and downs of the societies in which they live. Seldom aware of the intricate connection between the patterns of their own lives and the course of world history, ordinary men do not usually know what this connection means for the kinds of men they are becoming and for the kinds of history-making in which they might take part. They do not possess the quality of mind essential to grasp the interplay of man and society, of biography and history, of self and world. They cannot cope with their personal troubles in such ways as to control the structural transformations that usually lie behind them.

Surely, it is no wonder. In what period have so many men been so totally exposed at so fast a pace to such earthquakes of change? That Americans have not known such catastrophic changes as have the men and women of other societies is due to historical facts that are now quickly becoming "merely history." The history that now affects every man is world history. Within this scene and this period, in the course of a single generation, one-sixth of mankind is transformed from all that is feudal and backward into all that is modern, advanced, and fearful. Political colonies are freed; new and less visible forms of imperialism, installed. Revolutions occur, men feel the intimate grip of new kinds of authority. Totalitarian societies rise, and are smashed to bits—or succeed fabulously. After two centuries of ascendancy, capitalism is shown up as only one way to make society into an industrial apparatus. After two centuries of hope, even formal democracy is restricted to a quite small portion of mankind. Everywhere in the underdeveloped world, ancient ways of life are broken up and vague expectations become urgent demands. Everywhere in the overdeveloped world, the means of authority and of violence become total in scope and bureaucratic in form. Humanity itself now lies before us, the supernation at either pole concentrating its most coordinated and massive efforts upon the preparation of World War III.

The very shaping of history now outpaces the ability of men to orient themselves in accordance with cherished values. And which values? Even when they do not panic, men often sense that older ways of feeling and thinking have collapsed, and that newer beginnings are ambiguous to the point of moral stasis. Is it any wonder that ordinary men feel they cannot cope with the larger worlds with which they are so suddenly confronted? That they cannot understand the meaning of their epoch for their own lives? That—in defense of selfhood—they become morally insensible, trying to remain altogether private men? Is it any wonder that they come to be possessed by a sense of the trap?

It is not only information that they need—in this Age of Fact, information often dominates their attention and overwhelms their capacities to assimilate it. It is not only the skills of reason that they need—although their struggles to acquire these often exhaust their limited moral energy.

What they need, and what they feel they need, is a quality of mind that will help them to use information and to develop reason in order to achieve lucid summations of what is going on in the world and of what may be happening within themselves. It is this quality, I am going to contend, that journalists and scholars, artists and publics, scientists and editors are coming to expect of what may be called the sociological imagination.

The sociological imagination enables its possessor to understand the larger historical scene in terms of its meaning for the inner life and the external career of a variety of individuals. It enables him to take into account how individuals, in the welter of their daily experience, often become falsely conscious of their social positions. Within that welter, the framework of modern society is sought, and within that framework the psychologies of a variety of men and women are formulated. By such means, the personal uneasiness of individuals is focused upon explicit troubles, and the indifference of publics is transformed into involvement with public issues.

The first fruit of this imagination—and the first lesson of the social science that embodies it—is the idea that the individual can understand his own experience and gauge his own fate only by locating himself within his period, that he can know his own chances in life only by becoming aware of those of all individuals in his circumstances. In many ways, it is a terrible lesson; in many ways, a magnificent one. We do not know the limits of man's capacities for supreme effort or willing degradation, for agony or glee, for pleasurable brutality or the sweetness of reason. But in our time we have come to know that the limits of "human nature" are frighteningly broad. We have come to know that every individual lives, from one generation to the next, in some society; that he lives out a biography, and that he lives it out within some historical sequence. By the fact of his living he contributes, however minutely, to the shaping of this society and to the course of its history, even as he is made by society and by its historical push and shove.

The sociological imagination enables us to grasp history and biography and the relations between the two within society. That is its task and its promise. To recognize this task and this promise is the mark of the classic social analyst. It is characteristic of Herbert Spencer—turgid, polysyllabic, comprehensive; of E. A. Ross—graceful, muckraking, upright; of Auguste Comte and Emile Durkheim; of the intricate and subtle Karl Mannheim. It is the quality of all that is intellectually excellent in Karl Marx; it is the clue to Thorstein Veblen's brilliant and ironic insight, to Joseph Schumpeter's many-sided constructions of reality; it is the basis of the psychological sweep of W. E. H. Lecky no less than of the profundity and clarity of Max Weber. And it is the signal of what is best in contemporary studies of man and society.

No social study that does not come back to the problems of biography, of history, and of their intersections within a society has completed its intellectual journey. Whatever the specific problems of the classic social analysts, however limited or however broad the features of social reality they have examined, those who have been imaginatively aware of the promise of their work have consistently asked three sorts of questions:

1. What is the structure of this particular society as a whole? What are its essential components, and how are they related to one another? How does it differ from other varieties of social order? Within it, what is the meaning of any particular feature for its continuance and for its change?
2. Where does the society stand in human history? What are the mechanics by which it is changing? What is its place within, and its meaning for, the development of humanity as a whole? How does any particular feature we are examining affect, and how is it affected by, the historical period in which it moves? And this period—what are its essential features?

How does it differ from other periods? What are its characteristic ways of history-making?

3. What varieties of men and women now prevail in this society and in this period? And what varieties are coming to prevail? In what ways are they selected and formed, liberated and repressed, made sensitive and blunted? What kinds of "human nature" are revealed in the conduct and character we observe in this society in this period? And what is the meaning for "human nature" of each and every feature of the society we are examining?

Whether the point of interest is a great power or a minor literary mood, a family, a prison, a creed—these are the kinds of questions the best social analysts have asked. They are the intellectual pivots of classic studies of man in society—and they are the questions inevitably raised by any mind possessing the sociological imagination. For that imagination is the capacity to shift from one perspective to another—from the political to the psychological; from examination of a single family to comparative assessment of the national budgets of the world; from the theological school to the military establishment; from considerations of an oil industry to studies of contemporary poetry. It is the capacity to range from the most impersonal and remote transformations to the most intimate features of the human self—and to see the relations between the two. Back of its use, there is always the urge to know the social and historical meaning of the individual in the society and in the period in which he has his quality and his being.

That, in brief, is why it is by means of the sociological imagination that men now hope to grasp what is going on in the world, and to understand what is happening in themselves as minute points of the intersections of biography and history within society. In large part, contemporary man's self-conscious view of himself as at least an outsider, if not a permanent stranger, rests upon an absorbed realization of social relativity and of the transformative power of history. The sociological imagination is the most fruitful form of this self-consciousness. By its use, men whose mentalities have swept only a series of limited orbits often come to feel as if suddenly awakened in a house with which they had only supposed themselves to be familiar. Correctly or incorrectly, they often come to feel that they can now provide themselves with adequate summations, cohesive assessments, comprehensive orientations. Older decisions that once appeared sound now seem to them products of a mind unaccountably dense. Their capacity for astonishment is made lively again. They acquire a new way of thinking, they experience a transvaluation of values: In a word, by their reflection and their sensibility, they realize the cultural meaning of the social sciences.

Perhaps the most fruitful distinction with which the sociological imagination works is between the "personal troubles of milieu" and the "public issues of social structure." This distinction is an essential tool of the sociological imagination and a feature of all classic work in social science.

Troubles occur within the character of the individual and within the range of his immediate relations with others: They have to do with his self and with those limited areas of social life of which he is directly and personally aware. Accordingly, the statement and the resolution of troubles properly lie within the individual as a biographical entity and within the scope of his immediate milieu—the social setting that is directly open to his personal experience and, to some extent, his willful activity. A trouble is a private matter: Values cherished by an individual are felt by him to be threatened.

Issues have to do with matters that transcend these local environments of the individual and the range of his inner life. They have to do with the organization of many such milieux into the institutions of a historical society as a whole, with the ways in which various milieux overlap and interpenetrate to form the larger structure of social and historical life. An issue is a public matter: Some value cherished by publics is felt to be threatened. Often, there is a debate about what that value really is and about what it is that really threatens it. This debate is often without focus, if only because it is the very nature of an issue, unlike even widespread trouble, that it cannot very well be defined in terms of the immediate and everyday environments of ordinary men. An issue, in fact, often involves a crisis in institutional arrangements, and often, too, it involves what Marxists call "contradictions" or "antagonisms."

In these terms, consider unemployment. When, in a city of 100,000, only one man is unemployed, that is his personal trouble, and for its relief we properly look to the character of the man, his skills, and his immediate opportunities. But when, in a nation of 50 million employees, 15 million men are unemployed, that is an issue, and we may not hope to find its solution within the range of opportunities open to any one individual. The very structure of opportunities has collapsed. Both the correct statement of the problem and the range of possible solutions require us to consider the economic and political institutions of the society, and not merely the personal situation and character of a scatter of individuals.

Consider war. The personal problem of war, when it occurs, may be how to survive it or how to die in it with honor; how to make money out of it; how to climb into the higher safety of the military apparatus; or how to contribute to the war's termination. In short, according to one's values, to find a set of milieux and within it to survive the war or make one's death in it meaningful. But the structural issues of war have to do with its causes; with what types of men it throws up into command; with its effects upon economic and political, family and religious institutions, with the unorganized irresponsibility of a world of nation-states.

Consider marriage. Inside a marriage, a man and a woman may experience personal troubles; but, when the divorce rate during the first four years of marriage is 250 out of every 1,000 attempts, this is an indication of a structural issue having to do with the institutions of marriage and the family and other institutions that bear upon them.

Or consider the metropolis—the horrible, beautiful, ugly, magnificent sprawl of the great city. For many upper-class people, the personal solution to the problem of the city is to have an apartment with private garage under it in the heart of the city, and, forty miles out, a house by Henry Hill, garden by Garrett Eckbo, on a hundred acres of private land. In these two controlled environments—with a small staff at each end and a private helicopter connection—most people could solve many of the problems of personal milieux caused by the facts of the city. But all this, however splendid, does not solve the public issues that the structural fact of the city poses. What should be done with this wonderful monstrosity? Break it all up into scattered units, combining residence and work? Refurbish it as it stands? Or, after evacuation, dynamite it and build new cities according to new plans in new places? What should those plans be? And who is to decide and to accomplish whatever choice is made? These are structural issues; to confront them and to solve them requires us to consider political and economic issues that affect innumerable milieux.

Insofar as the economy is so arranged that slumps occur, the problem of unemployment becomes incapable of personal solution. Insofar as war is inherent in the nation-state system and in the uneven industrialization of the world, the ordinary individual in his restricted milieu will be powerless—with or without psychiatric aid—to solve the troubles this system or lack of system imposes upon him. Insofar as the family as an institution turns women into darling little slaves and men into their chief providers and unweaned dependents, the problem of a satisfactory marriage remains incapable of purely private solution. Insofar as the overdeveloped megalopolis and the overdeveloped automobile are built-in features of the overdeveloped society, the issues of urban living will not be solved by personal ingenuity and private wealth.

What we experience in various and specific milieux, I have noted, is often caused by structural changes. Accordingly, to understand the changes of many personal milieux, we are required to look beyond them. And the number and variety of such structural changes increase as the institutions within which we live become more embracing and more intricately connected with one another. To be aware of the idea of social structure and to use it with sensibility is to be capable of tracing such linkages among a great variety of milieux. To be able to do that is to possess the sociological imagination.

What are the major issues for publics and the key troubles of private individuals in our time? To formulate issues and troubles, we must ask what values are cherished yet threatened, and what values are cherished and supported, by the characterizing trends of our period. In the case both of threat and of support, we must ask what salient contradictions of structure may be involved.

When people cherish some set of values and do not feel any threat to them, they experience *well-being*. When they cherish values but do feel them to be threatened, they experience a crisis—either as a personal trouble or as a public issue. And, if all their values seem involved, they feel the total threat of panic.

But suppose people are neither aware of any cherished values nor experience any threat? That is the experience of *indifference*, which, if it seems to involve all their values, becomes apathy. Suppose, finally, they are unaware of any cherished values, but still are very much aware of threat? That is the experience of *uneasiness*, of anxiety, which, if it is total enough, becomes a deadly, unspecified malaise.

Ours is a time of uneasiness and indifference—not yet formulated in such ways as to permit the work of reason and the play of sensibility. Instead of troubles—defined in terms of values and threats—there is often the misery of vague uneasiness; instead of explicit issues, there is often merely the beat feeling that all is somehow not right. Neither the values threatened nor whatever threatens them has been stated; in short, they have not been carried to the point of decision. Much less have they been formulated as problems of social science.

In the 1930s, there was little doubt—except among certain deluded business circles—that there was an economic issue that was also a pack of personal troubles. In these arguments about the "crisis of capitalism," the formulations of Marx and the many acknowledged reformulations of his work probably set the leading terms of the issue, and some men came to understand their personal troubles in these terms. The values threatened were plain to see and cherished by all; the structural contradictions that threatened them also seemed plain. Both were widely and deeply experienced. It was a political age.

But the values threatened in the era after World War II are often neither widely acknowledged as values nor widely felt to be threatened. Much private uneasiness goes unformulated; much public malaise and many decisions of enormous structural relevance never become public issues. For those who accept such inherited values as reason and freedom, it is the uneasiness itself that is the trouble; it is the indifference itself that is the issue. And it is this condition, of uneasiness and indifference, that is the signal feature of our period.

All this is so striking that it is often interpreted by observers as a shift in the very kinds of problems that need now to be formulated. We are frequently told that the problems of our decade, or even the crises of our period, have shifted from the external realm of economics and now have to do with the quality of individual life—in fact, with the question of whether there is soon going to be anything that can properly be called individual life. Not child labor but comic books, not poverty but mass leisure, are at the center of concern. Many great public issues as well as many private troubles are described in terms of the "the psychiatric"—often, it seems, in a pathetic attempt to avoid the large issues and problems of modern society. Often, this statement seems to rest upon a provincial narrowing of interest to the Western societies, or even to the United States—thus ignoring two-thirds of mankind; often, too, it arbitrarily divorces the individual life from the larger institutions within which that life is enacted, and which on occasion bear upon it more grievously than do the intimate environments of childhood.

Problems of leisure, for example, cannot even be stated without considering problems of work. Family troubles over comic books cannot be formulated as problems without considering the plight of the contemporary family in its new relations with the newer institutions of the social structure. Neither leisure nor its debilitating uses can be understood as problems without recognition of the extent to which malaise and indifference now form the social and personal climate of contemporary American society. In this climate, no problems of the "private life" can be stated and solved without recognition of the crisis of ambition that is part of the very career of men at work in the incorporated economy.

It is true, as psychoanalysts continually point out, that people do often have the "increasing sense of being moved by obscure forces within themselves that they are unable to define." But it is *not* true, as Ernest Jones asserted, that "man's chief enemy and danger is his own unruly nature and the dark forces pent up within him." On the contrary: "Man's chief danger" today lies in the unruly forces of contemporary society itself, with its alienating methods of production, its enveloping techniques of political domination, its international anarchy—in a word, its pervasive transformations of the very "nature" of man and the conditions and aims of his life.

It is now the scientist's foremost political and intellectual task—for here the two coincide—to make clear the elements of contemporary uneasiness and indifference. It is the central demand made upon him by other cultural workmen—by physical scientists and artists, by the intellectual community in general. It is because of this task and these demands, I believe, that the social sciences are becoming the common denominator of our cultural period, and the sociological imagination, our most needed quality of mind.

CRITICAL THINKING QUESTIONS

Mills argues that someone who understands his or her personal experience within its social and historical context possesses the sociological imagination and is better off than the person who does not. Who do you think is better off—someone who has just been laid off from his job who possesses the sociological imagination or someone recently laid off who does *not* possess the sociological imagination? Why?

This reading was first published in 1959. What social problems is Mills most concerned about? Would these be considered social problems today, or have they been replaced by other concerns?

CHAPTER 2

Constructing Social Problems

Malcolm Spector and John I. Kitsuse

SOCIAL PROBLEMS AS ACTIVITIES

Fuller and Myers defined a social problem as "a condition which is defined by a considerable number of persons as a deviation from some norm, which they cherish" (1941b:320). We have discussed the methodological problems inherent in referring to numbers of people in the definition of social problems. How many people? What must they do in order for the sociologist to place the condition in the social problems category and begin the analysis? These questions are insoluble. If we remove the reference to numbers of people, what do we have left? What kinds of conditions are social problems?

Our view is that any definition of social problems that begins "social problems are those conditions..." will lead to a conceptual and methodological impasse that will frustrate attempts to build a specialized area of study. The question, then, is: if social problems cannot be conditions, what are they? Most succinctly, they are the activities of those who assert the existence of conditions and define them as problems.

It is helpful in developing a model for defining the subject matter for the study of social problems to refer to the study of occupations. This model is profitable for several reasons. The study of work and occupations is an area that is not beset with the terminological and definitional dilemmas that characterize the field of social problems. If we learn how that field manages to avoid these issues, perhaps we can construct a similar definition to structure the study of social problems.

While diverse theoretical views are represented in the study of occupations, the underlying sociological theory that guides our approach to social problems has also guided a major orientation of research on occupations, symbolic interactionism. The interactionist view in the sociology of occupations is evident in the writings of Hughes (1971) and his followers. This body of literature may provide us with theoretical analogues for our study of social problems. The study

11

of work and occupations is relevant in another way: social problems activities are the *work* of many people—journalists, doctors, politicians, social workers, consumer advocates, and union organizers. Many aspects of social problems may be approached through the study of the people who work in various stages of the process of creating social problems.

Our inquiry stands to profit from a convergence, or at least a compatibility, with the study of work and occupations which focuses on the activities by which men and women earn their livelihood. Whenever and wherever people are engaged in such activity, they provide the subject matter for the sociology of work. It does not matter whether only a few or a great many people are engaged in that activity. Conceptually, they are considered participants in the category "work." If very few practice the activity, we might observe, interview, and study them all. If a great number engage in the activity, we must find some means of drawing a sample. Even if only one person earns her livelihood at an activity, it is still possible to make it the subject of an occupational study—describing the activity, how she came to do the work, with whom she associates in performing her tasks, how her activities are affected by the presence or absence of co-workers or colleagues, and so on.

We want to define the subject matter of the sociology of social problems so that a researcher may carry through the analysis with the same reasonable procedure as the student of work and occupations. Just as the study of occupations examines how people earn their living, the study of social problems must look at how people define social problems. If a sociologist of occupations studying prostitution would look for people earning their livings at it, the sociologist of social problems would look for people engaged in defining (or promoting) the prostitution problem. The student of occupations sets out to describe work activity, elaborating its various forms and organization, and inventing concepts to make sense of and explain its variations. In the same way, the student of social problems should discover the nature of social problem activities and develop concepts that will most clearly and succinctly account for their special character. In each case, a distinctive kind of activity is singled out for attention: in the former case, the technical term for the activity is *work*. In the latter case, we must propose, define, and elaborate the technical term which we call claims-making activity.

A DEFINITION OF SOCIAL PROBLEMS

Our definition of social problems focuses on the process by which members of a society define a putative condition as a social problem. Thus, we define social problems as *the activities of individuals or groups making assertions of grievances and claims with respect to some putative conditions.* The emergence of a social problem is contingent upon the organization of activities asserting the need for eradicating, ameliorating, or otherwise changing some condition. *The central problem for a theory of social problems is to account for the emergence, nature, and maintenance of claims-making and responding activities.* Such a theory should address the activities of any group making claims on others for ameliorative action, material remuneration, or alleviation of social, political, legal, or economic disadvantage.

Let us comment briefly on the word *putative* in the above definition. The dictionary defines this word as "reputed, hypothesized, or inferred." We use the word to emphasize that any given claim or complaint is about a condition *alleged* to exist, rather than about a condition whose existence we, as sociologists, are willing to verify or certify. That is, in focusing attention on the claims-making process, we set aside the question of whether those claims are true or false.

In an analysis of the logic of this position in the related area of the sociology of deviance, Rains states:

> Like the term "alleged," "putative" is intentionally, even ostentatiously, careful talk, allowing one to speak of something without commitment to its actuality. As a way of handling the problem of how to speak about what "reactions to deviance" are reactions to, words like "putative" have similarly, if more pertinently served to beg the question. The phrase "reactions that impute mental illness" does not, after all, require mental illness in the same way that the phrase "reactions to mental illness" does. But just as "putative father" is an ambiguous term that may express several possible degrees of belief in a girl's claim, "putative deviation" permits a variety of not necessarily explicit theoretical stances toward the relationship between deviance and the societal reactions which impute it. (1975:3)

We are interested in constructing a theory of claims-making activities, not a theory of conditions. Thus, the significance of objective conditions for us is *the assertions made about them,* not the validity of those assertions as judged from some independent standpoint, as for example, that of a scientist. To guard against the tendency to slip back into an analysis of the condition, we assert that even the existence of the condition itself is irrelevant to and outside of our analysis. We are not concerned whether or not the imputed condition exists. If the alleged condition were a complete hoax—a fabrication—we would maintain a noncommittal stance toward it unless those to whom the claim were addressed initiated their own analysis and uncovered it as a hoax.

Having stated the matter in the most extreme, and seemingly unreasonable, fashion, let us try to make it appear more sensible. Some objection to this position may stem from the fact that certain conditions do exist in the real world—out there. Objections may also be based on the view that some putative conditions appear to be just the phenomena that sociologists are trained to discover and verify. Let us discuss the second point first.

Suppose the following claims are made by three different groups:

1. The admission policy of Paramount University Medical School systematically discriminates against female and minority applicants; thus it violates affirmative action guidelines.

2. The water in Brown River is polluted and constitutes an acute health hazard for the city's residents.

3. Interplanetary beings have landed and established bases in the remote mountain areas of Wyoming. They are preparing a massive strike against the United States.

A sociologist might feel competent to make a direct assessment of the validity of the first group's assertion, refer the second to a natural scientist, and assert that the claims of the third group are groundless, perhaps investigating the *activities* of this group as an instance of collective delusion. But let us phrase each of these questions differently: is the admission policy of Paramount University a social problem; is water quality of the Brown River a social problem; is the existence of interplanetary visitors a social problem? Phrased in this way, the verification of assertions about conditions is not a fundamental aspect of the sociologist's analysis of social problems. On what theoretical grounds are the facts of some conditions investigated and others dismissed as nonexistent? It would rarely occur to the sociologist to independently attempt to verify the alleged pollution of the river; still less to attempt to objectively confirm a claim about an interplanetary invasion. The fact that the sociologist has become qualified to certify the factual character of *some* claims about conditions does not provide the theoretical warrant for the view that certification of claims is a fundamental feature of social problems analysis. Yet, if the subject matter of social problems is claims-making activity, *the factual basis* of assertions about racist or sexist policies of medical schools is not any more relevant to their status as social problems than the factual basis of assertions about interplanetary invasions.

Two unfortunate consequences follow the sociologists' persistence in addressing the factual existence of imputed conditions as a basis for social problems certification. First, they often mistake their own participation in certifying a very small range of claims for a mandate to make authoritative statements in areas where they have no recognized competence. For example, on what basis can a sociologist claim the authority to comment on the question of the addictive qualities of marijuana or its genetic effects? Second, they inevitably put themselves in the position of borrowing findings from other disciplines whose reliability and validity they cannot evaluate. Richard Fuller, commenting more than a quarter of a century ago, saw clearly that this left the sociologist "open to the charge of professional fakery; i.e., the sociologist took his information and ideas from all the other sciences, and then proceeded to pass moral judgments on what ought to be done" (1938:416). His solution was to abandon the pretense that the sociologist "could hold himself out as an authority on everything from technological unemployment to dementia praecox.... He need not be an expert on social problems, but an expert on the sociology of social problems" (1938:424).

On these grounds, it is not such an extreme position to urge that sociologists of social problems set aside the issue of the objective basis of alleged conditions, even to the extent of remaining indifferent to their existence. Does this mean that we maintain such conditions do not exist, or that the sociologist or any other scientist should not attempt to document their existence and study their causes? Not at all. Whatever the factual basis of the various conditions imputed to exist, the claims-making and responding activities themselves are the subject matter of the sociology of social problems. We contend that these activities exist, and can be documented and analyzed from a sociological perspective.

CLAIMS-MAKING ACTIVITIES

The activity of making claims, complaints, or demands for change is the core of what we call social problems activities. Definitions of conditions as social problems are constructed by members of a society who attempt to call attention to situations they find repugnant and who try to mobilize the institutions to do something about them.

The dictionary defines a claim as:

1. an authoritative or challenging request;
2. a demand of a right or supposed right;
3. a calling on another for something due, or supposed to be due;
4. an assertion, statement or implication often made, or likely to be suspected of being made, without adequate justification. (*Webster's New International Dictionary*, 3d ed., s.v. "claim")

Claims-making is always a form of interaction: a demand made by one party to another that something be done about some putative condition. A claim implies that the claimant has a right at least to be heard, if not to receive satisfaction. A letter from a constituent to a member of congress urging support of some measure is a claim. So is a petition to the city council to fix potholes in the streets. So, also, is a resolution of a professional body calling for the end of a war in Indochina. Mundanely, claims-making consists of demanding services, filling out forms, lodging complaints, filing lawsuits, calling press conferences, writing letters of protest, passing resolutions, publishing exposés, placing ads in newspapers, supporting or opposing some governmental practice or policy, setting up picket lines or boycotts; these are integral features of social and political life.

All those who involve themselves in these activities participate in the process of defining social problems. As we shall discover, this may include a great variety of persons such as protest groups or moral crusaders who make demands and complaints; the officials or agencies to whom such complaints are directed; members of the media who publicize and disseminate news about such activities (as well as participate in them); commissions of inquiry; legislative bodies and executive or administrative agencies that respond to claims-making constituents; members of the helping professions, such as physicians, psychiatrists, social workers; and sometimes, social scientists who contribute to the definition and development of social problems. Later we will illustrate the participation of each of these groups in social problems activities.

Our definition of social problems cannot be applied by the sociologist without regard to the perspective of the participants who make and respond to claims. That is, the definition does not provide sociologists with a set of criteria that will enable them, "from the outside," to differentiate claims-making from non-claims-making activities. Sociologists' classification of an activity as claims-making is not based on a quality intrinsic to that activity, but rather on the inter-actional setting in which members make assertions and demands in the name of their right to responsive action. Thus, our definition requires that the sociologist ascertain how *participants* in an activity define that activity.

Usually it is not difficult for the sociologist to recognize and classify activi-ties cited as claims because *they are so recognized and interpreted by members as well.* That is, claims are a common-sense category, understood by members of a society and often associated with such terms as demands, complaints, gripes, and requests.

There are several reasons to stress that the technical term *claim* is also a member's category. However routine and ordinary an event may be, the partici-pants in an activity must construct its meaning as a claim. A complaint presented in the most conventional manner may sometimes be interpreted and dismissed as senseless, just as a bizarre act, such as the delivery of an amputated human ear, may be interpreted as a terrorist's demand for the release of political prison-ers. As Horowitz and Liebowitz (1968) have indicated, claims and complaints may be responded to as crime and deviance, implicitly denying their legitimacy, casting them in a different light, and activating an entirely different social insti-tutional response. Or, what might be presented as a claim from the participant's point of view may be defined by institutional authorities as symptoms of men-tal illness or insanity. Such a construction can effectively defuse the claims-making activity, relegating it to surveillance and control by law enforcement or psychiatric agencies.

Other examples more forcefully demonstrate the socially constructed nature of the category "claim." Activities outside of the usual conventions may be used to make claims, or may be interpreted as claims, whatever their intent. Members may succeed or fail to sustain a definition of these events as an instance of claims-making. For example, a journalist writes a story on the filthy condi-tions found in the kitchens of local restaurants. While the story neither explic-itly criticizes the health department or the proprietors of the restaurants, nor calls for action to be taken, both health officials and proprietors may respond to the charges and demands that they see as implicit in the story. The journalist's reportage is interpreted as a claim.

On the other hand, when firefighters are ambushed by snipers at a fire set to lure them to a particular location, the act may be attributed to or claimed by a local organization. But it may also remain undefined and unclaimed. If the group engaging in such activities issues no communication claiming credit or making demands, on what basis could we say that they were "calling on another for some-thing due?" In such instances, the press, police, and public officials often attempt to make sense of events by attributing them to some known terrorist group. Thus, a claim may be created by observers and added to the actual events in which no claims were, in fact, presented. In the same way, groups may claim credit for an event (a skyjacking, for example) where there is no evidence that they were actually responsible for it.

A number of years ago, in the middle of a class on Eastern religions, a student raised his hand and was called on by the professor. He rose and asked the professor what he thought of the post office. Not understanding the intention or relevance of the question to Eastern religions, the professor returned the question and asked the student what he thought of the post office that he would ask a question about it. The student made a long speech about how inefficient the post office was, citing numerous examples of waste, poor planning, and excess. The most memorable of his examples referred to the safety reflectors on the back doors of large postal trucks. The student informed the class that whereas such trucks may have up to sixteen such reflectors, it was perfectly obvious that two or three at most would have done the same job. The student had with him a large manila file that seemed to contain copious documentation of his outrage, as well as some correspondence with the postal authorities.

The situation created in this class was discomforting and required delicate management on the part of the professor. What was presented as a claim, grievance, or complaint was defined as an instance of bizarre behavior.

Neither the professor of religion nor the students in the class treated the claim as a claim or responded to its content or substance. Nothing about the speech itself, however, would allow an observer to decide that it was not a claim as we have been discussing that term. Had it been addressed to the postal authorities, to the General Accounting Office, or to others who investigate the misuse of funds, those authorities, and therefore the sociologist, would have clearly recognized it as a common type of complaint. This does not preclude that they might not decide later that its author was a crank. The example shows that when the choice of a forum is grossly inappropriate, people making claims will not be treated as claimants, but quite possibly as deranged, misguided, or insane people. It is not possible to predict in advance how such claims will be received, nor to specify which offices are the "appropriate" ones for a given complaint. The example illustrates that proffered claims may be regarded as symptoms, but it does not tell us how to predict when this would occur. Given the emergent and voluntaristic nature of social life, we are not likely ever to be able to make very strict predictive statements of this sort. Perhaps in another class at the same university (a class on social problems?) the speech would have been treated differently.

These marginal cases illustrate that claims are routinely defined by members, not by the sociologist-observer. When members use conventional forms to express complaints and demands, their recognition and registration as claims may be routine. When unconventional forms are used, considerable effort may be expended to define the event as a claim. Some events not intended as claims may be so classified and responded to. Some events intended as claims may be so ambiguous that no one can make much sense of them as such. For example, terrorist activities that threaten to destroy the "fascist insect" may resist any interpretation so that a specific individual or agency could take any action as an accommodative response.

Claims-making most readily brings to mind the demands that crusaders for various social reform and social movements make on governmental agencies and officials. Such activities fall well within our conception of social problems, and we shall occasionally use such examples to illustrate or highlight a point. However, there are a wide variety of other contexts and forums in which social problems claims may be raised. For example, while legislatures have been pressed by activists to decriminalize homosexual acts between consenting adults, the American Psychiatric Association has also responded to demands from within and outside of the profession to declare that homosexuality per se is not an illness. Also, a committee of the American Library Association demanded that the Library of Congress cease classifying books on gay liberation under the heading "sexual perversion." All of these are examples of social problems claims and provide us with data for the development of a sociology of social problems.

CRITICAL THINKING EXERCISE

Choose a social problem, and describe the claims-making activities that make it a social problem.

REFERENCES

Fuller, Richard (1938) "The Problem of Teaching Social Problems," *American Journal of Sociology*, vol. 44 (November) 415–435.

Fuller, Richard and Richard Myers (1941) "The Natural History of a Social Problem," *American Sociological Review*, vol. 6 (June) 320–328.

Horowitz, Irving L. and Martin Liebovitz (1968) "Social Deviance and Political Marginality," *Social Problems*, vol. 15 (Winter) 280–296.

Hughes, Everett C. (1971) *The Sociological Eye*. Chicago: Aldine.

Rains, Prudence (1975) "Imputations of Deviance: A Retrospective Essay on the Labeling Perspective," *Social Problems*, vol. 23 (October) 1–11.

CHAPTER 3

An Introduction to the Sociology of Social Problems

Robert Heiner

To begin our study in the sociology of social problems, we should note that "social problems" is a subdiscipline of sociology. Sociology is a very broad field, encompassing such subdisciplines as the sociology of the family, of crime and delinquency, of race relations, of the environment, of education, of law, of medicine, of science, of knowledge, and yes, even of sociology itself. Sociology is so broad that most sociologists specialize in just one or two subdisciplines. The point is that the sociology of social problems is a subdiscipline; it is *not* simply a current events course. The sociologist who specializes in social problems is not a news journalist or simply a social commentator; he or she brings to the analysis of current events the perspectives, tools, and theories specific to his or her sociological training.

THE SOCIOLOGICAL PERSPECTIVE

Sociology is a social science, and as a science, it attempts to approach its subject matter objectively. The social sciences include such disciplines as sociology, psychology, and anthropology. The natural sciences include such disciplines as biology, chemistry, and physics. The social sciences are often called "soft" sciences, or accused of being mere "fluff," referring to the fact that they are less scientific or less objective than the natural, or "hard," sciences. Indeed, there is truth to these charges. Value judgments do come into play more often in the social sciences than in the natural sciences. The social sciences are more subjective because humans are conducting the research and humans are the subject of the research. One cannot study oneself objectively. However, the natural sciences are not totally objective either. Implicit judgments underlie the conduct of research in the natural sciences, such as, What is important to know? What is the best way to study it? What constitutes sufficient evidence? *Important, best, sufficient*—these are all value judgments.

We can, then, conclude that the social sciences are less scientific than the natural sciences because they are less objective. However, we cannot conclude that the social sciences are not truly sciences on the basis of their lack of objectivity (as the term *fluff* implies) because if we use objectivity as our primary criterion, then the natural sciences are not sciences either; in fact, there would be no such thing as science. What the natural sciences and the social sciences have in common is that they systematically strive for objective understanding.

This is an important point in the sociological study of social problems because most people assume that "social problems" are bad and need to be eliminated. Indeed, the very use of the word "problem" promotes such connotations. However, if we approach the study of social problems assuming that they are bad, we are not being objective and we will not achieve a sociological understanding.

Let us take crime, for example. Most students of social problems and of criminology begin their study of crime presuming that it is bad and needs to be eliminated. *Bad* is a value judgment, and it impedes our objective understanding of the phenomenon of crime. One who presumes crime is bad is likely to overlook many of the "good" aspects of crime. For example, crime provides us with nearly three million jobs in the local, state, and federal criminal justice systems as well as in private security.[1] Perhaps it could be argued that without crime these people could find other jobs. However, many people who work in these areas like their jobs, so for them crime is good. Emile Durkheim[2] and Kai Erikson[3] both argue that crime plays an essential role in uniting a society against common enemies and in establishing the moral boundaries of a community. To the extent that crime performs these functions, it is good. Further, sociologists have pointed out the role organized crime has played in American history in terms of providing ethnic minorities with a ladder to the middle class.[4] Through organized crime, minority members have acquired wealth, and with that wealth they have established legitimate businesses, hiring others of their own kind who were previously excluded from the workplace. This process began with the Irish in the late nineteenth century, then the Jews at the turn of the century, then the Italians, and now Hispanics and African Americans. If you are of Jewish, Irish, or Italian descent, perhaps you or someone you know can afford to be in college because your or his or her grandparent was hawking drugs in the 1920s (i.e., alcohol during Prohibition). Likewise, 20 or 30 years from now, more Hispanic and African American kids may be able to afford to go to college because their parent or grandparent was hawking crack in the 1980s. Consequently, crime has been good for millions of immigrants and minorities in American history. Only a small proportion of them participated in organized crime, but countless more were helped into legitimate business by the participation of a few.

To suggest that crime has its positive aspects is not to argue that the United States' relatively high crime rates are reason to rejoice, nor is it to suggest that crime should be encouraged; but it does suggest that the layperson's assumption that crime is bad and needs to be eliminated is a limited and limiting view. One who takes this perspective will not likely be open to a more complete understanding of the phenomenon. The same can be said of all social problems. Thus, as social scientists, it is important that we suspend some of our moral beliefs and value judgments as we pursue a fuller, more objective understanding of social problems. Unfortunately, "problem" is a value-laden term; to the layperson, it connotes an element of undesirability. The sociologist striving for some degree of objectivity, therefore, defines the phrase *social problem* very carefully. Sociologically, *a social problem is a phenomenon regarded as bad or undesirable by a significant number of people or a number of significant people who mobilize to remedy it.* To understand the scientific advantages of this definition, it is important to understand the concept of *social structure.*

In a society, there are individuals, groups, and institutions. These individuals, groups, and institutions are all related to one another. These relationships may be very strong or very weak, very direct or very indirect. The totality of these individuals, groups, and institutions and the relationships between them make up the social structure. It is presumed that there are rules governing these relationships. Sociology is the study of these rules, and a sociological theory is an attempt to describe such a rule.

Now, let us get a little abstract and graphically depict a social structure (Figure 3.1). The social structure is arbitrarily represented as a grid (A), a set of intersecting rules and relationships. Contained within this social structure is a phenomenon (B) that is a *potential* social problem. According to our sociological definition, this phenomenon does not become an actual social problem until it is defined as such by a group (C). To repeat our definition, a social problem is a phenomenon regarded as bad or undesirable (B in the diagram) by a significant number of people or a number of significant people (C in the diagram) who mobilize to eliminate it. The group (C), which is either significant in size or significant in composition, is often called a social movement organization. So important is this group that in their classic formulation Malcolm Spector and John Kitsuse define

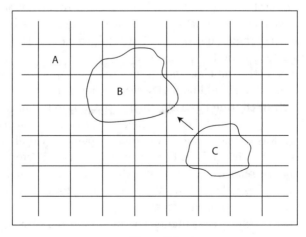

Figure 3.1

a social problem solely in terms of its activities: "Thus we define social problems as the activities of individuals or groups making assertions of grievances and claims with respect to some putative conditions."[5]

To understand why this group forms, one must understand the social structure (A). The point of this conceptualization is that a phenomenon (B) does not become a social problem because of its inherent badness; it becomes a social problem because of factors *external* to the problem itself—namely, the social structure (A) and the social movement organization (C). Here is the scientific advantage of this conceptualization: the sociologist cannot objectively say that phenomenon B is bad, but he or she can objectively say that group C says phenomenon B is bad. Hence, the sociologist is able to establish a degree of objectivity over the otherwise value-laden phrase *social problem*....

To illustrate the social problems perspective, let us take the example of child abuse. Children have been physically abused by the thousands for hundreds or thousands of years. There were brief periods in history when a group would organize on behalf of abused children; but for the most part, what we call "child abuse" was overlooked or tolerated by most of Western civilization throughout most of its history.[6] That is, it did not meet our definition of a social problem. One might be inclined to argue that child abuse was a social problem, even though it was not recognized as such, because countless children were being hurt, even killed, at the hands of their parents, and that is bad. However, *bad* is a value judgment. How badly do the children have to have been hurt and how many have to have been hurt for child abuse to constitute a social problem? We cannot objectively say. Where do we draw the line in terms of injury or numbers of injuries before we can call something a social problem? This is a matter of opinion, and science cannot answer this question.

It was not until the early 1960s that physicians began to organize, opposing the previous medical practice of overlooking evidence of child abuse. According to Pfohl,[7] there were a number of features of the medical profession that help to explain this timing. First, in the late 1950s, pediatric radiology had advanced to the point where long bone fractures could be identified. Long bone fractures travel up and down the bone and are almost certainly the result of periodic trauma occurring over a long period of time, fitting the pattern of child abuse. Before this advance in pediatric radiology, emergency room doctors encountering injuries resulting from abuse could be pretty certain that abuse was the cause; but they generally refrained from reporting their suspicions to the authorities. They were inclined to overlook child abuse because, at the time, what went on between family members was considered a family matter; parents had almost absolute property rights over their children. Furthermore, norms of doctor–patient confidentiality made the reporting of child abuse a difficult ethical decision. At the time, it was not clear exactly who was the patient: the child or the parents, who "owned" the child and were paying for the doctor. On the other hand, pediatric radiologists acted largely as consultants, having little or no direct contact with either the child or the parents. They also received little or no respect within the medical profession because they were "merely" consultants, they did not perform surgery, and their connection to life-or-death decisions was indirect. They, therefore, had something to gain by their "discovery" of child abuse. So they became the "experts," and they were often called into court to testify about life-and-death decisions involving children. Their prestige increased within the profession as a result of the discovery of child abuse. Soon, psychiatrists joined in the mobilization against child abuse. They, too, had previously enjoyed little prestige in the medical profession and could only stand to elevate themselves by aligning themselves with what was becoming a popular cause. Then, with the help of the media, the police, and various political leaders, child abuse became a full-blown social problem.

Note that we just explained how child abuse became a social problem without stating or implying that it is bad, without making a subjective evaluation of the harm that it causes. Instead, we explained how the phenomenon (B in Figure 3.1) became a social problem because a group (C), made up of pediatric radiologists and psychiatrists, mobilized against it. This group came about because of features and changes in the social structure (A). Remember that the social structure is made up of individuals, groups, institutions, and the relationships between them. That is what we described: the relationships between parents and their children, between doctors and parents, between doctors and children, between pediatric radiologists and the rest of the medical profession. Child abuse became a social problem not because of the harm done by the phenomenon but because of features external to the phenomenon.

A FEW DRAWBACKS

While sociology is a social science and while we strive to control our subjectivity, it must be noted that objectivity is an impossible goal. All of us are products of our society, and as such, we cannot study society objectively. We are subject to the same rules of society that we are trying to study. The social problems perspective should be recognized as merely a device, a flawed device, that enables us to achieve some degree of objectivity. Now let us take a look at the flaws in this device.

Our definition of a social problem is a good deal less than purely objective. According to this definition, a social problem is a phenomenon regarded as bad or undesirable by a significant number of people or a number of significant people who mobilize to eliminate it. The problem with this definition is, of course, the word *significant*. Significance is a value judgment. How many people make up a significant number? Also, how significant do the people involved have to be? Having this word in the definition allows the researcher to identify virtually any phenomenon he or she wants and to justify this identification by calling the group opposed to it "significant."

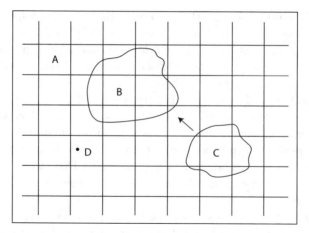

Figure 3.2

Let us take a look at the diagram again. It has been redrawn in Figure 3.2. Another flaw in the social problems perspective is that the sociologist lives, breathes, and conducts her or his research in that social structure. (The sociologist is now represented by the little speck [D] marked on the diagram.) In other words, the sociologist is not looking at the social structure from above, as you are looking at the diagram on this page. The sociologist is part of the social structure that she or he is studying, subject to the same norms, values, and beliefs that characterize that social structure. Consequently, his or her objectivity is compromised.

A FEW ADVANTAGES

These flaws notwithstanding, there are certain advantages to this perspective for the sociologist interested in social problems. The social problems perspective emphasizes that it is not the objective harm done by a phenomenon that makes it a social problem; instead, the activities of parties external to the phenomenon give it the status of a social problem, and those activities must be understood in terms of their social structural context. Therefore, this perspective allows us to ask two very important questions: (1) Why does a seemingly harmful phenomenon that has been around for a long time suddenly achieve the status of a social problem (e.g., child abuse)? (2) Why are some seemingly harmful phenomena considered social problems while other seemingly harmful phenomena are not? (For example, why is street crime so often defined as a social problem, while corporate crime is not?) These two questions ("why all of a sudden?" and "why this and not that?") are of fundamental concern from the sociological perspective referred to in this book as "critical constructionism." From the social problems perspective and from the critical constructionist perspective, the answers to these questions do not have to do with the relative harm done by the phenomenon.

CRITICAL CONSTRUCTIONISM

Critical constructionism is largely a synthesis of two very influential theories in sociology—namely, conflict theory and symbolic interactionism. It will be useful to review these theories before turning to our discussion of critical constructionism.

Conflict Theory

Conflict theory is derived largely from the works of Karl Marx. Writing at the time of the Industrial Revolution, Marx was concerned with the struggle between the bourgeoisie and the proletariat. The *bourgeoisie* owned the factories and the *proletariat* worked in them. The relationship between the two classes, according to Marx, was one of exploitation. With the state representing the interests of the bourgeoisie, the social structure itself favored the interests of the bourgeoisie; the proletariat were unable to do anything but work for them. All terms of employment favored the employers, and they worked their advantage to the hilt, underpaying their workers and treating them like replaceable parts. Modern conflict theory is concerned not only with the struggle between employers and employees but also with the struggle between all interest groups: rich and poor, white and black, men and women, etc.

Conflict theorists are concerned mostly with inequality. Those interested in social problems usually attribute them to inequality and to the use and abuse of power. *Power is the ability to influence the social structure.* Those with power—the elite—influence the social structure in ways that will enhance their power. Generally, the elite tend to use their power to prevent change and maintain the status quo. It is, after all, contemporary social arrangements—the present social structure, the status quo—that allow them their power. Those with relatively little power tend to accept the status quo, not necessarily because they are forced to, but more often because they believe in it. Our norms, values, and beliefs are products of the social structure. Therefore, the ability to influence the social structure is the ability to influence the way people think. People are socialized by society's basic institutions—government, education, religion, and the media—to think that those in power should be in power.

Like their predecessor, Marx, modern conflict theorists tend to be very critical of capitalism. Contrary to what most people think, the people in power, referred to earlier, are not the nation's political or military leaders. The real power in the United States, they argue, is in the hands of the capitalists, specifically the nation's corporate leaders. Controlling as much money and resources as they do, they are able to influence legislation and policy for their own interests. The free market economy of the United States, with its relative lack of regulations, benefits American corporations often at the expense of the American people. According to the neo-Marxists, the American people, on the other hand, often tend to believe that anything that is good for corporate America is good for them, not because this is true, but because that is what they have been socialized to believe.

It is not surprising, then, that conflict theory often comes across as a very terse critique of capitalism. Americans tend to be far less receptive to such ideas than their European counterparts. During the 30-plus years of the Cold War, everything Marxist was considered bad and most things capitalist were considered good. Besides being ideologically unpopular, conflict theory also suffers in that it is easily interpreted to suggest that the elite make up a united, all-powerful conspiracy. This, however, is not the intention of the conflict theorist. First of all, the elite are not all-powerful. Their ability to influence the social structure is not boundless. There is a certain give and take. All legislation and policy does not favor their interests; but their influence is such that the totality of legislation and policy, at least slightly, favors their interests. Second, few conflict theorists would suggest that the elite conspire to subjugate the rest of society. Instead, the elite have a *unity of interests* that makes it seem *as if* they conspire. That is, on average, the same policies that would benefit one powerful person will also benefit most powerful people; when each pursues his or her individual self-interest, it produces the same effect as a conspiracy.

Another feature of conflict theory that may or may not be problematic is the primacy it gives to the value of equality. There is an inherent value judgment implicit to most conflict theory. The pain and suffering that are the result of inequality are viewed negatively. Objectivity is often willingly suspended in the name of equality. In fact, many conflict theorists often take an activist role, feeling it is their moral duty to promote social and political change. Even though its objectivity may be compromised, conflict theory is generally highly regarded among sociologists. Many would argue that the human rights that conflict theorists study and promote are universal or inherent rights and, therefore, do not constitute subjective values. Whether this is true or not is a philosophical matter, but their perspective remains sociological because their emphasis is on the social structure and the inequality built into the relationships between individuals, groups, and institutions. Conflict theory's emphasis on social justice has added the elements of liberalism and humanitarianism for which sociology is renowned and for which it is sometimes reviled.

Symbolic Interactionism

Unlike conflict theory, which focuses on the broader social structure, symbolic interactionism focuses on the day-to-day interactions between people. Symbolic interactionism is considered a branch of social psychology because it focuses on the ways people think and give meaning to the world. Virtually all human interaction involves the act of interpretation. George Herbert Mead argued that human beings are different from other animals because their communication is based on language. The communication of other animals is genetically programmed; therefore, their utterances have inherent meaning. Human communication, on the other hand, is based on language; language is based on words; and words are symbols. A *symbol*, by definition, is something that signifies something else. Symbols, then, have no inherent meaning and, therefore, require interpretation.[8]

The act of interpretation is critical to all of our social experiences, not just the processing of language. Between us and our environment is our interpretation of the environment. People do not respond directly to the environment, instead they respond to their interpretation of the environment. The way we interpret the environment depends upon our past experiences. Since no two people have the same history of experiences, no two people interpret the same event or object exactly the same way. Hence, the word *college,* for example, has at least a slightly different meaning for everyone who uses it. Likewise, any given social problem will mean something different to all who conceive of it. Based on their different histories of experience, people will interpret and prioritize social problems differently.

Though no two people's experiences can be the same, members of different groups within the social structure will have experiences more similar to each other than they will to members of other groups. Their interpretations of the environment, therefore, will be more similar to each other's than to those of members of other groups. For example, members of the upper class have more experiences in common with one another than they do with members of the lower class. Therefore, upper-class and lower-class individuals are likely to label or define social problems differently.

We have already been introduced to the logic of symbolic interactionism in our discussion of the social problems perspective, illustrated in Figure 3.1. In this diagram, the potential social problem (B) does not become an actual social problem until it is defined, or *labeled,* as such by a significant number of people or a number of significant people (C). Like a symbol, the potential social problem (B) has no inherent meaning. Before it can become a social problem, it has to be interpreted as such by a significant group (C). Symbolic interactionism, then, directs our attention not to the social problem itself but to meanings that are assigned to it. This leads us directly to a discussion of critical constructionism.

Critical Constructionism

Some seemingly harmful phenomena meet our definition of a social problem, while other seemingly more harmful phenomena do not meet this definition. Put another way, some phenomena come to be interpreted by a significant number of people or a number of significant people as social problems that need to be addressed and some do not, irrespective of the amount of harm done by these phenomena. *Social constructionism* is concerned with how the meanings of social problems are constructed. Problem construction involves the following processes: the identification of a phenomenon as problematic, the providing of explanations for the causes of that phenomenon, and the persuasion of the public that the phenomenon is problematic and needs to be remedied. The social constructionist examines these processes. *Critical constructionism* is different from social constructionism only in that it emphasizes the role of elite interests in the process of problem construction. Borrowing from conflict theory, the critical constructionist argues that the way social problems are constructed, conceived, and presented to the public, more often than not, reflects the interests of society's elite more than those of the mainstream and often at the expense of those with the least power.

It was suggested earlier that the social problems perspective allows us to ask the question, Why are some seemingly harmful phenomena considered social problems and not other seemingly harmful phenomena? The example of street crime vs. corporate crime was given. Most Americans would consider it common sense that street crime is more "dangerous" than corporate crime. The critical constructionist might argue that street crime is considered more of a social problem than corporate crime because the groups that have the power to frame social problems have an interest in diverting public attention away from crimes committed by the upper class and directing it to crimes committed by the lower class. Thus, the way the crime problem is constructed reflects the interests of the elite (whose crimes do more harm), to the detriment of the poor (who are punished more severely for their crimes).

Symbolic interactionists argue that all interpretations of reality are influenced by our experiences. To put it more strongly, all knowledge is socially constructed. All constructions of social problems are, therefore, worthy of constructionist analysis. Without denying this position, however, the critical constructionist is most concerned with those constructions of social problems that are in the popular domain—namely, those that receive a great deal of media attention—and how those constructions are influenced by elite interests. Popular constructions of social problems are those that sway social policy, and elite interests are most in need of critical scrutiny because they are so often obscured or confused with societal interests. Consistent with conflict theory from which it is derived, critical constructionism strives to give voice to the less powerful groups in society, a voice that is typically overwhelmed in public debate by the resources of those groups with more power.

Though the term *critical constructionism* may be unfamiliar, this type of analysis is not new to sociology. Many of its components were described by Marx and later developed further by Antonio Gramsci. Gramsci, a socialist, was incarcerated by the Fascist government in Italy in the 1920s, in the words of the prosecutor, "to stop that brain from working for twenty years."[9] Gramsci wrote many of his ideas down in what have come to be known as "the prison notebooks." Gramsci addressed what many have argued is a critical flaw in the work of Marx, the question of "inevitability." Marx argued that it was inevitable that the workers would rise up in revolution and overthrow their capitalist oppressors. Such a revolution did not take place in a great many countries, including the United States. In these countries, Gramsci argued, the capitalist elite have been able to thwart a revolution through their influence on institutions associated with the production of knowledge and culture. Gramsci called this influence "hegemony," and through their hegemony, the elite are able to shape what the public considers "common sense."[10] For example, in the United States, it is considered common sense that the country is both the "the land of the free" and "the land of opportunity" despite, as we shall see, evidence to the contrary. However, as long as

Americans believe these to be matters of common sense, they feel no need to change the status quo, let alone revolt against the capitalists. Thus, Gramsci and the critical constructionists are in agreement that, through their influence on the production of cultural knowledge, the elite are able to influence the public's perceptions of social problems to their own advantage.

Critical constructionists do not argue that the social problems that are successfully constructed are inconsequential and harmless. Instead, they argue that our view of the problems that exist in society has been distorted by the power relations involved in their construction. In this regard, critical constructionism is not very useful in terms of providing solutions to problems; but it is useful in terms of providing a perspective that allows us to decipher what the real problems are in society and to prioritize them on a rational basis, a basis that is concerned with the societal welfare and that does not weigh more heavily in favor of society's elite.

CRITICAL THINKING QUESTION

According to this reading, a phenomenon is not a "social problem" until it is defined as such by a significant group of people. What are the advantages and disadvantages of such a definition?

NOTES

1. *Sourcebook of Criminal Justice Statistics.* Washington, D.C.: U.S. Department of Justice, Bureau of Justice Statistics, 1994.
2. Emile Durkheim, *The Rules of Sociological Method.* Translated by S. A. Solovay and J. H. Mueller, edited by G. E. G. Catlin. New York: Free Press, 1966.
3. Kai Ericson, *Wayward Puritans.* New York: Macmillan, 1966.
4. Daniel Bell, "Crime as an American Way of Life," *Antioch Review,* vol. 13, 1953, 131–154.
5. Malcolm Spector and John I. Kitsuse, *Constructing Social Problems.* New York: Aldine de Gruyter, 1987, 75.
6. Lloyd de Mause, *The History of Childhood.* New York: Psychohistory Press, 1974.
7. Steven J. Pfohl, "The 'Discovery' of Child Abuse," in D. H. Kelly (ed.), *Deviant Behavior,* 3rd ed. New York: St. Martin's, 1989, 40–51.
8. George Herbert Mead, *Mind, Self, and Society.* Edited by C. W. Morris. Chicago: University of Chicago Press, 1934.
9. Neil McInnes, "Antonio Gramsci," *Encyclopedia of Philosophy,* vol. 3. New York: Macmillan and Free Press, 1967, 376–377.
10. Antonio Gramsci, *Selections from the Prison Notebooks.* Translated and edited by Q. Hoare and G. N. Smith. New York: International Publishers, 1971.

CHAPTER 4

The Problem of Journalism

Robert W. McChesney

Democratic theory generally posits that society needs a journalism that is a rigorous watchdog of those in power and who want to be in power, can ferret out truth from lies, and can present a wide range of informed positions on the important issues of the day. Each medium need not do all of these things, but the media system as a whole should make this caliber of journalism readily available to the citizenry. How a society can construct a media system that will generate something approximating democratic journalism is a fundamental problem for a free society, as powerful interests tend to wish to dominate the flow of information.

In this chapter I attempt to provide a political-economic framework for explaining why contemporary U.S. journalism is such a failure on...the above counts. I first look at the rise of professional journalism roughly a hundred years ago, and some of the problems for democracy inherent in the manner in which it developed in the United States. I then assess the two-pronged attack on the autonomy of professional journalism that has taken place over the past generation....I argue, these...factors explain [in part] the pathetic state of U.S. journalism in the early twenty-first century. The implications of my argument are that a commitment to anything remotely resembling bona fide democracy requires a vastly superior journalism, and we can only realistically expect such a journalism if there are sweeping changes in media policies and structures to make such a journalism a rational expectation.

I aspire to demonstrate the importance of political-economic analysis in journalism studies. It is commonly thought that the political economic critique of U.S. journalism is centered on looking at how large media corporations, media concentration, and advertisers corrupt the public service of journalism, undermine its professionalism, and keep it from being serious and nonpartisan, if not objective. Some critics of the political-economic approach argue that the critique is therefore of limited value, because it has a tendency to overplay its hand, and downplay the importance of professional values in journalism. These charges are misguided. On the one hand, the notion of professional journalism is a relatively recent phenomenon, and one with an important history. It did not fall from the sky and land in the newsroom of the *New York Times*. On the other hand, it is a political-economic critique that best explains the rise and nature of professional journalism as it has come into practice in the United States. Political economy is not the *only* analysis that explains professionalism, but it is indispensable to any analysis.[1] At any rate, the bottom line is clear: grasping the origins and nature of professional journalism is the necessary starting point for any critique of contemporary journalism, political economic or otherwise, that is worth its salt.

THE RISE OF PROFESSIONAL JOURNALISM

The notion that journalism should be politically neutral, nonpartisan, professional, even "objective," did not emerge until the twentieth century. During the first two or three generations of the Republic such notions for the press would have been nonsensical, even unthinkable. The point of journalism was to persuade as well as inform, and the press tended to be highly partisan. The free press clause in the First Amendment to the constitution was seen as a means to protect dissident political viewpoints, as most newspapers were closely linked to political parties. It was understood that if the government could outlaw or circumscribe newspapers, it could effectively eliminate the ability of opposition parties or movements to mobilize popular support. It would kill democracy. What few Americans know is that the government actively subsidized the press through printing well into the nineteenth century, and postal subsidies to this day. A partisan press system has much to offer a democratic society as long as there are numerous well-subsidized media providing a broad range of opinions.[2]

During the nineteenth century, the logic of newspaper publishing changed from being primarily political to being primarily commercial. The press system remained explicitly partisan, but it increasingly became an engine of great profits as costs plummeted, population increased, and advertising—which emerged as a key source of revenues—mushroomed. During the Civil War, President Lincoln faced press criticism—from some newspapers in the Northern states—that would make the treatment of Lyndon Johnson during Vietnam, Richard Nixon during Watergate or Bill Clinton during his impeachment seem like a day at the beach.[3] A major city like St. Louis, for example, had at least ten daily newspapers for much of the middle- to late-nineteenth century. Each newspaper tended to represent the politics of the owner and if someone was dissatisfied with the existing choices, it was not impossible to launch a new newspaper. By contemporary standards, it was a fairly competitive market.

But it was only a matter of time before there would be a conflict between the commercial economics of the press and its explicitly partisan politics. It became a growing problem during the Gilded Age. Following the logic of accumulation, the commercial press system became less competitive and ever more clearly the domain of wealthy individuals, who usually had the political views associated with their class. Commercialism also fostered corruption, as newspapers turned to sensationalism and outright lying to generate sales.[4] Throughout this era, socialists, feminists, abolitionists, trade unionists, and radicals *writ large* tended to regard the mainstream commercial press as the mouthpiece of their enemies, and established their own media to advance their interests. Consider, for example, the United States in the early 1900s. Members and supporters of the Socialist Party of Eugene V. Debs published some 325 English and foreign language daily, weekly, and monthly newspapers and magazines. Most of these were privately owned or were the publications of one of the 5,000 Socialist Party locals. They reached a total of more than two million subscribers.[5] *Appeal to Reason*, the socialist newspaper based in Kansas, alone had a readership of nearly a million.[6]

From the Gilded Age through the Progressive Era, an institutional sea change transpired in U.S. media not unlike the one taking place in the broader political economy. The dominant newspaper industry became increasingly concentrated into fewer chains and the majority of communities only had one or two dailies. The economics of advertising-supported newspapers erected barriers to entry that made it virtually impossible for small, independent newspapers to succeed, despite the protection of the constitution for a "free press." The dissident press, too, found media market economics treacherous, and lost much of its circulation and influence throughout the first third of the twentieth century, far in excess of the decline in interest in "dissident" politics. (How much the collapse of the independent press contributed to the demise of popular politics is a matter of no small importance in media studies.)

At the beginning of the twentieth century these developments led to a crisis for U.S. journalism. It was one thing to posit that a commercial media system worked for democracy when there were numerous newspapers in a community, when barriers to entry were relatively low, and when immigrant and dissident media proliferated widely, as was the case for much of the nineteenth century. For newspapers to be partisan at that time was no big problem because there were alternative viewpoints present. But it was quite another thing to make such a claim by the early twentieth century when many communities only had one or two newspapers, usually owned by chains or very wealthy and powerful individuals. Everywhere concentration was on the rise, and almost nowhere were new dailies being launched successfully to enter existing markets. For journalism to remain partisan in this context, for it to advocate the interests of the owners and the advertisers who subsidized it, would cast severe doubt on the credibility of the journalism. Likewise, sensationalism was less of a problem when there were several other newspapers in the community to counter it.

During the Progressive Era, criticism of the capitalist press reached fever pitch in the United States and was a major theme of muckrakers and progressive social critics, to an extent never equaled subsequently.[7] Leading reformers, like Robert LaFollette of Wisconsin, argued that the commercial press was destroying democracy in its rabid service to the wealthy. As Henry Adams put it, "The press is the hired agent of a moneyed system, set up for no other reason than to tell lies where the interests are concerned." Criticism extended across the political spectrum; in the 1912 presidential race all three challengers to President Taft—Debs, Roosevelt, and Wilson—criticized the capitalist bias of the press. In 1919 Upton Sinclair published his opus, *The Brass Check,* which provided the first great systematic critique of the limitations of capitalist journalism for a democratic society. Sinclair's book was filled with example after example of explicit lying and distortion of the labor movement and socialist politics by the mainstream press.[8] In short, it was widely thought that journalism was explicit class propaganda in a war with only one side armed. The parallel critique of the press argued that greedy publishers encouraged a fraudulent sensationalistic journalism that played very loose with the truth to generate sales. In combination, the widespread acceptance of these beliefs was very dangerous for the business of newspaper publishing, as many potential readers would find newspapers incredible, propagandistic, and unconvincing.

It was in the cauldron of controversy, during the Progressive Era, that the notion of professional journalism came of age. Savvy publishers understood that they needed to have their journalism appear neutral and unbiased, notions entirely foreign to the journalism of the Republic's first century, or their businesses would be far less profitable. They would sacrifice their explicit political power to lock in their economic position. Publishers pushed for the establishment of formal "schools of journalism" to train a cadre of professional editors and reporters. None of these schools existed in 1900; by 1920, all the major schools such as Columbia, Northwestern, Missouri, and Indiana were in full swing. The revolutionary and unprecedented notion of a separation of the editorial operations from the commercial affairs—termed the separation of church and state—became the professed model. The argument went that trained editors and reporters were granted autonomy by the owners to make the editorial decisions, and these decisions were based on their professional judgment, not the politics of the owners and the advertisers or their commercial interests to maximize profit. As trained professionals, journalists would learn to sublimate their own values as well. Readers could trust what they read and not worry about who owned the newspaper or that there was a monopoly or duopoly in their community.[9] Indeed, if everyone followed professional standards, press concentration would become a moot issue. Who needed more than one or two newspapers if every paper basically would end up running the same professionally driven content? Owners could sell their neutral monopoly newspapers to everyone in the community and rake in the profits.

It took decades for the professional system to be adopted by all the major journalistic media. And during the 1930s and 1940s, prominent journalists like George Seldes and Haywood Broun struggled for a vision of professional journalism that was ruthlessly independent of corporate and commercial influence, a vision that collapsed with the smashing of popular politics following the Second World War. The first half of the twentieth century is replete with owners like the *Chicago Tribune's* Colonel McCormick, who used their newspapers to advocate their fiercely partisan (and, almost always, far-right) views. When the Nazis came to power, for example, the *Tribune's* European correspondent defected to the Germans so he could do pro-Nazi shortwave radio broadcasts to the United States.[10] But by midcentury even laggards like the *Tribune* had been brought into line. In the famed Tribune Building in Chicago, urban legend has it that editorial workers and the business side of the paper were instructed to use separate elevators, so the editorial integrity of the newspaper would not be sullied. What is important to remember is that professional journalism looked awfully good compared to what it immediately replaced. The emphasis on nonpartisanship and factual accuracy, the discrediting of sensationalism, who could oppose that? It has been and is roundly hailed as the solution to the problem of journalism.

Over time it has become clear that there was one problem with the theory of professional journalism, an insurmountable one at that. The claim that it was possible to provide neutral and objective news was suspect, if not entirely bogus. Decision making is an inescapable part of the journalism process, and some values have to be promoted when deciding why one story rates front-page treatment while another is ignored.[11] This does not mean that some journalism cannot be more nonpartisan or more accurate than others; it certainly does not mean that nonpartisan and accurate journalism should not have a prominent role to play in a democratic society. It only means that journalism cannot actually be neutral or objective, and unless one acknowledges that, it is impossible to detect the values at play that determine what becomes news, and what does not. The way journalism evolved in the United States was to incorporate certain key values into the professional code; there was nothing naturally objective or professional about those values. In core respects they responded to the commercial and political needs of the owners, although they were never framed in such a manner. To the extent journalists believe that by following professional codes they are neutral and fair—or, at least, they need not entertain the question of bias—they are incapable of recognizing and addressing this inherent limitation of the craft. Scholars have identified three deep-seated biases that are built into the professional code that journalists follow, and that have decidedly political and ideological implications.[12] These biases remain in place to this day; indeed, they are stronger than ever.

First, to remove the controversy connected with the selection of stories, professional journalism regards anything done by official sources, e.g., government officials and prominent public figures, as the basis for legitimate news. In the partisan era of journalism, newspapers would stand behind story selection as representing their values, what they thought was important. Such an attitude was anathema in professional times. Relying on sources as the basis for legitimate news helped solve that problem. Then, if chastised by readers for covering a particular story, an editor could say, "Hey, don't blame us, the governor (or any other official source) said it and we merely reported it." It also has the important added benefit of making the news fairly easy and inexpensive to cover—merely put reporters where official sources congregate and let them report what they say. This is a crucial factor in explaining why coverage of the U.S. presidency has grown dramatically during the twentieth century: there are reporters assigned to the White House and they file stories regularly, regardless of what is taking place. In the late nineteenth century, coverage of the president occupied maybe 2 or 3 percent of the "news hole" in U.S. newspapers. By the middle-to-late twentieth century, the president dominated 10 to 25 percent of the news, depending upon the scope of the survey.

The limitations of this reliance upon official sources are self-evident. It gives those in political office (and, to a lesser extent, business) considerable power to set the news agenda by what they speak about and, just as important, what they keep quiet about. When a journalist dares to raise an issue that no official source is talking about, he or she is accused of being unprofessional, and attempting to introduce his or her own biases into the news. Shrewd politicians and powerful figures learn how to use journalistic conventions to their advantage.[13] Journalists find themselves where they cannot antagonize their sources too much, or they might get cut off and become ineffectual. Political journalism has often degenerated to simply reporting what someone in one party says, and then getting a reply from someone on the other side of the aisle, or who takes a dissenting position within the community of official sources. All in all, the reliance on official sources gives the news a very conventional and mainstream feel, and does not necessarily lead to a rigorous examination of the major issues.

As the old saying goes, the media do not necessarily tell you what to think, but they tell you what to think about, and how to think about it. If one wants to know why a story is getting covered, and why it is getting covered the way it is, looking at sources will turn up an awfully good answer a high percentage of the time. It is not just about whether a story will be covered at all, but, rather, how much attention a story will get and the tone of the coverage. In view of the fact that legitimate sources tend to be restricted to political and economic elites, this bias sometimes makes journalists appear to be stenographers to those in power—exactly what one would expect in an authoritarian society with little or no formal press freedom.

Many working journalists recoil at these statements. Their response would be that professional reliance on official sources is justifiable as "democratic" because the official sources are elected or accountable to people who are elected by the citizenry. This is not a dictatorship. The reporter's job is to report what people in power say and let the reader/viewer decide who is telling the truth. The problem with this rationale for stenography is that it forgets a critical assumption of free press theory: even leaders determined by election need a rigorous monitoring, the range of which cannot be determined solely by their elected opposition. Otherwise the citizenry has no way out of the status quo, no capacity to criticize the political culture as a whole. If this watchdog function grows lax, corruption invariably grows, and the electoral system decays.

In addition to this reliance on official sources, experts are also crucial to explaining and debating policy, especially in complex stories. As with sources, experts are drawn almost entirely from the establishment. Studies on the use of news sources and experts invariably point to the strong mainstream bias built into the news. An analysis of national TV broadcast news for 2001, for example, found that the sources and experts used were overwhelmingly white, male, Republican, and wealthy. The emphasis upon Republicans can be explained mostly by the Republican administration. The news covers people in power. They also have seemingly accepted business domination of the political economy as legitimate. There were 955 representatives of corporations on the newscasts as opposed to thirty-one representatives of labor.[14]

A second flaw in journalism is that it tends to avoid contextualization like the plague. This was the great strength of partisan journalism: it attempted to take every important issue and place it in a larger political ideology, to make sense of it. But under professional standards, to provide meaningful context and background for stories, if done properly, will tend to commit the journalist to a definite position and enmesh the journalist (and medium) in the controversy professionalism is determined to avoid. Coverage tends to be a barrage of facts and official statements. What little contextualization professional journalism does provide tends to conform to official source consensus premises. The way to assure that news selection not be perceived as ideologically driven is to have a news hook or a news peg to justify a news story. If something happens, it is news. This meant that crucial social issues like racism or environmental degradation fell through the cracks of journalism unless there was some event—like a demonstration or the release of an official report—to justify coverage, or unless official sources wanted to make it a story so they could talk about it repeatedly. For those outside power to generate a news hook was and is often extraordinarily difficult. The 1968 report of the Kerner Commission on Civil Disorders, for example, specifically cited the poor coverage and lack of contextualization by journalism of civil rights issues over the years as strongly contributing to the climate that led to the riots of the 1960s.[15]

Both of these factors helped to stimulate the birth and rapid rise of the public relations (PR) industry, the purpose of which was to surreptitiously take advantage of these two aspects of professional journalism. It is not an accident that the PR industry emerged on the heels of professional journalism. By providing slick press releases, paid-for "experts," ostensibly neutral-sounding but bogus citizens groups, and canned news events, crafty PR agents have been able to shape the news to suit the interests of their mostly corporate clientele. Powerful corporate interests that have a distinct concern about government regulation spend a fortune to see that their version of science gets a wide play in the news...as objective truth.[16] Media owners welcome PR, as it provides, in effect, a subsidy for them by providing them with filler at no cost. Surveys show that PR accounts for anywhere from 40 to 70 percent of what appears as news. Because PR is only successful if it is surreptitious, the identity of the major players and knowledge of their most successful campaigns is unknown to the general public. During the 1990s the PR industry underwent a major consolidation, and today the three largest advertising agency companies, which now offer full-service corporate communication to their clients, own eight of the ten largest U.S. PR firms.[17]

The combined effect of these two biases and the prominence of spin is to produce a grand yet distressing paradox: journalism, which, in theory, should inspire political involvement, tends to strip politics of meaning and promote broad depoliticization. It is arguably better at generating ignorance and apathy than informed and passionately engaged citizens.[18] Politics becomes antiseptic and drained of passion, of connection to the lives people lead. At its worst, it feeds a cynicism about the value and integrity of public life.[19] So it is that on some of those stories that receive the most coverage, like the Middle East or the Clinton health-care proposal in the early 1990s, Americans tend to be almost as ignorant as on those subjects that receive far less coverage.[20] The journalism is more likely to produce confusion than understanding and informed action. This creates a major dilemma for journalism over time. It is well understood that democracy needs journalism; viable self-government in our times is unthinkable without it. What is less well perceived is that journalism requires democracy. Unless there is a citizenry that depends upon journalism, that takes it seriously, that is politically engaged, journalism can lose its bearings and have far less incentive to do the hard work that generates the best possible work. The political system becomes less responsive and corruption grows. Thus we can restate the paradox of professional journalism as follows: journalism in any meaningful sense cannot survive without a viable democracy. This implies journalism must become aggressively and explicitly critical of the anti-democratic status quo, it must embrace once again the old adage of "afflicting the comfortable and comforting the afflicted." In short, the logic suggests that to remain democratic, to continue to exist, journalism must become... unprofessional.

The third bias of professional journalism is more subtle but arguably the most important: far from being politically neutral, within the constraints of the first two biases, it smuggles in values conducive to the commercial aims of the owners and advertisers as well as the political aims of the owning class. Ben Bagdikian refers to this as the "dig here, not there" phenomenon.[21] So it is that crime stories and stories about royal families and celebrities become legitimate news. (These are inexpensive to cover and they never antagonize people in power.) So it is that the affairs of government are subjected to much closer scrutiny than the affairs of big business. And of government activities, those that serve the poor (e.g., welfare) get much more critical attention than those that serve primarily the interests of the wealthy (e.g., the CIA and other institutions of the national security state), which are more or less off-limits. This focus on government malfeasance and neglect of corporate misdeeds plays directly into the hands of those who wish to give more power and privileges to corporations, and undermine the ability of government to regulate in the public interest. As Ed Baker observes, professional practices, along with libel laws, "favor exposing governmental rather than private (corporate) wrongdoing."[22] This, too, plays into the promotion of cynicism about public life. The corporate scandals of 2002 finally forced certain corporate excesses into the news, but what was immediately striking was how all the criminal activity had taken place for years without a shred of news-media interest. The genius of professionalism in journalism is that it tends to make journalists oblivious to the compromises with authority they routinely make.

Establishing if there actually *is* a pro-corporate bias in the news is not an easy task, and has been a source of more than a little controversy over the years. Although studies show the topic of corporate power is virtually unmentioned in U.S. political journalism, it is highly controversial to accuse journalism of a pro-corporate bias.[23] In the 1990s, for the first time, what amounts to a controlled experiment shed new light on the debate. Charles Lewis was an award-winning journalist who left network television to form the Center for Public Integrity (CPI) in the early 1990s. Receiving funding from foundations, Lewis assembled a large team of investigative journalists, and had them do several detailed investigative reports each year. The purpose was to release the reports to the news media and hope for coverage and follow-up investigative work. Lewis notes that when his group releases exposés of government malfeasance, they tend to receive extensive coverage and follow-up. The CPI broke the story, for example, about President Clinton's "leasing" the Lincoln Bedroom in the White House to major campaign contributors. When the CPI issues a report on corporate malfeasance, in contrast, Lewis says the press conference is virtually empty and there is almost no coverage or follow-up. What makes this striking is that the exact same journalists do these reports.[24] Were Lewis unprincipled, he would logically discontinue doing corporate exposés.[25]

Imagine if the president or the director of the FBI ordered news media not to issue any critical examinations of corporate power or class inequality in the United States. It would be considered a grotesque violation of democratic freedoms and a direct challenge to the viability of the Republic. It would constitute a much greater threat to democracy than Watergate; one would probably have to return to the Civil War and slavery to find a comparable threat to the union. The American Civil Liberties Union (ACLU) would go ballistic. Yet, when the private sector control of journalism, through professional practices, generates virtually the exact same outcome, it goes unmentioned and unrecognized in political culture. It is a non-issue.

Although the professional code incorporates these three general biases, it is also malleable; it is not fixed in stone. Over the years it has been influenced by factors such as the rise of radio and television, or new communication technologies.[26] It is also true that the organized activities of the mass of people can have the ability to influence the shape of journalism. In moments of resurgence for social movements, professional journalism can improve the quantity and quality of coverage. Certainly there was a notable shift in coverage of issues surrounding African Americans and women from the 1950s to the 1970s, reflecting the emergence of the civil rights and feminist movements. It works in the other direction, too. In the 1940s, for example, when the U.S. labor movement was at its zenith, full-time labor editors and reporters abounded on U.S. daily newspapers. There were several hundred of them. Even ferociously anti-labor newspapers, like the *Chicago Tribune*, covered the labor beat. The 1937 Flint sit-down strike that launched the United Autoworkers and the trade union movement was a major news story across the nation. By the 1980s, however, labor had fallen off the map and there were no more than a couple of dozen labor beat reporters remaining on U.S. dailies. The story was simply no longer covered. Hence the 1989 Pittstown sit-down strike—the largest since Flint—was virtually unreported in the U.S. media, and its lessons unknown. As the labor movement declined, coverage of labor was dropped. People still work, poverty among workers is growing, workplace conflicts are as important as ever, but this is no longer as newsworthy as it was when organized labor was more powerful.[27]

...Professional journalism hit its high-water mark in the United States from the 1950s into the 1970s. During this era journalists had relative autonomy to pursue stories and considerable resources to use to pursue their craft. There was a strong emphasis upon factual accuracy, which is all to the good. The best journalism of the professional era came (and still comes) when there were debates among official sources or when an issue was irrelevant to elite concerns. In these cases, professional journalism could be sparkling. Likewise, during this golden age of professional journalism, the political culture, official sources, especially though not exclusively in the Democratic Party, were considerably more liberal than they would be by the 1980s. Along with the increase in social activism overall, this opened up opportunities for journalists to take risks and cover stories that would be much more difficult as the entire political class became increasingly enthralled with the market. So someone like Ralph Nader routinely received extensive and fairly sympathetic press coverage for his consumer campaigns during the 1960s and early 1970s. The consumer and environmental legislation he is responsible for pushing into law during this period is little short of astounding by contemporary standards. By the 1990s he had basically been scripted out of the political culture and journalism, leading him to enter electoral politics to express his frustration with the status quo.

But one should not exaggerate the quality of journalism or the amount of autonomy journalists had from the interests of owners, even in this "golden age." Even at the height of the golden age there was an underground press predicated upon the problems in contemporary journalism, and hard-edged criticism of the flaws of existing journalism abounded. In every community there was a virtual Sicilian code of silence for the local commercial media, for example, regarding the treatment of the area's wealthiest and most powerful individuals and corporations. Media owners wanted their friends and business pals to get nothing but kid-glove treatment in their media and so it was, except for the most egregious and boneheaded maneuver. Likewise, newspapers, even prestigious ones like the *Los Angeles Times*, used their power to aid the economic projects of the newspaper's owners.[28] And pressure to shape editorial coverage to serve the needs of major advertisers was a recurring problem.

If the system of professional journalism has had deep-seated biases built into its code that have deadened it as a democratic force, that does not mean that there have not been many good, and some great, journalists who nevertheless have done brilliant work. Decade after decade newsrooms have produced outstanding journalists whose contributions to building a democratic and just society have been immeasurable.[29] In recent times, one thinks of the work of the *Philadelphia Inquirer's* Donald Bartlett and James Steele.[30] Some of the most impressive work often has come in the form of books, ranging from those of Rachel Carson and Robert Caro to Studs Terkel and Betty Friedan. The list is really quite long. To some extent, this reflects the ability of books to convey detailed reports, but it also highlights how many great journalists had to leave the routine of standard newsroom journalism in order to do the stories they deemed important. Their work points out what can be done but generally is not being done. Along these lines, it is worth noting that many of the twentieth-century's finest journalists— Ben Bagdikian, George Seldes, A. J. Liebling, I. F. Stone, David Halberstam, Bill Moyers, and William Greider—have been among its foremost press critics. In short, the great work has been done not because of the system as much as in spite of it....

CRITICAL THINKING QUESTIONS

Using this reading as a guideline, contrast the types of bias characterizing the American news media before and after the movement to professionalize journalism. How did the professionalization lead to the current forms of bias? How does this reading relate to the themes developed in the previous readings in the volume? How could the journalistic biases described above have contributed to the economic crisis first reported in 2008?

NOTES

This chapter first appeared in a slightly different form as Robert W. McChesney, "The Problem of Journalism: A Political Economic Contribution to an Explanation of the Crisis in Contemporary US Journalism," *Journalism Studies* 4/3 (2003): 299–29. Some of this material was also used in chapters 2 and 3 of Robert W. McChesney, *The Problem of the Media.*

1. For critics of the political economic approach, see: Daniel C. Hallin, *We Keep America on Top of the World* (New York: Routledge, 1994), 11–13; Michael Schudson, *The Power of News* (Cambridge, MA: Harvard University Press, 1995), 4. For different approaches that draw invaluable material, see Richard L. Kaplan, *Politics and the American Press: The Rise of Objectivity, 1865–1920* (Cambridge: Cambridge University Press, 2002); and David T. Z. Mindich, *Just the Facts: How "Objectivity" Came to Define American Journalism* (New York: New York University Press, 1998).
2. Jeffrey L. Pasley, *"The Tyranny of Printers": Newspaper Politics in the Early American Republic* (Charlottesville: University Press of Virginia, 2001).
3. Harry J. Maihafer, *War of Words: Abraham Lincoln and the Civil War Press* (Washington, DC: Brassey's, 2001).
4. Gerald J. Baldasty, *The Commercialization of News in the Nineteenth Century* (Urbana: University of Illinois Press, 1992); Gerald J. Baldasty, *E. W. Scripps and the Business of Newspapers* (Urbana: University of Illinois Press, 1999).

5. Rodger Streitmatter, *Voices of Revolution: The Dissident Press in America* (New York: Columbia University Press, 2001).

6. John Graham, ed., *"Tours for the Revolution": The Appeal to Reason, 1895–1922* (Lincoln: University of Nebraska Press, 1990).

7. Tom Goldstein, ed., *Killing the Messenger: 100 Years of Media Criticism* (New York: Columbia University Press, 1989), ix.

8. Upton Sinclair, *The Brass Check* (Urbana: University of Illinois Press, 2003).

9. For the classic statement on professional journalism, see Joseph Pulitzer, "Selection from the College of Journalism," in *Killing the Messenger,* ed. Tom Goldstein (New York: Columbia University Press, 1989), 190–99. (Originally published in *North America Review,* May 1904).

10. Horst J. P. Bergmeier and Rainer E. Lotz, *Hitler's Airwaves: The Inside Story of Nazi Radio Broadcasting and Propaganda Swing* (New Haven: Yale University Press, 1997), 70–73.

11. The classic treatments of this topic include: Gaye Tuchman, *Making News: A Study in the Construction of Reality* (New York: Free Press, 1978); Herbert J. *Guns, Deciding What's News* (New York: Pantheon Books, 1979); Mark Fishman, *Manufacturing the News* (Austin: University of Texas Press, 1980). For a more recent critique from a Canadian perspective, see Robert A. Hackett and Yuezhi Zhao, *Sustaining Democracy? Journalism and the Politics of Objectivity* (Toronto: Garamond Press, 1998).

12. I am indebted to Ben Bagdikian for much of what follows. See Ben H. Bagdikian, *The Media Monopoly* (Boston: Beacon Press, 2000).

13. Stephen Ponder, *Managing the Press: Origins of the Media Presidency, 1897–1933* (New York: Palgrave, 1998).

14. Ina Howard, "Power Sources," *Extra!* June 2002.

15. Commission on Civil Disorders, "The Role of the Mass Media in Reporting of News about Minorities," in Goldstein, *Killing the Messenger,* 200–27.

16. Stuart Ewen, *PR! A Social History of Spin* (New York: Basic Books, 1996); Sheldon Rampton and John Stauber, *Trust Us, We're Experts: How Industry Manipulates Science and Gambles with Your Future* (New York: Putnam, 2001); Alicia Mundy, *Dispensing with Truth: The Victims, the Drug Companies, and the Dramatic Story behind the Battle over Fen-Phen* (New York: St. Martin's Press, 2001).

17. Suzanne Vranica, "Publicist Group Bolsters Its PR Holdings," *Wall Street Journal,* May 30, 2001.

18. For a brilliant discussion of this and its implications for democracy, see Christopher Lasch, *The Revolt of the Elites and the Betrayal of Democracy* (New York: W. W. Norton, 1995), chapter 9.

19. Joseph N. Cappella and Kathleen Hall Jamieson, *Spiral of Cynicism: The Press and the Public Good* (New York: Oxford University Press, 1997).

20. James Fallows, *Breaking the News: How the Media Undermine American Democracy* (New York: Vintage, 1996).

21. Bagdikian, *Media Monopoly.*

22. Edwin C. Baker, *Media, Markets and Democracy* (New York: Cambridge University Press, 2002), 106.

23. George Farah and Justin Elga, "What's *Not* Talked About on Sunday Morning? Issue of Corporate Power Not on the Agenda," *Extra!* September/October 2001, 14–17.

24. Interview with Charles Lewis, in *Orwell Rolls over in his Grave,* documentary by Robert Pappas.

25. For examples of the CPI's work, go to http://www.publicintegrity.org.

26. See, for example, Edward Jay Epstein, *News from Nowhere: Television and the News* (New York: Vintage Books, 1973); Bill Kovach and Tom Rosenstiel, *Warp Speed: America in the Age of Mixed Media Culture* (Century Foundation Press, 1999); W. Lance Bennett, *News, the Politics of Illusion* (New York: Longman, 2001); Jeffrey Scheuer, *The Sound Bite Society: Television and the American Mind* (New York: Four Walls Eight Windows, 1999).

27. Harold Meyerson, "If I Had a Hammer: Whatever Happened to America's Working Class?" *Los Angeles Times*, September 2, 2001.

28. Jon Fine, "California Dreaming, Scheming," *Advertising Age,* April 30, 2001, 81.

29. See, for example, Judith Serrin and William Serrin, eds., *Muckraking! The Journalism That Changed America* (New York: New Press, 2002); Nancy J. Woodhull and Robert W. Snyder, eds., *Defining Moments in Journalism* (New Brunswick, NJ: Transaction Publishers, 1998).

30. For a collection of their reports collected into a book, see Donald L. Bartlett and James B. Steele, *America: What Went Wrong* (Kansas City, MO: Andrews McMeel, 1992).

PART II

The Economics of Inequality

Conventional wisdom holds that the United States is as strong as it is because of the value it places of market freedom. In a free market, according to Adam Smith, with a minimum of government interference, competition will ensure that the best products and services are made available at the best possible prices; further, Smith claims that there is no better means of distributing resources throughout a society. These conditions ensure that the most talented, innovative, and ambitious individuals will thrive and, consequently, that society will thrive as well. These conditions ensure that the most opportunities will be available to the most people and the American Dream will become a reality for all those who are deserving.

Jeff Faux challenges some of these suppositions in his article on the "governing class." He argues that the system is set up to favor the rich and, therefore, the market is somewhat less free and opportunities to advance oneself in the class hierarchy are somewhat less accessible than is commonly believed. As the elite have become increasingly rich and powerful over the past several decades, they have come increasingly to reserve the privileges of wealth and power for themselves, further reducing the viability of the American Dream for the rest of society. Moreover, he cites evidence that in many advanced industrialized countries where there is more government intervention in the economy and less concentration of wealth at the top, there are actually as many or more opportunities to advance oneself as in the United States.

Faux points out that the elite have managed to concentrate more of their wealth and power by shifting economic risks away from themselves and onto the middle and working classes. The consequent insecurity produced by the shifting of risk is the focus of the second reading in this part, by Jacob Hacker. In the post–World War II era, an unwritten "social contract" governed the relations between employers and employees in most American companies. The contract "read" that if employees dedicated their working careers to a company, that company would ensure them privileges based on seniority, provide them and their families with health care, and guarantee them a pension upon retirement. The company took on considerable financial risk to ensure a dedicated, loyal, hardworking labor force, and the American economy prospered. The working class, middle class, and upper class all shared in this prosperity until the 1970s, when a series of recessions rocked the American economy and when outsourcing labor to Third World countries became increasingly attractive to American corporations. As Hacker documents, corporations began cutting their workers loose from the social contract. Since then, the upper class has seen a meteoric rise in their share of the wealth and the working and middle classes have become more susceptible to catastrophic declines in their financial prospects. Hacker wrote this selection before the current economic crisis; of course, the problem of insecurity has been greatly exacerbated since then.

Most Western European countries, on the other hand, offer far more in terms of security. Unions are strong, labor laws make it very difficult to fire an employee, and the state ensures health care is available to all and usually ensures free education at all levels and a generous pension upon retirement. In the next article, Robert Kuttner describes how he believes he has found in Denmark an economy that allows for the blending of the best of American economic principles with the best of the welfare state principles found in its neighboring European countries. The keys to the success of the Danish economy, he argues, are manifold. Unlike their European counterparts, it is not difficult for a Danish employer to lay off an employee. This gives the business sector much more flexibility to adapt to new technologies and an ever-changing business environment in a globalized economy. On the other hand, high taxes—higher tax rates than most American would tolerate—provide a generous safety net for those out of work and for "highly customized" job retraining. The result, says Kuttner: a flexible, highly productive, well-paid workforce. Kuttner provides an important caveat, however: Economies evolve slowly and are highly reflective of the cultures in which they arise. The Danish economy reflects Danish history and values and could not easily be transferred to another culture. That does not mean, however, that there is nothing for us to learn from the Danish economy.

Different aspects of a country's economic model can be exported across national boundaries. Deregulation—that is, minimal government intervention in the economy—was one particular aspect of the American model that was exported around much of the world in the last two decades. The most recent subprime mortgage meltdown and credit crisis revealed the flaws in the extreme noninterventionist approach of American capitalism, and many countries are coming to regret their emulation of the American model.

In the next article, sociologist Joan Ferrante discusses the plight of the world's poor. Many Americans think that the United States has been very generous in helping the poor in foreign countries through foreign aid. But, in fact, the United States does relatively little in this regard and could do a lot more. Further, many who deal with issues relating to global poverty argue that, through its domestic and foreign policies, the United States does more to hurt the poor than to help them. By subsidizing U.S. farmers and encouraging agricultural exports, U.S. products often undercut prices in the poor countries and undermine local economies. Furthermore, the United States–based World Bank often requires Third World countries to open their markets to exports and cut back on social programs as a condition of foreign debt repayment. In countries that are already astonishingly poor, cutbacks in welfare provisions, health care, and education can have devastating effects and only serve to keep the poor poor. Ferrante, however, draws our attention to the United Nation's Millennium Development Project and to programs that do offer some hope for success in some of these countries.

CHAPTER 5

The Governing Class

Jeff Faux

CLASS UNCONSCIOUSNESS

The influence of money on American politics is a fact of life. It would follow that the rich have more influence on public decisions than the rest of us. It would also seem to follow that the rich, as a class, act together in their common interest.

Yet the idea of the rich as a political class is quickly dismissed by the punditry as obsolete Marxist "conspiracy theory." The accusation that someone is waging "class warfare" is one of the most effective conversation stoppers in American political life.

The promotion of shared class interest is natural human behavior; people who are alike tend to socialize with each other, reinforce each other's views of the world, and act together when their common interests are at stake. It would be odd if the richest and most influential individuals did not act in their common interest. Indeed, Adam Smith himself was a conspiracy theorist. As he famously observed, "People of the same trade seldom meet together, even for merriment and diversion, but the conversation ends in a conspiracy against the public."[1]

The constraints on the public discussion of economic class seem to apply primarily to those at the top. The poor are studied to death by government agencies and liberal foundations as a substitute for a serious national effort to combat poverty. We know who the poor are, what they eat, how they behave. The ostensible purpose of the research is to guide policies aimed at changing the behavior of those at the bottom.

Another, more commercially motivated research industry studies the middle class, breaking it into small niches (for example, upwardly mobile urban white women between twenty-five and thirty, retired seniors in the Southwest, non-college-graduate males in medium-sized cities, and so on). Most of this research—conducted at universities, as well as private survey research firms—is driven by the desire of corporate managers, politicians, and others who sell to mass markets to better identify the most profitable "niches." As with studies of the poor, research on the middle class is also aimed at attitude and behavioral change—in this case, to get consumers to buy certain products or vote for certain candidates.

In contrast, there is comparatively little serious research on the composition and behavior of the American elite. In the academic world, departments of sociology, political science, and economics are parts of the university system run by people of or near the governing class. Scrutinizing and publishing reports on their behavior as a class might suggest some practical-change agenda as well, a prospect that they would clearly rather not encourage.

Of course, political, sports, and entertainment figures, including business celebrities like Donald Trump and Ted Turner, fill the pages of newspapers and magazines and soak up TV airtime and tabloids. They are icons to be worshipped or envied as individuals, but not a class to be examined for its collective impact on our lives....

THE TOP FIFTY THOUSAND

Conventional wisdom asserts that America is a middle-class country, because that's what most Americans say they are.

When pollsters ask Americans if they are lower, middle, or upper class, 80 to 90 percent typically select "middle." In fact, the middle 80 percent of the distribution of income in America covers a huge range. In 2002, it spanned $10,620 to $114,112.

The media often stretches the range further. Steve Case, the former chair and CEO of America Online, was frequently referred to in the press as coming from the "middle class." Yet as G. William Domhoff notes, "His father was a corporate lawyer and his mother a descendant of a sugar plantation owner. He grew up in an exclusive Honolulu neighborhood, attended a high-status private school in his teens and graduated from Williams College, his father's alma mater. He received his start at the company that later became AOL through his older brother, already established as an investment banker and a member of the company's board of directors."[2] In another common confusion of "class," Bill Gates is celebrated as a college "dropout" who made good. But Gates's story is not what most of us think about when we hear the word "dropout." He is the son of a well-to-do corporate lawyer and went to a private prep school, before entering Harvard. He dropped out to form Microsoft.[3] Bill Clinton's origins were more modest, but they hardly deserve the label "poor" or "humble" the media often gives them. His mother was a registered nurse and his father a partner in an auto dealership, which in most of 1950s America were above-average circumstances. Writer Garry Wills notes, "This was no Dogpatch, as one can tell from the number of Clinton's childhood friends who went on to distinguished careers."[4]

The initial response to pollsters is clearly limited by the choices presented. When respondents are offered a fourth choice, "working class," the results shift. According to the National Opinion Research Center of the University of

Chicago, in 1998, in the middle of an economic boom, 45 percent of the public considered themselves "working class" whereas 46 percent said they were "middle class." Five percent said they were lower and 4 percent upper class.[5]

The term "working class" carries a huge ideological burden in American culture. It is commonly associated with images of downsized blue-collar industrial workers, who in 2003 represented only 12 percent of the labor force. So the survey results undoubtedly understate the extent to which people think of themselves as working, rather than middle, class.

Another way to define "working class" is to separate those whose income depends on work from those whose income is derived from investment. In the early 1990s, Robert Reich estimated that 80 percent of the workforce was labor-dependent and 20 percent composed of wealthy people who lived off their investments or "symbolic analysts," that is, highly paid professionals who sold their specialized services in the global market. Sociologists Robert Perucci and Earl Wysong come up with similar numbers, identifying 20 percent of the population as "privileged." These are people with high incomes, extensive power on the job, and income security. The vast majority of these are a "credentialed" class of managers and highly paid professionals. At the top is a super-rich class of 1 to 2 percent of Americans who live on investment income and are protected by their vast wealth.[6]

Professor Michael Zweig of the State University of New York at Stony Brook divides the labor force into three broad classes, based largely on the power people have in and around their job. He estimates that in 1996 the working class—those with no power—represented the bottom 62 percent of the country's workers. Its members are now overwhelmingly in the service sector, almost half female, and roughly 10 percent unionized. He breaks the middle class into three groups: small businesspeople, supervisors and middle managers, and professionals. Together they make up 36 percent. Zweig estimates the "capitalist" class—the top managers and directors of corporations employing more than five hundred workers—at roughly two hundred thousand people. From this group he winnows out those who serve on the boards of directors of only one major corporation and adds some major political and cultural leaders affiliated with the major corporations. He concludes with an estimate of an American "ruling class" of roughly fifty thousand people[7]—1.7 percent of Americans.

Fifty thousand is clearly too many to comprise some secret conspiracy. But the class system in America is not born of a secret conspiracy. Domhoff observes, "Not everyone in this nationwide upper class knows everyone else, but everybody knows somebody who knows someone in other areas of the country, thanks to a common school experience, a summer at the same resort, membership in the same social club, or membership on the same board of directors. The upper class at any given historical moment consists of a complex network of overlapping social circles knit together by the members they have in common and by the numerous signs of equal social status that emerge from a similar lifestyle."[8]

BREAKING INTO THE RULING CLASS IS GETTING HARDER, NOT EASIER

But does it matter? The United States appears to be a mobile society, where people easily move up and down the socioeconomic ladder. So what if there are classes? If your position depends on your abilities and not the class that you were born into, what's the problem?

Compared to many other places in the world, and other times in history, America today certainly provides more opportunities for talented people to better themselves. Our history has many examples of people who climbed from humble origins to places of power and wealth. The Horatio Alger story of the poor boy who rises to riches represents an icon of the American experience.[9]

But the United States is not as mobile as the official catechism would have it, and the evidence is that it is getting less so. In the roughly three decades following World War II, the distribution of income and wealth became more equal and mobility among classes improved. Labor unions gave greater bargaining power to workers, educational opportunities were expanded, and government-subsidized housing gave working-class Americans access to a wealth-building asset. Then, after the 1970s, both trends reversed. For example, 74 percent of families that were in poverty at the beginning of the decade of the 1970s remained there at the end. During the decade of the 1990s, despite the fast overall economic growth and the increase in two-earner families, 77 percent remained poor. During the 1970s, 73 percent who started the decade in the top 20 percent remained there. In the 1990s, 77 percent stayed at the top. Sons of fathers in the bottom three-quarters of the socioeconomic scale were substantially less likely to rise out of their class in the 1990s than they were in the 1960s.[10]

James Heckman, a Nobel Prize-winning economist at the University of Chicago, concluded, "The big finding in recent years is that the notion of America being a highly mobile society isn't as true as it used to be."[11]

The persistence of inherited status is often rationalized as the natural result of genetically transmitted characteristics. Race and gender, for example, are significant determinants of economic status. We know that good-looking, intelligent people are more successful, and although we can argue over the degree to which good looks and intelligence are inherited, that genes play some role is not in doubt. Still, the overwhelming evidence in the last twenty years is that inherited *status* is more important than inherited genes. In an exhaustive analysis of the research, professors Samuel Bowles and Herbert Gintis concluded in 2002 that "wealth, race, and schooling are important to the inheritance of economic status, but IQ is not a major contributor, and…the genetic transmission of IQ is even less important."[12]

Conventional wisdom among the globalist elite is that inequality is the price a society must pay for increasing social mobility, reflecting greater opportunity. Thus, for example, the governing class never seems to tire of telling Americans how lucky they are compared with the citizens of Western Europe who are so protected from competition that they have no incentive to succeed. Yet, although the United States has the highest level of income inequality among all advanced societies,[13] a child born to poverty actually has a greater chance of moving up the class ladder in Western Europe and Canada than in the United States. Economist Miles Corak, who analyzed dozens of studies on this point, told the *Wall Street Journal* in May 2005, "The U.S. and Britain appear to stand out as the least mobile societies among the rich countries studied."[14] France and Germany, regularly ridiculed by the American elite for economic policies that supposedly discourage ambition, actually provide more room for mobility than does the United States. Canada and the Scandinavian countries, home of high taxes and generous welfare, are, according to the numbers, even greater lands of individual opportunity.[15]

Yet over the last thirty years the gap between the EU's and U.S.'s GDP per hour narrowed from 35 to 7 percent. Productivity per hour of work in Austria, Denmark, and Italy is at U.S. levels. In France, Belgium, Germany, Norway, and Ireland it is higher.[16] Returns on investment in Europe have been the match of America's for the previous decade. Moreover, this has been accomplished without the huge amount of overseas borrowing that has sustained the American economy. As a special report by the *Economist* in June 2004 concluded, "The widely held belief that the euro area economies have persistently lagged America's is simply not supported by the facts."[17]

It is precisely this economic dynamism that has allowed Europe to maintain its social safety net and economic democracy in spite of a more competitive world. You can become a billionaire quicker in America, but your chances of living a longer, more secure life, with time for your family and friends, free from the anxiety of economic ruin if you get sick, and a higher-quality education for your children, are much greater in Western Europe. European workers have taken more of their productivity gains in leisure—primarily in longer holidays and shorter workweeks. Over their lifetimes, Americans work an estimated 40 percent more hours than do workers in France, Germany, and Italy.

The immediate cause of reduced economic mobility in the United States has been the closing off of avenues of escape from low-wage jobs. The traditional job paths into the middle class—unionized industrial jobs and unskilled government service—have shrunk. While opportunities for further upward mobility have declined, rising costs have priced people in the lower end of the income distribution out of the market for a college education, the springboard for the next generation.

In the decade of the 1990s, after adjusting for inflation, the annual cost of undergraduate tuition plus room and board rose 21 percent at public colleges and 26 percent at private ones.[18] The annual cost of sending a child to Harvard is now $41,500. Of course, subsidies and loans are available for the extraordinary child of poverty. But for the only moderately gifted person from poor or ordinary families, opportunities are slipping away. For example, they must compete with children from families who can afford to pay $400 an hour to a tutor who knows how to raise SAT scores. Then they must compete against children who simply go to the best schools because their parents went there. The *Economist* reported in late 2004 that "legacies"—children admitted because their parents are alumni—made up a significant share of the student body. "In most Ivy League institutions, the eight supposedly most select universities of the northeast, 'legacies' make up between 10% and 15% of every class. At Harvard they are over three times more likely to be admitted than others. The students in America's places of higher education are increasingly becoming an oligarchy tempered by racial preferences."[19]

Children of wealthier families are further fast-tracked by the growing importance of internships—the new apprentice system for careers in the most competitive and attractive fields, such as communications, entertainment, and politics. Each year, several thousand young people come to Washington to work for no money, or very little, in order to make career connections and add to their résumés for prestigious graduate schools. They work for congressional offices, at the White House, at newspapers and TV stations, think tanks, NGOs, lobbying firms, and for political consultants. Mark Oldman, co-founder of a career counseling center, told the *New York Times*, "It used to be that internships used to be a useful enhancement to one's resumes. Now it's universally perceived as an essential stepping stone to career success."[20]

But fewer college students can afford to take unpaid internships. At the very least, they have to pay for housing, food, and transportation away from home in an expensive city. For the large numbers who have to make as much money as possible in the summer to help pay for the rising costs of college, taking an unpaid internship is close to impossible.

Not, of course, entirely impossible. As in many areas of life in the United States, the extraordinarily committed person from modest means has a shot at success. In the summer of 2004, the *Washington Post* interviewed one student who worked two paying jobs as well as a full-time unpaid internship—eighty-nine hours a week. But by and large, the apprenticeship for careers in public policy is being reserved for children of families with the means. Those who must wait tables, deliver packages, or do other work to earn a living on their "vacation" fall behind in the race to find a place at the top of power structure.

GAPS BETWEEN CLASSES

As the class structure of American society hardens, the gap between those at the top and the rest of the economy is widening. In 2002, the average income of the very top one-tenth of 1 percent of income earners—about 145,000 taxpayers—was over $3 million. It had more than doubled since 1980. This group's share of all income also more than doubled. The share of income going to the rest of those in the top 10 percent also rose, but much less. The share of income going to the bottom 90 percent fell.[21] Wealth is even more concentrated. In 2001, the top 1 percent of households held 33 percent of all Americans' assets and 40 percent of all financial assets.[22]

Those who insist that America is a classless society point to the spread of corporate stock ownership as evidence that we are becoming a nation of capitalists—an "ownership society," as George W. Bush terms it. But in 2001 the wealthiest 1 percent of households held 33 percent of all corporate shares. Since they own most of the stock—and presumably have more access to information—the benefits of the great stock market boom went primarily to those at the top. Obviously owning just a few of the ten billion outstanding shares of General Electric does not give you any real clout with the company or get you an invitation to the White House.

Still, it is true that corporate stock ownership has widened over the past decade. By 2001, 52 percent of all households owned stock. Of these holdings 70 percent was *indirect*, that is, in mutual funds or 40l(k) plans. The broadening of stock ownership has been primarily driven by the shift away from defined-benefit *pension* plans—where the company invests and guarantees the pension payment—to the 40l(k), which is not a pension at all but a personal savings plan to which the employer makes a defined *contribution*. The risks that there might not be enough in the pension plan to retire on have shifted to the employee from the employer.

But the risks do not get shifted to those who rule at the top. Instead, in addition to allowing the corporate managers and owners to escape their traditional obligations to their longtime employees, the 40l(k) has provided opportunities for the corporate manager class to loot the life savings of their workers. As with so many companies that proclaimed themselves leaders of the "New Economy," Enron's executives created a corporate culture that celebrated the enterprise as one big, classless family. But the underlying economic relationship was class warfare; the corporation's managers were selling virtually worthless stock at high prices into their own workers' 40l(k) plans. Inevitably the bubble had to burst, and top executives who understood the company's finances bailed out—leaving the workers' 40l(k)s chock-full of virtually worthless stock. To add insult to injury, the people at the very top of the Enron pyramid got guaranteed-benefit pensions. Ex-CEO Ken Lay, for example, gets $457,000 a year for life.

CEO mismanagement of pension systems is endemic. In early 2005 the Pension Benefits Guarantee Corporation, the government agency that is supposed to insure private pensions, estimated that American corporations were underfunding their pensions to the tune of $450 billion. Meanwhile the agency was $60 billion in the red and facing a huge collapse of pensions in the airline industry. But, as in the Enron case, the CEOs who had been paid to take the risk offloaded it onto the employees. While United Airlines was reneging on almost $7 billion in pensions owed to more than 100,000 employees, the board gave its president an ironclad pension guarantee of $4.5 million. The board of Delta was equally generous to its CEO. US Airways went one better; six months before the corporation went bankrupt the board voted its CEO, Stephen Wolf, a $15 million golden parachute.[23]

"Certain things in life never seem to change," commented *New York Times* business writer Gretchen Morgenson, "and one of the most unfortunate constants is that when corporations behave badly, their rank-and-file workers are hit hardest. Executives always seem to vanish from the accident scene, toting their munificent pay packages; ordinary workers are left with little or nothing."[24]

Meanwhile, the upward redistribution of income continues because the system treats the class of corporate CEOs differently than it treats the rest of the workers. Roughly 60 percent of corporate directors are themselves CEOs of large corporations and are anxious to protect the prerogatives of their peer group. Conservatively measured, the pay of the average CEO rose from 26 times the pay of the typical worker in 1965 to over 310 times in 2000.[25]

Clearly, the owners and top managers of the nation's largest corporations have increased their bargaining power over those who work for them. In the last thirty years, union membership has dropped from 24 percent to 13 percent of the labor force—less than 10 percent in the private sector. As the collective bargaining position of labor has weakened, so has its political clout. The minimum wage, unemployment compensation, and the right to strike are among the legal rights that have been eroded.

The business media routinely rationalizes such disparities on the grounds that the individuals getting these salaries are "worth it." The "market" makes the decision. Thus, CEO salaries are said to reflect not a class society but a meritocracy. Since talent and aptitude for hard work are unequally distributed, so are the rewards.

In the early 1990s, many corporate boards announced that they had "reformed" the determination of CEO salaries by tying them to the corporation share price, considered the market's best measure of the company's value. In the dizzying Wall Street boom, CEO salaries and bonuses soared. Still, company-by-company analyses show little specific relationship between CEO pay and share prices. By 1999, *Business Week* magazine concluded that the connection between CEO salaries and company performance "has been all but severed in today's system."[26] The observation was prescient; when the market crashed in 2000 and stagnated for the next four years, CEO salaries kept going up.

If we don't pay the CEO a high salary, say the CEOs who make up a majority of boards of directors, they will be lured away by a competitor. Thus, in 1999, the board of Motorola gave its CEO, Christopher Galvin, $59.8 million in cash and stock. The chair of the compensation committee said they were worried about losing Galvin in this highly competitive market. Yet Galvin did not appear to be much of a "flight risk." His grandfather founded the company and his father had been CEO before him.[27]

The notion that the growing inequality between the majority of working Americans and those at the top of the income scale is purely a result of a failure of workers to keep up with technology also has been a fundamental governing-class doctrine for several decades. And for several decades the doctrine has been undermined by the facts. As economists Lawrence Mishel, Jared Bernstein, and

Sylvia Allegretto have shown, the technology claim fails by virtually every economic measure applied over the last two decades. Just as the change in the ratio of wages in Mexico and the United States cannot be explained because of differences in productivity, so the change in income between workers and managers, and the change among workers themselves, cannot be explained by variations in productivity.[28]

Despite the evidence, the subject of "who gets what in America" is today dominated by the claim that income is distributed according to one's contribution to productivity—if the rich make so much, it has to be because they are more productive. The result gives the governing class a way to minimize public discussion of what everyone knows is true—that those with the most income and wealth have the most political power, and that they use that power to perpetuate themselves....

LOYALTY TO WHOM?

The corporation is an instrument to power and wealth of the class that manages it. When a particular corporate instrument dulls and wears out, it is discarded. In the end, loyalty to one's class trumps loyalty to any specific corporation. For example, for decades, large U.S. manufacturing companies have complained loudly that they are at a competitive disadvantage in the global economy because of the expensive and dysfunctional U.S. health care system. U.S. firms must pay for health insurance for their workers, which in other countries is covered by public insurance programs. A car can be made in Canada, for example, for roughly $1,000 less than in America because the Canadians have a publicly funded national health care system.

Publicly funded national health care would clearly be a major benefit to large American manufacturers, who have been steadily losing markets both here and abroad. Accordingly, Bill Clinton expected that these corporations would support his health care agenda and designed his specific proposals with them in mind. Robert Rubin and Lloyd Bentsen told him that giving priority to the passage of NAFTA would bring them further along. But the CEOs of the large insurance companies were adamantly opposed. They demanded that their peers in other industries take a stand against the Democratic effort to "socialize" health care. The manufacturers withdrew their support from Clinton, despite their desperate need to find a way to reduce their health care costs. This was truly class solidarity.

One afternoon in the late 1980s, I gave a lecture to several steel company executives on trends in the U.S. economy. With charts on the wall, I described how the Reagan economic policies had priced American steel out of the market and led to the collapse of several firms and the downsizing of half the industry. The vice president of a major company interrupted me. "You don't have to explain the damage Reagan did to the steel industry," he said. "We know all about it. We lived through it."

"Then why do you guys support him?" I asked.

He leaned back in his chair and smiled. "You have to understand," he said. "He cut our taxes. And we're a country club crowd."

CRITICAL THINKING QUESTIONS

Why is it that when liberal politicians propose to increase taxes on the rich, they are accused of promoting "class warfare"? And why is this accusation, in Faux's words, "one of the most effective conversation stoppers in American political life"?

This selection was written before the economic crisis of 2008–2009. Do you think it is more or less relevant today? Explain your answer.

NOTES

1. Angela Partington, ed., *The Oxford Dictionary of Quotations* (New York: Oxford University Press, 1996), p. 650.
2. G. William Domhoff, *Who Rules America?* (Berkeley: University of California Press, 2002), p. 27.
3. Ibid., p. 58.
4. Garry Wills, "The Tragedy of Bill Clinton," *New York Review of Books* 51, no. 13 (August 12, 2004).
5. Jack Metzgar, "Politics and the American Class Vernacular," *Working USA*, Summer 2003, p. 49.
6. Robert Perrucci and Earl Wysong, *The New Class Society* (Lanham, Md.: Rowman and Littlefield, 2003), pp. 28–29.
7. Michael Zweig, *The Working Class Majority* (Ithaca, N.Y.: ILR Press, 2000), chapter 1.
8. Domhoff, *Who Rules America?*, p. 67.
9. Actually, the hero of the typical Horatio Alger stories did not succeed through hard work, but through a combination of luck and personal courage, for instance, rescuing a young lady who turns out to be the bank president's daughter.
10. Aaron Bernstein, "Waking Up from the American Dream," *Business Week*, December 1, 2003.
11. Ibid.
12. Samuel Bowles and Herbert Gintis, "The Inheritance of Inequality," *Journal of Economic Perspectives* 16, no. 3 (Summer 2002): 3.
13. United Nations Development Program, *Human Development Report 2003: Millennium Development Goals: A Pact among Nations to End Poverty* (New York: Oxford University Press, 2003), p. 282, table 13.
14. David Wessel, "Moving Up: Challenges to the American Dream," *Wall Street Journal*, May 13, 2005.
15. See Miles Corak, ed., *Generational Income Mobility in North America and Europe* (New York: Cambridge University Press, 2004), and Anders Bjorklund and Marcus Jantti, "Intergenerational Income Mobility in Sweden Compared to the United States," *American Economic Review* 87, no. 5 (December 1997): 1017.

16. Jeffrey I. Bernstein, Richard G. Harris, and Andrew Sharpe, "The Widening Canada–US Manufacturing Productivity Gap," *International Productivity Monitor,* Fall 2002, www.csls.ca/ipm.asp.

17. "Mirror, Mirror, on the Wall—Europe vs. America," *Economist,* June 19, 2004. European shortfalls often reported on the U.S. side of the Atlantic are mostly differences in statistical method. For example, Americans count spending on computer software as an investment; Europeans count it as a current expense.

18. NCES/Digest of Education Statistics Tables and Figures 2002, http://nces.ed.gov/programs/digest/ (Student Charges and Student Financial Assistance Table 312; accessed September 2, 2004).

19. "Meritocracy in America: Ever Higher Society, Ever Harder to Ascend," *Economist,* December 29, 2004, p. 15.

20. Jennifer Lee, "Crucial Unpaid Internships Increasingly Separate the Haves from the Have-Nots," *New York Times,* August 10, 2004, sec. A.

21. David Cay Johnston, "Richest Are Leaving Even the Rich Far Behind," *New York Times,* June 5, 2005, p. 1.

22. Lawrence Mishel, Jared Bernstein, and Sylvia Allegretto, *The State of Working America* (Ithaca, N.Y.: ILR Press, 2005), p. 279.

23. "An Immodest Proposal," CNN news report, June 13, 2005.

24. Gretchen Morgenson, "Who Loses the Most at Marsh? Its Workers," *New York Times,* October 24, 2004.

25. Mishel, Bernstein, and Allegretto, *The State of Working America,* p. 112.

26. Sam Pizzagati, *Greed and Good: Understanding and Overcoming the Inequality That Limits Our Lives* (New York: Apex Press, 2004), p. 27.

27. Ibid., p. 73.

28. Mishel, Bernstein, and Allegretto, *The State of Working America,* pp. 151–156.

CHAPTER 6

The New Economic Insecurity
Jacob S. Hacker

I was born in a small college town in Oregon in the early 1970s—just before the oil shocks, stagflation, and upheaval of the decade. I remember gas lines snaking around the block near my family's rented home, and my mother's dismay as prices in the supermarket, like unemployment, just kept rising. Underlying the surface calm was a growing unease—a sense that the nation was unsettled. My first real political memory was the Iranian hostage crisis; the first election I remember was Reagan's rout of Carter in 1980. What I didn't realize as I rode my red Raleigh bike through the quiet streets of my neighborhood was that a larger shift was also occurring in the wider world. An era was ending. A thirty-year period of shared prosperity in the United States was giving way to a new age of insecurity.

Today, the Internet, newspapers, and the airwaves are filled with debates over American national security. Yet a different kind of security threat, the kind many of us got our first taste of in the seventies, is looming larger and larger in the American consciousness. It's a threat that strikes middle-class families..., workers recently laid off from well-paying jobs in high-tech, parents struggling under the costs of a child's unexpected health problems—in short, our next-door neighbors, our friends, the people we cross paths with everyday. The threat level started rising around the time of my youth, slowly eroding the confidence of middle-class Americans that they'd have stable jobs, generous benefits, and smooth upward mobility, and that their children would enjoy greater economic security than they'd enjoyed. But who killed economic security and why remains a mystery that we have only just begun to plumb.

We all know something about rising *inequality* in the United States, the growing space between the rungs of America's economic ladder. We hear about the soaring incomes of princely executives who garner hundreds of millions in compensation even as workers at the middle and bottom fall farther and farther behind. Yet we have heard much less about rising *insecurity*, the growing risk of slipping from the economic ladder itself. Perhaps that's because the stories here seem more random—blue-collar workers laid off after long years of service, college-educated middle managers whose upward trajectories have been abruptly halted, working families thrown off balance by catastrophic expenses, middle-class parents who find that health and retirement plans are shifting more costs and uncertainties onto them. It's easy to find the common thread when the subject is hardening divisions between two Americas—one marked by deprivation, the other by excess. It's harder to find it in stories of loss and anxiety whose common element is not constancy or stability, but sudden and often unexpected change.

Inequality and insecurity are deeply interwoven, but they are not the same. Inequality has indeed risen sharply. Between 1979 and 2003 the average income of the richest Americans more than doubled after adjusting for inflation, while that of middle-class Americans increased by only around 15 percent.[1] Nonetheless, it is possible to look at rising inequality and still paint a positive picture. After all, Americans at all points on the income ladder have gotten richer—just not at equal rates—and during this same period, our economy has expanded handsomely. A rising tide may not be lifting all boats as well as it did in the 1950s and 1960s, but it is lifting them nonetheless.

But another tide has been rising in the United States since my youth—the rising tide of economic risk. Americans may be richer than they were in the 1970s, but they are also facing much greater economic insecurity. And this insecurity is increasingly plunging ordinary middle-class families into a sea of economic turmoil.

Consider some of the alarming facts. Personal bankruptcy has gone from a rare occurrence to a routine one, with the number of households filing for bankruptcy rising from fewer than 290,000 in 1980 to more than two million in 2005.[2] The bankrupt are pretty much like other Americans before they file: slightly better educated, more likely to be married and have children, roughly as likely to have had a good job, and modestly less likely to own a home.[3] They are not the persistently poor, the downtrodden looking for relief. They are refugees of the middle class, frequently wondering how they fell so far so fast.

Americans are also losing their homes at record rates. Since the early 1970s, the mortgage foreclosure rate has increased fivefold.[4] From 2001 to 2005 an average of one in every sixty households with a mortgage fell into foreclosure a year—a legal process that begins when homeowners default on their mortgages and can end with homes being auctioned to the highest bidder in local courthouses.[5] David Lamberger, a Michigan resident who has worked in the auto industry most of his life, can testify to just how shattering the process can be. David and his wife, Mary, purchased their two-story home in the metro Detroit area as an investment in the future for themselves and their four children. When David lost his job at an auto parts maker, he declared bankruptcy to delay foreclosure on the house. But the money he made working at a used-car lot hasn't been sufficient to keep them afloat, and now he's on the verge of losing his family's modest home.[6] For David and scores of other ordinary homeowners, the American Dream has mutated into what former U.S. Comptroller of the Currency Julie L. Williams calls "the American nightmare."[7]

Meanwhile, the number of Americans who lack health insurance has increased with little interruption over the last twenty-five years as corporations have cut back on workplace coverage for employees and their dependents. Over a two-year period, more than 80 million adults and children—one out of three nonelderly Americans, 85 percent of them working or the kids of working parents—spend some time without the protection against ruinous health costs that insurance offers.[8] They are people like Mark Herrara, a union carpenter who went out on his own to become an independent contractor. Health insurance wasn't a priority when Herrara was using all his resources to get his business off the ground. Or at least it wasn't until he woke up one morning with a massive headache. Reluctant to go to the hospital for fear of the costs, he finally relented only to discover that he had suffered two strokes and his brain was bleeding. Ineligible for Medicaid, his bills now outstrip his pay several times over. "I've got a $225,000 debt and yeah, if I come into any money, well, the first people I got to pay back is for this medical coverage," says Herrara.[9]

At the same time that the financial threats associated with our jobs, our homes, and our health care have all increased, corporations have raced away from the promise of guaranteed benefits in retirement. Twenty-five years ago, 83 percent of medium and large firms offered traditional "defined-benefit" pensions that provided a predetermined monthly benefit for the remainder of a worker's life. Today, the share is below a third.[10] Instead, companies that offer pensions provide "defined-contribution" plans, such as the 401(k), in which returns are neither predictable nor assured. Defined-contribution pensions can earn big returns, but they also can mean big risks: the risk of stock market downturns, the risk of inadequate savings, the risk of outliving one's account balances. Between 1989 and 1998—a decade in which 401(k) coverage exploded and the stock market boomed—the share of families whose pension savings allowed them to replace at least half of their prior income in retirement actually declined, as old-style guaranteed pensions rapidly became a thing of the past.[11]

Perhaps most alarming of all, American family incomes are now on a frightening roller coaster, rising and falling much more sharply from year to year than they did thirty years ago. Indeed, the *instability* of American families' incomes has risen substantially faster than the *inequality* of families' incomes. In other words, while the gaps between the rungs on the ladder of the American economy have increased, what has increased even more quickly is how far people slip down the ladder when they lose their financial footing.

And this rising insecurity does not come with any obvious silver linings. The chance that families will see their income plummet has risen. The chance that they will experience long-term movement up the income ladder has not. For average families, the economic roller coaster takes them up and down. It doesn't leave them any higher than when they started. As David Lamberger, the Michigan man who is in the process of losing his house, puts it, "There have been years I made $80,000, and there have been years I made $28,000....Sometimes we're able to pay bills and get by, but then stuff from the slow times never goes away. You can't catch up, and it comes back to haunt you."[12]

What's more, while these up-and-down swings are more severe for workers like David Lamberger who lack a college education, the pace by which instability has increased since the 1970s has been almost exactly the same for workers who've received a college degree as it has been for those who never earned a high school diploma. Educated professionals may comfort themselves with the thought that they are more financially stable than the check-out clerk who never finished high school. But compared with educated professionals in the past, they are experiencing much greater income swings—swings in fact comparable to those experienced by less-educated workers in the 1970s.

And while national income and wealth have indeed grown handsomely during the era in which insecurity has risen, the economic standing of the American middle class has increased only modestly. The incomes of middle-class families aren't much higher today than they were in the 1970s—and they are much more at risk.

Americans may be willing to turn a blind eye to growing inequality, confident in the belief that their own standard of living is still rising. But economic insecurity strikes at the very heart of the American Dream. It is a fixed American belief that people who work hard, make good choices, and do right by their families can buy themselves permanent membership in the middle class. The rising tide of economic risk swamps these expectations, leaving individuals who have worked hard to reach their present heights facing uncertainty about whether they can keep from falling. Economic inequality may stir up our envy as we ogle the BMWs and McMansions of our richer neighbors, but the prospect of economic insecurity—of being laid off, or losing health coverage, or having a serious illness befall a family member—stirs up our anxiety. And anxiety, as we shall see, is just what millions of middle-class Americans increasingly feel.

AMERICA'S HIDDEN INSECURITY

All this is likely to come as a surprise to those who follow current economic debate. Yes, stories of economic hardship appear in the news. Yes, complaints about particular economic problems, from low savings to high gas prices, are ubiquitous. But the general tone of economic discussion today is decidedly sunny. Americans, we are told, are richer than they have ever been—and not just at the top of the economic ladder. Most working Americans, analysts claim with certainty, are far surpassing their parents' incomes. Back in the fifties and sixties, the optimists point out, owning a new kitchen appliance or installing one's children in a thin-walled bedroom in a Levittown Cape Cod was the height of middle-class luxury. Now, those same middle-income families have DVD players, air conditioners, a cell phone, a bedroom for each family member, and a second car—amenities that only the very rich in the mid-twentieth century could afford.[13]

Not only are middle-income Americans enjoying riches beyond the imagination of citizens of any nation or time, according to this familiar account, they are also living in an age of virtually unparalleled growth. Productivity is rising handily. The economy is humming along. And even as growth rises, inflation and unemployment remain low.[14] In late 2005, the *Wall Street Journal* headlined an online news story about the economy: "The Miracle Continues."[15]

There's just one problem: Americans don't believe the miracle exists. In poll after poll in recent years, Americans have heaped scorn on the happy talk and the sunny statistics. They have said that the country is on the wrong economic track. They have said that they expect the economy to get worse, not better. They have said that their own financial situation is weakening. And they have said that leaders on both sides of the partisan aisle are failing to address their most fundamental economic concerns.

In exit polls taken as Americans left the voting booth in 2004, for instance, less than a quarter of middle-class voters said that the job situation in their community had improved in the previous four years, and less than a third said their own family's financial situation had improved.[16] Forecasts of the election that crunched just the economic numbers predicted the incumbent president, George W. Bush, would win in a landslide.[17] But on Election Day he squeaked through with the smallest popular vote margin for a winning incumbent president since 1828. Since then, public ratings of the economy have dropped even farther, as have Bush's approval numbers. Today, for all the happy talk, a majority of Americans say that the economy is worsening, that it's a bad time to find a good job, and that economic conditions are "fair" or "poor," rather than "excellent" or even "good." As a Gallup Poll report noted in March 2006, "Americans continue to resist giving the nation's economy positive ratings, regardless of what so-called 'hard' economic indicators may show."[18]

Commentators have offered plenty of reasons to explain—or, more accurately, explain away—Americans' continuing grumpiness. According to the curmudgeonly columnist Robert Samuelson, the United States has become a land of whiners: "Americans have developed perfectionist standards. We expect total prosperity and are disappointed by anything less. There should be no doubts or deficiencies."[19] Others have pointed to the negativity of the news media as the culprit, or Americans' growing unease about the war in Iraq.[20] But perhaps the most popular explanation is that voters have simply not woken up and smelled the economic coffee. Fully four years since the recession of 2001, Americans, we are told, are still gripped by an outdated and irrational pessimism that blinds them to the bountiful riches of the Miracle Economy.

It is high time to embrace a simpler thesis: Americans don't think the economy is all that good because, as far as they're concerned, it's not. And the main reason why it's not that good is that Americans' economic lives are becoming more insecure even though the basic statistics are strong. In March 2004, for example, unemployment and inflation were both low. Yet roughly half of Americans agreed that "America no longer has the same economic security it has

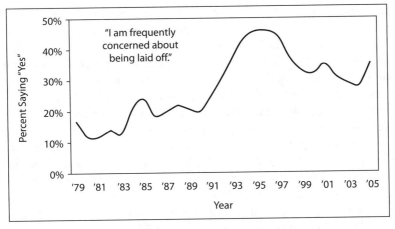

Figure 6.1 A Growing Perception of Job Insecurity
SOURCE: Towers Perrin. Reprinted with permission.

had in the past," while another fifth thought the statement could be true down the road. By contrast, just 27 percent believed that their economic complaints merely reflected the normal downside of the business cycle.[21]

This is not the first time that there has been a disconnect between basic economic statistics and what Americans say they are experiencing. Back in the mid-1990s, a similar—and similarly puzzling—process played out: Voters were far more negative about the economy than most statistics suggested they should be. In 1982, amid a severe recession that had pushed the unemployment rate up to nearly 10 percent, a poll by the private business research firm ISR found that only 12 percent of workers were "frequently concerned about being laid off." Yet in 1996, with the unemployment rate hovering around 5 percent—half what it was when the 1982 poll was done—the percentage of workers who said they were frequently concerned was 46 percent. Even in 2005, with the unemployment rate again at only 5 percent, the number of Americans worried that they would lose their jobs was still about three times as high as it was during the steep economic downturn of 1982 (see Figure 6.1).[22]

Americans, it seems, just don't get what the pundits are crowing about. And that's because the statistics that pundits love to cite don't capture what most Americans feel: a sense of ever-increasing financial risk.

THE RISK FACTOR

Pundits fixate on the current state of the economy: Is GDP growth accelerating or slowing? Is the job market expanding or contracting? Is the stock market rising or falling? These are important questions, but they are about the short-term waves of our economy—the movement on the surface, rather than the fundamental changes below. The Great Risk Shift isn't a wave—it's a rising tide that has increased the level of economic insecurity for nearly all Americans, in good times as well as bad.

Everyone knows what risk is when they experience it. When we first get behind the wheel of a car, or traverse the edge of a perilous cliff, we feel the butterflies in our stomach, the lightheadedness of fear. But conceptually, risk is not so easy to grasp. It turns all our conventional frames of reference on their head. We are used to thinking about averages, rather than about ranges; about what happens, rather than what could happen; about events at one point, rather than evolution over time—in sum, about levels, rather than dynamics.

Yet risk—the possibility of multiple outcomes, whether good or bad—is all about dynamics. Sophisticated investors in the stock market (the fearless surfers on the waves of risk) recognize this when they talk about the volatility of a stock as well as its return. If a stock has higher *volatility*, its price undergoes more substantial up and down shifts over time. These fluctuations in its price, or return, mean that the stock embodies greater risk for the investor, which is why savvy traders only snap up high-volatility stocks when they have high returns as well. Much of our increasingly sophisticated appreciation of risk comes from the efforts of economic players who deal with risk day in and day out to come up with new measures and new models for judging its magnitude and effects.

Risk is at the heart of some of capitalism's greatest successes. The entrepreneurs who financed the nation's first railroad tracks, prospected for oil, and bet on the success of microchips reaped outsized profits. Risk has also been the source of untold misery. For every story of a successful financial or business risk taken, there is one in which individuals lose their shirts. Risk is the reason companies go bankrupt, workers end up on the streets, and, at the extreme, financial markets crash. Seeing risk and understanding it, finding ways to quantify and share and manage it, gaining from its upsides while minimizing its downsides—these constitute some of the greatest achievements of the last two centuries. But while societies have the ability to master risk—to pool it across many people or address its root causes—societies also create risks: the risks of a dynamic investment market, the risks of interruption of earnings that arise in a division-of-labor economy in which people trade their work for pay, and, of course, the risks to health and the environment that modern production and consumption can pose.[23]

Economic insecurity lies on the dark side of risk. Although the term is rarely defined, *economic insecurity* can be understood as a psychological response to the possibility of hardship-causing economic loss. The psychology of insecurity is crucial, for it motivates many of our personal and social responses to risk—responses that can be either positive (buying insurance, building up private savings, forming a family) or negative (suffering anxiety, withdrawing from social life, postponing investments in the future because of fear of loss). Yet a feeling of insecurity is not enough to say someone is insecure. Insecurity requires real risk that threatens real hardship. We know that Americans think they are insecure. What I will show is that they have good reason to think so—that, like the investor who buys a highly volatile stock, Americans are facing much greater risk of substantial economic loss. The Great Risk Shift is the story of how a myriad of risks that were once managed and pooled by government and private corporations have been shifted onto workers and their families—and how this has created both real hardship for millions and growing anxiety for millions more.

Risk turns out to be a lot harder to capture precisely with people than with stocks. To know what the volatility of a stock is, we need only follow the ticker for a while (with the familiar caveat that past performance is no guarantee of future performance). To know what the volatility of families' economic standing is, however, we need to trace a representative set of families over time, preferably long periods of time. We need to follow these families through all the normal and abnormal events of life: births, deaths, relocations, the formation and destruction of families, and so on. We need, in short, to look at the economy the way people actually live it—as a moving picture, rather than an isolated snapshot.

That's not, however, what economic statistics typically do. Consider the growing body of research on inequality in the United States. We know the gap between the rich and the rest has grown dramatically over the last thirty years, reaching levels not seen since before the late 1930s. The spoils of our system are now so unevenly divided that we must reach back to the Robber Barons of the 1890s and Gatsbys of the 1920s for a similar comparison to today's gap between middle-income Americans and the super-rich. In 2003, the richest 1 percent of U.S. households averaged over $800,000 in annual income, or more than eighteen times the average for middle-income households. A quarter century ago, the richest 1 percent raked in less than twelve times as much as the middle class.[24]

Yet as arresting as this fact is, it's based on annual surveys that reach different people every year. These surveys can tell us how many people are rich and how many are poor, and how big the gap between the two is. But they cannot tell us whether the same people are rich or poor from year to year, or whether movement up (or down) the income ladder is greater or smaller than it used to be. We all know we'll never be as rich as Bill Gates. But can we depend, as our parents once did, on maintaining—or even better, steadily augmenting—our income share and standard of living? And how many people are experiencing the wild fluctuations in income (fluctuations that resemble some of our most volatile stocks) that David Lamberger's family has seen?

To answer these sorts of questions, we need to do more than take annual snapshots of income. We need to survey the same people over many years, following them even as they experience death, birth, marriage, pay raises, pay cuts, new jobs, lost jobs, relocations, and all the other events, good and bad, that mark the passage from childhood into old age. We need to see Mark Herrara ensconced in his union job as a carpenter as well as Mark Herrara, independent contractor, as he returns from the hospital, hundreds of thousands of dollars in debt. These kinds of surveys are called "panel surveys," and compared with the usual approach—contacting a different random group of people for each survey—they are exceedingly difficult to carry out. Surveyors must stay in contact with respondents (and their descendants) over long periods of time while periodically adding new respondents to keep the survey representative of a changing population.

Given the difficulties, it's perhaps understandable that no official economic statistic tries to assess directly the dynamics of family income. Curious citizens who spend a few hours on the websites of the Commerce Department or Census Bureau will come away with a wealth of snapshots of the financial health of American families—from annual wages and income to the gap between rich and poor. But they will search fruitlessly for even the most basic information about how the economic status of American families changes over time, much less about what causes these shifts. If they extend their search beyond official statistics, they will do better, but not much better. Many studies of income dynamics have been done. Yet when I began my research, nobody had looked at the simple question of whether the up-and-down swing of family incomes—the volatility of the American family stock, if you will—had risen or fallen over the last generation.

The answer can be found in the Panel Study of Income Dynamics (PSID)—a nationally representative survey that has been tracking thousands of families from year to year since the late 1960s. Nearly forty years into its operation, the survey has included more than 65,000 people, some of whom have been answering questions for their entire adult lives, others of whom have been in the survey since their birth. As a result, the PSID is uniquely well suited to examining how and why incomes rise and fall over time.

And what becomes immediately clear is that family incomes rise and fall a lot—far more than one would suspect just looking at static income-distribution figures. To take just one simple measure, during a ten-year period, Americans aged twenty-five to sixty-one have less than a fourth the income in the year they're poorest, on average, as they do in the year they're richest.[25] Over ten years, in other words, an average Betty who had $60,000 in her best year would have less than $15,000 in her worst. This striking disparity, it turns out, is a dramatic increase from even the relatively recent past: In the 1970s, as Figure 6.2 shows,

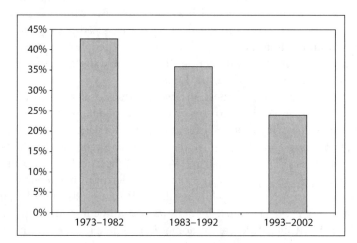

Figure 6.2 The Rising Ratio of Low-to-High Family Incomes over 10-Year Periods
SOURCE: Panel Study of Income Dynamics; Cross National Equivalent File. These are the average ratios of low-to-high family income over 10 years; the analysis follows household heads, with top and bottom 1 percent of observations trimmed.

the low was just shy of 50 percent below the high—meaning our average Betty would have around $30,000 in her worst year, rather than less than $15,000.

These up-and-down swings are what get missed when we use annual snapshots to look at the distribution of American family income. There are not just the well off and the poor. There are Americans who are doing well one year and poorly the next—and vice versa. In fact, a surprisingly big chunk of the income inequality that we see across families at any point in time is due to transitory shifts of family income, rather than to permanent differences across families.

This is a point that the Miracle Economy crowd loves: Sure, inequality is growing, they say, but mobility is alive and well, making any comparison of income groups misleading. The fact that Betty could make $20,000 one year and more than $60,000 in another just shows that the American Dream remains strong for those willing to pull themselves up by their own bootstraps.

But this conclusion is as wrongheaded as the image of a frozen class structure that is sometimes taken from income-distribution statistics. Upward mobility is real. Men like Mark Herrara do start their own businesses; David Lamberger does get his dream house. But upward mobility is usually not dramatic, and there is no evidence that it has increased substantially in the contemporary era of rising inequality.[26] Recently, the *Economist* magazine, no foe of American-style capitalism, reported that "a growing body of evidence suggests that the meritocratic ideal is in trouble in America. Income inequality is growing to levels not seen since the Gilded Age, around the 1880s. But social mobility is not increasing at anything like the same pace: would-be Horatio Algers are finding it no easier to climb from rags to riches, while the children of the privileged have a greater chance of staying at the top of the social heap."[27]

The evidence shows, moreover, that income mobility across generations is actually lower in the United States than in other affluent nations. According to recent studies, there is more social mobility in European nations such as Sweden than in the United States, and in fact only South Africa and Britain have as little mobility across generations.[28]

Plus, there's an even more glaring oversight of paeans to social mobility: What goes up also goes down. As we saw with David Lamberger, volatility of income can mean making $80,000 one year and freefalling to $28,000 the next—and the year of the freefall could be the year one loses not only one's job but also the family home.

The difference between these two scenarios is profound, because both research and common sense suggest that downward mobility is far more painful than upward mobility is pleasurable. In fact, in the 1970s, the psychologists Amos Tversky and Daniel Kahneman gave a name to this bias: "loss aversion."[29] Most people, it turns out, aren't just highly risk-averse—they prefer a bird in the hand to even a very good chance of two in the bush. They are also far more cautious when it comes to bad outcomes than when it comes to good outcomes of exactly the same magnitude. *The search for economic security is, in large part, a reflection of a basic human desire for protection against losing what one already has.*

Anybody who has watched the differing responses of a toddler to the pleasure of receiving a new toy and the pain of having one taken away knows about loss aversion. Yet it is something of a puzzle why adults behave like toddlers when it comes to things they own. After all, in classic economic theory, goods are simply tickets to enhanced welfare, and we should have no special attachment to things we already possess if other items could deliver welfare just as effectively. Aside from the "diminishing marginal utility" of income (the fact that every dollar buys slightly less happiness or well-being, making us value a $100 gain modestly less than we lament a $100 loss), people should, according to standard theory, value losses and gains in roughly equal terms.

Experiments show that few actual people think this way. Even when given a trivial item, we suddenly become willing to pay a much higher price to retain it than we were willing to shell out to buy it. (One clever study involved giving college students mugs and pencils—seemingly trivial items—and finding that they insisted on selling their gift for much more than they'd earlier said they would pay for it.) Researchers call this "endowment effect," and it helps explain myriad features of the economic world that are otherwise inexplicable: why, for example, wages don't generally fall during recessions; why stocks have histori- cally had to pay much higher returns than bonds to entice people to take on the increased risk of loss—and why insurance against economic injury remains the most popular and extensive of all the activities that modern governments engage in. (In 2001, for example, spending by public and private social programs like Medicare, Social Security, workplace retirement pensions, and unemployment insurance represented a quarter of our economy.[30])

The endowment effect is surprisingly strong. Americans are famously opportunity-loving. But when asked in 2005 whether they were "more concerned with the opportunity to make money in the future, or the stability of knowing that your present sources of income are protected," 62 percent favored stability and just 29 percent favored opportunity.[31] In 1996 the Panel Study of Income Dynamics asked participants a similar question. Which would you choose: your present job with your current income for life, or a new job that offered a fifty-fifty chance of doubling your income and a fifty-fifty chance of cutting your income by a third?

On paper, the deal was pretty good. If John was making $30,000 and won the gamble, he'd have $60,000—a comparative fortune. If he lost the gamble, he'd make $20,000—not great, but not terrible compared with what he had. If John didn't worry at all about risk, the choice would be easy: Since he has a fifty-fifty chance of ending up with $60,000 and a fifty-fifty chance of ending up with $20,000, the rational position would be to treat the gamble as offering $40,000 (the average of the two salaries)—an amount a third higher than his present income.

Few people who were asked whether they'd take the gamble were rational in this fashion: Only 35 percent said they would roll the dice. Lowering the poten- tial income loss budged some of the cautious, but surprisingly few. More than a third of respondents said they wouldn't accept even the most generous deal that the survey presented (which promised, on average, an almost 50 percent income increase). People like to gamble, but not, it seems, when they think that their long-term economic security is on the line.

Loss aversion is a well-known phenomenon in behavioral economics—the study of how people actually reason about economic choices. But the implications of loss aversion for our understanding of the ups and downs of economic life are often missed. What loss aversion means is that drops in income, even when later compensated for by equal or even larger gains, are intensely psychologically difficult. (Perhaps that's why a recent cross-national study finds that the best predictor of the self-reported happiness of a nation's citizenry isn't national income, but the extent of economic security.[32]) Upward mobility is nice; downward mobility is devastating, especially since it's on the downward trips that jobs, houses, savings, and the other things gained on the way up often get lost.

THE ECONOMIC ROLLER COASTER

Judged on these terms, what my evidence shows is troubling, to say the least. When I started out, I expected to see a modest rise in instability. But I was positively thunderstruck by what I found: Instability of before-tax family incomes had skyrocketed. *At its peak in the mid-1990s, income instability was almost five times as great as it was in the early 1970s.* And while it dropped during the boom of the late 1990s, it never fell below twice its starting level, and it shot up again in recent years (my data end in 2002) to three times what it was in the early 1970s. The rise is less pronounced when taxes are taken into account, but it's still dramatic.[33] Moreover, while instability and inequality have both risen substantially, instability has actually risen faster and farther than inequality. The gap between Bill Gates and Joe Citizen is a lot larger than it used to be, but it's actually grown less quickly than the gap between Joe Citizen in a good year and Joe Citizen in a bad year.

Isn't this just a problem of the less educated, the workers who've fallen farthest behind in our skills-based economy? The answer is no. Volatility is indeed higher for less educated Americans than for more educated Americans—slightly more than twice as high.[34] (It is also higher for blacks and Hispanics than for whites, and for women than for men.) Yet, surprisingly, volatility has risen by roughly the same amount across all these groups over the last generation. During the 1980s, people with less formal education experienced a large rise in volatility, while those with more formal education saw a modest rise. During the 1990s, however, the situation was reversed: Educated workers saw the instability of their income rise more, and by the end of the decade, as Figure 6.3 shows, the overall instability of their income had increased by almost as much from the 1970s baseline. The story of the 1990s is the generalization of the income instability that once afflicted mostly the less educated and disadvantaged. Increasingly, more educated workers are riding the economic roller coaster once reserved for the working poor.

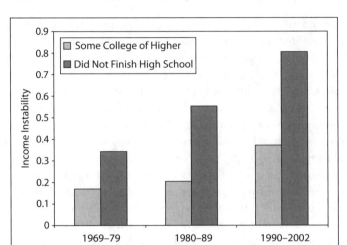

Figure 6.3 Instability Rise at Both High and Low Education Levels
SOURCE: Panel Study of Income Dynamics.

This suggests that growing economic instability cannot easily be chalked up to poor personal choices. It might be argued that workers without a college degree could have gotten additional education (although this would leave open the question of who exactly would fill the millions of jobs that require little advanced training or skills). But how can we say that about workers who did stay in school and yet still experience high levels of volatility? The forces that have created the new economic roller coaster—growing workplace insecurity, the new risks of the contemporary family, and the erosion of stable social benefits—have swept through the lives of almost every American. Prudent choices can reduce but not eliminate exposure to the growing level of economic risk. Indeed, many of the choices that expose Americans to risk—from going to school to seeking a better job to building a family—are precisely the ones that most greatly benefit families and society as a whole. Families can give up many of these risks only by giving up on the American Dream.

A major clue on this point is found in the Panel Study of Income Dynamic's questions about risk mentioned earlier, questions that measure the extent to which people are risk-seeking or risk-avoiding. If much of the volatility in income that we see in the PSID was caused by voluntary choices, then we would expect that people who are more worried about risk would be less likely to experience large income swings. After all, if you want to avoid risk and you have the power to do so, you are unlikely to put yourself in a position where your income is highly unstable. If you are risk-averse, you won't choose to go back to graduate school when you can continue working at the local bank, and you won't leave your cushy corporate job for that one-in-a-million opportunity to get your own business off the ground.

Yet the PSID data reveal few consistent relationships between how risk toler-ant someone is and how unstable their income is.[35] The risk tolerance of some-one in the PSID turns out to be a terrible predictor of their income experience. People who are highly risk-seeking experience wild income swings, but so too do people who are highly risk-averse—which is not at all what one would expect if income volatility were mostly voluntary. It's as if a cautious grandmother and reckless teenager were each equally likely to take up bungee jumping, a sure sign that something other than unfettered free choice is at work.

Maybe so, but couldn't family breakup be driving the results? If a family divorces, for example, does one family become two, each with a lower income? The answer is yes, divorce does cause some instability in my measure, but that's because divorce is a real risk to family incomes. The analysis looks at how unsta-ble people's incomes are, and family changes (birth, death, marriage, divorce, separation, and the like) are an important cause of income instability. Lest it be thought that rising divorce rates are the main reason for the rise in income insta-bility, however, it's worth pointing out that the U.S. divorce rate actually peaked in the early 1980s and fell in the 1990s—precisely when economic instability climbed.[36]

How can we make sure that we aren't confusing instability with income growth? If Americans are getting richer and richer, wouldn't that show up as greater income variance? The answer is no. (The premise of the question is also wrong—most Americans are not flying into the income stratosphere.) Just as with the volatility of a stock, the volatility of family incomes is meant to capture how much income bounces around its overall growth path. If the income of a family rises smoothly, then it's not counted as unstable. It has to swing, not just climb.[37]

DROP ZONE

Still, it's hard to think about income instability in the same way we think about stock volatility. When most of us contemplate the financial risks in our lives, we don't worry about the up-and-down movement of our finances around some long-term path, even though that's technically what financial risk is. We think about downside risks, about drops in our income—and understandably so: We are loss averse, in major part, because losing what we have can require wrenching adjustments. We have to cut back, to go without, to adjust our expectations, to rethink our lives. When losses are catastrophic, people have to confront what the anthropologist Katherine Newman calls "falling from grace"—to contend "not only with financial hardship, but also with the psychological, social, and practi-cal consequences" of losing our proper place.[38]

We can get a better sense of these "falls from grace" by looking specifically at drops in family income. About half of all families in the PSID experience a drop in real income over a two-year period, and the number has remained fairly steady. Yet families that experience an income drop fall much farther than they used to. In the early 1970s the typical income loss was a bit more than 25 percent of prior

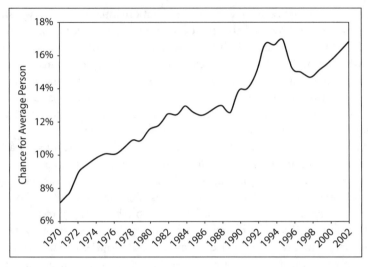

Figure 6.4 Americans' Chance of a 50 Percent or Greater Income Drop
SOURCE: Panel Study of Income Dynamics. Results are from a logistic regression predicting drops in household-size-adjusted family income among individuals aged 25–61.

income; by the late 1990s it was around 40 percent.[39] For a family earning $42,000 (the median income for U.S. households in 1999), a 40 percent loss would mean an income drop of almost $17,000. And remember, this is the median drop: Half of families whose incomes dropped experienced even larger declines.

Figure 6.4 uses somewhat fancier statistics to show what the chance of experiencing a 50 percent or greater family income drop is for an average person each year. The probability of a 50 percent or greater drop for an average person was just 7 percent in the 1970s. It's risen dramatically since, and while (like income volatility) it fell in the strong economy of the 1990s, it has recently spiked to record levels.[40] There is nothing extraordinary about "falling from grace." You can be perfectly average—with an average income, an average-sized family, an average likelihood of losing your job or becoming disabled—and you're still two-and-a-half times as likely to see your income plummet as an average person was thirty years ago.

The most dramatic consequence of "falling from grace" is poverty—subsistence at a level below the federal poverty line (for 2006, an annual income of slightly less than $10,000 for an individual and about twice that for a family of four).[41] Our conventional view of poverty envisions a distinct group—"the poor," "the truly disadvantaged," "the underclass"—whose experience of deprivation lasts for years, and perhaps even extends across generations. Yet long-term poverty, though real and worrisome, is rarer than we think. Most of the poor at any moment are not poor for long. Less than a tenth of Americans experience five consecutive years of poverty during their adult life.[42]

The flipside of this picture, however, is that poverty afflicts many more Americans at some point in their lives than is commonly believed. Take the U.S. child poverty rate of 20 percent—a rate three times higher than the norm in northern Europe. Most people look at this number and think that "only" one in five kids experience poverty in the United States. That's true in any given year, but the kids who are poor change from year to year. If we want to know how many kids experience poverty at some point in their childhood, we need to count up the total number who spend at least a year beneath the poverty line by the age of eighteen. The answer, it turns out, is shocking: More than *half* of American kids spend at least a year in poverty by the time they're eighteen—compared with less than a quarter of German children.[43]

The picture is similar for adults. Using the PSID, the sociologist Mark Rank has calculated that a stunning 58.5 percent of Americans will spend at least a year in poverty between the ages of twenty and seventy-five.[44] I have asked Rank whether this striking result somehow hinges on including cash-poor college students in the calculations, and he has assured me it does not. Indeed, even if *everyone* younger than twenty-five is excluded from the calculations, the chance of experiencing poverty by the age of seventy-five is still almost 50 percent.

Worse, the chance of spending at least a year in poverty has increased substantially since the late 1960s, even for workers in their peak earning years. People who were in their forties in the 1970s had around a 13 percent chance of experiencing at least a year in poverty during their forties. By the 1990s, people in their forties had more than a 36 percent chance of ending up in poverty—an almost threefold rise.[45]

These numbers illuminate the hidden side of the Miracle Economy: the growing economic insecurity faced by ordinary workers and their families. And unlike other possible measures, these statistics are as direct and comprehensive as they come. They tell us by exactly how much the roller coaster goes up and down, looking at every source of a family's income, from friends to employers to government. Rates of bankruptcy or home foreclosure (which have both increased dramatically in the last generation) might go up because financial meltdowns have lost their stigma or because people are making foolish choices about spending and debt. But nobody files for a major income drop or spends their way into a highly unstable income. Income instability is the DNA of economic insecurity, its basic building block.

Income instability is the building block of insecurity, but it is not the whole. Indeed, as dramatic and troubling as the trends we have examined are, they vastly *understate* the true depth of the problem. The up-and-down movement of income among working-age Americans is a powerful indicator of the economic risks faced by families today. Yet economic insecurity is also driven by the rising threat to families' financial well-being posed by budget-busting expenses like catastrophic medical costs, as well as by the massively increased risk that retirement has come to represent, as more and more of the responsibility of planning for the post-work years has shifted onto Americans and their families. When we take in this larger picture, we see an economy not merely changed but fundamentally transformed.

WHAT'S GOING ON?

Over the years as I've revisited the old neighborhood where I once rode my bike, it looks essentially unchanged—a city in amber. The supermarket is still there. Close by, other neighborhoods have sprouted large new homes amid long stretches of green. The surface is tranquil, even improved. The old gas station where I remember gas-crisis lines is gone; a microbrewery has moved in nearby. But beneath the calm facade is a growing canker. Families whose lawns remain manicured fear not being able to meet their next mortgage payment. Having seen their salaries drop once, if not more than once, they question their ability to hang on.

The Great Risk Shift is a classic murder mystery: Who killed economic security in the United States? The potential culprits are many, the motives murky, the evidence often circumstantial.... The answer is not as neat or simple as some murder mysteries, but then again we are talking about momentous shifts in our economy, our society, and our nation's social policies. A change as big as the Great Risk Shift does not usually stem from a single grand cause.

The mystery, it turns out, is not just why Americans have come to face greater economic risk. There are straightforward reasons why workers and their families experience heightened financial instability in today's economy and society. The big puzzle is why political and corporate leaders have been so slow to respond. In fact, the puzzle is even deeper than that. Political and corporate leaders haven't simply failed to respond; they've actually piled on new risks even as Americans have become increasingly less secure....

CRITICAL THINKING QUESTIONS

This selection was written before the economic crisis of 2008–2009. What facts and factors would you include if you were updating this selection? How do the historical trends documented by Hacker help provide a context for understanding current economic trends?

NOTES

1. Joel Friedman, Isaac Shapiro, and Robert Greenstein, "Recent Tax and Income Trends Among High Income Tax Payers" (Washington, DC: Center on Budget and Policy Priorities, 2006), available online at www.cbpp.org/4-10-06tax5.htm.
2. Data courtesy of Elizabeth Warren, Harvard Law School. The number of filings was inflated in 2005 by the rush of filings before the bankruptcy bill took effect. The number in 2004, however, still exceeded 1.56 million.

3. Elizabeth Warren, "Financial Collapse and Class Status: Who Goes Bankrupt?" *Osgoode Hall Law Journal* 41, no. 1 (2003).

4. Calculated from Peter J. Elmer and Steven A. Seelig, "The Rising Long-Term Trend of Single-Family Mortgage Foreclosure Rates" (Federal Deposit Insurance Corporation Working Paper 98-2, n.d.), available online at www.fdic.gov/bank/analytical/working/98-2.pdf.

5. Christian E. Weller, *Middle-Class Turmoil: High Risks Reflect Middle-Class Anxieties* (Washington, DC: Center for American Progress, December 2005), 3.

6. Suzette Hackney, "Families Fight for Their Homes," *Detroit Free Press*, October 15, 2005.

7. Joe Baker, "Foreclosures Chilling Many US Housing Markets," *RockRiver Times,* March 22–28, 2006, available online at www.rockrivertimes.com/index.pl?cmd=viewstory&id=12746&cat=2.

8. *One In Three: Non-Elderly Americans without Health Insurance, 2002–2003* (Washington, DC: Families USA Foundation, 2004), available online at www.familiesusa.org/issues/uninsured/about-the-uninsured.

9. *The Newshour with Jim Lehrer,* "Coping without Health Insurance," November 28, 2005, available online at www.pbs.org/newshour/bb/health/july-dec05/insurance_ll-28.html.

10. John H. Langbein, "Understanding the Death of the Private Pension Plan in the United States" (unpublished manuscript, Yale Law School, April 2006).

11. Edward Wolff, *Retirement Insecurity* (Washington, DC: Economic Policy Institute, 2002), excerpt available online at www.epinet.org/content.cfm/books_retirement_intro.

12. Hackney, "Families Fight for Their Homes."

13. Stephen Moore and Lincoln Anderson, "The Great American Dream Machine," *Wall Street Journal,* December 21, 2005, A18; Gregg Easterbrook, *The Progress Paradox: How Life Gets Better while People Feel Worse* (New York: Random House, 2003).

14. "Fact Sheet: Economic Growth Continues—Unemployment Falls Below 5 Percent," White House News Release, January 6, 2006, available online at www.whitehouse.gov/news/releases/2006/01/20060106.html.

15. Mark Gongloff, "The Afternoon Report: The Miracle Continues," *Wall Street Journal Online*, December 6, 2005.

16. Exit poll results are at www.cnn.com/ELECTION/2004/pages/results/states/US/P/00/epolls.O.html.

17. Ray C. Fair, "A Vote Equation and the 2004 Election," Yale University, October 2004, available online at http://fairmodel.econ.yale.edu/vote2004/vot!004.htm.

18. Frank Newport, "Republicans All Alone in Viewing the Economy as Good," Gallup Poll News Service, March 21, 2006.

19. Robert J. Samuelson, "Presidential Prosperity Games," *Washington Post*, December 21, 2005, A31.

20. Noel Sheppard, "According to the Media, Most Economic News Is Bad," Free Market Project, November 7, 2005, available online at www.freemarketproject.org/news/2005news20051107.asp; John D. McKinnon, "Bush Plugs Economy, Hinting at Thrust of 2006 Campaign," *Wall Street Journal*, December 6, 2005, A4.

21. NBC News and *Wall Street Journal* Poll, March 15, 2004, available via the Roper public opinion database (http://roperweb.ropercenter.uconn.edu/iPoll) as USNBCWSJ.04MAR.R31.

22. Other polls showed even higher concern: In response to a 1995 *New York Times* survey, 53 percent of Americans said their own job was insecure, nearly 83 percent said it was hard to find a good job in their community, and 48 percent feared that they would lose their own job *and* that it would be hard to find a good job in their area. The survey, "Economic Insecurity," is available via the Roper public opinion database (http://roperweb.ropercenter.uconn.edu/iPOLL) as USNYT95-012. The same basic pattern appears in public responses to the Gallup Poll, which has been asking a standard question about economic conditions since 1992. The share of Americans describing the economy as "only fair" or "poor" was extremely high in the early 1990s (peaking at 90 percent in 1992) and did not fall below a majority until late 1997. It remained low in 1998, 1999, and 2000, bottoming out at 25 percent in 2000, before shooting back up to its current high levels of 60–80 percent in 2001. This pattern matches up almost perfectly with the trends in pre-tax income volatility discussed later in this chapter. Indeed, between the beginning of 1992 (when Gallup Poll data begin) and the end of 2002 (when the income volatility data end), the correlation between negative public appraisals of the economy and income volatility is greater than 70 percent. Gallup Poll data available online at http://poll.gallup.com. The question wording is as follows: "How would you rate economic conditions in this country today—as excellent, good, only fair, or poor?"

23. This is the core theme of Ulrich Beck, *Risk Society: Towards a New Modernity*, trans. Mark Ritter (London: Sage, 1992).

24. Calculated from Congressional Budget Office (CBO), *Historical Effective Federal Tax Rates: 1979–2003* (Washington, DC: CBO, December 2005).

25. Like all the other figures reported in this chapter, these numbers are adjusted for inflation and exclude both questionable data—mainly, people who report zero or negative incomes—and people younger than twenty-five and older than sixty-one, so as to leave out college students and retirees. Unless otherwise noted, they also include all sources of cash income (including alimony) and account for government taxes and benefits.

26. See, for example, Andrew J. Rettenmaier and Donald R. Deere, "Climbing the Economic Ladder" (Washington, DC: The National Center for Policy Analysis, 2003), 17–18. Though the overall tone of the report is cheerful, a closer look at the data tells a less sunny story. While in a given year almost half of people in the middle three quintiles are likely to move to a different quintile, they are more likely to move to the quartile below the one they're in than the one above. Those in the bottom quartile, who by definition cannot fall to a lower quartile, are much less likely to move. Only 31 percent are likely to change quartiles, and most of these move up by only a single quartile.

27. "Ever Higher, Ever Harder to Ascend," *Economist*, December 29, 2004, available online at www.economist.com/world/na/displayStory.cfm?story_id=3518560.

28. Alan B. Krueger, "The Apple Falls Close to the Tree, Even in the Land of Opportunity," *New York Times*, November 14, 2002, C2.

29. Daniel Kahneman and Amos Tversky, "Prospect Theory: An Analysis of Decisions Under Risk," *Econometrica* 47, no. 2 (1979).

30. Willem Adema and Maxime Ladaique, "Net Social Expenditures, 2005 Edition," OECD Social Employment and Migration Working Paper No. 29 (Paris: Organization for Economic Cooperation and Development, 2005), table 6 ("gross social expenditure"), available online at www.oecd.org/dataoecd/56/2/35632106.pdf.

31. George Washington University Battleground 2006 Survey, March 24, 2005.

32. International Labor Office, *Economic Security for a Better World* (Washington, DC: Brookings, 2004).

33. For a description of the model used to calculate over-time income variance, see Robert A. Moffitt and Peter Gottschalk, "Trends in the Transitory Variance of Earnings in the United States," *Economic Journal* 112 (March 2002): 68–73. Data on taxes and government benefits are from the Cross-National Equivalent File, Cornell University, available online at www.human.cornell.edu/che/PAM/Research/Centers-Programs/German-Panel/Cross-National-Equivalent-File_CNEF.cfm. In these analyses, family income variables are adjusted for family size by dividing by the square root of family size—a common equivalence scale, reflecting the lesser costs per person of maintaining a larger family.

34. Not surprisingly, volatility is also higher for lower-income Americans. See Lily Batchelder, "Taxing the Poor: Income Averaging Reconsidered," *Harvard Journal on Legislation* 40 (2003): 395–452.

35. This is not to say that there are no relationships; people with higher incomes do seem less worried about the risk of economic loss than people with lower incomes, and people who have experienced substantial upward mobility are less worried about risk than those who have experienced flat or falling incomes.

36. Elmer and Seelig, "The Rising Long-Term Trend of Single-Family Mortgage Foreclosure Rates," 31.

37. What's more, all these results are based on analyses that transform income so that it is what statisticians call "mean-independent." This is just a fancy way of saying that the level of a family's income doesn't directly affect the measure of volatility. Take two families—each of whose income drops by 20 percent between two years. If family one has twice the income as family two, that 20 percent drop is going to be twice as large in dollar terms, even though the two families are experiencing exactly the same size change relative to their prior income. Using mean-independent measures fixes that, making it possible to compare volatility across people with different income levels and across years with different average income levels. All these analyses also use inflation-adjusted dollars, so year-to-year changes in the inflation rate don't show up as instability either.

38. Katherine S. Newman, *Falling from Grace: The Experience of Downward Mobility in the American Middle Class* (New York: Free Press, 1988).

39. Median drops in family income are estimated by looking at changes in post-tax family income over a two-year period among families experiencing income drops. As in the other PSID analyses, the sample is restricted to families with heads aged twenty-five to sixty-one with positive income. The table shows the median drops from 1969 to 2002.

Years	Median Drop in Family Income
1969–1971	27%
1970–1972	29%
1971–1973	29%
1972–1974	29%
1973–1975	27%
1974–1976	29%
1975–1977	29%
1976–1978	27%
1977–1979	26%
1978–1980	26%
1979–1981	26%
1980–1982	28%
1981–1983	30%
1982–1984	30%
1983–1985	28%
1984–1986	28%
1985–1987	31%
1986–1988	28%
1987–1989	25%
1988–1990	25%
1989–1991	27%
1990–1992	30%
1991–1993	39%
1992–1994	37%
1993–1995	35%
1994–1996	38%
1996–1998	44%
1998–2000	37%
2000–2002	38%

40. A logistic regression was used to estimate the average probability that an individual experiences at least a 50 percent drop in family-size-adjusted income over a two-year interval. The analysis controls for the demographic and social characteristics of individuals, as well as individuals' permanent family income levels (measured as the five-year moving average of family income). It also includes variables that account for different types of risks that may contribute to income drops, including unemployment, retirement, disability, illness, divorce, marriage, and the birth or adoption of children. A time-trend variable in the model captures any consistent change in the probability of income loss over time that cannot be accounted for by the other variables in the model. To predict the probability of income loss for each year for an "average" individual simply requires using the coefficients of the model to calculate the probability of an income drop of 50 percent or greater for an individual possessing the mean values on each of the variables. The rising trend shown in figure 6.4 is robust to the inclusion of individual fixed effects—that is, controlling for individual-specific attributes that are invariant over time but that may be correlated with the likelihood of an income drop.

41. U.S. Department of Health and Human Services 2006 Poverty Guidelines, available online at http://aspe.hhs.gov/poverty/06poverty.shtml.

42. Mark Rank, *One Nation, Underprivileged: Why American Poverty Affects Us All* (New York: Oxford University Press, 2004), 94.

43. Lee Rainwater and Timothy M. Smeeding, *Poor Kids in a Rich Country: America's Children in Comparative Perspective* (New York: Russell Sage Foundation, 2003), 52, 58.

44. Rank, *One Nation, Underprivileged*, 94.

45. Daniel Sandoval, Thomas A. Hirschl, and Mark R. Rank, "The Increase of Poverty Risk and Income Insecurity in the U.S. since the 1970's" (paper presented at the American Sociological Association Annual Meeting, San Francisco, CA, August 14–17, 2004).

CHAPTER 7

The Copenhagen Consensus

Robert Kuttner

Adam Smith observed in 1776 that economies work best when governments keep their clumsy thumbs off the free market's "invisible hand." Two generations later, in 1817, the British economist David Ricardo extended Smith's insights to global trade. Just as market forces lead to the right price and quantity of products domestically, Ricardo argued, free foreign trade optimizes economic outcomes internationally.

Reading Adam Smith in Copenhagen—the center of the small, open, and highly successful Danish economy—is a kind of out-of-body experience. On the one hand, the Danes are passionate free traders. They score well in the ratings constructed by pro-market organizations. The World Economic Forum's Global Competitiveness Index ranks Denmark third, just behind the United States and Switzerland. Denmark's financial markets are clean and transparent, its barriers to imports minimal, its labor markets the most flexible in Europe, its multinational corporations dynamic and largely unmolested by industrial policies, and its unemployment rate of 2.8 percent the second lowest in the OECD (the Organization for Economic Cooperation and Development).

On the other hand, Denmark spends about 50 percent of its GDP on public outlays and has the world's second-highest tax rate, after Sweden; strong trade unions; and one of the world's most equal income distributions. For the half of GDP that they pay in taxes, the Danes get not just universal health insurance but also generous child-care and family-leave arrangements, unemployment compensation that typically covers around 95 percent of lost wages, free higher education, secure pensions in old age, and the world's most creative system of worker retraining.

Does Denmark have some secret formula that combines the best of Adam Smith with the best of the welfare state? Is there something culturally unique about the open-minded Danes? Can a model like the Danish one survive as a social democratic island in a turbulent sea of globalization, where unregulated markets tend to swamp mixed economic systems? What does Denmark have to teach the rest of the industrial world?

These questions brought me to Copenhagen for a series of interviews in 2007 for a book I am writing on globalization and the welfare state. The answers are complex and often counterintuitive. With appropriate caveats, Danish ideas can indeed be instructive for other nations grappling with the enduring dilemma of how to reconcile market dynamism with social and personal security. Yet Denmark's social compact is the result of a century of political conflict and accommodation that produced a consensual style of problem solving that is uniquely Danish. It cannot be understood merely as a technical policy fix to be swallowed whole in a different cultural or political context. Those who would learn from Denmark must first appreciate that social models have to grow in their own political soil.

COMPASSIONATE CAPITALISM

At the center of the current Danish model is a labor-market strategy known as flexicurity. The idea is to reconcile job flexibility with employment security. The welfare state is often associated with rigid job protections: laws and union contracts making it illegal or prohibitively expensive to lay off workers. In much of the rest of Europe, labor-market rigidities have been blamed for high unemployment rates and for a welfare state of "insiders and outsiders," in which the well employed fiercely protect their jobs at the expense of those with little or nothing. It is here that Denmark offers its most ingenious blend of free markets and social democracy: despite heavy unionization, there are no regulations against laying off workers other than the requirement of advance notice.

In fact, Denmark has Europe's highest rate of labor turnover. What is more, much of it is voluntary. A 2005 Eurobarometer poll found that over 70 percent of Danes think it is a good thing to change jobs frequently, compared with less than 30 percent in neighboring Germany. Danish respondents reported that they had changed employers an average of six times, the highest figure in the European Union (EU). One in three Danes changes jobs every year. And with employers free to deploy workers as they wish and all Danes eligible for generous social benefits, there is no inferior "temp" industry, because there is no need for one. As precarious short-term contract employment has grown in most other countries, the number of Danes in temporary contracts has decreased since the mid-1980s. Where most other OECD nations have a knot of middle-aged people stuck in long-term unemployment, in Denmark, the vast majority of the unemployed return to work within six months, and the number of long-term unemployed is vanishingly small.

What makes the flexicurity model both attractive to workers and dynamic for society are five key features: full employment; strong unions recognized as social partners; fairly equal wages among different sectors, so that a shift from manufacturing to service-sector work does not typically entail a pay cut; a comprehensive income floor; and a set of labor-market programs that spend an astonishing 4.5 percent of Danish GDP on initiatives such as transitional unemployment assistance, wage subsidies, and highly customized retraining.

In return for such spending, the unions actively support both employer flexibility and a set of tough rules to weed out welfare chiselers; workers are understood to have duties as well as rights. Professor Per Kongshøøj Madsen, director of the Center for Labor Market Research at Aalborg University, observes that the income security guaranteed by the Danish state, as well as the good prospects for reemployment, enables Danes to comfortably take risks with new jobs.

For the United States, 4.5 percent of GDP would be about $600 billion a year. Current U.S. spending on all forms of government labor-market subsidies—of which meager and strictly time-limited unemployment compensation makes up the most part—is about 0.3 percent of GDP, less than $50 billion. The dynamic U.S. economy, in other words, has plenty of flexibility but little security. Denmark suggests that a different path is possible.

The Danish model squares another circle by reconciling free trade with economic security. This is not an easy feat. In a global system, corporations can move around in search of low taxes, cheap labor, and scant social regulation. Yet in Denmark, even trade unionists are passionate free traders. One of my more startling interviews was with Marina Hoffmann, chief economist of the Danish Metalworkers Union and former senior economic adviser to the most recent Social Democratic prime minister, Poul Nyrup Rasmussen. "We need to convince Danish industry to do more outsourcing," this trade union leader improbably told me. "We are a small country and we survive by exporting.... If a Danish multinational manufacturing corporation can be more competitive by outsourcing components, we will be more competitive as a nation." In other words, hiving off routine production jobs and moving them to China and eastern Europe can help keep higher-end, knowledge-based design and engineering jobs in Denmark. And as manufacturing becomes more automated, a national policy of professionalizing service-sector jobs takes up much of the slack. A nursing-home worker in Denmark, for example, gets far more training, status, and pay than one in the United States.

I encountered an equally surprising set of enthusiasms when I interviewed the director of the Confederation of Danish Employers, Henrik Bach Mortensen, whose support for union-management partnerships would be most unwelcome at, say, the U.S. Chamber of Commerce. Employers value the system, said Mortensen, both for its absence of industrial conflict and for its supply of good workers. The collaborative vocational training system, he noted, is essential for Danish competitiveness. This view was confirmed in an extensive survey of Danish employers conducted by Professor Cathie Jo Martin, of Boston University. Companies, she found, support the model because it brings them tangible benefits in the form of skilled and adaptive employees.

The productive work force helps both large and specialized Danish export industries thrive. Denmark is a global leader in such niche exports as hearing-aid production (through world-class companies such as Oticon), consumer electronics (Bang & Olufsen), insulin (Novo Nordisk), environmental technology, and finely engineered plumbing fixtures. As a seafaring nation, Denmark has global shipping giants such as Maersk, which ranks 138 on the Fortune Global 500 list. And in the service sector, Danish multinationals, such as the ISS Group, with 220,000 employees worldwide, are among the largest contractors for janitorial and security-guard services for office buildings, airports, and hospitals.

Wages in Denmark are about 70 percent above the OECD average, but the high productivity of the Danish work force justifies them. And because the Danish welfare state is financed primarily by income taxes and not payroll charges, overall labor costs to employers are moderated. But more than anything else, as Jøørgen Søøndergaard, director general of the Danish National Institute of Social Research, pointed out to me, it is Denmark's culture of collaboration that allows win-win outcomes for corporations and their employees alike.

In another typically Danish bit of ingenuity, a good deal of consumer choice is deliberately built into the social-welfare model, since Denmark is highly libertarian as well as partly socialist. Choices are offered to accommodate individual preferences, so that the model enhances liberty rather than imposing one-size-fits-all regimentation. Consumer choice also allows the discipline of competition to keep social providers on their toes and to retain the support of more affluent Danes for the model. Thus, there is good socialized medical care, but the basic package is complemented by private insurance, now used by about seven percent of the population, and Danes have a broad choice of doctors and hospitals. There is excellent free public education all the way through university and graduate school, but private and religious schools can get 85 percent government financing. In the United States, school vouchers are promoted by the right as a way of undermining the public-school system; in Denmark, state-financed private schools are accepted by the left as a safety valve.

THE GREAT DANES

To fully grasp its dynamics, the foreign observer needs to recognize the Danish model not as a silver bullet of clever public policymaking but as the product of a century of Danish political and cultural history. The modern Danish social system began with the labor compromise of September 1899. The previous decade had seen a bitter struggle between raw industrial capitalism and the rising labor movement. After an increasingly enervating series of strikes and lockouts, the Danish employers association and the central trade union federation, the LO, struck a historic bargain. The employers gave the unions legal recognition, which was soon ratified and reinforced by the state; the unions, in turn, recognized the employers' right to direct work, prefiguring the flexicurity model of a century later. Both agreed to a system of dispute resolution that prohibited both strikes and lockouts.

Denmark never again experienced the type of organized union busting characteristic of the United States and most nations outside northern Europe. Trade unions were empowered to be the bargaining agents of nearly all Danish workers, whether or not the workers chose to pay for individual membership (most did). Their ranks swelled to the point where unions came to consider themselves less an interest group than the stewards of a larger system. Growing union membership also made the closely allied Social Democrats the dominant governing party and the custodians of the social model. But even centrist and center-right parties did not challenge that model's core elements, because they were so highly valued by the populace. Over the course of the twentieth century, the model was continuously refined. The ideal of an egalitarian society with broad economic security took hold as an object of national pride.

This social consensus, however, requires constant tending. In the 1970s, Denmark's then overly generous lifetime social benefits collided with slow growth resulting from the OPEC oil shock. With the unemployment rate rising sharply, a taxpayer revolt broke out; the nationalist, antitax Progress Party became Denmark's second largest. When I visited Denmark in the late 1980s, to write an article on the faltering Scandinavian "third way," it was not clear whether the Danish model would survive. As late as 1993, the unemployment rate remained stuck at 12 percent.

In the early 1990s, a new Social Democratic government, under Prime Minister Poul Nyrup Rasmussen and Finance Minister Mogens Lykketoft, brokered macroeconomic and labor-market improvements in three rounds of reforms. Growth was restored, and the model was refined. They worked through a commission that drew on business, labor, academia, and the other major political parties, striking a series of compromises that were typically Danish.

At the time, some prime-age, able-bodied Danes were using unemployment and disability benefits to stay out of the labor force, often for life—an embarrassment to the work ethic and a practice that was rendering the system unaffordable and undermining its legitimacy. The unions agreed to support a crackdown on abuses: the eligibility time for unemployment compensation was reduced from nine years to four and individualized reemployment plans were created that required the unemployed to meet regularly with counselors to seek new jobs, often in new occupations. (The labor movement's commitment, after all, is to facilitating and rewarding work, not idleness.) This brand of tough love forced many of Denmark's unemployed to seek and find jobs. And in return, the Danish government increased resources for highly customized training and temporary wage subsidies, with special provisions for workers under the age of 25. An unemployed Dane who reports to a job center can qualify for such opportunities as adult apprenticeships and university-level education. Denmark today has the world's highest percentage of workers, 47 percent, in some form of continuing education. Employer freedoms were also reaffirmed, helping to bring down unemployment. As Lykketoft observed, "When companies are aware of the fact that it is possible to get rid of the manpower when market conditions change, they will not hesitate to hire new people at an upswing."

Despite the coincidence of timing and some superficially similar elements, the Danish reforms of the 1990s were not remotely like welfare reform in the United States. The Danish unemployment benefit for a median-income family of four can be 95 percent of the prior wage. In the United States, it is about 30–35 percent, and many workers do not qualify. Whereas Danes can draw benefits for four years, the typical U.S. limit is six months. With the exception of small pilot programs, neither the U.S. welfare system nor the U.S. unemployment system offers sufficient support to enable people to cover their living expenses while they are undergoing retraining. And in the United States, a shift from a manufacturing job to a service-sector job typically means a significant pay cut.

As the continuing refinements of Denmark's labor-market policy suggest, there is constant debate, self-evaluation, and policy reformulation in order to keep renewing the model's dynamism and the political consensus that underpins it. Success requires continuous social dialogue, on the shop floor as well as on the floor of the Danish parliament. The latest refinements to flexicurity are focused on raising spending on the training of unskilled workers, further limiting the duration of unemployment benefits, and increasing pressure on the unemployed to actively seek new work. At the same time, Denmark is determined not to end up with the kind of low-wage service sector typical of deregulated capitalism, for that would undercut the entire model. For example, there has been an ongoing national debate about housecleaners. Housecleaning is an occupation that cannot be upgraded much by training: at the end of the day, making beds, doing laundry, and vacuuming carpets is pretty basic work. In the 1990s, after considerable debate, the Danish government decided that the only way to prevent housecleaning from becoming a ghetto of low-wage jobs was to subsidize the pay. So the Danish taxpayer got not only employment security, good medical insurance, generous family leave, and a secure pension but subsidized housecleaning as well. In 2002, as a cost-saving measure, these subsidy benefits were limited to less affluent Danes.

THE FUTURE OF FLEXICURITY

Can the Danish system survive? Today, the model is at risk of being eroded by multiple forces. One is fiscal and demographic: as the population ages, it is hard to keep providing high-quality benefits without raising taxes to unacceptably high levels, because the ratio of working people to retired people dwindles. However, thus far the Danes have managed to keep the basic system intact with adjustments around the edges.

The more serious threats to the Danish model have to do with several facets of globalization other than trade. A primary issue is immigration. Denmark, with a population of 5.47 million, now has about 330,000 foreign-born residents (approximately six percent of the population), about half of whom are Muslim. The number of non-European immigrants has tripled since the 1970s. With higher birthrates than native-born Danes, immigrants and their descendants are projected to rise to nearly ten percent of the Danish population by 2020.

Reconciling solidarity with diversity is a big challenge, and although the Danes are a fairly tolerant people, immigration undermines the social model in a number of mutually reinforcing ways.

The political system that underpins the Danish model is rooted in social norms that are enforced by subtle peer pressure. People use public spaces in respectful ways. The country is almost preternaturally tidy. A taxi driver is likely to remind you to fasten your seat belt. Denmark's traditional Lutheran heritage, with its concern for community and its distrust of ostentation, reinforces modern social democratic policies. Most immigrants to Denmark come from very poor countries, often with very different traditions and social behaviors. Denmark is historically Lutheran but tolerant and secular. The Danes prize irony. They were a little shocked when the decision by the newspaper Jyllands-Posten to publish satirical cartoons on Islam in 2005 made their small country a lightning rod for Muslim anti-Western feeling. The whole episode reflected Denmark's tolerance of everything but intolerance and underscored a growing backlash against immigrants, some of whom share neither Danish norms nor broader Enlightenment values.

Low-skill immigrants also consume a disproportionate share of public services, and this in a society where much of the middle class already feels overtaxed. Danes get a lot back for their taxes, but there is not much margin for error. Add high unemployment, and the system risks fiscal collapse. Add too many immigrants, and more native-born taxpayers will stop supporting the model.

At a political level, the presence of immigrants increases partisan fragmentation, which undermines the process of national consensus building. The antitax, antiforeign Danish People's Party won 25 parliamentary seats in the November 2007 general election, down only slightly from the peak representation of the predecessor Progress Party in the mid-1970s, when unemployment increased sharply. The DPP wants to restrict some aspects of the Danish social model, including its high taxes and benefits for foreigners, and the current liberal-conservative minority coalition government depends on the party's support for its parliamentary survival. In 2007, the New Alliance Party made its debut, offering a libertarian program of welcoming foreigners and rejecting much of the welfare state. In last November's general election, New Alliance picked up five seats in the parliament. The immigration issue also splits the Social Democratic Party, the traditional champion of the Danish model. Its idealistic leaders tend to be immigrant-friendly, but many of its core working-class voters want a harder line on foreigners.

Immigration also presents a frontal challenge to flexicurity, which is based on the premise that virtually every worker can be trained for a good job. Not surprisingly, the hardest cases are recent immigrants with weak educational backgrounds, few if any skills, and often a reluctance even to learn Danish. The statistics are somewhat better for the second generation, whose members are more likely to have a decent basic education. Yet the children of immigrants continue to lag behind those of native-born Danes in school performance, and according to Peter Birch Søørensen, chair of the Danish Economic Council and a leading economist at the University of Copenhagen, many immigrant children still do not speak fluent Danish, and non-Western immigrant children tend to do far worse on standardized tests. The Danish Economic Council recently recommended that working-age immigrants be required to have at least a bachelor's degree in order to get a work permit in Denmark.

There is a race going on between the social integration of the children of immigrants and the patience of the Danish middle-class taxpayer. All the political leaders I interviewed agreed that Denmark's ability to reconcile its social model with immigration will depend on the success of integration. If immigrants remain an undigested lump of alien cultures in the midst of a generous welfare state, accepting its benefits but rejecting its cultural norms, support for the social system will erode.

A serious defection of the middle class would push the Danish model to a tipping point, as very nearly happened during the recession of the 1970s. Some Danes see this outcome as a deliberate goal of the current center-right government of Prime Minister Anders Fogh Rasmussen. Although it is not acting as crudely as the conservative governments of Margaret Thatcher in the United Kingdom and Ronald Reagan in the United States did, Rasmussen's government sometimes seems to be deliberately nudging the Danish model toward that tipping point. His coalition, which has been in power since 2001, has trimmed health and education benefits, increased social charges, and left citizens to rely more heavily on supplemental private insurance. "They have been very successful at pushing more people to private kindergartens, private hospitals, private old-age care, in a fiscal context of limited public resources," says Lykketoft. This is all done in the name of fiscal discipline and consumer choice, but it pushes affluent citizens toward the conclusion that they would be better off with fewer social benefits and lower taxes. "The risk is that the consensus starts to crack," Sorensen told me. The government has also promoted lower-cost, nonunion unemployment benefit plans, to discourage individual workers from joining unions, accelerating a slow decline in union membership. Still, the government is far from making a frontal assault on the basic model, which continues to enjoy broad support.

None of these strategies, however, embraces the other key elements that make flexicurity both a political and a policy success. Most seek to buffer the dislocations of trade on the cheap. But the Danish model cannot be understood as a strategy merely of "compensating losers" or even of reinforcing political consent for free trade. It is part of a far broader national commitment to maintaining a highly egalitarian society in which there are no bad jobs and to the use of ongoing labor-market subsidies to create a highly skilled and dynamic work force as the essence of global competitiveness. The other northern European nations have their own successful variants of active labor-market policy, but most of the proposals outside Scandinavia that invoke the Danish model would appropriate the flexibility without the security. None is politically serious about the necessary scale of public outlay or social collaboration. "I am skeptical about how much of the model can be exported," says Lars Rohde, director of the Danish labor-market system, "because it is the product of unique circumstances."

It is possible, however, to learn from Danish flexicurity. For instance, the United States and other industrial nations might grasp the logic of far more systematic investment in the work force as a strategy for attaining greater competitiveness, equality, and security. This could be understood as a way to overcome a well-known market failure: industry's refusal to invest enough in its employees because of a justifiable fear that they will take their newly acquired skills elsewhere. Far from interfering with the rest of the market's efficiency, public investment in the work force actually enhances the market's dynamism. It reduces the resistance of workers to changing jobs and subsidizes a more productive work force over time, just as government compensates for another well-known market failure when it subsidizes basic research.

For example, one could imagine a new U.S. administration embarking on a broad program of upgrading human service work, so that every job tending to the old, the young, or the sick would be a professionalized job on the Nordic model. This would require both government standards and significantly increased government outlays—on pre-kindergarten and child care, on better training and career prospects for paraprofessionals caring for the aged, and on workers in the lower tiers of the health-care system. This scale of commitment would produce over ten million middle-class service-sector jobs that could not be exported, replacing vanishing middle-class blue-collar jobs. Such an approach, however, would require a major political shift—progressive taxation, higher levels of public spending, and a renewed commitment to a far more egalitarian society.

Yet the United States cannot import Danish political or cultural history. Economic historians have a concept known as path dependence. The classic example is the QWERTY keyboard, which was created in 1873 with an oddly inefficient configuration of letters devised to keep typewriters' mechanical keys from sticking. Although more efficient keyboards were invented several decades ago, generations of Americans had grown up learning QWERTY, and we remain stuck with it. Path dependence reflects the dead hand of prior learning and lazy habits, as well as embedded economic and political power. Some would say that the market dominance of Microsoft's products over the technically more elegant Apple products is another case of path dependence and consumer lock-in.

So it is with social policy. Policy paths are heavily dependent on prior history, as Americans are reminded whenever they try to depart from the illogic of employer-provided medical insurance. Because of the unique social and political history behind it, Danish flexicurity policy cannot be imported whole by other countries. There are important differences between the welfare states of Scandinavia and those of Germany and France, whose labor safeguards are more protectionist and less flexible. Even greater are the differences with the United States, where unions try to protect what they have because there is no system for facilitating job transitions or for moderating extreme wage disparities. It is hard to imagine the United States importing Danish industry's embrace of trade union partners, or the Danish labor movement's comfort level with outsourcing, or the Danish taxpayer's tolerance of total tax rates of 50 percent. In an interrelated system, changing one element requires changing others.

Yet a national policy of greater competitiveness and greater equality based on dynamic investment in worker skills is too good an idea to ignore. Denmark breaks through stale notions about the inexorable tradeoff between equality and efficiency, as well as the conventional view shared by the American left and the American right that social justice and free trade are incompatible. If a U.S. administration had the political nerve to propose an active labor-market policy on a serious scale, it could not only narrow income gaps and increase overall productivity; it might also reclaim some of the lost support for a more managed brand of capitalism, revive the idea of a role for government in promoting equality as well as efficiency, reclaim trade unions as social partners, and build more compassion among Americans for those of different social strata.

Adam Smith is best known for his axiom that individual acts of selfishness aggregate to a general good. Even Smith, however, acknowledged that there are some economic necessities that market forces cannot provide, such as education. In 1759, long before he wrote *The Wealth of Nations*, Smith published the less well-known *Theory of Moral Sentiments,* a treatise on what a modern Danish social democrat might call social solidarity. "How selfish soever man may be supposed," Smith began, "there are evidently some principles in his nature, which interest him in the fortune of others, and render their happiness necessary to him." Reading those words of Adam Smith in Copenhagen did not feel odd at all.

CRITICAL THINKING QUESTION

Compare and contrast Danish and American society in terms of economic systems, employment practices, culture, and the welfare of the people. Which features of the Danish economic model do you think could or should be exported to the United States?

CHAPTER 8

Global Inequality and the Challenges of Reducing Extreme Poverty

Joan Ferrante

GLOBAL INEQUALITY, EXTREME POVERTY, AND EXTREME WEALTH

Global inequality refers to a situation in which income, wealth, and other valued resources are distributed unequally across countries and among the people living within each country on the planet. At one of end of the spectrum are those living in a state of extreme poverty. Extreme poverty is the most severe form of poverty such that the affected people cannot afford the basic human necessities (food, clothes, water, and shelter). Extreme poverty is characterized by malnutrition, chronic hunger, and disease. According to the United Nations the 1.2 billion people in the world who live on less than $1 per day live in extreme poverty. There are another 1.8 billion people who live on between $1 and $2 per day.

At the other end of the continuum are those who live in a state of extreme wealth, the most excessive form of wealth in which a very small minority of people (perhaps as few as the richest 400) possess enough money, material possessions, and resources such that a 4 percent levy on that wealth could provide adequate food, safe water, sanitation, and basic health care for the 1.2 billion poorest people on the planet. It would also include the richest 7.7 million people in the world (one-tenth of one percent of the world's population) whose average wealth is one million dollars (excluding the value of and whose combined wealth is estimated to be $28 trillion, a staggering amount when you consider that it represents 54 percent of gross world product [GDP] which is $51.4 trillion [Associated Press 2001; INQ7money.net 2004; U.S. Central Intelligence Agency 2005]).

The places in which people are born have an important effect on people's life chances. Obviously the chances a baby will survive the first year of life depend, in large part, on the country into which it is born. A baby born in Sweden has the best chance of surviving its first year of life as 3.44 of every 1000 babies born

---

Keynote address to the Pennsylvania Sociological Society

die before reaching the age of one; a baby born in Angola has the worst chance of surviving that first year as almost 200 of every 1000 babies born die within the first year.

One of the most startling examples of inequality across countries can be found when we compare the consumption patterns of the highest income countries (which contain 20 percent of the world's people) against the rest of the world, and especially the countries containing the poorest 20 percent. Consumers in the highest income countries account for 86 percent of total private consumption expenditures while those living among the poorest 20 percent account for 1.3% of this spending (United Nations 1988).

One way of conceptualizing the distribution of valued resources within countries is to compare the reported income held by the richest 10 percent of the population to that held by the poorest 10 percent. In the United States, the income of the richest 10 percent is 30.5 percent of all reported income; the income of the poorest 10 percent is 1.8 percent of all reported income. To put it another way, for every $1,000 earned by the poorest 10 percent, the richest 10 percent earn $16,600. Keep in mind that we are referring to earned income, not wealth. The greatest inequality gap between the richest and poorest 10 percent can be found in Namibia where the richest 10 percent earn 129 times more than the poorest 10 percent....

IS THERE A PLAN IN PLACE TO REDUCE GLOBAL INEQUALITY?

On September 18, 2000, the United Nations Millennium Declaration (2000) was signed and unanimously endorsed by the 189 members of the UN General Assembly. The document states:

> As leaders we have a duty…to all the world's people, especially the most vulnerable and, in particular the children of the world, to whom the future belongs.… We will spare no effort to free our fellow men, women, and children from the abject and dehumanizing conditions of extreme poverty, to which more than a billion are currently subjected.… We also undertake to address the special needs of the least developed countries including the small island developing states, the landlocked developing countries, and the countries of sub-Saharan Africa.

The Millennium Development Project includes 8 broad goals, 18 targets to be reached by 2015, and 48 indicators for measuring progress. For example, one goal is to eradicate extreme poverty and hunger. Two targets are associated with this goal:

Target 1: Halve, between 1990 and 2015, the proportion of people whose income is less than one dollar a day.

Target 2: Halve, between 1990 and 2015, the proportion of people who suffer from hunger.

Indicators for monitoring progress toward meeting these two targets include:

1. The proportion of population below $1 (PPP) per day: in 1990 that proportion was 27.9 percent. By 2015 that proportion should be 13.8 percent.
2. The prevalence of underweight children under five years of age: in 1990 that prevalence was 33 percent; in 2015 the prevalence should be 16.5 percent.
3. The proportion of population below minimum level of dietary energy consumption: in 1990 that proportion was 20 percent; in 2015 it should be 10 percent.

Other targets to be met by 2015 include:

• Eliminate gender disparity in primary and secondary education, preferably by 2005, and all levels of education no later than 2015.
• Reduce by three-quarters, between 1990 and 2015, the maternal mortality ratio.

REASONS TO BE PESSIMISTIC

Clearly these are ambitious goals. Their success hinges upon at least two major commitments from the world's richest countries: (1) they must invest .7 percent or seven-tenths of one percent of their annual Gross National Income in the Millennium Development Project, and (2) they must develop an open non-discriminatory trading system that addresses the needs of the lowest income economies by eliminating the subsidies, tariffs, and quotas that put their products at a disadvantage in the global market place.

Foreign Assistance Equal to .7 Percent of GNI

A 2005 UN Report identified the United States, Japan, and Italy as among the least generous donors in that they are furthest away from meeting the .7 percent target (Dagger 2005). On the bright side five countries—Denmark (.84%), Luxembourg (.85%), the Netherlands (.74%), Norway (.87%), and Sweden (.77%)—have met and exceeded that target. The .55 percent gap between the actual foreign assistance dollars allocated (.15) and the target of .7 percent accounts for 53 percent of the total shortfall in targeted donations (Sachs 2005).

[Those opposed to increasing foreign aid] argue that the United States has given and continues to give a disproportionate share of the money but it is misused, mismanaged, or otherwise wasted. While it is true that the United States is the largest donor in absolute dollars, its per capita spending and aid assistance as a percent of GNI makes it the least generous donor. Jeffrey D. Sachs, author of *The End of Poverty: Economic Possibilities for Our Times* and the UN Millennium Project Director and Task Force co-coordinator on Poverty and Economic Development, argues that the biggest myth held by most Americans is that the United States already gives so much money and that much, if not all, is wasted. Sachs maintains that the United States puts in "almost no funding, and it accomplishes almost nothing. And then we bemoan the waste. I don't know how to break through that misunderstanding. That's what I've been trying to do for many years, but it's very, very powerful in this country." Here is how Sachs (2005) assesses U.S. financial assistance to Africa:

> The U.S. aid to Africa is $3 billion this year. That $3 billion is roughly divided into three parts: The first is emergency food shipments. Of the billion or so in emergency food shipments, half of that, roughly $500 million, is just transport costs. So the commodities are maybe half a billion dollars. That's not development assistance, that's emergency relief. The second billion is the AIDS program, now standing at about $1 billion. That, on the whole, is a good thing. I would call it a real program. It's providing commodities; it's providing relief. It started late and it's too small, but it's there. The third billion is everything else we do for child survival, maternal survival, family planning, roads, power, water and sanitation, malaria; everything is the third $1 billion. Most of that, approaching 80 percent, is actually American consultant salaries. There's almost no delivery of commodities, for example. There's essentially zero financing to help a country build a school or build a clinic or dig a well.

Jeffrey Sachs' assessment is in stark contrast to the American public's belief that their government is contributing about 20.0 percent of its $2,224 trillion budget (or $498 billion) in financial assistance to other countries (Office of Management and Budget 2005). Could the UN and Jeffrey Sachs be mistaken? According to U.S. Department of State, the two are not. Table 8.1 shows that the amount of foreign financial assistance that the United States allocated in 2005 is $17.9 billion which represents .9 percent of the national budget or .15 percent of a $12.224 trillion GNI.

A review of how the $17.9 billion in assistance is allocated (Table 8.2) suggests that most of it cannot be classified as development-related aid. Rather the assistance goes toward disaster/famine relief, refugee programs, military training and financing, and narcotics control (U.S. Department of State 2005).

Trade Concessions

The wealthiest economies in the world are resisting the request to dismantle a trade system that is structured to their advantage and to the advantage of some of the wealthiest segments of their populations. In particular, the United States, Japan, the European Union countries, and other high-income countries subsidize agriculture and other sectors like steel and textiles such that its producers are paid more than world market value for their products. Considerable attention has been given to agricultural subsidies in which farmers in high-income countries receive an estimated $250 billion in support. In 2002 the EU spent an estimated $100.6 billion, Japan $43.9 billion and the United States $39.6 billion in agricultural subsidies (Abbott 2003). It is well documented that most of the subsidies go to the corporate farmer, not small growers. For example, Riceland

Table 8.1 Official Foreign Assistance Dollars by Donor Country and as a Percentage of Gross National Income

COUNTRY	OFFICIAL FOREIGN ASSISTANCE BY DONOR COUNTRY IN MILLIONS OF U.S. DOLLARS, 2003	FOREIGN ASSISTANCE DOLLARS AS A PERCENT OF A COUNTRY'S GROSS NATIONAL INCOME
United States	13,290	.15
Japan	8,880	.20
France	7,253	.41
United Kingdom	6,282	.34
Germany	5,324	.28
Netherlands	3,981	.80
Italy	2,433	.17
Sweden	2,400	.79
Norway	2,042	.92
Canada	2,031	.24
Spain	1,961	.23
Belgium	1,853	.60
Denmark	1,714	.84
Switzerland	1,299	.39
Australia	1,219	.25
Finland	558	.35
Austria	505	.20
Ireland	504	.39
Greece	362	.21
Portugal	320	.22
Luxembourg	194	.81
New Zealand	165	.23

Source: Organization for Economic Development and Co-operation, 2005.

Foods, Inc. (the top recipient) received $519.2 million in subsidies between 1995 and 2003 (Environmental Working Group 2005).

In addition to subsidies, tariffs and quotas are applied to imported goods that compete with protected products making the lower-cost imported goods equivalent in price or more expensive than the domestic version. Consider sugar. The EU protects its sugar industry such that domestic growers earn double, sometimes triple, the world market price. Because subsidies encourage overproduction, EU growers dump an estimated six million tons of surplus sugar each year in to the world market at artificially low prices. The United States, while not a major exporter of sugar, applies tariff and quotas on imported sugar to protect its sugar growers (Thurow and Windsock 2005). Subsidies, tariffs, and quotas on sugar help to keep prices on the world market artificially low and prices within protected markets artificially high. Of course, sugar is not the only protected commodity. Others include rice, textiles, and steel. The United Nations estimates that this system of subsidies, tariffs, and quotas cost poor nations an estimated

Table 8.2 Summary of U.S. Foreign Assistance Funding by Category

TYPE OF ASSISTANCE	FY 2005 AID ($ MILLIONS)	PERCENT
Bilateral Economic Assistance	9,766	49.4
Child Survival Health Programs	1,538	7.8
Development Assistance	1,488	7.5
Economic Support	2,481	12.6
Transition Initiatives	49	0.2
FREEDOM Support Act	556	2.8
Support for Eastern European Democracy	393	2.0
Global HIV/AIDS Initiative	1,374	7.0
Millennium Change Account*	1,488	7.5
Nonproliferation, Anti-Terrorism, De-mining*	399	2.0
Multilateral Economic Assistance	325	1.6
International Organizations and Programs	325	1.6
Humanitarian Assistance	2,334	11.8
International Disaster and Famine Assistance	367	1.9
Migration and Refugee Assistance	794	4.0
Food for Peace	1,173	5.9
Military Assistance	6,285.4	31.8
International Military Education and Training	79.5	0.4
Foreign Military Financing	5,991.6	30.3
Peacekeeping Operations	214.3	1.1
Law Enforcement Assistance	1,051	5.3
International Narcotics Control and Law Enforcement	326	1.6
Andean Counter Drug Initiative	725	3.7
TOTAL	$19,761†	100.00

Source: U.S. Department of State and U.S. Agency of International Development, 2005.

*Money has been budgeted but not yet allocated.

†The amount is actually $17,874 when the money promised but not allocated is subtracted from the total.

$50 billion annually in lost export revenue, which has the effect of negating the $50 billion in aid given to these economies on a yearly basis.

Such policies do not just affect the workers in the poorest countries but affect workers in the protected markets. For example, Brach and Kraft Foods closed their U.S.-based candy plants and outsourced more than 1,000 jobs to Argentina and Canada where sugar can be purchased at lower world market prices (Kher 2002). Moreover, in the United States, the highest tariffs are often placed on goods purchased by low-income consumers. That is, tariffs are usually lowest on luxury items and highest on essential items such as shoes and clothing, especially on the cheaper varieties. For example, there is a 2.4 percent tariff on women's silk underwear and a 16.2 percent tariff on the polyester variety. There is a 1.9 percent tariff on silk suits, a 12 percent tariff on wool suits, and a 29 percent tariff on polyester suits. There is a 5.3 percent tariff on snakeskin handbags and an 18 percent tariff on plastic-sided handbags. There is no tariff on silver-handled forks and a 15 percent tariff on stainless steel ones. While the poor within the U.S. pay more, so do the poor in the lowest income economies when their governments apply tariffs to essential products coming into the countries. In Viet Nam bicycles are essential purchases for the rural poor but the 50 percent tariff makes the cost prohibitive as the cheapest bicycle costs about twice the monthly income of those in rural communities. Likewise the 25 percent tariff that some sub-Saharan governments place on mosquito nets prevents the poor from taking proven action to prevent malaria, a disease which kills almost 1 million people a year in that region of the world.

REASONS TO BE OPTIMISTIC

The Millennium Goals are ambitious and, by the UN's own admission, it is unlikely they will be met by 2015. But that does not mean the effort is a failure. In fact there are a number of features that make this effort remarkable. The Millennium Development Project has brought together over 250 experts to devise a plan to accomplish the eight broad goals. It includes soil experts, medical doctors, malariologists (malaria experts), and hydrologists (safe drinking water). The team has laid out 17 Quick Wins, or doable actions that could bring immediate and measurable results. Examples of Quick Wins include

- "Eliminating school and uniform fees to ensure that all children, especially girls, are not out of school because of their families' poverty.
- Providing impoverished farmers in sub-Saharan Africa with affordable replenishments of soil nitrogen and other soil nutrients.
- Providing free school meals for all children using locally produced foods with take-home rations.
- Distributing free, long-lasting, insecticide-treated bed-nets to all children in malaria-endemic zones to cut decisively the burden of malaria" (United Nations Millennium Project 2005).

There is also the Millennium Village Project connected to the Earth Institute at Columbia University. One dozen Earth Institute experts work with local leaders to apply a package of proven interventions aimed at helping "pilot" villages escape extreme poverty within five years at a total cost of $110 per person including government and community contributions. Two villages—one in Kenya and the other in Ethiopia—are currently serving as test cases. Proven interventions include "increasing food production through a host of soil fertility measures; obtaining a village vehicle for transporting villagers to hospitals for emergency medical treatment, gaining easier access to markets, and providing electricity through rechargeable lanterns; improving access to water; providing nutritious lunches for all school children; establishing a health clinic to provide basic services including distribution of anti-retro viral drugs and bed nets for malaria prevention; and establishing a community center" (Earth Institute News 2004).

In evaluating efforts to end extreme poverty, one must also look beyond the UN-sponsored efforts. There are thousands of creative and successful efforts aimed at reducing poverty that offer hope. Some examples include:

Positive Deviants: Save the Children staff member Jerry Stein was charged with a seemingly impossible assignment—save starving children in Vietnam. He drew inspiration from the theory of positive deviants—those individuals whose exceptional behaviors and practices enable them to get better results than their neighbors with the exact same resources. Stein identified those Vietnamese children whose weight (relative to their age) suggested they were well-nourished. He observed the children's mothers and learned that they were behaving in ways that defied conventional wisdom. Among other things, the mothers were (1) using alternative food sources available to everyone (they were going to the rice paddies to harvest tiny shrimp and crab and they were picking sweet-potato greens—considered low-class food—and mixing both food sources with rice); (2) feeding their children when they had diarrhea even though traditional practices said not to this, and (3) making sure their children ate, rather than "hoping children would take it upon themselves to eat." The strategy of observing positive deviants as a problem-solving technique reached 2.2 million Vietnamese in 276 villages. In addition this model has been used in at least 20 countries where malnutrition is widespread (Dorsey and Leon 2000).

Micro Lending: In 1976 micro lending was first piloted in Bangladesh, a country whose economy is among the poorest. The goal was to examine the possibility of extending tiny loans to the poorest of the rural poor women. The hoped for outcome was to eliminate money lenders' exploitation of the poor and create opportunities for self-employment among the unemployed rural population of Bangladesh. Today the bank has 1,175 branches with an estimated 2.4 million borrowers living in 41,000 villages (about 60 percent of all villages in Bangladesh). An estimated 90 percent of borrowers repay the loans (Grumman 2005).

Barefoot College: In 1972 Bunker Roy founded the Barefoot College in India. The completely solar-electrified college, built by local population, serves over 125,000 people. The college encourages practical knowledge and skills (learning by doing, as opposed to paper learning). One program has trained more than 100 "barefoot engineers" (illiterate and semi literate) to install and manage solar energy equipment in 136 remote Himalayan villages (ANI-Asian News International 2001). The program has transformed the lives of an estimated 16,000 people. Among other things villagers no longer have to walk two days each month to secure kerosene fuel (Barefoot College 2005).

Conditional Cash Transfer: This is a relatively new model for addressing the needs of the poorest segments of Peru's population. To be eligible a family must have a child 14 years of age or younger and live in a community that lacks running water, electricity, health service, or some other basic need. Participating families receive $30 per month on the condition that they do certain things, like enroll their children in school and make sure that they are vaccinated. While $30 seems like a small amount of money, it doubles the monthly income of participating households. By the end of 2005, Peru expects to serve 98,000 families or 400,000 people living in a state of extreme poverty. Ultimately Peru expects to reach one half of the 2.5 million of its poorest people. Similar programs are underway in Chile, Columbia, Jamaica, Nicaragua, and Uruguay (Chauvin 2005).

In reviewing various actions to end extreme poverty, one strategy is to "think small, and tackle it through millions of practical steps" (Colebatch 2005). I have come to believe in this advice and find it exciting and uplifting to identify "solutions" to poverty and inequality. Over the past few years, I have identified at least five organizations that are taking effective and practical steps to end poverty and I have invested in them. I think it is important to share with introduction to sociology students "solutions" I have come to admire and believe in enough to support. Those organizations are:

Mary Magdalen House is an oasis of hospitality in downtown Cincinnati's Over-the-Rhine which provides a safe and pleasant place for people without homes in need of a shower, toilet, a change of clean clothes, a mail address, a place for someone to leave them phone messages, and other amenities associated with home.

SOTENI is a small Cincinnati-based NGO with ties to Kenya. Its goal is to strengthen the fight against AIDS by sharing lessons, resources, and inspiration, and mobilizing the caring power of U.S. and Kenyan-based individuals, groups, organizations, communities, and governments. I invested in a program that sponsors Kenyan orphans by paying for their school fees, uniforms, supplies, food and medical care.

Heifer International has a micro enterprise program in which resource-poor communities receive no-interest "living loans" of farm animals. Loan recipients start milk processing plants, weaving centers, honey-making collectives, and many other kinds of income- and employment-generating enterprises.

Matthew 25 Ministries is a Cincinnati-based NGO that provides "nutritional food to the hungry, clean water to the thirsty, clothing to the naked, affordable shelter to the homeless, medical care to the ill, and humanitarian supplies to prisoners." My investment was applied to sending pallets of humanitarian aid across the globe such as school supplies, soap, clothing, medical supplies and more to those in need.

6th District Elementary School is a Northern Kentucky school that serves low income students, most of whom are on school lunch programs. The school's budget was about $300 per year, not even enough to buy each child a box of crayons. I invested in their art program so that students could have access to basic art supplies and reference materials for art classes.

CONCLUSION

After hearing this information, I hope that newcomers to the discipline come away with a basic understanding of

- Global inequality
- Extreme wealth
- Extreme poverty
- The Millennium Project
- The powerful structural and institutional forces that block the realization of this plan
- The organizations and grassroots efforts working to solve the problem of poverty by "changing the system, spreading the solution, and persuading entire societies to take new leaps" (Ashoka 2004). For all of us who get discouraged by the institutional and structural barriers that stand in the way of progress, we can place hope in those who will not rest until they make an impact.

CRITICAL THINKING QUESTION

What are some popular misperceptions about U.S. aid to poor countries?

REFERENCES

Abbott, Charles. 2003. "Farm Subsidies Common Globally, Bypassing Small Farms." *Forbes* (August 6). www.forbes.com/business/newswire/2003/08/06/rtll050636.html.

Ashoka, 2004. "What Is a Social Entrepreneur?" www.ashoka.org/fellows/social-entrepeneur.cfm.

Associated Press. 2001. "Ranks of the Wealthy Grow Worldwide." *New York Times* (May 15): C12.

Barefoot College. 2005. http://www.barefootcollege.org/.

Chauvin, Lucien. 2005. "Peru Gives Its Poor More Money, but There's a Catch." *Christian Science Monitor* (October 14). www.csmonitor.com/2005/1014/p01s03-woam.html.

Colebatch, Tim. 2005. "Fight against Poverty a Campaign of 'Small Steps.'" *The Age* (October 15). www.theage.com.au.

Dorsey, David and Jana Leon. 2000. "Positive Deviant." Fast Company. http://www.fastcompany.com/online/41/stemin.html.

Dugger, Celia W. 2005. "UN Report Cites U.S. and Japan as the 'Least Generous Donors.'" *New York Times* (September 8): A4.

Earth News Institute News. 2004. "Earth Institute Launches Its First Millennium Village—A New Approach to Ending Global Poverty." The Earth Institute at Columbia University. www.earthinstitute.columbia.edu/news/2004/storvlO-19-04.

Environmental Working Group. 2005. *Farm Subsidy Database.* www.ewg.org/farm.

Golman Environmental Prize. 2002. www.goldmanprize.org.

Grameen. 2005. "Grameen Bank at a Glance." www.grameen info.org.

INQ7money.net. 2004. "World's Millionaires Increased to 7.7 Million in 2003" (June 17). www.monev.inq7.net.

Kher, Unmesh. 2002. "Sugar Subsidy: U.S. Sugar Tariffs Cost Consumers and Workers." Time.com (February 25). www.time.com/time/global/feb2002/articles/sweet.html.

Millennium Project Task Force on Trade. 2005. *Trade for Development: Achieving the Millennium Development Goals.* Earth Scan.

Office of Management and Budget. 2005. Budget of the United States Government, FY 2006. www.whitehouse.gov/omb/budget/fy2006/tables.html.

Organization for Economic Co-operation and Development. 2005. "Official Development Aid by Countries in US Dollars, 2003." www.pbs.org/now/politics/aiddollars.html.

Sachs, Jeffrey. 2005. "Interview: Can We End Global Poverty?" Federal News Service, Inc. www.truthabouttrade.org.

Thurow, Roger and Geoff Winestock. 2005. "Bittersweet: How an Addiction to Sugar Subsidies Hurts Development." *A World Connected.* www.aworldconnected.org/article.php/242.html.

United Nations. "Changing Today's Consumption Patterns—For Tomorrow's Human Development." *Human Development Report.* www.undp.org/hydro/98.htm.

United Nations Millennium Declaration. 2000. "Resolution Adopted by the General Assembly." Fifty-fifth Session (September 18, 2005).

United Nations Millennium Project. 2005. "What Are the 'Quick Wins'?" www.unmillenniumproiect.org/facts/qa8e.htm.

United States Central Intelligence Agency. 2005. *World Factbook: The World.* www.odci.gov/cia/publications/factbook.

U.S. Department of State and U.S. Agency of International Development. 2005. *U.S. Foreign Assistance Reference Guide* (January).

PART III

Social Inequalities

Two articles on gender inequality begin this section. Amy Gluckman shows us that women's rights and gender inequalities vary tremendously around the world. While women have made substantial strides in the United States, the speed with which these changes have come have varied across the states, women are still underrepresented in the higher paying professions, and the gap between men's and women's pay has far from vanished. In her discussion of the status of women throughout the rest of the world, it may come as a surprise to some that women generally do more of the world's work than men. Gluckman also directs our attention to the relationship between wealth inequality and the other debilitating inequalities faced by women throughout most of the world. In a similar vein, Isobel Coleman argues for the important effects that advancing women's rights in poor countries will have in addressing other social and economic problems endemic to these societies. Women's empowerment, she argues, would contribute to the economic well-being of the poor in the developing countries, enhance global stability, and support U.S. interests in foreign affairs.

As the Gluckman article addresses the gender wealth gap, the article by Meizhu Lui describes the modern-day wealth gap between the white majority and racial and ethnic minorities. Wealth accumulates over generations and, therefore, reflects a history of discrimination. Lui provides a brief historical overview of policies that have hindered the accumulation of wealth in the hands of minorities. Even if all present-day discrimination were to disappear tomorrow, racial and ethnic disparities in wealth would remain for generations to come. This presents an ethical dilemma for today's society and its policymakers: Given that the inequality brought about by generations of legalized discrimination will last for generations to come, do we owe minority groups any kind of restitution or policies that will help to level the playing field today or in the near future?

The next two articles deal with inequalities in access to two vital social services: education and health care. American children are guaranteed the right to primary and secondary education, but we stand apart from almost all other nations in that the guarantee is not written into the national constitution but instead is guaranteed by each and every state constitution. Thus, the responsibility for educating the nation's children belongs primarily to the states. As Michael Engel demonstrates, the result is huge disparities in funding and the quality of education from state to state and, ultimately, from city to city, town to town, and neighborhood to neighborhood. Not surprisingly, these disparities often fall along racial lines. After describing the strikingly inadequate conditions of Alliyah's elementary school in New York City, with mostly minority students, Jonathan Kozol notes,

> At the time I met Alliyah in the school-year 1997–1998, New York's Board of Education spent about $8,000 yearly on the education of a third grade child in a New York City public school. If you could have scooped Alliyah up out of the neighborhood where she was born and plunked her down within a fairly typical white suburb of New York, she would have received a public education worth about $12,000 every year. If you were to lift her up once more and set her down within one of the wealthiest white suburbs of New York, she would have received as much as $18,000 worth of public education every year and would likely have had a third grade teacher paid approximately $30,000 more than was her teacher in the Bronx.[1]

Aside from a school system where the bulk of the responsibility for education resides in the individual states, the United States also stands apart from its industrialized counterparts in that the provision of health care is not guaranteed to all citizens. As James Russell explains, while the United States spends more per capita on health care, we compare poorly in terms of critical measures of the population's health: life expectancy, infant mortality, maternal mortality, and so on. Unfortunately, the dismal statistics for the poor and uninsured increase our mortality and morbidity rates, resulting in poor national averages and lowered health prospects for the overall population when compared to our industrial counterparts.

Almost all Americans agree that everyone has a fundamental right to an education, yet many disagree with the right to health care. Europeans, Canadians, Australians, and people from other nations view these American positions as inconsistent. It would seem that the right to health care is as fundamental as the right to an education, if not more so. After all, what good is an education if you are too sick to learn, too sick to apply what you have learned, or dead?

NOTE

1. Kozol, Jonathan. *The Shame of the Nation: The Restoration of Apartheid Schooling in America*. New York: Three Rivers Press, 2005, pp. 44–45.

CHAPTER 9

Women and Wealth: A Primer

Amy Gluckman

Put "wealth" and "women" into the same sentence, and contradictory images jump to mind: from Cleopatra, Marie Antoinette ("let them eat cake"), or Oprah to an anonymous Asian, Latin American, or African woman lugging buckets or bales along a rugged path. Each of these images bears some truth: women's relationship with wealth is not a simple one. Women have, historically, held every possible juxtaposition with wealth and property. They have been property themselves, essentially sold in marriage, and in some instances inherited upon a husband's death by his brother or other male relative. They have almost universally faced restricted rights to own, control, and inherit property compared to men. Yet women have also been fabulously wealthy, and in not insignificant numbers—sometimes benefiting from family-owned wealth, occasionally wealthy in their own right. Today, according to a recent report in Datamonitor, more than half of Britain's millionaires are women.

Furthermore, women's access to wealth is always conditioned by race, ethnicity, class, and all of the other parameters that shape the distribution of wealth in any society. Her gender is never the sole factor that shapes a woman's acquisition or use of property.

Marriage in particular has acted as a double-edged sword for women. On one hand, marriage typically gives a woman access to a man's income and wealth, affording her a higher standard of living than most social orders would have allowed her to achieve on her own. On the other hand, women have widely lost rights to own, control, and inherit wealth when they married. And when divorced or widowed, women have sometimes lost the access that marriage afforded them to their husbands' property without gaining any renewed rights to the property of their natal families.

Discriminatory laws and customs in many parts of the world have broken down, although it's sobering to remember how recent this change has been. In the United States, the first state to enact a comprehensive law removing restrictions on property ownership by married women was New York, in 1848. (Mississippi passed a limited statute in 1839. In a clear illustration of the complicated nexus of race, class, and gender that always shapes wealth ownership, the Mississippi law was primarily focused on giving married women the right to own slaves; the law was likely intended to offer plantation owners a way to avoid having their slaves seized to pay the husband's debts.) Other states were still passing similar laws up to 1900, and discrimination on the basis of sex and marital status in granting credit was made illegal at the federal level only in 1974. And of course, custom and economic institutions continued to discriminate against women in the ownership and control of property, access to credit in their own names, and related matters long after laws had been changed.

Around the world, many countries have only recently granted women—or married women in particular—property rights. A 2000 U.N. report lists Bolivia, the Dominican Republic, Eritrea, Malaysia, Nepal, Uganda, Tanzania, and Zimbabwe among countries that have recently passed laws recognizing women's ownership of land, for example. Many countries still lack statutes giving women an express right to own land or other wealth in their own names.

FREE BUT NOT EQUAL

Even with the right to own wealth, women have not necessarily had the means to accumulate any. Among the factors key to building assets are income, education, and inheritance—and, of course, in each of these, women face obstacles, whether customary or legal.

In the rich countries, women today have largely the same educational attainment as men—up to, but not including, the highest levels. In the United States, for example, more girls than boys graduate from high school, and more women than men are enrolled in bachelor's degree programs. But there are still far more men than women who hold advanced degrees, especially in lucrative fields such as engineering, business, law, and medicine. Women workers remain concentrated in female-dominated occupations that continue to pay less than male-dominated occupations requiring the same degree of skill, preparation, and responsibility. This is a key reason for the persistent gender pay gap. The median income of U.S. men working full-time, year-round was $38,275 in 2001; the equivalent figure for women was $29,215, or only 76% of men's pay.

Women in the global South continue to face far larger education and income gaps, although with great variation among countries. For example, Yemen, Pakistan, and Niger all have female-male adult literacy ratios under 60%, while Jordan, Sri Lanka, and Cameroon all have ratios of 95% or above. Income data disaggregated by sex is not available for many countries, according to the most recent U.N. Human Development Report. But the report's rough estimates show a substantial gender gap in income in every country. And in many developing countries, women continue to hold only limited rights to inherit property.

Plenty of factors account for women's lack of wealth accumulation across the globe, but working too little is certainly not one of them. Women work longer hours every day than men in most countries, according to time-use studies assembled by the United Nations. The unequal work burden is most pronounced in rural areas, where women typically work 20% more minutes a day than men. Environmental problems in many countries have exacerbated women's work burden; a Population Reference Bureau report notes that "Given the variety of women's daily interactions with the environment to meet household needs, they are often most keenly affected by its degradation. In the Sudan, deforestation in the last decade has led to a quadrupling of women's time spent gathering fuelwood. Because girls are often responsible for collecting water and fuelwood, water scarcity and deforestation also contribute to higher school dropout rates for girls."

WOMEN'S WEALTH HOLDINGS: WHAT WE KNOW

Today's wealth distribution reflects the accumulation of assets over years, even generations. So it will take time before the uneven but dramatic changes in women's status over the past few decades will show up in the wealth statistics. Given that, what is the distribution of wealth by gender today?

The first thing to note is that we really don't know what it is, for a number of reasons. First, data on personal wealth are scarce. Most countries do not systematically collect data on wealth ownership. Among the few countries that do are the United States, Sweden, Germany, and Britain.

Where data *are* regularly collected, the unit is typically the household, not the individual. Thus the assets of most married couples are assigned to both wife and husband equally in wealth surveys, obscuring any differences in the two spouses' authority to manage or benefit from those assets or to retain them if the marriage ends. This leaves gender comparisons possible only between unmarried men and unmarried women, a minority of the adult population.

In many countries, property ownership is governed by customary or informal rules rather than legal title. The term "ownership" itself is a simplification; ownership is really a bundle of rights that don't necessarily reside in the same person. In statutory systems and particularly in customary systems, women may have limited ownership rights; for example, a woman may have the right to use a piece of property but not to transfer or bequeath it. This limits the value of any simple, quantitative snapshot of wealth distribution by gender. Instead, a complex qualitative portrait is necessary.

Given all of these limitations, what *do* we know?

In the United States, the significant gap is between married and unmarried people. Married-couple households have median net worth far more than two times that of households headed by unmarried adults. However, there is also a gender gap between unmarried men and unmarried women. The median net worth of single female-headed households in 2001 was $28,000; of single male-headed households, $47,000. And this gap has to be viewed in relation to the greater financial responsibilities of single women: a greater portion of single-female headed households include children under 18. There is also a vast wealth gap between white women and women of color: the median net worth of house-holds headed by single white women was $56,590 in 2001; of households headed by single African-American women, $5,700; and of households headed by single Hispanic women, $3,900.

The young baby-boomer cohort, looked at separately, shows nearly no wealth gap between unmarried men and women...This suggests that women are catch-ing up—at least in a rich country like the United States. This is not surprising, as women are moving toward parity with men in several of the factors corre-lated with higher net worth, such as education and income. However, the income gap has long been smaller between young women and men than between older women and men, at least in part because the workforce participation of women—who typically bear greater parenting responsibilities than men—becomes more uneven over time. As the young boomers age, how much the wealth gap is really shrinking will become more clear.

For the global South, systematic personal wealth data simply do not exist. But it's possible to assess some of the factors that are shaping the distribution of wealth by gender in poor and middle-income nations. The transition to for-mal systems of property ownership has had complex effects in many poor, pre-dominantly rural countries. In theory, holding legal title to land can benefit small farmers—many of whom around the world are women. With a legal title, a farmer can use the land as collateral and thereby gain access to credit; she can also more confidently invest in improvements. However, in the process of for-malizing land titles, governments have often taken land that was customarily under a woman's control and given the title to it to a man. Likewise, land reform programs have often bypassed women. Women were "left out of the agrarian reforms of the 1960s and 1970s" in Latin America, according to a U.N. report, because household heads, to whom land titles were given, were simply assumed to be men. Women do 60% to 80% of the agricultural labor throughout the devel-oping world, but are not nearly as likely to be actual landowners: the percentage of agricultural landowners who are women ranges from 3% in Bangladesh to 57% in Namibia, and their average holdings are smaller than men's.

Lacking formal title to land, women have very limited access to agricultural credit. The same is true outside of agriculture: of the 300 million low-income self-employed women in the global South, hardly any have access to credit (aside from moneylenders, who typically charge exorbitant interest rates that can range up to 100% a month). Microcredit programs have sprung up in many countries and are making a dent in this problem, but just a dent. Although it's now worth some $2.5 billion, the microcredit sector reaches only an estimated 3% of those across the global South (both women and men) who could benefit from it.

Liberalization and structural adjustment policies pressed on third world governments have been hard on women's economic status. Consider the case of Mexico where, following the introduction of economic liberalization in the mid-1980s, growth has been slow for everyone. But women have suffered dis-proportionately. With the opening of lots of export-oriented *maquiladoras,* women's share of industrial jobs grew. But women's industrial wages fell from

80% of men's in 1984 to 57% of men's in 1992. At the same time, the bland term "structural adjustment" means, in practice, often-huge cutbacks in public services such as health care, education, and aid to the poor. Women (and children) are typically more dependent on these programs than men, and so suffer more when they are cut.

WHAT IS WEALTH GOOD FOR?

Does it matter if women have less wealth and less capacity to acquire and control assets than men? Most adult women across the globe are married, and for most married women, these forms of gender-specific discrimination do not prevent them from enjoying a family standard of living underwritten by their husbands' income and wealth. But a woman's ability to own property in her own name turns out to be more important than it might appear. Women with property are less vulnerable to all of life's vicissitudes. Owning property can protect women affected by HIV/AIDS from destitution, for example; the International Center for Research on Women is currently documenting this association.

And asset ownership changes the balance of power between women and men. In a study of 500 urban and rural women in Kerala, India, Pradeep Panda of the Centre for Development Studies, Trivandrum, and Bina Agarwal of the Institute of Economic Growth, Delhi, found that women who are wealthless are considerably more vulnerable to domestic violence than women who own property. The study's remarkable results are worth quoting at length:

> The study's findings did bear out the fact, that ownership of immovable property by women is associated with a dramatically lower incidence of both physical and psychological harassment, as well as long-term and current violence. For example, as many as 49% of the women who owned neither land nor house suffered long-term physical violence, compared with 18% and 10% respectively of those who owned either land or a house, and 7% of those who owned both.

> The effect of property ownership on psychological violence is even more dramatic. While 84% of property-less women suffered abuse, the figure was much lower (16%) for women who owned both land and a house.

> The ownership of property also offers women the option of leaving an abusive environment—of the 179 women experiencing long-term physical violence, 43 left home. The percentage of women leaving home was much higher among the propertied (71%) than among those without property (19%). Moreover, of the women who left home, although 24 returned, 88% of the returning women were property-less. Few propertied women returned.

> So, not only are propertied women less likely to experience marital violence, they are also able to escape further violence. Hence, property ownership serves both as a deterrent and as an exit option for abused women....

It has long been a shibboleth in the U.S. women's movement that all women can face domestic violence regardless of their economic circumstances. But owning and controlling some wealth surely offers women in rich countries the same kinds of protection the Kerala study revealed: a stronger position in the marital power dynamic, and the ability to exit. And owning some property no doubt underwrites a woman's ability to struggle against patriarchal institutions in other ways too, at least on an individual level, and to achieve her own potential. Virginia Woolf wrote a century ago that a woman who wanted to create needed a modest (unearned) income and a room of her own; Woolf's vision is no less true today.

But today most women around the world still don't have the modest unearned income or the room of their own—and not only because of their gender. What then would a progressive feminist agenda around wealth look like? Of course, it would address all of the remaining customs, statutes, and institutional barriers that limit women's economic rights relative to men's. But it would also seek to reorient all economic institutions toward the provision of social forms of wealth and the deconcentration of private wealth. Only a dual agenda like this can offer any hope—for achieving either gender equity *or* a decent standard of living—to a majority of the world's women.

CRITICAL THINKING QUESTIONS

What, according to Gluckman, is the relationship between women's inequality in wealth and other social problems affecting women? What do you think she means by "social forms of wealth" referred to in the concluding paragraph?

CHAPTER 10

The Payoff from Women's Rights

Isobel Coleman

THE COST OF INEQUALITY

Over the past decade, significant research has demonstrated what many have known for a long time: women are critical to economic development, active civil society, and good governance, especially in developing countries. Focusing on women is often the best way to reduce birth rates and child mortality; improve health, nutrition, and education; stem the spread of HIV/AIDS; build robust and self-sustaining community organizations; and encourage grassroots democracy.

Much like human rights a generation ago, women's rights were long considered too controversial for mainstream foreign policy. For decades, international development agencies skirted gender issues in highly patriarchal societies. Now, however, they increasingly see women's empowerment as critical to their mandate. The Asian Development Bank is promoting gender-sensitive judicial and police reforms in Pakistan, for example, and the World Bank supports training for female political candidates in Morocco. The United States, too, is increasingly embracing women's rights, as a way not only to foster democracy, but also to promote development, curb extremism, and fight terrorism, all core strategic objectives.

Women's status has advanced in many countries: gender gaps in infant mortality rates, calorie consumption, school enrollment, literacy levels, access to health care, and political participation have narrowed steadily. And those changes have benefited society at large, improving living standards, increasing social entrepreneurship, and attracting foreign direct investment.

Yet significant gender disparities continue to exist, and in some cases, to grow, in three regions: southern Asia, the Middle East, and sub-Saharan Africa. Although the constraints on women living in these areas—conservative, patriarchal practices, often reinforced by religious values—are increasingly recognized as a drag on development, empowering women is still considered a subversive proposition. In some societies, women's rights are at the front line of a protracted battle between religious extremists and those with more moderate, progressive views. Deep tensions are evident in Saudi Arabia, Iraq, and Afghanistan, for example, and to a lesser extent in Nigeria, Pakistan, and Indonesia. Their resolution will be critical to progress in these countries, for those that suppress women are likely to stagnate economically, fail to develop democratic institutions, and become more prone to extremism.

Washington appreciates these dangers, but it has struggled to find an appropriate response. Since September 11, 2001, largely thanks to growing awareness of the Taliban's repression of Afghan women, gender equality has become a greater feature of U.S. policy abroad. But the Bush administration's policies have been inconsistent. Although Washington has linked calls for democracy with increased rights for women, especially in the Middle East, it has done too little to enforce these demands. It has supported women's empowerment in reform-oriented countries such as Morocco, but it has not promoted it in countries less amenable to change such as Saudi Arabia. Although women's rights feature prominently in U.S. reconstruction plans for Afghanistan and Iraq, Washington has not done enough to channel economic and political power to women there.

Given the importance of women to economic development and democratization—both of which are key U.S. foreign policy objectives, Washington must promote their rights more aggressively. In particular, it must undertake, consistently and effectively, more programs designed to increase women's educational opportunities, their control over resources, and their economic and political participation. With overwhelming data now showing that women are critical to development, good governance, and stable civil life, it is time that the United States does more to advance women's rights abroad.

A HIGH-RETURN INVESTMENT

Gender disparities hit women and girls the hardest, but ultimately all of society pays a price for them. Achieving gender equality is now deemed so critical to reducing poverty and improving governance that it has become a development objective in its own right. The 2000 UN Millennium Development Goals, the international community's action plan to attack global poverty, lists gender equality as one of its eight targets and considers women's empowerment essential to achieving all of them. Nobel Prize–winning economist Amartya Sen has argued that nothing is more important for development today than the economic, political, and social participation of women. Increasingly, women, who were long treated as passive recipients of aid, are now regarded as active promoters of change who can help society at large. And various studies specifically show that the benefits of promoting women are greatest when assistance focuses on increasing their education, their control over resources, and their political voice.

Although there is no easy formula for reducing poverty, many argue that educating girls boosts development the most. Lawrence Summers, when he was chief economist at the World Bank, concluded that girls' education may be the investment that yields the highest returns in the developing world. Educated women have fewer children; provide better nutrition, health, and education to their families; experience significantly lower child mortality; and generate more income than women with little or no schooling. Investing to educate them thus creates a virtuous cycle for their community.

Educating women, especially young girls, yields higher returns than educating men. In low-income countries, investing in primary education tends to pay off more than investing at secondary and higher educational levels, and girls are more concentrated at lower levels of the education system than are boys. So closing the gender gap in the early years of schooling is a better strategy than promoting other educational reforms that allow gender gaps to remain. Similarly, children benefit more from an increase in their mother's schooling than from the equivalent increase in their father's. Educating mothers does more to lower child mortality rates, promote better birth outcomes (for example, higher birth weights) and better child nutrition, and guarantee earlier and longer schooling for children.

Girls' education also lowers birth rates, which, by extension, helps developing countries improve per capita income. Better-educated women bear fewer children than lesser-educated women because they marry later and have fewer years of childbearing. They also are better able to make informed, confident decisions about reproduction. In fact, increasing the average education level of women by three years can lower their individual birth rate by one child. Studies show that in India, educating girls helps lower birth rates even more effectively than family planning initiatives.

Female education also boosts agricultural productivity. World Bank studies indicate that, in areas where women have very little schooling, providing them with at least another year of primary education is a better way to raise farm yields than increasing access to land or fertilizer usage. As men increasingly seek jobs away from farms, women become more responsible for managing the land. Because women tend to cultivate different crops than their husbands do, they cannot rely on men for training and need their own access to relevant information. As land grows more scarce and fertilizers yield diminishing returns, the next revolution in agricultural productivity may well be driven by women's education.

It is no coincidence, then, that in the last half-century, the regions that have most successfully closed gender gaps in education have also achieved the most economically and socially: eastern Asia, southeastern Asia, and Latin America. Conversely, regions with lagging growth—southern Asia, the Middle East, and sub-Saharan Africa—have also lagged in their investments in girls' education. Today, illiteracy among adult females is highest in southern Asia (55 percent), the Arab world (51 percent), and sub-Saharan Africa (45 percent). Simulation analyses suggest that, had these three regions closed their gender gaps in education at the same rate as eastern Asia did from 1960 to 1992, their per capita income could have grown by up to an additional percentage point every year. Compounded over three decades, that increase would have been highly significant.

Giving women more control over resources also profits the community at large because women tend to invest more in their families than do men. Increases in household income, for example, benefit a family more if the mother, rather than the father, controls the cash. Studies of countries as varied as Bangladesh, Brazil, Canada, Ethiopia, and the United Kingdom suggest that women generally devote more of the household budget to education, health, and nutrition, and less to alcohol and cigarettes. For example, increases in female income improve child survival rates 20 times more than increases in male income, and children's weight-height measures improve about 8 times more. Likewise, female borrowing has a greater positive impact on school enrollment, child nutrition, and demand for health care than male borrowing.

These differences help explain why extending microfinance (small-scale lending with little or no collateral) to women has become such a powerful force for development. Mohammed Yunus founded Grameen Bank in Bangladesh—and launched the microfinance wave—by reasoning that if loans were granted to poor people on appropriate and reasonable terms, "millions of small people with their millions of small pursuits [could] add up to create the biggest development wonder." Yunus deliberately promoted microfinancing for women for reasons of equity: women are generally poorer and more credit-constrained than men, and they have limited access to the wage labor market and an inequitable share in decision-making at home. But he was also moved by sound economics: women pay their loans back more consistently than men.

Microfinance has been lauded for alleviating poverty in a financially sustainable way. But its greatest long-term benefit could be its impact on the social status of women. Women now account for 80 percent of the world's 70 million microborrowers. And studies show that women with microfinancing get more involved in family decision-making, are more mobile and more politically and legally aware, and participate more in public affairs than other women. Female borrowers also suffer less domestic violence—a consequence, perhaps, of their perceived value to the family increasing once they start to generate income of their own.

Allowing women to participate in politics also benefits democracy—and not only because it advances their civil rights. Intriguing new studies suggest that women in power make different policy choices than their male counterparts, with profound implications for the local allocation of public resources and, thus, for development. Esther Duflo, an economist at the Massachusetts Institute of Technology, has examined the impact of a constitutional amendment that India passed in 1993, which requires states to devolve more power over expenditures to panchayats (local councils) and reserve a third of council leadership positions for women. Duflo found that when women are in charge, the panchayat invests more in infrastructure that is directly relevant to women's needs. This is not to say that women's priorities are somehow better than men's, only that they are different and that in countries in which women are neglected, putting them in charge may begin to redress the imbalance.

The research of Steven Fish, a political scientist at the University of California at Berkeley, into why Muslim countries are generally less democratic than other countries reveals other benefits of female political participation. Fish has found that robust democracy is exceedingly rare in societies that display a large gender gap in literacy rates and a skewed gender ratio (usually a marker of inferior nutrition and health care for girls and infanticide or sex-selective abortion). He argues that societies that marginalize women generally count both fewer anti-authoritarian voices in politics and more men who join fanatical religious and political brotherhoods—two factors that stifle democracy.

ONE AT A TIME

Given the importance of women to economic and political development, it is no surprise that they are on the front line of modernization efforts around the world. But empowering women is rarely easy: it produces tensions everywhere, because it often collides with the twin powers of culture and religion.

Today, much scrutiny is given to the impact of Islam on women, often as evidence of a deep cultural rift between the West and conservative Muslim societies. But the real cultural rift may be within the Muslim world: between highly traditional rural populations and their more modernized urban compatriots or between religious fundamentalists and more moderate interpreters of Islam. Such tensions can be felt in countries ranging from Nigeria to Indonesia, but nowhere are they starker than in the Middle East.

Mustafa Kemal Atatüürk, the founder of modern Turkey, may be the best-known leader to have pushed his country into modernity by transforming the role of women in society. After the abolition of the Ottoman caliphate in 1924, Atatüürk promoted an aggressive program of secularization, replacing sharia with European constitutional law, prohibiting traditional Muslim dress, abolishing religious schools, and turning education into a state monopoly. Believing that women are intrinsically important to society, he launched many reforms to give them equal rights and more opportunities. A new civil code abolished polygamy and recognized the rights of women to inherit, divorce, and get custody of their children. Segregation in education was ended, and women were given full political rights. By the mid-1930s, Turkey had 13 female judges and 18 female parliamentarians. It was the first country in the world to appoint a female justice to its highest court, and in the mid-1990s, a woman was elected prime minister.

Similarly, when Tunisia won its independence in 1956, President Habib Bourguiba adopted an authoritarian, top-down approach to empower women as part of broader efforts to modernize the country. In his first year, he adopted a revolutionary Code of Personal Status that greatly enhanced women's rights: it banned polygamy, required a girl's consent for marriage, raised the minimum marriage age to 17, and allowed women to request divorce. At the time, these were progressive measures not only for Tunisia, but also for the world. And they stood in especially stark contrast to the laws then in force in Morocco, which gained independence from France at the same time but adopted a highly restrictive personal status law (moudawana) that institutionalized many conservative constraints on women.

Tunisia's enlightened policies toward women have contributed to its markedly superior record on developing human capital and economic growth. Today, the country's overall literacy rate is 70 percent (80 percent for men and 60 percent for women), compared to only 48 percent in Morocco (60 percent for men and 35 percent for women). Tunisia's better-educated work force has helped the country attract more foreign direct investment. And tens of thousands of Tunisian women have brought their families into the middle class by working in export-oriented light manufacturing and foreign service centers. Not surprisingly, Tunisia's population growth rate has been notably lower than Morocco's, which accounts in part for its stronger gains in per capita income.

The aggressive promotion of women's rights has not come without a significant backlash. Because the notion of female empowerment is often strongly associated with secularism and Western values, it has generated widespread resistance in certain societies, among both men and women. To appeal to religious conservatives, leaders throughout the Arab world have long given them significant influence over women, usually by letting them oversee family law and personal status codes. But now that the importance of women to economic and political development is becoming increasingly clear, several young, Western-educated reformist leaders—King Mohamed VI of Morocco, King Abdullah of Jordan, and Sheik Hamad of Qatar—are reclaiming control over these areas. These leaders are engaged in the delicate exercise of pushing women forward without alienating their still highly conservative constituencies. Their efforts were boosted by the groundbreaking Arab Human Development Report 2002, which attributed the Arab world's economic and political stagnation in part to gender inequality.

Women in Morocco have made some remarkable advances in recent years. In the mid-1990s, with the support of the World Bank, Morocco launched a program promoting women's participation in development by increasing girls' education, health care for mothers and their children, and economic and political opportunities for women. It guaranteed that women would get 10 percent of the seats in the lower house of parliament in the 2002 elections. This quota helped raise the number of female representatives from 2 to 35 a notable achievement in the Arab world, which has the lowest percentage of women parliamentarians anywhere (about 3 percent). Several international organizations, including the National Democratic Institute and the UN Development Fund for women, helped train the female candidates.

Women's groups have also been encouraged to play a more active role in Moroccan politics. In recent years, they have lobbied hard to reform the moudawana, and despite vehement opposition from fundamentalists, Mohammed VI established a "royal consultative committee" to assist their efforts. In January, the Moroccan parliament enacted one of the most progressive women's rights laws in the region, allowing women to marry without their father's consent, initiate divorce, and share with their husbands responsibility over family matters. The minimum marriage age was raised from 15 to 18, and the practice of polygamy severely restricted.

Similarly, in Jordan, King Abdullah is improving the education of women and increasing their participation in the work force and in politics. The government has eliminated any gender gap in primary school enrollment, and girls now out-number boys in secondary and tertiary education. Queen Rania, Abdullah's wife, has actively promoted microfinance initiatives, and under her patronage, in late 2003, Jordan hosted the region's first microfinance conference. The government has also implemented limited electoral quotas, reserving 6 out of 110 seats in parliament for women.

Nowhere, however, is women's reform more startling than in tiny Qatar, an otherwise highly conservative Wahhabi state. Sheik Hamad has launched a number of political reforms, including the country's first popular elections in 1999, in which both men and women were allowed to vote and run for office. Hamad and his wife, Sheika Mouza, have also encouraged educational reform. The government hired the Rand Corporation to advise on restructuring the country's educational system, and it launched the Education City Initiative, which has invited several American universities to set up local branches in Qatar (including the Virginia Commonwealth School of Arts and the Weill Cornell Medical College). Women now make up nearly 70 percent of the country's university students. Although Qatar's population is less than a million, the effects of its reforms are likely to ripple beyond its borders.

These reforms have not gone unnoticed in neighboring Saudi Arabia, for example, where religious conservatives still maintain strict control over women's access to public life. Saudi society is nearly completely segregated: in health care, education, and the work force. Women are treated as minors: they must have a male chaperon in public, they are not allowed to drive, and they need permission from their closest male relative to travel. The Saudi government has recently agreed to issue women identity cards, but only with the permission of a male guardian. The notorious mutaween (religious police) patrol malls to ensure that women are fully covered in public. In a tragic incident in Mecca in 2002, 15 schoolgirls were killed in a fire after mutaween allegedly forced them back inside the burning building because they were not appropriately covered.

But the Mecca fire prompted a national debate over religious extremism, after which control over the education of Saudi girls was transferred from religious authorities to the Ministry of Education. And that controversy helped revive long-standing calls for change. Female literacy in Saudi Arabia has risen from 2 percent in the mid-1960s, when universal female education was introduced (over vehement protest from the religious authorities), to more than 70 percent today. Women now account for nearly 60 percent of all university students, and they increasingly question the constraints on their lives. In January 2003, Saudi women signed a petition demanding that the government recognize their legal and civil rights. These efforts are beginning to pay off. The government, risking the wrath of religious conservatives, recently offered to let women take part in elections scheduled for later this year.

The demands of Saudi women may be helped along by new economic circumstances that are fueling the pressure for change. (A joke circulating around Riyadh says that the woman most sought after these days is the one with a job.) As GNP per capita has plunged from $25,000 in 1984 to roughly $8,500 today, more

Saudis are wondering why half the country's human capital should be so severely handicapped. Indeed, a World Bank study on labor markets in the Middle East indicates that the increased participation of women in the work force can raise the average household income by as much as 25 percent without raising unemployment. So it is an encouraging sign that 10 percent of private Saudi businesses today are believed to be run by women.

Still, the Saudi debate over women's rights is often a proxy for difficult and dangerous debates over civil liberties, religious extremism, and human rights more generally, which are largely stifled. Talk of women's liberation encounters powerful resistance and recurring backlashes. Women played a major role in the recent Jeddah Economic Forum, which featured a keynote address by Lubna al Olayan, a prominent businesswoman, calling for greater economic and political rights for women. But soon after the conference, Saudi Arabia's grand mufti, or highest religious authority, issued a fatwa denouncing the public role of women. (It could not have helped that al Olayan also appeared on the front page of several leading Saudi newspapers with her head uncovered.)

Fundamentalists draw such a close link between women's empowerment and Western decadence that reformists such as Crown Prince Abdullah must be exceedingly careful when they endorse the former not to appear to be condoning the latter. For now, the role of women continues to be a line in the sand between those who want to modernize the country and those who seek to impose a harsh, medieval version of Islam in the kingdom.

A FAIRER FUTURE

...For the sake of consistency and credibility, the United States must promote international efforts intended to advance the role of women worldwide. It should lead the implementation of UN Resolution 1325, unanimously passed by the General Assembly in 2000, which committed the UN to giving women a greater role in peacekeeping and post-conflict transitions. More important, the United States should finally endorse the 1981 Convention to Eliminate Discrimination Against Women, the only global treaty that deals exclusively with the rights of women, which 175 countries, including every industrialized democracy but the United States, have ratified. U.S. critics of the treaty have called it "antifamily," even though nothing in it contradicts traditional family values. They have also argued that the United States does not need it, since U.S. laws go well beyond what it recommends. So why not ratify it? By failing to support the agreement, Washington undermines its professed commitment to women's rights and exposes itself to charges of hypocrisy.

The United States should also dramatically increase funding to improve the status of women in regions where gender gaps are widest and assistance is most needed: the Middle East, southern Asia, and sub-Saharan Africa. Given the demonstrated high returns on investments in girls' education, the United States should, as its top development priority, work to eliminate gender gaps in primary education (USAID support for basic education is roughly $250 million). Likewise, it should expand support for microfinancing beyond its current level of roughly $200 million. Women's health and family planning deserve more funding too, particularly in countries such as Afghanistan where maternal mortality rates are alarmingly high. Adequate primary, maternal, and reproductive health care is critical to women's empowerment, especially in areas with high rates of adolescent marriage.... Finally, the United States should use the Middle East Partnership Initiative, a $150 million program to advance democracy in the Middle East, which promotes programs for female literacy and health, as well as business and political training, as a model for more activist, pro-women policies in other parts of the world.

With the Millennium Challenge Account, the United States is now undertaking the largest expansion of foreign development aid in more than a generation. It should seize this opportunity to leverage its aid for the benefit of women's rights, by incorporating specific gender measures into the criteria that determine eligibility for funds. None of the 16 current criteria specifically takes account of women's status, but these could easily be adjusted. A country's maternal mortality ratio and its female primary school completion rate are both good indicators of gender equality there.

Similarly, the United States could promote respect for women's rights by making adherence to them a more explicit condition for U.S. military and economic aid. The State Department should be tasked with writing country reports tracking worldwide progress on key gender measures such as girls' literacy, maternal health, gender ratios, and political participation, much as it already does on human rights. Funding data collection on gender disparities is also important. Such information is lacking in many countries, and improving it could, by itself, help close gender gaps resulting from neglect.

"The worldwide advancement of women's issues is not only in keeping with the deeply held values of the American people," Powell has said, "it is strongly in our national interest as well." The United States has advocated women's rights as a moral imperative or as a way to promote democracy. In so doing, it might have compounded the difficulty of its task, by irking conservative religious forces or the authoritarian regimes it otherwise supports. But now Washington can also make an economic case for women's rights, which may be more acceptable to traditionalists. Promoting women's rights because they spur development and economic growth is a powerful way for the United States to advance its foreign policy in the future while minimizing the ideological debates that have frustrated it in the past.

CRITICAL THINKING QUESTIONS

Before reading this article, how high was women's empowerment ranked in your mind's list of global priorities? After reading this article, has that ranking changed? Why or why not?

CHAPTER 11

Doubly Divided: The Racial Wealth Gap

Meizhu Lui

R ace—constructed from a European vantage point—has always been a basis on which U.S. society metes out access to wealth and power. Both in times when the overall wealth gap has grown and in times when a rising tide has managed to lift both rich and poor boats, a pernicious wealth gap between whites and nonwhite minorities has persisted.

Let's cut the cake by race. If you lined up all African-American families by the amount of assets they owned minus their debts and then looked at the family in the middle, that median family in 2001 had a net worth of $10,700 (excluding the value of automobiles). Line up all whites, and *that* median family had a net worth of $106,400, almost 10 times more. Less than half of African-American families own their own homes, while three out of four white families do. Latinos are even less wealthy: the median Latino family in 2001 had only $3,000 in assets, and less than half own their own homes.

We do not know how much Native Americans have in assets because so little data has been collected, but their poverty rate is 26% compared to 8% for whites, even though more than half own their own homes. Nor is much information collected about Asian Americans. What we do know is that their poverty rate is 13%, and that 60% of Asian Americans own their own homes, compared to 77% of whites.

Almost 40 years after the passage of the 20th century's major civil rights legislation, huge wealth disparities persist. However, the myth that the playing field was leveled by those laws is widespread. For anyone who accepts the myth, it follows that if families of color are not on an economic par with whites today, the problem must lie with *them*.

But the racial wealth gap has nothing to do with individual behaviors or cultural deficits. Throughout U.S. history, deliberate government policies transferred wealth from nonwhites to whites—essentially, affirmative action for whites. The specific mechanisms of the transfer have varied, as have the processes by which people have been put into racial categories in the first place. But a brief review of American history, viewed through the lens of wealth, reveals a consistent pattern of race-based obstacles that have prevented Native Americans, African Americans, Latinos, and Asians from building wealth at all comparable to whites.

NATIVE AMERICANS: IN THE U.S. GOVERNMENT WE "TRUST"?

When European settlers came to what would become the United States, Indian tribes in general did not consider land to be a source of individual wealth. It was a resource to be worshipped, treasured, and used to preserve all forms of life. Unfortunately for them, that concept of common ownership and the way of life they had built around it would clash mightily with the idea that parcels of land should be owned by individuals and used to generate private profit.

After the American Revolution, the official position of the new U.S. government was that Indian tribes had the same status as foreign nations and that good relations with them should be maintained. However, as European immigration increased and westward expansion continued, the settlers increasingly coveted Indian land. The federal government pressured Native Americans to sign one treaty after another giving over land: In the United States' first century, over 400 Indian treaties were signed. Indians were forcibly removed, first from the south and then from the west, sometimes into reservations.

Eventually, the Indians' last large territory, the Great Plains, was essentially handed over to whites. In one of the clearest instances of land expropriation, the 1862 Homestead Act transferred a vast amount of land from Indian tribes to white homesteaders by giving any white family 160 acres of land for free if they would farm it for five years. Of course, this massive land transfer was not accomplished without violence. General William Tecumseh Sherman, of Civil War fame, wrote: "The more [Indians] we can kill this year, the less will have to be killed the next year, for the more I see of these Indians, the more convinced I am that they all have to be killed or be maintained as a species of paupers." (Ironically, the Homestead Act is often cited as a model government program that supported asset-building.)

Out of the many treaties came the legal concept of the U.S. government's "trust responsibility" for the Native nations, similar to the relationship of a legal guardian to a child. In exchange for land, the government was to provide for the needs of the Native peoples. Money from the sale of land or natural resources was to be placed in a trust fund and managed in the best interests of the Indian tribes. The government's mismanagement of Indian assets was pervasive; yet, by law, Indian tribes could not fire the designated manager and hire a better or more honest one.

The Dawes Act of 1887 was designed to pressure Indians to assimilate into white culture: to adopt a sedentary life style and end their tradition of collective land ownership. The law broke up reservation land into individual plots and forced Indians to attempt to farm "western" style; "surplus" land was sold to whites. Under this scheme, millions more acres were transferred from Native Americans to whites.

After 1953, the U.S. government terminated the trust status of the tribes. While the stated purpose was to free Indians from government control, the new policy exacted a price: the loss of tribally held land that was still the basis of some tribes' existence. This blow reduced the remaining self-sufficient tribes to poverty and broke up tribal governments.

Thus, over a 200-year period, U.S. government policies transferred Native Americans' wealth—primarily land and natural resources—into the pockets of white individuals. This expropriation of vast tracts played a foundational role in the creation of the U.S. economy. Only in recent years, through the effective use of lawsuits to resurrect tribal rights assigned under the old treaties, have some tribes succeeded in building substantial pools of wealth, primarily from gaming businesses. This newfound casino wealth, though, cannot make up for the decimation of Native peoples or the destruction of traditional Native economies. Native Americans on average continue to suffer disproportionate poverty.

AFRICAN AMERICANS: SLAVES DON'T OWN, THEY ARE OWNED

From the earliest years of European settlement until the 1860s, African Americans were assets to be tallied in the financial records of their owners. They could be bought and sold, they created more wealth for their owners in the form of children, they had no rights even over their own bodies, and they worked without receiving any wages. Slaves and their labor became the basis of wealth creation for plantation owners, people who owned and operated slave ships, and companies that insured them. This was the most fundamental of wealth divides in American history.

At the end of the Civil War, there was an opportunity to create a new starting line. In the first few years, the Freedmen's Bureau and the occupying Union army actually began to distribute land to newly freed slaves: the famous "40 acres and a mule," a modest enough way to begin. But the Freedmen's Bureau was disbanded after only seven years, and the overwhelming majority of land that freed slaves had been allotted was returned to its former white owners. Unable to get a foothold as self-employed farmers, African Americans were forced to accept sharecropping arrangements. While sharecroppers kept some part of the fruits of their labor as in-kind income, the system kept them perpetually in debt and unable to accumulate any assets.

In 1883, the Supreme Court overturned the Civil Rights Act of 1875, which had given blacks the right to protect themselves and their property. By 1900, the Southern states had passed laws that kept African Americans separate and unequal, at the bottom of the economy. They began migrating to the North and West in search of opportunity.

Amazingly, some African-American families did prosper as farmers and businesspeople in the early 20th century. Some African-American communities thrived, even establishing their own banks to build savings and investment within the community. However, there was particular resentment against successful African Americans, and they were often targets of the vigilante violence common in this period. State and local governments helped vigilantes destroy their homes, run them out of town, and lynch those "uppity" enough to resist, and the federal government turned a blind eye. Sometimes entire black communities were targeted. For example, the African-American business district in north Tulsa, known as the "Black Wall Street" for its size and success, was torched on the night of June 21, 1921, by white rioters, who destroyed as many as 600 black-owned businesses.

The Depression wiped out black progress, which did not resume at all until the New Deal period. Even then, African Americans were often barred from the new asset-building programs that benefited whites. Under Social Security, workers paid into the system and were guaranteed money in retirement. However, domestic and agricultural work—two of the most significant black occupations—were excluded from the program. Unemployment insurance and the minimum wage didn't apply to domestic workers or farm workers either. Other programs were also tilted toward white people. The Home Owners' Loan Corporation was created in 1933 to help homeowners avoid foreclosure, but not a single loan went to a black homeowner.

Following World War II, a number of new programs provided a ladder into the middle class—for whites. The GI Bill of Rights and low-interest home mortgages provided tax-funded support for higher education and for homeownership, two keys to family wealth building. The GI Bill provided little benefit to black veterans, however, because a recipient had to be accepted into a college—and many colleges did not accept African-American students. Likewise, housing discrimination meant that homeownership opportunities were greater for white families; subsidized mortgages were often simply denied for home purchases in black neighborhoods.

In *The Cost of Being African American*, sociologist Thomas Shapiro shows how, because of this history, even black families whose incomes are equal to whites' generally have unequal economic standing. Whites are more likely to have parents who benefited from the land grants of the Homestead Act, who have Social Security or retirement benefits, or who own their own homes. With their far greater average assets, whites can transfer advantage from parents to children in the form of college tuition payments, down payments on homes, or simply self-sufficient parents who do not need their children to support them in old age.

These are the invisible underpinnings of the black-white wealth gap: wealth legally but inhumanely created from the unpaid labor of blacks, the use of violence—often backed up by government power—to stop black wealth-creating activities, tax-funded asset building programs closed to blacks even as they, too, paid taxes. The playing field is not level today. For example, recent studies demonstrate that blatant race discrimination in hiring persists. But even if the playing field were level, the black/white wealth gap would still be with us.

LATINOS: IN THE UNITED STATES' BACKYARD

At the time of the American Revolution, Spain, not England, was the largest colonial landowner on the American continents. Unlike the English, the Spanish intermarried widely with the indigenous populations. In the 20th century, their descendants came to be identified as a distinct, nonwhite group. (In the 1800's, Mexicans were generally considered white.) Today, Latinos come from many countries with varied histories, but the relationship of Mexicans to the United States is the longest, and people of Mexican descent are still the largest Latino group in the United States (67% in 2002).

Mexico won its independence from Spain in 1821. Three years later, the Monroe Doctrine promised the newly independent nations of Latin America "protection" from interference by European powers. However, this doctrine allowed the United States itself to intervene in the affairs of the entire hemisphere. Ever since, this paternalistic relationship (reminiscent of the "trust" relationship with Native tribes) has meant U.S. political and economic dominance in Mexico and Central and South America, causing the "push and pull" of the people of those countries into and out of the United States.

Mexicans and Anglos fought together to free Texas from Mexican rule, creating the Lone Star Republic of Texas, which was then annexed to the United States in 1845. Three years later, the United States went to war against Mexico to gain more territory and continue fulfilling its "manifest destiny"—its God-given right—to expand "from sea to shining sea." Mexico lost the war and was forced to accept the 1848 Treaty of Guadalupe Hidalgo, which gave the United States half of Mexico's land. While individual Mexican landowners were at first assured that they would maintain ownership, the United States did not keep that promise, and the treaty ushered in a huge transfer of land from Mexicans to Anglos. For the first time in these areas, racial categories were used to determine who could obtain land. The English language was also used to establish Anglo dominance; legal papers in English proving land ownership were required, and many Spanish speakers suffered as a result.

In the twentieth century, government policy continued to reinforce a wealth gap between Mexicans and whites. The first U.S.-Mexico border patrol was set up in 1924, and deportations of Mexicans became commonplace. Like African Americans, Latino workers were disproportionately represented in the occupations not covered by the Social Security Act. During World War II, when U.S. farms needed more agricultural workers, the federal government established the Bracero program, under which Mexican workers were brought into the United States to work for sub-minimum wages and few benefits, then kicked out when their labor was no longer needed. Even today, Mexicans continue to be used as "guest"—or really, reserve—workers to create profits for U.S. agribusiness.

The North American Free Trade Agreement, along with the proposed Central American Free Trade Agreement and Free Trade Agreement of the Americas, is the newest incarnation of the Monroe Doctrine. Trade and immigration policies are still being used to maintain U.S. control over the resources in its "backyard," and at the same time to deny those it is "protecting" the enjoyment of the benefits to be found in papa's "front yard."

ASIAN AMERICANS: PERPETUAL FOREIGNERS

The first Asian immigrants, the Chinese, came to the United States at the same time and for the same reason as the Irish: to escape economic distress at home and take advantage of economic opportunity in America. Like European immigrants, the Chinese came voluntarily, paying their own passage, ready and willing to seize the opportunity to build economic success in a new land. Chinese and Irish immigrants arrived in large numbers in the same decade, but their economic trajectories later diverged.

The major reason is race. While the Irish, caricatured as apes in early cartoons, were soon able to become citizens, the Naturalization Act of 1790 limited eligibility for citizenship to "whites." Asians did not know if they were white or not—but they wanted to be! The rights and benefits of "whiteness" were obvious. Other Americans didn't know whether or not they were white, either. Lawsuits filed first by Chinese, then by Japanese, Indian (South Asian), and Filipino immigrants all claimed that they should be granted "white" status. The outcomes were confusing; for example, South Asians, classified as Caucasian, were at first deemed white. Then, in later cases, courts decided that while they were Caucasian, they were not white.

A series of laws limited the right of Asians to create wealth. Chinese immigrants were drawn into the Gold Rush; the Foreign Miners Tax, however, was designed to push them out of the mining industry. The tax provided 25% of California's annual state budget in the 1860s, but the government jobs and services the tax underwrote went exclusively to whites—one of the first tax-based racial transfers of wealth. And with the passage of the Chinese Exclusion Acts in 1882, the Chinese became the first nationality to be denied the right to join this immigrant nation; the numbers of Chinese-American citizens thus remained small until the 1960s.

The next wave of Asians came from Japan. Excellent farmers, the Japanese bought land and created successful businesses. Resentment led to the passage of the 1924 Alien Land Act, which prohibited noncitizens from owning land. Japanese Americans then found other ways to create wealth, including nurseries and the cut flower business. In 1941, they had $140 million of business wealth.

World War II would change all that. In 1942, the Roosevelt administration forced Japanese Americans, foreign-born and citizen alike, to relocate to internment camps in the inland Western states. They had a week to dispose of their assets. Most had to sell their homes and businesses to whites at fire sale prices—an enormous transfer of wealth. In 1988, a successful suit for reparations gave the survivors of the camps $20,000 each, a mere fraction of the wealth that was lost.

Today, Asians are the group that as a whole has moved closest to economic parity with whites. (There are major variations in status between different Asian nationalities, however, and grouping them masks serious problems facing some groups.) While Asian immigrants have high poverty rates, American-born Asians have moved into professional positions, and the median income of Asians is now higher than that of whites. However, glass ceilings still persist, and as Wen Ho Lee, the Chinese-American nuclear scientist who was falsely accused of espionage in 2002, found out, Asians are still defined by race and branded as perpetual foreigners.

The divergent histories of the Irish and the Chinese in the United States illustrate the powerful role of race in the long-term accumulation of wealth. Irish Americans faced plenty of discrimination in the labor market: consider the "No Irish Need Apply" signs that were once common in Boston storefronts. But they never faced legal prohibitions on asset ownership and citizenship as Chinese immigrants did, or the expropriation of property as the Japanese did. Today, people of Irish ancestry have attained widespread material prosperity and access to political power, and some of the wealthiest and most powerful men in business and politics are of Irish descent. Meantime, the wealth and power of the Chinese are still marginal.

Throughout history federal policies—from constructing racial categories, to erecting barriers to asset building by nonwhites, to overseeing transfers of wealth from nonwhites to whites—have created the basis for the current racial wealth divide. If the gap is to be closed, government policies will have to play an important role.

It's long past time to close the gap.

CRITICAL THINKING QUESTION

For each group—Native Americans, African Americans, Hispanic Americans, and Asian Americans—identify what you think is the most important reason members of the group trail whites today in the accumulation of wealth. Should legal barriers to the accumulation of wealth among minorities in the past have any bearing on policymaking in the present?

CHAPTER 12

School Finance: Inequality Persists

Michael Engel

The states vary widely among themselves in terms of support for public education, and there are multiple ways of measuring that variation. According to the federal government's National Center for Education Statistics (NCES), median per pupil expenditure in 2003–2004 ranged from $5,862 in Utah to $14,667 in Alaska; the national median was $7,860. A more significant statistic, calculated by the Census Bureau, is the amount spent by each state per $1,000 of personal income. This measures spending against how much the state's population can potentially afford. In 2003–2004, Florida was at the bottom with $34.36, and Alaska was at the top with $62.92. The figure for the nation as a whole was $43.68.

Perhaps more important is the inequality in spending among school districts *within* each state. The "federal range ratio" for school spending, as reported by the NCES, compares per pupil expenditure in districts spending the least and those spending the most. In Montana, for example, districts at the fifth percentile (those that spend less per pupil than 95% of the districts in the state) spend $5,526 per pupil, versus $19,400 per pupil at the 95th percentile; thus Montana's federal range ratio is 2.51, the highest in the country. (A federal range ratio of zero would denote equal spending across all districts; a federal range ratio of one describes a state where districts at the 95th percentile spend twice as much per pupil as districts at the 5th percentile.) States with relatively low range ratios—for instance, Maryland at 0.32 and Florida at 0.38—are the most "egalitarian."

Putting these three sets of figures together offers a detailed picture of educational inequality in the United States. Interestingly, West Virginia, one of the poorest states in the union, spends more than the median amounts *and* has the lowest federal range ratio in the country. The state's school districts are county-wide, which may explain its relatively equitable school funding: wealthier suburban towns cannot fund their own schools well without also supporting the schools in nearby cities.

So far, these data reveal the wide spreads between high- and low-budget school districts. But *which* children are getting the short end of the stick? Here we can look to the Education Trust, whose analysts have calculated the state and local dollars per pupil available to the highest- versus the lowest-poverty school districts and to the districts with the highest versus the lowest minority populations in each state (for 2004). They found that in about half of the states, the one-fourth of school districts with the highest share of poor students had less in state and local dollars to spend per pupil than the one-fourth of districts with the lowest share of poor students.

The variation from one state to another is striking. At the more egalitarian end of the spectrum are states such as New Mexico, Massachusetts, Minnesota, and New Jersey, where the highest-poverty districts have between $1,000 and $2,000 *more* to spend per pupil than the lowest-poverty districts. At the other end are Illinois, New Hampshire, New York, and Pennsylvania, where the highest-poverty districts have between $1,000 and $2,000 *less* to spend per pupil than the lowest-poverty districts.

As the Education Trust analysts note, though, it costs more—not the same—to provide an equal education to poor children. So these figures actually understate the disparity. The report offers the same comparisons cost-adjusted by 40% to account for the higher expense of educating poor children. Using the cost-adjusted figures, the highest-poverty districts have less to spend per pupil than the lowest-poverty district in two-thirds of the states. The adjusted figures show a funding gap in Illinois and New York that exceeds $2,000 per pupil. (Just imagine how an additional $60,000 a year could transform the educational environment for a class of 30 fourth graders!) In terms of discrimination against both the poor and minorities, the worst offenders are Arizona, Illinois, Montana, New Hampshire, New York, Texas, and Wyoming. States that rank high in shortchanging minority districts include Kansas, Nebraska, North Dakota, South Dakota, and Wisconsin.

In states with large urban centers surrounded by wealthy suburbs, the differences in school funding can be especially dramatic. Among the 69 school districts within 15 miles of downtown Chicago, for instance, the city itself ranks 50th in per-pupil spending, according to NCES data. Chicago spends $8,356 per pupil; compare that to $18,055 for Evanston and $15,421 for Oak Park, both wealthy suburbs. In fact, Illinois has a terrible record in every respect, but the state Supreme Court has twice explicitly rejected any judicial responsibility for reform. Among the 41 school districts in New York state within 20 miles of downtown Manhattan, New York City ranks 37th, with spending of $13,131 per pupil, compared with Great Neck at $20,995, Lawrence at $22,499, and Manhasset at $22,199. Even among suburbs, poorer ones with larger minority populations such as Mount Vernon fall far behind whiter and more prosperous communities. In New York, court battles continue while the legislature stalls, ignoring deadlines for reform already set by the courts.

These inequalities extend even to differences in funding within school districts, mostly in the form of teacher salary differentials. A 2005 report by the Education Trust-West *California's Hidden Teacher Spending Gap* concluded that "the concentration of more experienced and more highly credentialed teachers (along with their corresponding high salaries) in whiter and more affluent schools drives huge funding gaps between schools—even between schools within the very same school district."

Financial inequality in U.S. public schools is not an anomaly, nor is it the result of a lack of possible remedies. States have undertaken countless so-called reforms over the past 20 years—to little effect. Only a few states, however, have taken any *serious* steps to guarantee even an adequate, much less an equal, education for all their children.

COURTROOM REMEDIES

As of 2003, cases challenging the constitutionality of education finance systems had been heard in the courts of 44 states; in 18 of those states, the systems were declared unconstitutional. In 12 states the courts refused to act at all. The court decisions are all over the map in terms of setting standards of adequacy, equity, or equality, requiring legislative action, or prescribing specific remedies. Often it has taken a series of decisions over a number of years to force any change at all. The main overall effect of these rulings has been to push reluctant state legislatures, including those in some states where courts had not yet issued decisions, to modify their educational finance systems.

The outcomes, again, are all over the map, but very few have enacted serious and thorough reforms. For the most part, states have merely tinkered with the existing methods of aiding local schools. The most prevalent method—used in forty-one states—is foundation aid, which sets a statewide minimum per-pupil expenditure and appropriates state funds to make up the difference between that amount and the amounts localities are able (or required) to raise from property taxes. Each state uses a different formula, some so complex as to defy comprehension. Most reforms have involved a change in that formula to benefit poor districts, or a higher foundation level financed by increased state appropriations, or separate and additional grant programs.

A less common and even more complex method is known as "district power equalizing," which essentially guarantees a minimum property tax base to each community. In other words, the state determines the amount of revenue that is to be raised by any given local property tax rate and offers aid to communities whose property tax base is too poor to reach that level. Thus if the state determines a 5% rate should raise $10 million, a community that can only raise $7 million at that tax rate will receive $3 million in state aid. A more radical version, such as the one enacted in Vermont, provides for "recapturing" and redistributing the excess revenues raised by wealthier communities.

Some states combine both methods. In any case, although several states, such as New Jersey and Massachusetts, have managed to improve their formulas to the benefit of poorer communities, none of these adjustments address the basic cause of inequality, namely, reliance on local funding. Overall, in that regard there has been no improvement in twenty years. The state share of public school funding across the nation peaked at 49% in 1985; the federal share peaked at 9% in 1980. Federal aid to elementary and secondary education was $41 billion in 2003, a paltry 2% of the entire federal budget. To the extent that communities continue to have to rely on local property taxes to fund their schools, there is no question that serious inequities will persist.

At least four states, however, have gone beyond the norm. It is instructive to examine their experience with devising school funding systems that ostensibly aim for equality, that is, making sure that no district has a significant financial advantage over any other.

Hawaii is unique in the nation in that the whole state is one school district, and the state government is responsible for appropriating funds to the individual schools. On the surface, this appears to be a perfect example of equal education. Unfortunately, it is not. Until quite recently, funds were appropriated on an enrollment basis, without allowing for the extra costs involved in educating students in high-poverty areas or those with special needs. Moreover, Hawaii ranks 50th in terms of the percent of total state and local government revenues allocated for public education. Per pupil expenditure is just slightly above the national median, and the state ranks 35th in spending per $1,000 of personal income. Thus Hawaii resembles a number of southern states in uniformly under-funding all its public schools.

Kansas adopted a new school finance system in 1992, prompted by a lower court decision invalidating the existing one. The School District Finance and Quality Performance Act set a uniform statewide property tax rate, and established a $3,600 foundation funding level per pupil. The pupil count was weighted to take into account factors such as poverty. State aid was to make up the difference between that foundation level and what each community could raise with the property tax. But an escape hatch was provided by allowing a "local option budget" for communities to raise additional monies, up to 25% over the foundation level. The subsequent failure of the state to fully fund this reform led to widespread use of the local option budget. Richer communities were thus able to raise more money, so pre-existing inequalities continued. According to the Education Trust report, Kansas had one of the largest minority funding gaps in the country in 2003, and the poverty gap increased substantially between 1997 and 2003. The Kansas courts are thus still involved in the issue of educational finance.

Michigan's reforms were not inspired by any court actions. Rather, facing widespread anger over high property taxes, in 1993 Republican governor John Engler bit the bullet by getting the legislature to eliminate the property tax as the basis for school funding. He then forced the issue further by slashing the state education budget, creating a financial crisis for the schools. As a result, voters in 1994 approved a 2% sales tax increase to fund education. Reform legislation set a statewide property tax rate, and localities were not allowed to exceed that rate. State aid would be based on a foundation plan. The result was that the state share of school spending more than doubled. But property taxes still accounted for one-third of school budgets, and with the rate frozen by state mandate, communities with low property values still fell behind. Combined with insufficient state funding (per pupil spending is below the national median), this means that although progress was achieved, Michigan still has a way to go to provide equal and adequate funding to the schools serving its poorest children.

Vermont's Act 60 came closest to bringing schools toward the ideal of educational equality. In 1995, the state's supreme court ruled that the existing finance system violated the state constitution. Two years later the legislature responded with Act 60, the most radical reform in the country. The new law set a statewide property tax rate and foundation spending level. Localities were allowed to levy additional property taxes, but if revenues from a locality exceeded the foundation amount, that excess reverted to the state and was put into a "sharing pool" used to aid poorer communities. This was essentially a district power equalizing program with a socialist twist. Rich communities were hit hard, and their budget process became guesswork since they had no way of knowing in a timely way how much property tax revenue they would be able to keep for the following year. A political uproar ensued; Act 60 was succeeded by Act 68 in 2004, which kept the statewide property tax and increased the state sales tax, but ended the sharing pool. How this will play out is as yet not clear, but as of 2003–2004, Vermont ranked 2nd in per $1000 spending and 8th in per pupil spending with a relatively low poverty gap.

PROSPECTS FOR CHANGE

The complexity and confusion of school finance systems and of all of the efforts to reform them obscure a simple and obvious solution, which no state has chosen: progressive taxation. If public schools were funded entirely by state and local taxes whose effective rates increase with income and wealth, if state aid was weighted sharply in favor of districts with higher educational costs, if federal aid was increased and similarly appropriated, and if strict limits were placed on local supplementation, financial inequality among schools would be history.

To free-market ideologues and neoclassical economists, these alternatives are obviously anathema. But they are rarely mentioned even by liberal or progressive politicians concerned about educational inequality. For they involve confronting two of the most sensitive issues in American politics: taxes and race. All state and local revenue systems in the United States are regressive to one extent or another. And as Jonathan Kozol points out, racial segregation makes it easy for the majority of public officials, and of whites in general, to ignore the disastrous conditions in predominantly black schools.

It would thus take enormous public pressure to force the government to choose a new course and pursue financial equality. If that were done, we could build a system of public schools that would offer all students genuinely equal opportunity to learn, and the false promise…of "No Child Left Behind"…could actually become a reality.

Sources: Jonathan Kozol, *Savage Inequalities* (Crown, 1991); *The Shame of the Nation* (Crown, 2005); John Yinger, ed., *Helping Children Left Behind* (MIT Press, 2004); Education Trust, *The Funding Gap 2005*, *The Funding Gap 2006*; Education Trust—West, *California's Hidden Teacher Spending Gap* (2005); US Census Bureau, *Survey of Local Government Finances* (www.census.gov/govs/www/estimate.html); U.S. Dept. of Education, National Center for Education Statistics, *Education Finance Statistics Center* (www.nced.ed.gov/edfin); National Conference of State Legislatures, *Education Finance Database* (www.ncsl.org/programs/educ/ed_finance); Hawaii Superintendent of Education, *16th Annual Report* (2005); Teachers College, Columbia University, National Access Network (www.schoolfunding.info/).

CRITICAL THINKING QUESTIONS

What do you think accounts for the complexity of methods used by the states to determine school funding? What are some possible effects of the unequal funding of education on American society?

CHAPTER 13

Double Standards in Health Care

James W. Russell

"It is vital for people to be protected from having to choose
between financial ruin and loss of health."

—WORLD HEALTH ORGANIZATION[1]

Each year eighteen thousand people die in the United States because of lack of
health insurance coverage.[2] With forty-five million citizens lacking health
insurance coverage and not counting many millions more whose coverage is inadequate, it is undeniable that the American system is seriously deficient compared to
its European counterparts, where all citizens have full coverage. The problem goes
further. The United States has the world's most expensive health care system (see
Table 13.1). Americans pay an average annual cost of $5,724 per person for their
health care, well over twice as high as the average Western European cost of $2,471.

If there is any area of social policy in which Americans are likely to be aware
that their system has flaws, it is in health care. Americans generally acknowledge that their high and rising cost of health care is a problem and they are less
satisfied with their health system than on average are Western Europeans. Only
40 percent of Americans are satisfied with their health care system compared to
57 percent of Western Europeans (Table 13.1).

But Americans are less likely to lay the cause on the privatized nature of their
health system, assuming that medical care is expensive by its very nature. The
majority of health care spending in Europe is publicly financed. In the United
States the majority is privately financed (Table 13.1). The major actors in the
American health system—insurance companies, pharmaceutical corporations,
and physicians—derive the world's highest health-related profits and incomes,
largely because they are immune to government regulation or control as they are
in Europe. American physicians are the world's highest paid. On average they
receive 5.5 times the income of average workers. In contrast, German physicians,
the highest paid in Europe, receive only 3.4 times the average income of workers.
In other European countries the income disproportions are less: Switzerland, 2.1;
France, 1.9; Sweden, 1.5; United Kingdom, 1.4.[3]

Americans acknowledge that the growing number of uninsured persons is
a problem. But they are less likely to be aware that their expensive system ranks

Table 13.1 Health Care System Financing and Cost

	PERCENT PUBLIC FINANCING	PER CAPITA COST	PERCENT PUBLIC SATISFIED WITH HEALTH CARE SYSTEM
Andorra	70.5	$1,908	—
Austria	69.9	$2,220	83
Belgium	71.2	$2,515	77
Denmark	82.9	$2,583	76
Finland	75.7	$1,943	74
France	76.0	$2,736	78
Germany	78.5	$2,817	50
Greece	52.9	$1,814	19
Ireland	75.2	$2,367	48
Italy	75.6	$2,166	26
Luxembourg	85.4	$3,066	72
Malta	71.8	$965	—
Monaco	79.6	$4,258	—
Netherlands	65.6	$2,564	73
Norway	83.5	$3,409	—
Portugal	70.5	$1,702	24
San Marino	79.2	$3,094	—
Spain	71.3	$1,640	48
Sweden	85.3	$2,512	59
Switzerland	57.9	$3,446	—
United Kingdom	83.4	$2,160	56
European average	*74.4*	*$2,471*	*57*
United States	44.9	$5,274	40

Sources: World Health Organization, *The World Health Report* 2005 (Geneva: World Health Organization, 2005). Annex Tables 5, 6; Organization for Economic Cooperation and Development (OECD). *Health Data* 2005 (Paris: OECD, 2005).

poorly in quality as well as coverage. Two issues are involved in determining the quality of health care: the quality of a health care system and the average health conditions of a citizenry. The World Health Organization (WHO) ranked in order the quality of the health care systems of 191 countries. All twenty-one Western European systems ranked higher than the United States (Table 13.2).

American health conditions are inferior to those in Europe in terms of infant mortality and longevity, the two most common measures used in international comparisons. Of one thousand babies born live, seven die within their first year of life in the United States compared to an average 4.9 in Western Europe. The average American life span of 77 years is 2.9 years less than the average Western European life span of 79.4.

DEVELOPMENT OF NATIONAL
HEALTH INSURANCE

Modern health systems began during the last part of the nineteenth century. Before then there was little professional health coverage for whole populations and no national plans to provide such coverage. Families cared for, and pooled

Table 13.2 Health Care System Quality and Outcomes

	WHO RANKING	INFANT MORTALITY	LIFE EXPECTANCY
France	1	4	80
Italy	2	5	81
San Marino	3	—	81
Andorra	4	—	81
Malta	5	6	79
Spain	7	4	80
Austria	9	4	79
Norway	11	3	79
Portugal	12	5	77
Monaco	13	—	81
Greece	14	5	79
Luxembourg	16	5	79
Netherlands	17	5	79
United Kingdom	18	5	79
Ireland	19	6	78
Switzerland	20	5	81
Belgium	21	8	79
Sweden	23	4	81
Germany	25	4	79
Finland	31	3	79
Denmark	34	8	77
European average		*4.9*	*79.4*
United States	37	7	77

Sources: World Health Organization, *The World Health Report 2000* (Geneva: World Health Organization, 2000), Annex Table 1 and *The World Health Report 2005*, Annex Tables 1, 2b.

their financial resources to provide for, sick members. Religious and other charities might be available to help the poor. In Europe and the United States, early labor unions set up sickness funds for members.

German Chancellor Bismarck established the prototype of national health insurance in 1883, in large part to counter the public support the socialist labor unions were gaining from the popularity of their sickness funds. Mandatory contributions from employers and employees funded the Bismarckian system. By the 1920s a number of European countries, including Belgium, Norway, and Britain, had followed the German example and set up similar models. None of the systems, though, were extensive enough to cover their entire national population nor were their benefits comprehensive enough to cover all situations. In 1930 social health insurance still covered less than half of the working populations of Europe.[4]

The Soviet Union, beginning in 1917, and post-World War II Eastern European communist countries were the first to establish comprehensive health systems that covered entire populations. Those accomplishments stimulated Western European leaders to establish their own comprehensive systems. In the same way that Chancellor Bismarck wanted to counter the influence of socialist labor unions, post-war Western European leaders sought to counter the influence and appeal of communist parties that were significant in a number of major countries, including Italy and France.

In 1946, following recommendations from the 1942 Beveridge Report, Britain passed the National Health Service Act. Sweden passed similar legislation the same year. By establishing centralized, government-owned health systems, the British and Swedish approaches differed from the Bismarckian social insurance approach. Both represented the first noncommunist approaches to universal health care coverage.

The state thus was the major actor in the development of the Western European health systems by either mandating establishment of social insurance funds tied to workplaces or establishing national health services. Social insurance offered mandated coverage to employed workers; national health services to all citizens. In time the social insurance systems would develop supplementary government-financed plans to extend coverage to unemployed and other sectors of the population ineligible for workplace-related insurance.

Following passage of the 1935 Social Security Act in the United States, several bills were introduced but never passed in Congress to extend Social Security provisions to health care for the entire population. American labor union leaders supported these attempts to establish national health insurance. But by the 1950s they adapted to the apparent reality that it was unlikely to be accomplished. Instead, health insurance became one of the issues for which they bargained with management. It became one of the advantages of union membership, since unionized workplaces were more likely to have health insurance as a fringe benefit. Health insurance development in the United States thus partially followed the Bismarckian model in that for the most part it was tied to employment as a fringe benefit. But unlike in Europe, the United States government never established or mandated coverage for all workers or the population as a whole, leaving such coverage up to the outcome of private market-driven activities, labor union collective bargaining, or employer largesse.

If the European health systems were established by government actions, the American system evolved out of patchwork private market opportunities around health insecurities and residual government actions that protected particular populations such as veterans, the elderly, and the poor.

COMPARATIVE HEALTH SYSTEMS

There are three health system models in Europe and the United States. These exist on a continuum between the most market driven and the most government controlled. At the two ends of the continuum are privately organized, for-profit health care that exists in the United States and national health systems— sometimes called the Beveridge model—that exist in the Scandinavian countries, the United Kingdom. Italy, Spain, and Portugal. In between, but closer to the government pole, are the social insurance systems that exist in Germany, France, and the Benelux countries.

In the private health care system of the United States, health care is treated as a commodity that is sold to consumers on market principles. The four major health care actors—physicians, insurance companies, hospitals, and providers of medical goods, such as pharmaceutical companies—operate as private businesses. State involvement and regulation is minimized. Individuals purchase health care services as commodities according to how much they can afford. Those who are ineligible for or who cannot afford health insurance go without.

Most Americans who have health insurance have it as a fringe benefit of their employment. Having health benefits tied to employment is seen by American conservatives as a way to encourage work. Instead of being a right, health insurance is a reward reserved for those who work. It is treated as a commodity that is available only to those who perform adequately in the marketplace.

The obvious problem of tying health insurance to the workplace is that it will not cover the unemployed. There is no national requirement in the United States, unlike in Europe, that employers actually include health insurance as a fringe benefit. This has become readily apparent, as a number of employers have begun to cease offering insurance altogether as it has become increasingly more expensive or they've begun to require workers to pay out of pocket greater portions of the costs. In a number of cases, employers have begun to cease paying the insurance costs of retirees.

Unlike European social insurance models in which the state mandates that employers and employees contribute to a fund, there is no such state mandate in the United States. Employee health insurance exists only if employers voluntarily offer it to their workers, or workers extract it as a fringe benefit from them. Therein lies the reason why so many working Americans lack health insurance.

In the social insurance model (Germany, France, the Benelux countries), there are a multiplicity of different health funds attached to unions, cooperatives, charities, and private companies. Employees and employers share payments into different such social insurance funds. Social insurance models have obtained universal coverage by virtue of two features. First, they are mandatory. Employers must offer social insurance plans and employees must enroll in them. Second, for those who are unemployed or otherwise ineligible for workplace-related coverage, governments have compulsory tax-financed back-up plans.

National health services—in the Scandinavian countries, the United Kingdom, Italy, Spain, and Portugal—organize health care as a publicly controlled service much like the provision of public education. Individuals pay for health care services through their taxes and are eligible to receive them by virtue of being residents or citizens of the country, thereby ensuring universal coverage. Governments own hospitals and may directly employ physicians on salaries.

None of the country health systems, though, are pure representations of any of the models. All have complex combined features. All have state and private funding. Doctors on government salary coexist with doctors in private practice. Private insurance plans exist alongside social insurance. This has led analysts to conclude that while there are pure models of different types of health systems, in practice all countries combine features from the different models.[5]

The United States, which has the most privately organized system, also has government-financed Medicare insurance for the elderly and Medicaid insurance for the poor. All of the European countries with social insurance or national health systems also allow supplemental private insurance to be sold. If the United States uses government-based insurance to partially compensate for the failure of the private market to find it profitable to cover all citizens, European countries allow private insurance companies to make businesses out of providing coverage for gaps in national coverage. From the point of view of citizens, purchasing supplementary private insurance is a way of topping off their basic plans. The difference is that whereas the private market on its own cannot cover citizens who lack purchasing power, government plans could become more comprehensive if that became a budgeted priority depending upon political conditions.

Mixed systems in Europe in which private insurance is allowed a role are a compromise between state-administered provision of basic needs and the market. They ensure universal coverage while allowing freedom of choice of coverage according to the different purchasing powers of consumers. Mixed provision systems, though, inevitably compromise egalitarian access, since they allow more choices for basic necessities to those with higher incomes.

Switzerland provides an unusual example of a European country that has achieved universal coverage with mainly private insurance. But for that to be achieved, the Swiss government had to implement regulatory and supplementary actions that violate pure free market principles. It requires its citizens to purchase health insurance in the same way that states of the United States require their motorists to purchase automobile insurance. Government regulations then require that private insurance plans pool their funds so that risks are shared equally. That avoids companies' selling policies only to healthy citizens. Swiss national or canton governments then provide coverage for citizens who are unable to purchase private insurance.

REFORM POLICY

Two questions underlie the politics of health policy: what type of primary model—national health service, social insurance, or private—a country will have and what type of secondary features it will adopt as reforms. Reforms in themselves are neither good nor bad. While often being presented publicly as purely pragmatic responses to technical problems, reforms usually carry consequences for underlying social policy goals.

In Europe, the primary issue for health care reform is the extent to which privatization and market features will expand within the otherwise state-controlled or regulated health care landscape. It is common to argue in the United States that the generous European welfare state is no longer affordable in an era of globalized competition. That argument, though, is difficult to sustain for health care policy when Europe has achieved universal higher quality coverage at less than half the cost of the American privatized system. Those who would reform in the direction of the American privatized model seek either to reduce state spending or to increase opportunities for private health businesses.

The underlying question is where the line will be between socialized coverage that is available for all citizens and privatized coverage that is available for only those who can afford it. Private insurance companies and their ideological allies would like to expand the latter. However, the inevitable consequences of adopting more features of privatized health care systems in Europe will be increased health inequality.

In the United States, the two glaring problems are increasing coverage and containing costs. With forty-five million—15 percent of the population—without health care coverage, the immediate necessity is to devise a national plan that will expand coverage to the entire population. It is not just a question, though, of expanding token coverage—insurance that covers only a few health problems or in which there are substantial costs borne out of pocket by consumers. It must be coverage in which people are, in the words of the World Health Organization, "protected from having to choose between financial ruin and loss of health."[6] At the same time, the out-of-control costs of American health care caused primarily by private profiteering must be reined in.

To obtain those goals, the United States could adopt features of either the European social insurance or national health system models. Most of the American health system is closest to the social insurance model since it is workplace based. The most obvious reform to expand coverage based on that model would be to make it mandatory as it is in Europe. All American workplaces would be required to have health plans. To contain the costs of those plans, the government would have to regulate and negotiate the permitted charges of insurance companies, physicians, and other providers. Socializing insurance risk pools could contain costs further.

There are a number of heath care reform advocates in the United States who would prefer a Canadian-style single payer system in which the government establishes a tax-funded health insurance agency that covers all citizens. Such a centralized body would then be able to negotiate fees with physicians and other private providers. At the same time the single-payer system falls short of a European national health system model, since it allows private physicians and other providers.[7]

Kaiser Permanente, a nonprofit insurance company, provides a model that is close to a European national health system approach for reforming health care in the United States. Henry J. Kaiser, an eccentric capitalist who sought a cost-effective way to provide health care for his workers, founded it in 1945. Kaiser wanted to make profit off of the work of his workers, not their health care needs. Healthy workers were more profitable workers.

What made Kaiser Permanente unusual in the American health care landscape was that from its beginning it emphasized preventive care and placed its doctors on salary. This made it like a European national health service and controversial in the American context, causing it to be denounced as socialistic. But it was able to more efficiently deliver health care services at lower costs than its traditional market-driven counterparts.

Kaiser physicians received lower incomes than those in private practice. But the tradeoff for them was that they worked fewer hours and could concentrate on providing health care without being distracted by problems of running a business, as are physicians in private practice.

In the early decades of Kaiser Permanente, there were marked differences in the experience of having it rather than traditional health insurance. It cost less. It was centralized, usually in a Kaiser hospital. It was prepaid. Kaiser members simply showed their identification cards and were treated. In traditional private insurance plans, members would pay up front and then be reimbursed, requiring a mountain of forms to keep track of. In traditional plans, physicians often charged higher fees than what the insurance would pay, causing unpredictable and aggravating out-of-pocket expenses for patients. In Kaiser there were no extra charges.[8]

Kaiser's emphasis on not for profit preventive health care has produced a potential model for health care reform. Kaiser members are generally more satisfied with their plans than are members of for-profit insurance plans. As a result of its preventive practices, including monitoring and controlling blood pressure and cholesterol, Kaiser members in Northern California have a 30 percent lower death rate from heart disease than the general population.[9]

In the end any reform that will actually make a difference in terms of resolving the serious problems of the American health care system will have to expand the government sector. The most effective way but least likely of political success would be to establish a system in which citizens would pay a new dedicated tax, as Medicare is paid, to finance government health insurance instead of them or their employers continuing to pay for increasingly more expensive private insurance as they do now. Less effective but more politically possible, would be to expand the coverage of existing government programs such as Medicare. Either way, any reform will have to rein in current private profiteering.

CRITICAL THINKING QUESTIONS

What reforms, if any, would you like to see in the American health care system? Why? What obstacle(s) in implementation do you foresee?

NOTES

1. World Health Organization, *World Health Report 2000* (Geneva: World Health Organization, 2000), 24.
2. Institute of Medicine of the National Academies, *Insuring America's Health* (Washington, DC: National Academies Press, 2004), 8.
3. Uwe E. Reinhardt, Peter S. Hussey, and Gerard F. Anderson, "Cross-National Comparisons of Health Systems Using OECD Data, 1999," *Health Affairs*, vol. 21, no. 3 (2002): 175.

4. Cited in Richard Freeman, *The Politics of Health in Europe* (Manchester: Manchester University Press, 2000), 26.

5. See Freeman, *The Politics of Health in Europe*, 5; and Robert H. Blank and Viola Burau, *Comparative Health Policy* (Hampshire, UK: Palgrave Macmillan, 2004), 22.

6. World Health Organization, *World Health Report 2000*, 24.

7. In June 2005 the Canadian Supreme Court ruled that the Quebec part of the national tax-based single-payer health care system was in violation of the province's bill of rights because it forbids private health insurance. Critics charged that the single-payer system was plagued by shortages of services. The purpose of the Quebec case was to allow private insurance companies to sell policies to cover the shortages. Defenders of the Canadian system correctly argue that introduction of private insurance will inevitably lead to health inequality between those who can and cannot afford the policies. Such shortages as do exist could be resolved by greater public funding without introducing health inequality.

8. Originally, private insurance companies simply passed the extra charges of physicians and other providers on to the consumers. In line with national efforts to rein in health care costs, private health insurance companies in the 1990s began to control physician and provider fees more closely. They directly contracted physicians into their networks. In return for receiving the business of the insurance plan's members, the physicians were required to charge only negotiated set fees.

9. Steve Lohr, "Is Kaiser the Future of American Health Care?," *New York Times*, October 31, 2004, section 3, 1. In line with its emphasis on prevention, Kaiser Permanente referred to itself as a health maintenance organization or HMO. Ironically, for-profit health insurance companies began to develop their own versions of HMOs in the 1980s in order to lower health costs. Their versions differed, though, in that they were being used to maintain or increase profits rather than deliver cost-effective preventive health care. In the eyes of the public, the term HMO, which originally had a progressive connotation, became increasingly identified with corporate greed.

PART IV

Problems of the Family

Discussions about present-day social problems often trace the causes of these problems back to the current state of "the family." Crime, drugs, family violence, teenage pregnancy, and more are blamed on faulty child-rearing resulting from the "breakdown" of the family. But assumptions about the erosion of the family—or of family values—are based on historical assumptions that are frequently inaccurate. In the first reading in this part Stephanie Coontz discusses many of these inaccuracies. It would seem that throughout most of history all generations have seen a previous generation as representing the golden age of family. Yet all generations of family have had their advantages and their disadvantages as well.

Those who long for the "good ole days of family" today are usually harkening back to some distorted image of the family of the 1950s with father as the breadwinner, mother as the housewife, and two or more dependent children. Coontz makes references to television shows with which many younger readers many not be familiar; but many of these shows appeared in syndication for decades, and most baby boomers were raised with a steady diet of idealized images of the family of the 1950s. This idealized image of the family neglects the pressures put on women to deny any ambitions to fulfill themselves outside of the household; neglects the pressures put on men to ensure the financial well-being of their family alone; neglects the pressure put on people to stay in violent, loveless, or unhappy marriages; and neglects the fact that millions of families could not afford to forgo the income of a housewife/mother. The idealized image of the 1950s family is still significant today to the extent that it influences the decisions of policymakers who are part of the baby boom generation.

In the next reading, Robert Drago addresses the relationship between work and family, especially as it pertains to women and caregiving. Often, women who stay at home to take care of children are perceived as not "working"; discussions of gender equality are almost exclusively confined to the paid labor force; and the most prominent measure of the economic health of our country, the gross domestic product, accounts only for labor that involves the exchange of money. Women working outside the home can expect to come home and start their "second shift." Women's productivity, then, is likely to go underacknowledged and undercompensated. With their work undervalued, the work itself becomes all the more stressful. Drago offers a perspective and a definition of work that might help bring balance to the work and family lives of both women and men.

The phrase "family values" is often bantered about in American political discourse, often by those who harken back to the idealized family of the 1950s and would like to see moms at home overseeing their children's moral development. In the next article, Brittany Shahmehri describes Swedish family leave policy. It is often the same people extolling family values who oppose expanding American family leave policies that would indeed allow parents more time to stay at home, nurture, supervise, and bond with their children. American family leave policies are, to say the least, negligible—virtually nonexistent—compared to almost all of the countries in Western Europe. Judging by the way they allocate their resources, these countries would seem to place a much higher priority on family values than does the United States.

In some ways consistent with the United States' relative failure to invest in its children, the last article in this part argues that American families are becoming less child-centered. More children are being born out of wedlock, more are living with single parents than in the past, and the number of children living with unmarried couples is on the rise. To some, such trends are themselves social problems; to others, they forebode more problems in the future; and to others, they are seen as no cause for alarm. See what you think.

CHAPTER 14

The Way We Wish We Were: Defining the Family Crisis

Stephanie Coontz

When I begin teaching a course on family history, I often ask my students to write down ideas that spring to mind when they think of the "traditional family." Their lists always include several images. One is of extended families in which all members worked together, grandparents were an integral part of family life, children learned responsibility and the work ethic from their elders, and there were clear lines of authority based on respect for age. Another is of nuclear families in which nurturing mothers sheltered children from premature exposure to sex, financial worries, or other adult concerns, while fathers taught adolescents not to sacrifice their education by going to work too early. Still another image gives pride of place to the couple relationship. In traditional families, my students write—half derisively, half wistfully—men and women remained chaste until marriage, at which time they extricated themselves from competing obligations to kin and neighbors and committed themselves wholly to the marital relationship, experiencing an all-encompassing intimacy that our more crowded modern life seems to preclude. As one freshman wrote: "They truly respected the marriage vowels"; I assume she meant *I-O-U*.

Such visions of past family life exert a powerful emotional pull on most Americans, and with good reason, given the fragility of many modern commitments. The problem is not only that these visions bear a suspicious resemblance to reruns of old television series, but also that the scripts of different shows have been mixed up: June Cleaver suddenly has a Grandpa Walton dispensing advice in her kitchen; Donna Stone, vacuuming the living room in her inevitable pearls and high heels, is no longer married to a busy modern pediatrician but to a small-town sheriff who, like Andy Taylor of "The Andy Griffith Show," solves community problems through informal, old-fashioned common sense.

Like most visions of a "golden age," the "traditional family" my students describe evaporates on closer examination. It is an ahistorical amalgam of structures, values, and behaviors that never coexisted in the same time and place. The notion that traditional families fostered intense intimacy between husbands and wives while creating mothers who were totally available to their children, for example, is an idea that combines some characteristics of the white, middle-class family in the mid-nineteenth century and some of a rival family ideal first articulated in the 1920s. The first family revolved emotionally around the mother-child axis, leaving the husband-wife relationship stilted and formal. The second focused on an eroticized couple relationship, demanding that mothers curb emotional "overinvestment" in their children. The hybrid idea that a woman can be fully absorbed with her youngsters while simultaneously maintaining passionate sexual excitement with her husband was a 1950s invention that drove thousands of women to therapists, tranquilizers, or alcohol when they actually tried to live up to it.

Similarly, an extended family in which all members work together under the top-down authority of the household elder operates very differently from a nuclear family in which husband and wife are envisioned as friends who patiently devise ways to let the children learn by trial and error. Children who worked in family enterprises seldom had time for the extracurricular activities that Wally and the Beaver recounted to their parents over the dinner table; often, they did not even go to school full-time. Mothers who did home production generally relegated child care to older children or servants; they did not suspend work to savor a baby's first steps or discuss with their husband how to facilitate a grade-schooler's "self-esteem." Such families emphasized formality, obedience to authority, and "the way it's always been" in their childrearing.

Nuclear families, by contrast, have tended to pride themselves on the "modernity" of parent-child relations, diluting the authority of grandparents, denigrating "old-fashioned" ideas about childraising, and resisting the "interference" of relatives. It is difficult to imagine the Cleavers or the college-educated title figure of "Father Knows Best" letting grandparents, maiden aunts, or in-laws have a major voice in childrearing decisions. Indeed, the kind of family exemplified by the Cleavers...represented a conscious *rejection* of the Waltons' model.

THE ELUSIVE TRADITIONAL FAMILY

Whenever people propose that we go back to the traditional family, I always suggest that they pick a ballpark date for the family they have in mind. Once pinned down, they are invariably unwilling to accept the package deal that comes with their chosen model. Some people, for example, admire the discipline of colonial families, which were certainly not much troubled by divorce or fragmenting individualism. But colonial families were hardly stable: High mortality rates meant that the average length of marriage was less than a dozen years. One-third to one-half of all children lost at least one parent before the age of twenty-one; in the South, more than half of all children aged thirteen or under had lost at least one parent.[1]

While there are a few modern Americans who would like to return to the strict patriarchal authority of colonial days, in which disobedience by women and children was considered a small form of treason, these individuals would doubtless be horrified by other aspects of colonial families, such as their failure to protect children from knowledge of sexuality. Eighteenth-century spelling and grammar books routinely used *fornication* as an example of a four-syllable word, and preachers detailed sexual offenses in astonishingly explicit terms. Sexual conversations between men and women, even in front of children, were remarkably frank. It is worth contrasting this colonial candor to the climate in 1991, when the Department of Health and Human Services was forced to cancel a proposed survey of teenagers' sexual practices after some groups charged that such knowledge might "inadvertently" encourage more sex.[2]

Other people searching for an ideal traditional family might pick the more sentimental and gentle Victorian family, which arose in the 1830s and 1840s as household production gave way to wage work and professional occupations outside the home. A new division of labor by age and sex emerged among the middle class. Women's roles were redefined in terms of domesticity rather than production, men were labeled "breadwinners" (a masculine identity unheard of in colonial days), children were said to need time to play, and gentle maternal guidance supplanted the patriarchal authoritarianism of the past.

But the middle-class Victorian family depended for its existence on the multiplication of other families who were too poor and powerless to retreat into their own little oases and who therefore had to provision the oases of others. Childhood was prolonged for the nineteenth-century middle class only because it was drastically foreshortened for other sectors of the population. The spread of textile mills, for example, freed middle-class women from the most time-consuming of their former chores, making cloth. But the raw materials for these mills were produced by slave labor. Slave children were not exempt from field labor unless they were infants, and even then their mothers were not allowed time off to nurture them. Frederick Douglass could not remember seeing his mother until he was seven.[3]

Domesticity was also not an option for the white families who worked twelve hours a day in Northern factories and workshops transforming slave-picked cotton into ready-made clothing. By 1820, "half the workers in many factories were boys and girls who had not reached their eleventh birthday." Rhode Island investigators found "little half-clothed children" making their way to the textile mills before dawn. In 1845, shoemaking families and makers of artificial flowers worked fifteen to eighteen hours a day, according to the *New York Daily Tribune*.[4]

Within the home, prior to the diffusion of household technology at the end of the century, house cleaning and food preparation remained mammoth tasks. Middle-class women were able to shift more time into childrearing in this period only by hiring domestic help. Between 1800 and 1850, the proportion of servants to white households doubled, to about one in nine. Some servants were poverty-stricken mothers who had to board or bind out their own children. Employers found such workers tended to be "distracted," however; they usually preferred young girls. In his study of Buffalo, New York, in the 1850s, historian Lawrence

Glasco found that Irish and German girls often went into service at the age of eleven or twelve.[5]

For every nineteenth-century middle-class family that protected its wife and child within the family circle, then, there was an Irish or a German girl scrubbing floors in that middle-class home, a Welsh boy mining coal to keep the home-baked goodies warm, a black girl doing the family laundry, a black mother and child picking cotton to be made into clothes for the family, and a Jewish or an Italian daughter in a sweatshop making "ladies'" dresses or artificial flowers for the family to purchase.

Furthermore, people who lived in these periods were seldom as enamored of their family arrangements as modern nostalgia might suggest. Colonial Americans lamented "the great neglect in many parents and masters in training up their children" and expressed the "greatest trouble and grief about the rising generation." No sooner did Victorian middle-class families begin to withdraw their children from the work world than observers began to worry that children were becoming *too* sheltered. By 1851, the Reverend Horace Bushnell spoke for many in bemoaning the passing of the traditional days of household production, when the whole family was "harnessed, all together, into the producing process, young and old, male and female, from the boy who rode the plough-horse to the grandmother knitting under her spectacles."[6]

The late nineteenth century saw a modest but significant growth of extended families and a substantial increase in the number of families who were "harnessed" together in household production. Extended families have never been the norm in America; the highest figure for extended-family households ever recorded in American history is 20 percent. Contrary to the popular myth that industrialization destroyed "traditional" extended families, this high point occurred between 1850 and 1885, during the most intensive period of early industrialization. Many of these extended families, and most "producing" families of the time, depended on the labor of children; they were held together by dire necessity and sometimes by brute force.[7]

There was a significant increase in child labor during the last third of the nineteenth century. Some children worked at home in crowded tenement sweatshops that produced cigars or women's clothing. Reformer Helen Campbell found one house where "nearly thirty children of all ages and sizes, babies predominating, rolled in the tobacco which covered the floor and was piled in every direction."[8] Many producing households resembled the one described by Mary Van Kleeck of the Russell Sage Foundation in 1913:

> In a tenement on MacDougal Street lives a family of seven—grandmother, father, mother and four children aged four years, three years, two years and one month respectively. All excepting the father and the two babies make violets. The three year old girl picks apart the petals; her sister, aged four years, separates the stems, dipping an end of each into paste spread on a piece of board on the kitchen table; and the mother and grandmother slip the petals up the stems.[9]

Where children worked outside the home, conditions were no better. In 1900, 120,000 children worked in Pennsylvania mines and factories; most of them had started work by age eleven. In Scranton, a third of the girls between the ages of thirteen and sixteen worked in the silk mills in 1904. In New York, Boston, and Chicago, teenagers worked long hours in textile factories and frequently died in fires or industrial accidents. Children made up 23.7 percent of the 36,415 workers in southern textile mills around the turn of the century. When reformer Marie Van Vorse took a job at one in 1903, she found children as young as six or seven working twelve-hour shifts. At the end of the day, she reported: "They are usually beyond speech. They fall asleep at the tables, on the stairs; they are carried to bed and there laid down as they are, unwashed, undressed; and the inanimate bundles of rags so lie until the mill summons them with its imperious cry before sunrise."[10]

By the end of the nineteenth century, shocked by the conditions in urban tenements and by the sight of young children working full-time at home or earning money out on the streets, middle-class reformers put aside nostalgia for "harnessed" family production and elevated the antebellum model once more, blaming immigrants for introducing such "un-American" family values as child labor. Reformers advocated adoption of a "true American" family—a restricted, exclusive nuclear unit in which women and children were divorced from the world of work.

In the late 1920s and early 1930s, however, the wheel turned yet again, as social theorists noted the independence and isolation of the nuclear family with renewed anxiety. The influential Chicago School of sociology believed that immigration and urbanization had weakened the traditional family by destroying kinship and community networks. Although sociologists welcomed the increased democracy of "companionate marriage," they worried about the rootlessness of nuclear families and the breakdown of older solidarities. By the time of the Great Depression, some observers even saw a silver lining in economic hardship, since it revived the economic functions and social importance of kin and family ties. With housing starts down by more than 90 percent, approximately one-sixth of urban families had to "double up" in apartments. The incidence of three-generation households increased, while recreational interactions outside the home were cut back or confined to the kinship network. One newspaper opined: "Many a family that has lost its car has found its soul."[11]

Depression families evoke nostalgia in some contemporary observers, because they tended to create "dependability and domestic inclination" among girls and "maturity in the management of money" among boys. But, in many cases, such responsibility was inseparable from "a corrosive and disabling poverty that shattered the hopes and dreams of...young parents and twisted the lives of those who were 'stuck together' in it." Men withdrew from family life or turned violent; women exhausted themselves trying to "take up the slack" both financially and emotionally, or they belittled their husbands as failures; and children gave up their dreams of education to work at dead-end jobs.[12]

From the hardships of the Great Depression and the Second World War and the euphoria of the postwar economic recovery came a new kind of family ideal that still enters our homes in "Leave It to Beaver" and "Donna Reed" reruns.... [T]he 1950s were no more a "golden age" of the family than any other period in American history....I...argue that our recurring search for a traditional family model denies the diversity of family life, both past and present, and leads to false generalizations about the past as well as wildly exaggerated claims about the present and the future.

THE COMPLEXITIES OF ASSESSING FAMILY TRENDS

If it is hard to find a satisfactory model of the traditional family, it is also hard to make global judgments about how families have changed and whether they are getting better or worse. Some generalizations about the past are pure myth. Whatever the merit of recurring complaints about the "rootlessness" of modern life, for instance, families are *not* more mobile and transient than they used to be. In most nineteenth-century cities, both large and small, more than 50 percent—and often up to 75 percent—of the residents in any given year were no longer there ten years later. People born in the twentieth century are much more likely to live near their birthplace than were people born in the nineteenth century.[13]

This is not to say, of course, that mobility did not have different effects then than it does now. In the nineteenth century, claims historian Thomas Bender, people moved from community to community, taking advantage...of non-familial networks and institutions that integrated them into new work and social relations. In the late twentieth century, people move from job to job, following a career path that shuffles them from one single-family home to another and does not link them to neighborly networks beyond the family. But this change is in our community ties, not in our family ones.[14]

A related myth is that modern Americans have lost touch with extended-kinship networks or have let parent-child bonds lapse. In fact, more Americans than ever before have grandparents alive, and there is good evidence that ties between grandparents and grandchildren have become stronger over the past fifty years. In the late 1970s, researchers returned to the "Middletown" studied by sociologists Robert and Helen Lynd in the 1920s and found that most people there maintained closer extended-family networks than in earlier times. There had been some decline in the family's control over the daily lives of youth, especially females, but "the expressive/emotional function of the family" was "more important for Middletown students of 1977 than it was in 1924." More recent research shows that visits with relatives did *not* decline between the 1950s and the late 1980s.[15]

Today 54 percent of adults see a parent, and 68 percent talk on the phone with a parent, at least once a week. Fully 90 percent of Americans describe their relationship with their mother as close, and 78 percent say their relationship with their grandparents is close. And for all the family disruption of divorce, most modern children live with at least *one* parent. As late as 1940, 10 percent of American children did not live with either parent, compared to only one in twenty-five today.[16]

What about the supposed eclipse of marriage? Neither the rising age of those who marry nor the frequency of divorce necessarily means that marriage is becoming a less prominent institution than it was in earlier days. Ninety percent of men and women eventually marry, more than 70 percent of divorced men and women remarry, and fewer people remain single for their entire lives today than at the turn of the century. One author even suggests that the availability of divorce in the second half of the twentieth century has allowed some women to try marriage who would formerly have remained single all their lives. Others argue that the rate of hidden marital separation in the late nineteenth century was not much less than the rate of visible separation today.[17]

Studies of marital satisfaction reveal that more couples reported their marriages to be happy in the late 1970s than did so in 1957, while couples in their second marriages believe them to be much happier than their first ones. Some commentators conclude that marriage is becoming less permanent but more satisfying. Others wonder, however, whether there is a vicious circle in our country, where no one even tries to sustain a relationship. Between the late 1970s and late 1980s, moreover, reported marital happiness did decline slightly in the United States. Some authors see this as reflecting our decreasing appreciation of marriage, although others suggest that it reflects unrealistically high expectations of love in a culture that denies people safe, culturally approved ways of getting used to marriage or cultivating other relationships to meet some of the needs that we currently load onto the couple alone.[18]

Part of the problem in making simple generalizations about what is happening to marriage is that there has been a polarization of experiences. Marriages are much more likely to be ended by divorce today, but marriages that do last are described by their participants as happier than those in the past and are far more likely to confer such happiness over many years. It is important to remember that the 50 percent divorce rate estimates are calculated in terms of a forty-year period and that many marriages in the past were terminated well before that date by the death of one partner. Historian Lawrence Stone suggests that divorce has become "a functional substitute for death" in the modern world. At the end of the 1970s, the rise in divorce rates seemed to overtake the fall in death rates, but the slight decline in divorce rates since then means that "a couple marrying today is more likely to celebrate a fortieth wedding anniversary than were couples around the turn of the century."[19]

A similar polarization allows some observers to argue that fathers are deserting their children, while others celebrate the new commitment of fathers to childrearing. Both viewpoints are right. Sociologist Frank Furstenberg comments on the emergence of a "good dad–bad dad complex": Many fathers spend more time with their children than ever before and feel more free to be affectionate with them; others, however, feel more free simply to walk out on their families.

According to 1981 statistics, 42 percent of the children whose father had left the marriage had not seen him in the past year. Yet studies show steadily increasing involvement of fathers with their children as long as they are in the home.[20]

These kinds of ambiguities should make us leery of hard-and-fast pronouncements about what's happening to the American family. In many cases, we simply don't know precisely what our figures actually mean. For example, the proportion of youngsters receiving psychological assistance rose by 80 percent between 1981 and 1988. Does that mean they are getting more sick or receiving more help, or is it some complex combination of the two? Child abuse reports increased by 225 percent between 1976 and 1987. Does this represent an actual increase in rates of abuse or a heightened consciousness about the problem? During the same period, parents' self-reports about very severe violence toward their children declined 47 percent. Does this represent a real improvement in their behavior or a decreasing willingness to admit to such acts?[21]

Assessing the direction of family change is further complicated because many contemporary trends represent a reversal of developments that were themselves rather recent. The expectation that the family should be the main source of personal fulfillment, for example, was not traditional in the eighteenth and nineteenth centuries.... Prior to the 1900s, the family festivities that now fill us with such nostalgia for "the good old days" (and cause such heartbreak when they go poorly) were "relatively undeveloped." Civic festivals and Fourth of July parades were more important occasions for celebration and strong emotion than family holidays, such as Thanksgiving. Christmas "seems to have been more a time for attending parties and dances than for celebrating family solidarity." Only in the twentieth century did the family come to be the center of festive attention and emotional intensity.[22]

Today, such emotional investment in the family may be waning again. This could be interpreted as a reestablishment of balance between family life and other social ties; on the other hand, such a trend may have different results today than in earlier times, because in many cases the extrafamilial institutions and customs that used to socialize individuals and provide them with a range of emotional alternatives to family life no longer exist.

In other cases, close analysis of statistics showing a deterioration in family well-being supposedly caused by abandonment of tradition suggests a more complicated train of events. Children's health, for example, improved dramatically in the 1960s and 1970s, a period of extensive family transformation. It ceased to improve, and even slid backward, in the 1980s, when innovative social programs designed to relieve families of some "traditional" responsibilities were repealed. While infant mortality rates fell by 4.7 percent a year during the 1970s, the rate of decline decreased in the 1980s, and in both 1988 and 1989, infant mortality rates did not show a statistically significant decline. Similarly, the proportion of low-birth-weight babies fell during the 1970s but stayed steady during the 1980s and had even increased slightly as of 1988. Child poverty is lower today than it was in the "traditional" 1950s but much higher than it was in the nontra-ditional late 1960s.[23]

WILD CLAIMS AND PHONY FORECASTS

Lack of perspective on where families have come from and how their evolution connects to other social trends tends to encourage contradictory claims and wild exaggerations about where families are going. One category of generalizations seems to be a product of wishful thinking. As of 1988, nearly half of all fami-lies with children had both parents in the work force. The two-parent family in which only the father worked for wages represented just 25 percent of all fami-lies with children, down from 44 percent in 1975. For people overwhelmed by the difficulties of adjusting work and schools to the realities of working moms, it has been tempting to discern a "return to tradition" and hope the problems will go away. Thus in 1991, we saw a flurry of media reports that the number of women in the work force was headed down: "More Choose to Stay Home with Children" proclaimed the headlines; "More Women Opting for Chance to Watch Their Children Grow."[24]

The cause of all this commotion? The percentage of women aged twenty-five to thirty-four who were employed dropped from 74 percent to 72.8 percent between January 1990 and January 1991. However, there was an exactly equal decline in the percentage of men in the work force during the same period, and for both genders the explanation was the same. "The dip is the recession," explained Judy Waldrop, research editor at *American Demographics* magazine, to anyone who bothered to listen. In fact, the proportion of *mothers* who worked increased slightly during the same period.[25]

This is not to say that parents, especially mothers, are happy with the pres-sures of balancing work and family life. Poll after poll reveals that both men and women feel starved for time. The percentage of women who say they would prefer to stay home with their children if they could afford to do so rose from 33 per-cent in 1986 to 56 percent in 1990. Other polls show that even larger majorities of women would trade a day's pay for an extra day off. But, above all, what these polls reveal is women's growing dissatisfaction with the failure of employers, schools, and government to pioneer arrangements that make it possible to com-bine work and family life. They do not suggest that women are actually going to stop working, or that this would be women's preferred solution to their stresses. The polls did not ask, for example, how *long* women would like to take off work, and failed to take account of the large majority of mothers who report that they would miss their work if they did manage to take time off. Working mothers are here to stay, and we will not meet the challenge this poses for family life by inventing an imaginary trend to define the problem out of existence.

At another extreme is the kind of generalization that taps into our worst fears. One example of this is found in the almost daily reporting of cases of child molestation or kidnapping by sexual predators. The highlighting of such cases, drawn from every corner of the country, helps disguise how rare these cases actually are when compared to crimes committed within the family.

A well-publicized instance of the cataclysmic predictions that get made when family trends are taken out of historical context is the famous *Newsweek* contention that a single woman of forty has a better chance of being killed by a terrorist than of finding a husband. It is true that the proportion of never-married women under age forty has increased substantially since the 1950s, but it is also true that the proportion has *decreased* dramatically among women over that age. A woman over thirty-five has a *better* chance to marry today than she did in the 1950s. In the past twelve years, first-time marriages have increased almost 40 percent for women aged thirty-five to thirty-nine. A single woman aged forty to forty-four still has a 24 percent probability of marriage, while 15 percent of women in their late forties will marry. These figures would undoubtedly be higher if many women over forty did not simply pass up opportunities that a more desperate generation might have snatched.[26]

Yet another example of the exaggeration that pervades many analyses of modern families is the widely quoted contention that "parents today spend 40 percent less time with their children than did parents in 1965." Again, of course, part of the problem is where researchers are measuring from. A comparative study of Muncie, Indiana, for example, found that parents spent much more time with their children in the mid-1970s than did parents in the mid-1920s. But another problem is keeping the categories consistent. Trying to track down the source of the 40 percent decline figure, I called demographer John P. Robinson, whose studies on time formed the basis of this claim. Robinson's data, however, show that parents today spend about the same amount of time caring for children as they did in 1965. If the total amount of time devoted to children is less, he suggested, I might want to check how many fewer children there are today. In 1970, the average family had 1.34 children under the age of eighteen; in 1990, the average family had only .96 children under age eighteen—a decrease of 28.4 percent. In other words, most of the decline in the total amount of time parents spend with children is because of the decline in the number of children they have to spend time with![27]

Now I am not trying to say that the residual amount of decrease is not serious, or that it may not become worse, given the trends in women's employment. Robinson's data show that working mothers spend substantially less time in primary child-care activities than do nonemployed mothers (though they also tend to have fewer children); more than 40 percent of working mothers report feeling "trapped" by their daily routines; many routinely sacrifice sleep in order to meet the demands of work and family. Even so, a majority believe they are *not* giving enough time to their children. It is also true that children may benefit merely from having their parents available, even though the parents may not be spending time with them.

But there is no reason to assume the worst. Americans have actually gained free time since 1965, despite an increase in work hours, largely as a result of a

decline in housework and an increasing tendency to fit some personal requirements and errands into the work day. And according to a recent Gallup poll,
most modern mothers think they are doing a better job of communicating with
their children (though a worse job of house cleaning) than did their own mothers and that they put a higher value on spending time with their family than did
their mothers.[28]

NEGOTIATING THROUGH THE EXTREMES

Most people react to these conflicting claims and contradictory trends with
understandable confusion. They know that family ties remain central to their
own lives, but they are constantly hearing about people who seem to have *no* family feeling. Thus, at the same time as Americans report high levels of satisfaction
with their own families, they express a pervasive fear that other people's families
are falling apart. In a typical recent poll, for example, 71 percent of respondents
said they were "very satisfied" with their own family life, but more than half
rated the overall quality of family life as negative: "I'm okay; you're not."[29]

This seemingly schizophrenic approach does not reflect an essentially intol-
erant attitude. People worry about families, and to the extent that they associate
modern social ills with changes in family life, they are ambivalent about innova-
tions. Voters often defeat measures to grant unmarried couples, whether heterosexual or homosexual, the same rights as married ones. In polls, however,
most Americans support tolerance for gay and lesbian relationships. Although
two-thirds of respondents to one national poll said they wanted "more traditional
standards of family life," the same percentage rejected the idea that "women should
return to their traditional role." Still larger majorities support women's right to
work, including their right to use child care, even when they worry about relying on day-care centers too much. In a 1990 *Newsweek* poll, 42 percent predicted
that the family would be worse in ten years and exactly the same percentage predicted that it would be better. Although 87 percent of people polled in 1987 said
they had "old-fashioned ideas about family and marriage," only 22 percent of
the people polled in 1989 defined a family solely in terms of blood, marriage, or
adoption. Seventy-four percent declared, instead, that family is any group whose
members love and care for one another.[30]

These conflicted responses do not mean that people are hopelessly confused.
Instead, they reflect people's gut-level understanding that the "crisis of the family" is more complex than is often asserted by political demagogues or others
with an ax to grind. In popular commentary, the received wisdom is to "keep
it simple." I know one television reporter who refuses to air an interview with
anyone who uses the phrase "on the other hand." But my experience in discussing
these issues with both the general public and specialists in the field is that people
are hungry to get beyond oversimplifications. They don't want to be told that
everything is fine in families or that if the economy improved and the government mandated parental leave, everything would be fine. But they don't believe
that every hard-won victory for women's rights and personal liberty has been

destructive of social bonds and that the only way to find a sense of community is to go back to some sketchily defined "traditional" family that clearly involves denying the validity of any alternative familial and personal choices.

Americans understand that along with welcome changes have come difficult new problems; uneasy with simplistic answers, they are willing to consider more nuanced analyses of family gains and losses during the past few decades. Indeed, argues political reporter E. J. Dionne, they are *desperate* to engage in such analyses.[31] Few Americans are satisfied with liberal and feminist accounts that blame all modern family dilemmas on structural inequalities, ignoring the moral crisis of commitment and obligation in our society. Yet neither are they convinced that "in the final analysis," as David Blankenhorn of the Institute for American Values puts it, "the problem is not the system. The problem is us."[32]

Despite humane intentions, an overemphasis on personal responsibility for strengthening family values encourages a way of thinking that leads to moralizing rather than mobilizing for concrete reforms. While values are important to Americans, most do not support the sort of scapegoating that occurs when all family problems are blamed on "bad values." Most of us are painfully aware that there is no clear way of separating "family values" from "the system." Our values may make a difference in the way we respond to the challenges posed by economic and political institutions, but those institutions also reinforce certain values and extinguish others. The problem is not to berate people for abandoning past family values, nor to exhort them to adopt better values in the future— the problem is to build the institutions and social support networks that allow people to act on their best values rather than on their worst ones. We need to get past abstract nostalgia for traditional family values and develop a clearer sense of how past families actually worked and what the different consequences of various family behaviors and values have been. Good history and responsible social policy should help people incorporate the full complexity and the tradeoffs of family change into their analyses and thus into action. Mythmaking does not accomplish this end.

CRITICAL THINKING QUESTIONS

Coontz is a historian, writing 20 years ago about fears stirred by changes then taking place in the family. Such fears are often resolved by the passage of time as social policy addresses the disruption produced by social change or as people get used to the change. Have most of the concerns that Coontz addressed been resolved since she wrote this selection? Explain your answer.

How does the kind of marriage that will likely typify your generation differ from that which typified your parents' generation? What are the advantages and disadvantages of each generation of family?

NOTES

1. Philip Greven, *Four Generations: Population, Land, and Family in Colonial Andover, Massachusetts* (Ithaca, N.Y.: Cornell University Press, 1970); Vivian Fox and Martin Quit, *Loving, Parenting, and Dying: The Family Cycle in England and America, Past and Present* (New York: Psychohistory Press, 1980), p. 401.

2. John Demos, *A Little Commonwealth: Family Life in Plymouth Colony* (New York: Oxford University Press. 1970), p. 108; Mary Ryan, *Cradle of the Middle Class: The Family in Oneida County, New York, 1790–1865* (New York: Cambridge University Press, 1981), pp. 33, 38–39; Carroll Smith-Rosenberg, *Disorderly Conduct: Visions of Gender in Victorian America* (New York: Oxford University Press, 1985), p. 24.

3. Frederick Douglass, *My Bondage and My Freedom* (New York: Dover, 1968), p. 48.

4. David Roediger and Philip Foner, *Our Own Time: A History of American Labor and the Working Day* (London: Greenwood, 1989), p. 9; Norman Ware, *The Industrial Worker, 1840–1860* (New York: Quadrangle, 1964), p. 5; Barbara Wertheimer, *We Were There: The Story of Working Women in America* (New York: Pantheon, 1977), p. 91; Sean Wilentz, *Chants Democratic: New York City and the Rise of the Working Class, 1788–1850* (New York: Oxford University Press, 1984), p. 126.

5. Faye Dudden, *Serving Women: Household Service in Nineteenth-Century America* (Middletown, Conn.: Wesleyan University Press, 1983), p. 206; Susan Strasser, *Never Done: A History of American Housework* (New York: Pantheon, 1982); Lawrence Glasco, "The Life Cycles and Household Structure of American Ethnic Groups,: in *A Heritage of Her Own: Toward a New Social History of American Women*, ed. Nancy Cott and Elizabeth Pleck (New York: Simon & Schuster, 1979), pp. 281, 285.

6. Robert Bremner et al., eds., *Children and Youth in America: A Documentary History* (Cambridge: Harvard University Press, 1970), vol. 1, p. 39; Barbara Cross, *Horace Bushnell: Minister to a Changing America* (Chicago: University of Chicago Press, 1958); Ann Douglas, *The Feminization of American Culture* (New York: Knopf, 1977), p. 52.

7. Peter Laslett, "Characteristics of the Western Family Over Time," in *Family Life and Illicit Love in Earlier Generations*, ed. Peter Laslett (New York: Cambridge University Press, 1977); William Goode, *World Revolution and Family Patterns* (New York: Free Press, 1963); Michael Anderson, *Family Structure in Nineteenth-Century Lancashire* (Cambridge, England: Cambridge University Press, 1971); Tamara Hareven, ed., *Transitions: The family and the Life Course in Historical Perspective* (New York; Academic Press, 1978); Tamara Hareven, "The Dynamics of Kin in an Industrial Community," in *Turning Points: Historical and Sociological Essays on the Family*, ed. John Demos and S. S. Boocock (Chicago: University of Chicago Press, 1978); Linda Gordon, *Heroes of Their Own Lives: The Politics and History of Family Violence, 1880–1960* (New York, Viking, 1988).

8. Helen Campbell, *Prisoners of Poverty: Women Wage Workers, Their Trades and Their Lives* (Westport, Conn.: Greenwood Press, 1970), p. 206.

9. Rosalyn Baxandall, Linda Gordon, and Susan Reverby, eds., *America's Working Women* (New York: Random House, 1976), p. 162.

10. Rose Schneiderman, *All for One* (New York P. S. Eriksson, 1967); John Bondnar, "Socialization and Adaption: Immigrant Families in Scranton," in *Growing up in America: Historical Experiences*, ed. Harvey Graff (Detroit: Wayne State Press, 1987),

pp. 391–92; Robert and Helen Lynd, *Middletown: A Study in Modern American Culture* (New York: Harcourt Brace Jovanovich, 1956), p. 31; Barbara Wertheimer, *We Were There: The Story of Working Women in America* (New York: Pantheon, 1977); pp. 336–43; Francesco Cordasco, *Jacob Riis Revisited: Poverty and the Slum in Another Era* (Garden City N.Y.: Doubleday, 1968); Campbell, *Prisoners of Poverty and Women Wage-Earners* (Boston: Arnoff, 1893); Lynn Weiner, *From Working Girl to Working Mother: The Female Labor Force in the United States, 1829–1980* (Chapel Hill: University of North Carolina Press, 1985), p. 92.

11. For examples of the analysis of the Chicago School, see Ernest Burgess and Harvey Locke, *The Family: From Institution to Companionship* (New York: American Book Company, 1945); Ernest Mowrer, *The Family: Its Organization and Disorganization* (Chicago: University of Chicago Press, 1932); W. I. Thomas and F. Znaniecki, *The Polish Peasant in Europe and America*, 5 vols. (Boston: Dover Publications, 1918–20). On families in the Depression, see Steven Mintz and Susan Kellogg, *Domestic Revolutions: A Social History of American Family Life* (New York: Free Press, 1988), pp. 133–49, quote on p. 136.

12. Glen Elder, Jr., *Children of the Great Depression: Social Change in Life Experience* (Chicago: University of Chicago Press, 1974), pp. 64–82; Lillian Rubin, *Worlds of Pain: Life in the Working-Class Family* (New York: Basic Books, 1976), p. 23; Edward Robb Ellis, *A Nation in Torment: The Great American Depression, 1929–1939* (New York: Coward McCann, 1970); Ruth Milkman, "Women's Work and the Economic Crisis," in *A Heritage of Her Own: Toward a New Social History of American Women*, ed. Nancy Cott and Elizabeth Pleck (New York: Simon & Schuster, 1979), pp. 507–41.

13. Rudy Ray Seward, *The American Family: A Demographic History* (Beverly Hills: Sage 1978); Kenneth Winkle, *The Politics of Community: Migration and Politics in Antebellum Ohio* (New York: Cambridge University Press, 1988); Michael Weber, *Social Change in an Industrial Town: Patterns of Progress in Warren, Pennsylvania, from the Civil War to World War I* (University Park: Pennsylvania State University Press, 1976), pp. 139–48; Stephen Thernstrom, *Poverty and Progress* (Cambridge: Harvard University Press 1964).

14. Thomas Bender, *Community and Social Change in America* (New Brunswick: Rutgers University Press, 1978).

15. Edward Kain, *The Myth of Family Decline: Understanding Families in a World of Rapid Social Change* (Lexington, Mass.: D. C. Heath, 1990), pp. 10, 37; Theodore Caplow, "The Sociological Myth of Family Decline," *The Tocqueville Review* 3 (1981): 366; Howard Bahr, "Changes in Family Life in Middletown, 1924–77, *Public Opinion Quarterly* 44 (1980): 51.

16. *American Demographics*, February 1990; Dennis Orthner, "The Family in Transition," in *Rebuilding the Nest: A New Commitment to the American Family*, ed. David Blankenhorn, Steven Bayme, and Jean Bethke Elshtain (Milwaukee: Family Service America, 1990), pp. 95–97; Sar Levitan and Richard Belous, *What's Happening to the American Family?* (Baltimore: Johns Hopkins University Press, 1981), p. 63.

17. Daniel Kallgren, "Women Out of Marriage: Work and Residence Patterns of Never Married American Women, 1900–1980" (Paper Presented at Social Science History Association Conference, Minneapolis, Minn., October 1990), p. 8; Richard Sennett, *Families Against the City: Middle Class Homes in Industrial Chicago, 1872–1890* (Cambridge: Harvard University Press, 1984), pp. 114–15.

18. Mary Jo Bane, *Here to Stay: American Families in the Twentieth Century* (New York: Basic Books, 1976); Stephen Nock, *Sociology of the Family* (Englewood Cliffs, N. J.: Prentice Hall, 1987); Kain, *Myth of Family Decline*, pp. 71, 74–75; Joseph Veroff, Elizabeth Douvan, and Richard Kulka, *The Inner American: A Self Portrait from 1957 to 1976* (New York: Basic Books, 1981); Norval Glenn, "The Recent Trend in Marital Success in the United States," *Journal of Marriage and the Family* 53 (1991); Tracy Cabot, *Marrying Later, Marrying Smarter* (New York: McGraw-Hill, 1990); Judith Brown, *Sanctions and Sanctuary: Cultural Perspectives on the Beating of Wives* (Boulder, Colo.: Westview Press, 1991); Maxine Baca Zinn and Stanley Eitzen, *Diversity in American Families* (New York: Harper & Row, 1987).

19. Dorrian Apple Sweetser, "Broken Homes: Stable Risk, Changing Reason, Changing Forms," *Journal of Marriage and the Family* (August 1985); Lawrence Stone, "The Road to Polygamy," *New York Review of Books*, 2 March 1989, p. 13; Arlene Skolnick, *Embattled Paradise: The American Family In an Age of Uncertainty* (New York: Basic Books, 1991), p. 156.

20. Frank Furstenberg, Jr., "Good Dads–Bad Dads: Two Faces of Fatherhood," in *The Changing American Family and Public Policy*, ed. Andrew Cherlin (Washington, D.C.: Urban Institute Press, 1988); Joseph Pleck, "The Contemporary Man," in *Handbook of Counseling and Psychotherapy*, ed. Murray Scher et al. (Beverly Hills Sage, 1987).

21. National Commission on Children, *Beyond Rhetoric*; *A New Agenda for Children and Families* (Washington. D.C.: GPO, 1991), p. 34; Richard Gelles and Jon Conte, "Domestic Violence and Sexual Abuse of Children," in *Contemporary Families; Looking Forward, Looking Back*, ed. Alan Booth (Minneapolis: National Council on Family Relations, 1991), p. 328.

22. Arlene Skolnick, "The American Family: The Paradox of Perfection," *The Wilson Quarterly* (Summer 1980); Barbara Laslett, "Family Membership: Past and Present," *Social Problems* 25 (1978); Theodore Caplow et al., *Middletown Families: Fifty Years of Change and Continuity* (Minneapolis: University of Minnesota Press, 1982), p. 225.

23. *The State of America's Children, 1991* (Washington, D.C.: Children's Defense Fund, 1991), pp. 55–63; *Seattle post-Intelligencer*, 19 April 1991; National Commission on Children, *Beyond Rhetoric*, p. 32; *Washington Post National Weekly Edition*, 13–19 May 1991; James Wetzel, *American Youth: A Statistical Snapshot* (Washington, D.C.: William T. Grant Foundation, August 1989), pp. 12–14.

24. *USA Today*, 12 May 1991, p 1A; Richard Morin, "Myth of the Drop Out Mom," *Washington Post*, 14 July 1991; Christine Reinhardt, "Trend Check," *Working Woman*, October 1991, p. 34; Howard Hayghe, "Family Members in the Work Force," *Monthly Labor Review* 113 (1990).

25. Morin, "Myth of the Drop Out Mom"; Reinhardt, "Trend Check," p. 34.

26. "Too Late for Prince Charming," *Newsweek*, 2 June 1986, p 55; John Modell, *Into One's Own: From Youth to Adulthood in the United States, 1920–1975* (Berkeley: University of California Press, 1989), p. 249; Barbara Lovenheim, *Beating the Marriage Odds; When you Are Smart, Single, and Over 35* (New York: William Morrow, 1990), pp. 26–27; *U.S. News & World Report*, 29 January 1990, p. 50; *New York Times*, 7 June 1991.

27. William Mattox, Jr., "The Parent Trap," *Policy Review* (Winter 1991): 6, 8; Sylvia Ann Hewlett, "Running Hard Just To Keep Up," *Time* (Fall 1990), and *When the Bough Breaks: The Cost of Neglecting Our Children* (New York: Basic Books, 1991), p. 73; Richard Whitmore, "Education Decline Linked with Erosion of Family," *The Olympian*,

1 October 1991; John Robinson, "Caring for Kinds," *American Demographics*, July 1989, p. 52; "Household and Family Characteristics: March 1990 and 1989," *Current Population Reports*, series P-20, no. 447, table A-1. I am indebted to George Hough, Executive Policy Analyst, Office of Financial Management, Washington State, for finding these figures and helping me with the calculations.

28. John Robinson, "Time for Work," *American Demographics*, April 1989, p. 68, and "Time's UP," *American Demographics*, July 1989, p. 34; Trish Hall, "Time on Your Hands? You May Have More Than You Think," *New York Times*, 3 July 1991, pp. C1, C7; Gannett News Service Wire Report, 27 August 1991.

29. *New York Times*, 10 October 1989, p. A18.

30. E. J. Dionne, Jr., *Why Americans Hate Politics* (New York: Simon & Schuster, 1991), pp. 110, 115, 325; *The Olympian*, 11 October 1989; *New York Times*, 10 October 1989; Time, 20 November 1989; *Seattle Post-Intelligencer*, 12 October 1990; Jerold Footlick, "What Happened to the Family?" *Newsweek Special Issue*, Winter/Spring 1990, p. 18.

31. Dionne, Why *Americans Hate Politics*.

32. David Blankenhorn, "Does Grandmother Know Best?" *Family Affairs* 3 (1990): 13, 16.

CHAPTER 15

Striking a Balance

Robert W. Drago

A book first published in 1970, *Our Bodies, Our Selves,* addressed women's health issues.[1] Among the book's claims was that medical research was biased in favor of men. Government research funding in particular was directed towards diseases that afflicted men, and most medical research subjects were men. Resulting treatments were more effective, not surprisingly, for men than women. After two decades of criticism, the U.S. Department of Health and Human Services responded to this bias in medical research by creating the Office of Research on Women's Health to ensure that diseases affecting women were given equal priority, and that women were included as research subjects in government funded studies.

The story demonstrates the broad reach of norms, in this case even influencing medical researchers who place a high value on objectivity. These norms were first challenged by the book and later by a broad range of advocates. We have moved from a situation where women were routinely excluded from major medical studies as recently as the 1980s, including a famous study linking aspirin with a reduced incidence of heart disease. By the 1990s, most participants in studies sponsored by the National Institutes of Health were women. The challenge, however, did not lead to complete gender equality in health care. Indeed, the report from the U.S. General Accounting Office (2000) that documents women's increased participation in studies also shows that few of the resulting publications inform us as to whether, for example, women exhibit different side effects than men in clinical trials of new drugs. Progress has not been complete, but what progress has been achieved has been due to the exposure of norms—to the recognition that women are not just mothers.

A more contemporary medical story reinforces this conclusion. Historically, the major exception to male bias in medical research fit the norm of motherhood. The vast majority of fertility studies concentrated on women,[2] and today, virtually every woman reading this book is aware that her biological clock for childbearing begins to run down at age 35. In addition, the widespread dissemination of information on women's biological clocks was fodder for the backlash against women's entry into the workforce. Women were told they should give up their careers in favor of childrearing.[3] The backlash invoked the norm of motherhood against the rapidly diffusing ideal worker norm.

However, it turns out that men's aging also plays a role in fertility. A study published in 2002 established that men also have a biological clock, and that it begins to run down at age 35.[4] The results of this study have not, however, led to a rash of media stories about men returning to the home, nor have the results led to television movies about young men desperately seeking partners before their clocks run out. These facts fit legal scholar Nancy Dowd's argument that contemporary fatherhood norms are nowhere near as clear or strong as the motherhood norm.

The key claim of this chapter is that the norms of the ideal worker, motherhood, and individualism have shaped our views of work, family, and life. Norms influence not only research, but also the language we use to describe the issues. To start the process of challenging the three norms, we need to rethink the words we use.[5] Such a rethinking leads us to stop viewing balance as a trade-off between work and family or work and life—a view closely linked to the ideal worker norm. Reframing the issues also allows us to reframe our conception of an ideal family as something that can only be sustained by the unpaid work of women—instead we can redefine the family in a way that both challenges the norm of motherhood and helps us to value caregiving. Most critically, in the following discussion we will start to approach a new conception of balance as something that involves a mixture of paid work, unpaid work, and leisure, a definition that makes sense of earlier research, conforms to common understandings of the term, and can help us move towards a better life.

WHAT IS WORK?

If a woman tells us she is "working too hard" and "overworked," we would usually interpret the statement as implying that she is stressed out because of her job. We view employment as work. Even the titles of popular magazines like *Working Mother* belie this implicit understanding.

Even where crucial differences exist, employment is usually treated as work. Consider practitioners and researchers in the area of work and family studies. Practitioners are often hired by corporations to develop and implement on-site child care, flextime, telecommuting, and child and elder care resource and referral services. Researchers address these programs along with broader issues of time and stress around work and family commitments. By the mid-1990s practitioners switched from the label "work-family" to that of "work-life" professionals,[6] while academics continue to describe themselves as performing "work-family" research.[7] This schism between practitioners and researchers makes life complicated for those attempting to communicate across the boundaries of the business and academic worlds. Nonetheless, the difference is rooted in an important shared assumption: that demands made by employment are to blame for the imbalance in our lives. Both groups believe a lever is needed to counter long hours on the job. The difference between work-family researchers and work-life practitioners concerns whether the most effective lever emphasizes family, and particularly motherhood, or instead focuses on life and the value of leisure.

Both sides of the field implicitly believe employment is too demanding. But is that belief justified? The answer is a qualified "not really." Work-family researcher Ellen Galinsky and colleagues at the Families and Work Institute recently completed a national study of overwork. They concluded that overwork was associated with higher levels of employee mistakes at work, elevated levels of anger directed at the employer and at co-workers, and poorer health outcomes including stress and depression. However, they also concluded that:

> Employees who have jobs that provide them more opportunities to continue to learn, whose supervisors support them in succeeding on the job, who have the flexibility they need to manage their job and their personal and family life, and who have input into management decision-making are less likely to be over-worked. This is true even when they work long hours and have very demanding jobs.[8]

As a more direct check, I tested for any correlation between a related measure of overwork and the usual number of hours worked per week in the 2002 National Study of the Changing Workforce. Paid work hours were indeed positively related to perceptions of overwork, but the correlation was not strong—paid work hours explained only five-and-a-half to 6% of the variance among people who said they were overworked.[9] Clearly, something else is going on.

Hours of employment have indeed lengthened for some. Although increasing numbers of professional men and women fit within the definition of the ideal worker norm in recent decades, this group still represents less than one-fifth of all employees.[10] Further, the average American employee has experienced shrinking vacation time: the average annual weeks worked by all prime-age employees (those between 25 and 54) rose by more than two weeks per year from 1976 to 2000.[11] Nonetheless, as the weak link between hours of employment and perceptions of overwork suggests, it is difficult to believe that imbalance is solely due to long hours of employment.

We can gain a better understanding of these phenomena if we include time spent on tasks for the family and in the home in our definition of work. Feminist economist Margaret Reid provided a good definition long ago, arguing that work is any *"activity...that...might be delegated to a paid [employee]."*[12] Because many household and caregiving tasks in middle-class families are farmed out to child care centers, nannies, household cleaning services, and nursing homes, her definition implies that time spent on parenting, housework, and care for ailing relatives should be counted as work.

Even though this definition of work is not widespread, it is far from novel. Although later research on overwork by other authors ignored housework and care,[13] the book that initiated the overwork debate did not. Feminist economist Juliet Schor's *The Overworked American* included an entire chapter on family tasks and counted relevant hours of housework and care in her calculations of working time.

Economist Nancy Folbre (2001) documented a related battle, which goes back more than half a century, over whether housework and care should be included in our accounting of national economic output. The omission of housework and care from calculations of our Gross National Product (GNP) and employment statistics leads to unsettling descriptions of reality: a man who quits a paid job to care for his kids, for instance, goes from being a productive to a nonproductive member of society. Worse still, two househusbands, living next door to each other, could hire each other to switch houses and perform the same work, and they would suddenly switch from being non-productive to valuable members of society even though they are doing precisely the same tasks as before. To resolve these problems, many economists have argued that housework and care should be included in the national accounts.[14]

But tossing housework and care for children and other family members into the same conceptual basket as employment carries with it some complexities. Some household activities such as cleaning, cooking, laundry, and grocery shopping both feel and look like work.[15] Other aspects of unpaid work involve unique responsibilities—for example, a parent cannot hire someone else to watch a child's play at school, and an elderly parent in need of care may place great value on the fact that a son (or more likely a daughter) is providing the care. In relatively few paid jobs is a particular individual so irreplaceable.

Adding up paid and unpaid work also misses the unique ways in which care and employment complement and conflict with each other. Earlier research finds that care work in the home can buffer the ill effects of employment stress, and vice-versa.[16] Research shows that individuals can feel some relief from their job stress even when they are engaged in potentially stressful work in their homes, and vice-versa. The change in tasks is one part of this and the change of people with whom the individual interacts is another. Variety fosters mental health.[17]

Therefore, even if care for dependents is work, it exhibits characteristics that suggest it is a distinct job or occupation. In this view, employed parents and those caring for ill partners or ailing elders are not simply working long hours. Instead, they are moonlighting, or holding down a second job after hours. Essentially, employed parents and others caring for families while earning a paycheck are moonlighting without pay.

To capture this distinction between tasks performed for the family and those for the employer, I differentiate "paid" from "unpaid" work. This distinction focuses our attention on the presence or absence of an employment relationship and is consistent with the arguments of economists who believe that housework and care for family should be counted as work, albeit unpaid, in the national accounts.

The paid and unpaid work distinction is similar to that drawn by sociologist Arlie Hochschild, who documented in *The Second Shift* the unpaid work

---

BOX 15.1

Leisure at Work

Employees may strive to achieve balance through leisure time at work. For example, where personal computers are used in the workplace, employees may play Solitaire while on the job. Leisure is often purposefully provided by corporations as a buffer against the imbalance associated with the ideal worker norm. Arlie Hochschild (1997) discovered that modern corporations persuade employees to put in long hours in part by providing leisure and a social life on the job, such as social time during meetings and non-work including picnics and sports teams for employees. Similarly, Harvard management professor Leslie Perlow (1997) studied the dot.coms of California's Silicon Valley in the 1990s, and found companies garnering extremely long hours from employees in part by providing toys, entertainment and workout centers, well-stocked kitchens, and even sleeping quarters.

In an earlier study, we discovered leisure in the workplace in a surprising way. As part of the Time, Work, and Family project, we administered time use diaries to elementary school teachers in the late 1990s (Drago et al. 1999). The teachers were asked to write down all of their activities for a 24-hour period. An unexpected finding was that teachers over the age of 50 were putting in the longest hours for their schools. Neither monetary compensation nor future promotion opportunities could explain why teachers nearing retirement would increase their work hours. The fact that many of these teachers were mothers whose children had left the nest provides part of the answer—unpaid work responsibilities had decreased, leaving more space for paid work. But even after adding in hours of unpaid work for the family, we still found the older teachers putting in a longer workday, suggesting that some of the time spent at and for the school was in fact leisure. These teachers achieved balance in part by "working" long hours.

Parenting has elements of leisure, but so do many paid jobs.

---

performed by many employed women. If housework is not treated as work, the average American woman appears to work fewer hours than the typical man. But if housework is classified as work, then women work longer hours than men. Many other work-family scholars have also argued that we need to recognize the value of unpaid work.[18]

Some readers may object to the term unpaid work with the claim that care for family is fun, as journalist Elinor Burkett did in her popular 2000 book, *The Baby Boon*. In this view, any unpaid work is more properly cast as leisure. However, this line of argument typically ignores housework and is rarely made with regard to care for an ill, infirm, or disabled family member. It instead hones in on parenting and, as a parent myself, I admit to occasionally having fun with my daughters. We might also counter the claim that family work is in fact leisure by noting that many jobs provide leisure as well (see Box 15.1). But at heart, objections to the claim that unpaid work *is* work are firmly rooted in the norm of motherhood and the related notion that care is done for love rather than money. It is no accident that critics like Burkett focus on parenting, ignoring other unpaid care and housework performed for families. The motherhood norm explains why it is women rather than men who are the real targets of these attacks on employed parents.

There is, however, a grain of truth in such arguments. If we take the concept of unpaid work seriously, then employed caregivers are indeed moonlighting without pay. Such moonlighting consumes time and effort and tends to diminish employee performance. Following this logic, some corporations require employees to sign contracts stating that they will not moonlight. For example, a lawyer advises companies to

> distribute a written policy prohibiting [moonlighting] with the understanding that violators are subject to immediate termination. No exceptions. No excuses. This practice might seem harsh and it might cause employees to hide their activities. Remember, though, moonlighting creates a risk for your firm without any possible reward.[19]

To be consistent, and if we take the notion of unpaid work seriously, such moonlighting prohibitions could be extended to parents and other caregivers. As the lawyer implies above, such commitments generate substantial risks and no rewards for employers.

I am not actually suggesting employers implement prohibitions against parenting. Fortunately, such policies are not just immoral; they are also likely illegal.[20] But if we take seriously the notion that family commitments require time, energy, and emotional involvement, then it follows that less time, energy, and emotion is left for employment.[21] As one faculty member at Penn State University told us in a recent study regarding academic faculty with family responsibilities:

> I think with my students I used to be a very caring teacher...And this was before I had my second child.... [S]omebody recently said that [there were negative comments about my teaching.] She said, "well, you are just not warm and fuzzy with them." So I said, "Aah, well, I have got two kids and they are the ones who get that."[22]

Distinguishing between paid and unpaid work helps us to understand imbalance in our lives. On the one hand, by including child and elder care alongside employment in the definition of work, we are likely to get a better handle on the meaning of overwork and imbalance: individuals overburdened by the demands of employment and family are likely to be stressed out. On the other hand, by distinguishing paid and unpaid work, we recognize that we will not understand imbalance simply by adding up work for families and employers: the jobs involved are fundamentally different.

ALL IN THE FAMILY

The way we define family is crucial to understanding which unpaid work commitments are viewed as legitimate, and who receives various legal protections associated with family status.

Any definition we use needs to account for the fact that American families have become increasingly diverse. According to the U.S. Census Bureau, married couples with children comprised 40% of all households in 1970, but only 24% of households by the year 2000. Whether or not they had children, 71% of all households were married couples in 1970, a figure that declined to 53% by 2000. Individuals living alone were the fastest growing household form. That group climbed from 17 to 26% of all households over the period.[23] The rate of divorce approximately doubled during the period and, although it leveled off during the 1990s, around half of all first marriages are now predicted to end in divorce.[24]

Looking at individual children instead of households gives a slightly different view of family diversity. As of 2002, only 21% of all children in the United States lived with a homemaker mother and breadwinning father. Almost one-quarter as many children lived with single fathers (5%). More children lived with single mothers (23%), and the largest single group of kids lived with dual-earner parents (43%).[25] Families are indeed becoming more diverse.

These differences, however, mask a constant. The vast majority of women in the United States, some 81%, still become biological mothers at some point.[26] The United States has experienced a long-term decline in fertility but, even so, the average American women can now expect to bear around two children.[27] That figure would be even higher if adoptive and step-motherhood was included. Motherhood *per se* is not disappearing.

So just what is a family? During the 1970s and 1980s, most research on work and family asked how the entry of married mothers into the labor force affected their children.[28] The implicit definition of family involved a heterosexual, married couple with children. But within this context, most research was shaped by the norm of motherhood. Men's work and family relationships were largely ignored.

The Family and Medical Leave Act (FMLA) of 1993 moves beyond the spouse and child vision of families found in most work-family research. The FMLA covers about half of all employees and ensures that their job will be secure while permitting them to take up to 12 weeks per year of unpaid leave to care for "immediate family," a term defined in the Act to include those caring for their parents, spouses, and children.[29] The FMLA definition of families emerged from a process of creating a broad political consensus around the meaning of family.[30] That definition centers on the reality and expectation of care: when one family member is ill, we expect another member to drop everything to help out. Management professor Teresa Rothausen concludes a review of family as found in organizational research by recommending a similar understanding of family based on the notion of "responsibility for dependents."

Taking Rothausen's view as a starting point, I define a "family" as *two or more people with a relationship such that the regular provision or receipt of unpaid work occurs and, in particular, is expected by all parties when needed.*[31] This definition is intended to be inclusive of the broad range of cases that individuals themselves would label as involving family relationships. It counts most households as families, all cohabiting couples as families or parts of families regardless of marital status or sexual orientation, captures the wide range of legal parenting relationships covered by the FMLA, and includes most members of families involved in divorce. It also captures geographically distant relationships where individuals are on call when required due to illness or catastrophic events.

By taking a broad approach, this definition of family challenges the norm of motherhood and promotes a new norm of inclusion. That norm is implicit in the FMLA, but this definition of family goes beyond the FMLA in its treatment of cohabitation and sexual orientation. Recent work by Christopher Carrington, a professor of human sexuality, found that virtually all of the issues that confront heterosexual couples also affect gay and lesbian couples. If one partner was ill, the other was responsible for care, and someone still had to take out the garbage regardless of sexual orientation. The case of cohabitation by opposite sex couples is the same. Where unpaid work responsibilities look like family commitments, they probably are.

Although the FMLA does not cover cohabitation, even the most contentious types of cohabitating couples—those involving gays and lesbians—are, fortunately, treated as families by many of the country's largest corporations. According to a Human Rights Campaign Foundation report, the number of Fortune 500 firms rated high on partner benefits and employee training to reduce discrimination against same-sex couples more than quadrupled in recent years, rising from only 13 firms in 2002, to more than 100 corporations in 2005.[32]

Defining families on the reality and expectation of unpaid work is inclusive of many family relationships, but also serves to limit the number of people counted as family members. First, absentee parents who provide only financial support to a family are not themselves members of the family. Second, biological parents without contact with their co-parent or children are not family members. Third, individuals living alone and neither expecting to nor actually providing or receiving unpaid work are not family members.

The absentee parent exclusion follows from Nancy Dowd's research on fatherhood. Dowd argued that limiting our view of fatherhood to breadwinning, as is now implicit in much divorce law and child support provisions, is limiting. It constrains the many fathers who wish to engage in parenting but are pushed into a purely breadwinning role, adversely affects the many children who do not receive care from their absentee fathers, and forces many employed mothers to bear the full brunt of the second shift. In Dowd's view and mine, a father should provide unpaid work to be considered a family member.

Relatedly, biological parents who are not in contact with their children are not members of families—it is impossible to provide care when needed if the need is never known. This exclusion historically covered the relationship between most adoptive children and their biological parents, a situation that is changing as more and more biological parents are taking on and being provided roles as active members of adoptive families (see Box 15.2).

═════ **BOX 15.2** ═════

Adoption and Family Relations

If even biological parents are excluded from the definition of family when they are neither involved nor expected to be involved with care of their children, does this imply that biological parents of adoptive children are not "real" parents?

In *The Adoption Revolution* (2000), Adam Pertman, Director of the Evan B. Donaldson Foundation, examines these relationships in the context of increasing exchanges of medical information and enhanced contact between the children and their biological parents in recent years. The biological parents, the adopted children themselves, and the adoptive parent or parents are referred to together as the adoption "triad."

Historically, adoptions in the United States were mainly "closed," such that the biological parents and adoptive children were denied any opportunity to make contact with each other. Almost inevitably, however, as the child grew to adulthood, he or she would seek to make contact, attempts that have been greatly facilitated in recent years by the growth of the Internet. Not all contacts are positive, but most are and in no case covered by Pertman did the adoptive child seek to abandon his or her adoptive parents (as some feared). To avoid related pain, suffering, doubts, and fears among adoptive children, many adoptions are now "open," with the three parts of the triad in regular if not frequent contact.

Is a triad also a family? For mothers, some unpaid work in the form of childbearing and perhaps breastfeeding early in the child's life provides grounds for claiming family membership, a claim that biological fathers typically do not share. Regardless of those claims, the promise of the open adoption movement, which Pertman advocates, is that the information necessary to initiate or reinitiate family membership is made available to all parties.

The definition of family used here can help us to understand family processes around adoption. Specifically, the definition suggests that open adoption would allow individuals *themselves* to resolve the question of family membership. Efforts to keep adoption closed effectively deny this choice.

The third exclusion from the definition of family—of single individuals—means that a burgeoning portion of the American populace is and should be cut off from whatever provisions we as a society provide to families. While the claim is formally correct, it is worth noting that lone individuals still seek and deserve balance in their lives.

Finally, volunteer work does not fall into the family category, although it indeed involves unpaid work (see Box 15.3).[33]

By focusing on the provision or expectation of unpaid work, we hone in on the ways families are created—through the development of relationships. We also focus our attention on the key mechanism through which families influence an individual's ability to achieve balance—through the provision of unpaid work.

BOX 15.3

Can Volunteers Achieve Balance?

Back in the 1960s, my mother, akin to many other married women living in the suburbs, performed much unpaid work for the family, undertook volunteer work as director of a women's chorus and in other ways, and had some leisure time as well. Did she lead a balanced life?

It is probably safe to answer "yes," since my mother would say that she had achieved balance. Indeed, she still directs a chorus to this day, and gets a fair amount of help in that endeavor from my now-retired father. For the married, stay-at-home mothers currently raising around one-fifth of America's children, volunteer work often serves to create balance, and our schools in particular often benefit greatly form this source of unpaid work.

For older women in financially secure positions, the volunteer approach may make sense. But young women employ this strategy at their peril. Not only will they often lose power in the family when they quit paid employment, but they also place themselves at severe economic risk in case of divorce or the death of their partner. Even where divorce does not occur, the woman's employment opportunities become increasingly limited the longer she remains out of the workforce. A recent report compared the hourly earnings of women who had taken no time out of the workforce with those who had stepped out for at least four years. Women who worked continuously averaged $15.72 per hour, while those with at least four years out averaged $9.25, a wage penalty of over 40%.[1]

Most adults perform some volunteer activities regularly (see later in this chapter). And for adults without family commitments, volunteer activity is central to leading a balanced life. Nonetheless, women considering substantial volunteer contributions when they are young should do so cautiously: they will often pay an unexpected, and steep, price when they re-enter the paid workforce.

----

[1]See Rose and Hartmann (2004).

WHERE IS LIFE?

I was shivering in a cold stadium in a small town in Pennsylvania, watching a girls' soccer game, and an obnoxious fan's yelling was making me madder by the minute. The phrase that came to mind was "Get a life!" Implicitly, I was charging him with leading an imbalanced life. The logic of the thought was that this father was living his life through his daughter, and that he needed to gain a broader perspective—one that would make his daughter's achievements slightly less important to him.

When people utter the phrase, "get a life," it more typically follows a tale of someone answering a cell phone during a child's event, interrupting a casual dinner with friends to respond to a beeper, or answering emails late at night. In these cases, the phrase implies the individual is allowing paid work to invade and consume the rest of life, and should instead leave employment responsibilities at the workplace.

Tweak these stories even slightly and most of us would view them positively. Suppose it were a mother at the soccer game who rushed onto the field when her daughter was injured. Suppose the cell phone permitted a father to escape the workplace long enough to attend his child's piano recital. Suppose the beeper was alerting a chemist to the fact that she had just won the Nobel Prize. Or suppose that answering email late at night allowed someone more time during the day to care for an ailing parent. In none of these cases would we dismiss the behavior with the phrase, "get a life!"

All of these stories, and our likely responses, involve a shared valuing of balance. Cast as malevolent, the stories are about violations of our notions of balance. Seen more positively, the stories are about the ways we strive to create balance under difficult circumstances.

To pin down this notion of balance, we need to move beyond the belief that we either must attempt to balance work and family, or instead to balance work and life. As argued earlier, these approaches are dead-ends because both trace difficulties in our lives solely to employment, and pit individuals with families against individuals who have minimal or no family commitments. We instead need an approach to balance that incorporates both paid and unpaid work—and leisure.

"Leisure" includes activities beyond work and the performance of physical activities such as sleep and personal health care. I therefore define a *balanced life as including components of paid and unpaid work and leisure.* This definition provides a new understanding of the term "balance," where balance means people are expected to engage in unpaid work beyond paid employment, that people bearing the burdens of unpaid work are expected to engage in paid employment, and that everyone should enjoy some leisure.

Imbalance in our lives occurs when we are missing leisure, unpaid work, or paid work. Some readers might be surprised that I include paid work on this list. Don't people dream of striking it rich and telling the boss to shove it? Research shows that this is not necessarily so, and that paid work, in fact, is a very necessary part of leading healthy lives. Feminist path breaker Betty Friedan wrote about several cases involving women who did not engage in paid work and labeled it "the problem with no name." That problem centered around the isolation, powerlessness, and often trivialized lives that middle-class suburban housewives led. Friedan, along with other second-wave feminists of the 1960s and 1970s, recommended employment as the answer.[34] Later studies confirmed that the lack of paid employment among mothers was a source of imbalance: non-employed mothers exhibit significantly lower levels of psychological well-being than those who are employed.[35] Indeed, most individuals claim they would continue to perform paid employment even if they won a large sum of money.[36] These findings support the assertion that a balanced life includes paid work.

A larger literature documents the ill effects of lives that are filled with paid and unpaid work but little leisure. One set of literature addresses the ill effects of very long hours of paid work, a sure recipe for imbalance because both unpaid work and leisure are shortchanged.[37] But, as mentioned earlier, it is not typically hours of paid work alone that create a sense of stress and overwork. The more usual culprit is long hours of paid work for an employer combined with unpaid work for a family, the problem Arlie Hochschild identified in *The Second Shift* and Juliet Schor documented in *The Overworked American*. In our study of elementary school teachers, we found that teachers performing large amounts of unpaid child care and housework for their families cut back on their time working for the school but also significantly reduced their time for leisure, sleep, and eating.[38] These lives are unbalanced.

People without families also need balance. Such individuals can achieve balance by performing unpaid work for their communities in addition to paid employment and having leisure. If this claim is correct, we should find some evidence of individuals pursuing balance through volunteer efforts. Such evidence indeed exists. Using recent telephone interview data collected each night over the course of eight days from a random sample of adults in the United States, human development researchers David Almeida and Daniel McDonald calculated the total amount of unpaid working time for family and community. They found the average respondent performing 22 hours of unpaid work per week and, most strikingly, only 4% of the sample performed no unpaid work. The 4% figure implies that a majority of individuals without families are typically engaging in community service. As we might expect, married men perform more unpaid work than single men if child care is counted. However, after excluding child care, men who are single perform *more* unpaid work than those who are married. This unpaid work signifies an effort to achieve balance.

If we accept this definition of balance, we still need to determine how many hours we should devote to each category. Are 35 hours of employment too little or too much? Are 20 hours per week of unpaid work about right? Should we each have 30 hours of leisure each week?

I believe these parameters of balance have not been defined because no single set of numbers exists. Some jobs and some families include more leisure than others; someone caring for a dying parent likely experiences less leisure than a performer in a Broadway show, though both undeniably engage in work as well. Unpaid work commitments to families change as individuals move through processes of partnering with others, raising children, and aging. Religious commitments, hobbies, and patterns of community involvement also shift over time, making the numeric measure of balance a moving target.

An implication of the ambiguous nature of balance is that only individuals themselves can define and detect balance. To help individuals achieve balance, we need to know what balance means to each person at a particular point in time. Individuals have to inform each other regarding that meaning. And that information needs to be acted upon.

Traditional economists would respond to these arguments by claiming that people already balance their lives as well as possible. In analyses like that of Gary Becker, individuals rationally choose courses of action to do the best they can. If they could do better, they would already have done so.

My claim that imbalance exists and can be changed rests on the role of norms. I believe that people can learn about norms and behavior, and, as a result, change them. Harmful norms such as these inhibit us from doing the best we can.

Consider the recent experiences of a young couple I know. We'll call them George and Sarah. The couple completed their college degrees, married, and found jobs. A baby arrived a few years later. Sarah quit her job to care for the child, and George continued to put long hours into employment. Sarah's behavior reflected the norm of motherhood. George's behavior fit the ideal worker norm. And neither parent gave much thought to any governmental role in terms of helping with care, consistent with the norm of individualism.

This outcome was lamentable. Sarah was the more ambitious member, while her husband was more patient. Even if they were going to divide tasks so thoroughly, their abilities dictated that the father stay at home and the mother serve as the breadwinner. The motherhood norm overruled this possibility, and the closer application of the ideal worker norm to men also worked against the possibility.

The outcome reflected neither the couple's abilities nor their values. This couple, along with a solid majority of young men and women, believed that parents should share equally in the care of their children.[39] Norms prevented the couple from acting on these values. If they are like more than 85% of all adult Americans, they also believe that the government should have provided paid leave for the parents when the baby was born.[40] If they lived in any European nation, both the mother and father could have taken paid leave.[41] But, in this case, as events unfolded, the possibility of governmental supports was never discussed, and even the unpaid leave available under the FMLA was not used.

This couple's inability to strike a balance was partially but not totally due to norms blinding them to various options. Ignorance of norms is an important element, but it does not tell the entire story. Objective circumstances, or what economists label "constraints," also play a role as well. The government does not (except in California) provide paid family leave for new parents to maintain their incomes while caring for infants or ill children. Employers rarely offer the option of reduced hours to new parents. The claim here is not that we should ignore objective circumstances, but instead the subtler one that the widespread nature of norms permits them to influence both individual behavior and the constraints facing individuals. Corporations may find the provision of reduced hours options expensive if they still need to pick up the full tab for health insurance when an employee cuts back (and pay the costs of training temporary employees to pick up the slack); but they are also influenced by the ideal worker norm, and hold negative views of employees who express a desire for reduced hours.

The words and terminology we use for various purposes have a profound influence on our actions. The options we consider, and the options we value, are constructed in part by the words we employ to describe and discuss problems. At the most fundamental level, achieving a better life requires that we shift the terms of the debate away from work and family or work and life, to instead focus on the value of balance as a mix of paid work, unpaid work, and leisure. The care, gender, and income gaps press us to explore these opportunities.

CRITICAL THINKING QUESTION

Drago writes, "Distinguishing between paid and unpaid work helps us to understand imbalance in our lives." Explain his reasoning.

NOTES

1. See Boston Women's Health Book Collective (1970).
2. ASRM (1996).
3. See Faludi (1991).
4. See Dunson, Colombo, and Baird (2002).
5. As Perry-Jenkins, Repetti, and Crouter state, the thorniest questions confronting work-family researchers today concern the "theoretical issues of definition and meaning regarding the weighty terms of work' and 'family'" (2000, p. 993).
6. For example, the major practitioner organization in the field, the Alliance for Work-Life Progress was formed in a merger involving the National Work Family Alliance in 1996. I was on the Board of the Alliance for Work-Life Progress for several years.
7. See, e.g., the Sloan Work and Family Research Network, housed at Boston College's Center for Work and Family at www.bc.edu/wfnetwork/.
8. Galinsky, Bond, Kim, Backon, Brownfield, and Sakai (2005), p. 5.
9. The questions, asked of 2,770 wage and salary employees, concerned whether the individual usually "felt overwhelmed by how much you had to do at work," had "been asked by your supervisor or manager to do excessive amounts of work," and had "to work on too many tasks at the same time." Cronbach's alpha for the additive scale is .751. The adjusted R-squared for a linear regression predicting perceived overwork from usual weekly hours on the main job is .062, while the comparable figure when usual weekly hours on all jobs is considered is .056. Curve estimation to test for quadratic effects only increases the adjusted R-squared figures by a maximum of .005.
10. See figures in Chapter 5 of Drago's book *Striking a Balance* (see Acknowledgments).
11. The average annual weeks worked for these employees rose from just over 45 weeks in 1976 to just under 48.5 weeks in 2000. See Bluestone (2003).
12. See Reid (1934), p. 11. The italics are mine, and the word "employee" has been substituted for the word "worker" in the quotation to preclude the use of the term being defined within the definition.
13. For instance, see Robinson and Bostrom (1994) or Jacobs and Gerson (1998; 2001).
14. Among the relevant economists are Nobel Prize winners Simon Kuznets and James Tobin (see Eisner 1989 and Folbre 2001). In a slightly different form, this problem arose much earlier in the context of developing the U.S. census during the 19th century, as documented by Folbre (1991).
15. See Barnett and Yu-Chu Shen (1997).
16. See Barnett and Hyde (2001).
17. This connection has been documented in thousands of studies, particularly as regards the linkage between job satisfaction and task variety. See Srivastva et al. (1975) for an early summary.
18. See Milkie and Peltola (1999) for the claim that women work longer hours than men if and only if unpaid work is counted. Books by work-family scholars favoring the view that unpaid work is still work include Bailyn (1993), Folbre (1994, 2001), Fried (1998), Fletcher (1999), Garey (1999), Harrington (1999), Heymann (2000), and Bookman (2003).

19. See Singer (1999).
20. See Williams and Segal (2002) for relevant U.S. case law.
21. The argument regarding emotional conflicts first appeared in Hochschild (1983).
22. See Drago, Crouter, Wardell, and Willits (2001), p. 27.
23. Figures are estimates from the March supplement to the Current Population Survey. See Fields and Casper (2000), p. 3.
24. See Kreider and Fields (2002).
25. See Fields (2002).
26. See Bachu and O'Connell (2001), p. 1.
27. For the long-term decline, and the leveling off to around two births per woman in recent decades, see Ameristat (2003).
28. For a history of the field, see Stebbins (2001), and particularly Chapter One on the early focus of the research.
29. Under the FMLA, a wide variety of parenting relationships are covered, including those associated with biological, adoptive, foster, and step-parents, as well as employees *in loco parentis*—holding day-to-day parenting responsibilities when a child is young.
30. For a history of the FMLA, see Wisensale (2001).
31. The "expectation" part of the definition is crucial. Absent this part, healthy, productive adults who join together as a couple would not be viewed as a family, even if they were married.
32. See Human Rights Campaign Foundation (2006). Relevant organizations include Aetna Insurance, American Airlines, Apple Computer, Inc., Eastman Kodak Co., Intel Corporation, J.P. Morgan Chase & Co., Lucent Technologies, NCR Corporation, and the Nike and Xerox corporations. As of this writing, gay marriage is legal in the state of Massachusetts. It is possible that we will see gay marriage legalized in other states, thereby giving such families official sanctioning. But regardless of legality, gay couples can form families according to the definition used here.
33. In terms of the definition of family, volunteering is unpaid work, and such work may occur on a regular basis. However, volunteers are not *expected* to perform unpaid work for a specific individual or group for an indefinite period. When a volunteer provides notice that the activity is ending, he or she receives thanks for the unpaid work provided. When a family member quits, as can occur during a divorce, the expectation and the implicit promise of unpaid work is often denied and broken.
34. See Friedan (1963), Simone de Beauvoir (1961) or, more recently, Bergmann (1986). For a contrary view within second wave feminism, see Greer (1970).
35. On higher levels of psychological well-being among employed as opposed to non-employed mothers, see Barnett and Baruch (1985).
36. A 2005 Gallup poll asked employees what they would do if they won $10 million, and less than 40% claimed that they would not engage in paid work afterwards. See Gallup (2006).
37. On the ill psychological effects of long paid work hours, see Parcel and Menaghan (1994).
38. See Drago, Caplan, and Costanza (2000).
39. For example, the 2002 National Study of the Changing Workforce data finds 54% of employed men aged 30 or younger either disagreeing or strongly disagreeing with the statement, "It is better for everyone involved if the man earns the money and the woman takes care of the home and children." The comparable figure for young,

employed women was 68.8%. These figures were derived from the "2002, 1997 and 1992 National Study of the Changing Workforce, Public-Use Files Version 1.0," New York: Families and Work Institute, 2004.

40. See Zero To Three (2000), p. 164.

41. See Gornick and Meyers (2003), Chapter 5.

REFERENCES

Ameristat. 2003. "U.S. Fertility Trends: Boom and Bust and Leveling Off." Washington DC: Population Reference Bureau, www.prb.org.

ASRM (American Society for Reproductive Medicine). 1996. *Age and Fertility: A Guide for Patients*. Patient Information Series. Birmingham AL: ASRM.

Bachu, Amara and Martin O'Connell. 2001. "Fertility of American Women: June 2000," *Current Population Reports;* P20-543RV. Washington DC: U.S. Census Bureau.

Bailyn, Lotte. 1993. *Breaking the Mold: Women, Men, and Time in the New Corporate World*. New York: Free Press.

Bluestone, Barry and Bennett Harrison. 1982. *The Deindustrialization of America*. New York: Basic Books.

Boston Women's Health Book Collective. 1970. *Our Bodies, Ourselves*. New York: Simon & Schuster.

Drago, Robert, Robert Caplan, David Costanza, Tanya Brubaker, Darnell Cloud, Naomi Harriss, Russell Kashian, and T. Lynn Riggs. 1999. "New Estimates of Working Time for Elementary School Teachers," *Monthly Labor Review* 122(4), 31–40.

Drago, Robert, Robert Caplan, and David Costanza. 2000. "The Time, Work and Family Project: A Study of Teachers," The Pennsylvania State University Work/Family Working Paper #00–02. University Park, PA: Pennsylvania State University (January).

Drago, Robert W., Ann C. Crouter, Mark Wardell, and Billie S. Willits. 2001. "Final Report for the Faculty and Families Project," Pennsylvania State University Work/Family Working Paper #01–02. University Park, PA: Pennsylvania State University (March).

De Beauvoir, Simone. 1961. *The Second Sex*. New York: Bantam Books.

Dunson, David B., Bernardo Colombo and Donna D. Baird. 2002. "Changes with Age in the Level and Duration of Fertility in the Menstrual Cycle," *Human Reproduction* 17(5), 1399–1403.

Eisner, Robert. 1989. *The Total Incomes System of Accounts*. Chicago: University of Chicago Press.

Faludi, Susan. 1991. *Backlash: The Undeclared War against American Women*. New York: Crown.

Fields, Jason. 2002. "Children's Living Arrangements and Characteristics: March 2002," *Current Population Reports*, P20–547. Washington DC: U.S. Census Bureau.

Fields, Jason and Lynne M. Casper. 2000. "America's Families and Living Arrangements: Population Characteristics," *Current Population Reports*, P20-537. Washington, DC: U.S. Census Bureau.

Fletcher, Joyce K. 1999. *Disappearing Acts: Gender, Power, and Relational Practice at Work*. Cambridge, MA: MIT Press.

Folbre, Nancy. 1991. "The Unproductive Housewife: Her Evolution in Nineteenth-Century Economic Thought," *Signs: Journal of Women in Culture and Society* 16(3), 463–484.

Folbre, Nancy. 1994. *Who Pays for the Kids? Gender and the Structures of Constraint.* New York & London: Routledge.

Folbre, Nancy. 2001. *The Invisible Heart: Economics and Family Values.* New York: New Press.

Freeman, Richard B. 1999. *The New Inequality: Creating Solutions for Poor America.* Boston, MA: Beacon Press.

Fried, Mindy. 1998. *Taking Time: Parental Leave Policy and Corporate Culture.* Philadelphia, PA: Temple University Press.

Friedan, Betty. 1963. *The Feminine Mystique.* New York: Dell.

Galinsky, Ellen. 1999. *Ask the Children: What America's Children Really Think about Working Parents.* New York: William Morrow.

Galinsky, Ellen, James T. Bond, Stacy S. Kim, Lois Backon, Erin Brownfield, and Kelly Sakai. 2005. *Overwork in America: When the Way We Work Becomes Too Much,* Executive Summary. New York: Families and Work Institute.

Gallup Organization. 2006. "Gallup Brain, Question Profile, Question qn25," *Gallup Poll Social Series—Work and Education,* 8/8/2005–8/11/2005. Princeton, NJ: Gallup Organization, http://institution.gallup.com.

Garey, Anita Ilta. 1999. *Weaving Work and Motherhood.* Philadelphia, PA: Temple University Press.

Gornick, Janet C. and Marcia K. Meyers. 2003. *Families that Work: Policies for Reconciling Parenthood and Employment.* New York: Russell Sage Foundation.

Greer, Germaine. 1970. *The Female Eunuch.* New York: McGraw-Hill.

Heymann, Jody. *Widening Gap Why America's Working Families Are in Jeopardy—And What Can Be Done About It.* New York: Free Press.

Hochschild, Arlie. 1983. *The Managed Heart: Commercialization of Human Feeling.* Berkeley: University of California.

Human Rights Campaign Foundation. 2006. "'Best Places to Work' Gives Choices to Gay, Lesbian, Bisexual and Transgender Job Seekers." Washington, DC: HRCF, www.hrc.org.

Jacobs, Jerry A. and Kathleen Gerson. 1998. "Who Are the Overworked Americans?" *Review of Social Economy* 56(4), 442–459.

Kreider, Rose M. and Jason M. Fields. 2002. "Number, Timing, and Duration of Marriages and Divorces: 1996," U.S. Census Bureau Current Population Reports (February).

Milkie, Melissa A. and Pia Peltola. 1999. "Playing All the Roles: Gender and the Work-Family Balancing Act," *Journal of Marriage and the Family* 61(2), 476–490.

Parcel, Toby I. and Elizabeth G. Menaghan. 1994. *Parents Jobs and Children's Lives.* New York: Aldine de Gruyter.

Perry-Jenkins, Maureen, Rena L. Repetti, and Ann C. Crouter. 2000. "Work and Family in the 1930s," *Journal of Marriage and the Family* 62, 981–998.

Perlow, Leslie A. *Finding Time: How Corporations, Individuals, and Families Can Benefit from New Work Practices.* Ithaca, NY: Cornell University Press.

Pertman, Adam. 2000. *Adoption Nation: How the Adoption Revolution Is Transforming America.* New York: Basic Books.

Reid, Margaret. 1934. *Economics of Household Production.* New York: John Wiley & Sons.

Robinson, John, and Ann Bostrom. 1994. "The Overestimated Workweek? What Time Diary Measures Suggest," *Monthly Labor Review* 117(8), 11–23.

Rose, Stephen J. and Heidi I. Hartman. 2004. "Still a Man's Labor Market: The Long-Term Earnings Gap," Research Report No. C355, Washington, DC: Institute for Women's Policy Research, www.iwpr.org.

Singer, Eric L. 1999. "Outside In: The Risks Inherent in Moonlighting." Lisle, IL:

Wildman, Harrold, Allen and Dixon, www.aepronet.org/es/esl.html. Srivastva, Suresh, et al. 1975. *Job Satisfaction and Productivity.* Cleveland, OH: Case Western Reserve University.

Williams, Joan and Nancy Segal. 2002. "The New Glass Ceiling: Mothers—and Fathers—Sue for Discrimination," Report of the Program on Gender, Work and Family. Washington, DC: American University.

Wisensale, Steven K. 2001. *Family Leave Policy: The Political Economy of Work and Family in America.* Armond, NY: M.E. Sharpe.

Zero to Three, Civitas, and BRIO Corporation. 2000. *What Grown-Ups Understand about Child Development: A National Benchmark Survey.* Washington, DC: Zero to Three.

CHAPTER 16

More Than Welcome: Families Come First in Sweden

Brittany Shahmehri

Recently, my husband's laptop needed repair, and he called technical support to arrange for service. When he explained the problem, the phone representative at the multinational computer company said, "I'm going to recommend level-two support, but the technician will have to call you tomorrow to schedule an appointment. Today he's home with his sick kid."

When we still lived in the US, my husband might have wondered what a sick child had to do with his laptop. But last year we moved to Sweden, where parents not only are legally entitled to stay home with their sick children, but also get paid for doing so. Most amazing is that there's no shame in it. For fathers as well as mothers, it is assumed that when your child is sick, you are going to take care of him or her. That's more important than fixing someone's laptop on the spot. The computer company knows it and my husband's employer knows it. In almost every circumstance, the laptop can wait a day.

Even visiting tourists can see that Sweden has a child-friendly culture. A stroller logo is as common as the wheelchair logo in public restrooms and elevators. Buses accommodate strollers, and trains have places for children to play. (By the way, the children ride free.) Gas stations often have tiny working toilets as well as the standard toilets, as do zoos and other places that cater to children. "Amazing," I thought, the first time I visited.

But on closer examination, all of this is just window dressing. Sweden has one of the most generous parental leave policies in the world. Parents of each newborn or newly adopted child share 450 paid days to care for that child. The childcare system is of extremely high quality, offers a wide range of options, and is subsidized for all families. Parents are legally entitled to work reduced hours at their current jobs until their children reach the age of eight (when they formally enter school), and can take up to 60 paid days to take care of sick children. Toss in protected time to nurse a baby on the job and tuition-free universities, and to an American working parent, it sounds like Utopia!

WHY SUCH WIDESPREAD SUPPORT?

According to Dr. Irene Wennemo, a Swedish family policy expert, the question of supporting families in Sweden is generally framed in terms of how the state should implement policies and what level of resources should be invested. "It's very accepted here that the state should be responsible for the living standard of children," Wennemo told me. "Children aren't a private thing; society has a responsibility for part of the cost."

Most of the reasons for this are self-evident. Children are members of society. It's not good for people, especially children, to live in poverty. Children should have equal opportunities. It's necessary for society that people have children, so it should be easy to combine working and having children. It's good for men and women to have equal access to both work and family.

"If you want a society in which it is accepted that both partners go out and work, then you have to take people's needs seriously," states Gunnar Andersson, a sociologist at Lund University. "Both school and child care must be really good, and there must be much more flexibility for all."[1]

"This is what our parents worked for," explains Anneli Elfwén, a Swedish midwife with two young sons. In the 1950s most Swedish women stayed home with the children. When women began to enter the workforce in the late 1960s, the need for stronger family policy became clear. The modern versions of parental leave policy and subsidized child care were implemented in the early 1970s and met with wide popular support. When I asked Elfwén why support for family policy was so widespread, she laughed, "Maybe we get it in the breastmilk. It's very natural for us."

HOW IT WORKS

When Elfwén's first son, Simon, was born in 1995, Elfwén was entitled to the same parental leave benefits that are offered to all Swedish families. She and her husband could share the 450 days of leave as they pleased, though one month was reserved for her, and one for her husband; and if either of them chose not to take their individual time, they would forfeit it.

One of the most unique aspects of Swedish parental leave is that it can be taken part time. Elfwén and her husband used the flexibility in their schedules to extend the time Simon spent at home with one of his parents. Between paid leave, flexible jobs, and the help of grandparents, the Elfwéns juggled a two-career, two-parent family. When their second son, Olle, was born in 1998, he, too, was entitled to 450 days of his parents' time. This made it possible for Elfwén to maintain the career that she loves, while keeping her children home until they were about three. The parental leave made all the difference.

Parents can continue to work reduced hours until their children reach the age of eight. This option was chosen by a couple I know, both schoolteachers. The mother took one day a week off, the father one day, and they staggered their hours on remaining days, so that their children spent less time in child care. Both parents were able to maintain professional lives while sharing the responsibility for raising their children.

CHOICES IN CHILD CARE

When it was time for the Elfwéns to decide on a preschool for Simon, they selected a Waldorf school with low student-teacher ratios and organic vegetarian meals. There are also traditional preschools, Christian schools, Montessori schools, cooperative schools, and even daycare centers that focus on gender equality. Families pay the county rather than the childcare center, and the amount depends on each family's household income. This means that, with few exceptions, parents can send their child to any childcare center without consideration to finances. So a single mother studying at university might pay $30.00 a month far her child to attend a school, while a family with three children and a household income of $40,000 would pay around $240 a month to have their three children in the same school. As of 2002, there will be a cap of $115 a month for the first child, ramping down according to income.

Of course, things are not perfect. It can be difficult to find a spot in the middle of the year, so it's necessary to plan ahead. The school we chose for my four year old did not suit him, so we kept him home while waiting for a place in a new school. In looking at the options, however, we were impressed with the low student-teacher ratios at all the preschools we visited, and the consistently high quality of care.

SEPARATE TAXATION AND CHILD ALLOWANCES

A few other odds and ends round out the package. People are taxed individually in Sweden, so a woman's income won't fall into a high tax bracket just because the household income is high. In addition, cash payments take the place of tax deductions for children. Each month, about $95.00 per child is deposited into the account of every family with a child, from the unemployed to the royal family. Families with more than two children receive a small bonus, so for my three children, we get a cash payment of $300 a month. Many families turn the money over to their children when they reach the age of 15 so they can learn to handle a checking account and manage their clothing and leisure purchases.

THE EMPLOYER'S ROLE

In Sweden, creating balance between work and family life is not left solely to the government and individual families. Section five of the Swedish Equal Opportunity Act reads, ""An employer shall facilitate the combination of gainful employment and parenthood with respect to both female and male employees." Employers, in other words, are legally obligated to help employees combine parenthood and work. Employees who believe that an employer has directly violated this principle can take their case to the office of the Equal Opportunity Ombudsman (JämO).

Claes Lundkvist filed one of the eight cases registered with JämO last year regarding parenthood and employment. Lundkvist, a broadcast journalist for Swedish Radio, generally took his children to daycare each morning, and his wife, a physiotherapist with her own business, picked them up at the end of the day. But a new contract required Lundkvist to transfer to a branch more than an hour away. His working hours were inflexible as well. "My wife was very stressed taking all the responsibility," Lundkvist says. "It didn't work." After looking at JämO's Web page, he decided to pursue the issue.

The involvement of fathers as parents should be encouraged, according to JämO: "Employers may have an old-fashioned view of parenthood, or think that 'your wife can take care of that,' when the husband wants to be free to care for sick children or asks for more flexible working hours in order to combine work and family."[2] Changing the attitude of such employers is one of JämO's goals. JämO accepted Lundkvist's case, recognizing that without some adjustment in his new situation, his ability to combine work and family would be seriously impaired. The case initially met with resistance from Lundkvist's employers, and as he was a contract worker, JämO's power was limited. Lundkvist has since, however, negotiated a solution that does offer some flexibility.

With each case filed, the resulting publicity strengthens the public debate about men's rights and responsibilities as fathers. "It's hard to change gender roles," says Tommy Ferrarini, a PhD student at the Institute of Social Research in Stockholm who is currently doing research on family policy. But Ferrarini believes measures such as parental leave time allotted for the father shift social expectations: "It puts pressure on the employers when something becomes a right. It's all very individualized.... [This means] increased individual autonomy for the mother, the father, and the children. You give both parents the possibility of self-fulfillment."

WHAT FAMILY POLICY MEANS FOR WOMEN

Swedish mothers don't think they are doing it all, and they don't think the system is perfect. Some women have jobs that are more flexible than others; some are happier with their child care than others. While men are doing a larger share of the housework than in the past, couples still fight about who does the laundry. You'd be hard-pressed to find a Swedish mom who would call herself a superwoman.

Observing the situation, however, I see women who come pretty close to fulfilling the American "superwoman" myth. The vast majority of women have careers. With the help of their partners, they juggle children and work and birthday parties and still manage to make it to aerobics every week.

In the US, in contrast, the superwoman myth operates in a male-dominated corporate culture, and society views accepting help as a weakness. If you are granted a day off, you should be grateful. If your husband takes two unpaid weeks at the birth of a child, he should be grateful. If his company calls after a week and asks him to come back early (as my husband's company did), he should apologize when he says no, and then thank them for understanding.

In Sweden, you can certainly say "thank you" if you like, but no one has done you any favors. Among CEOs and entrepreneurs, you may see a more male-dominated culture, but even there, people are still likely to take a good portion of the five to eight weeks vacation they receive annually.

Swedish women face many of the same problems as their American counterparts. Their career advancement slows while children are young, and juggling everything can be very challenging. But women in Sweden do not have to do it alone. Families are supported by society, both financially and culturally. This means that women also give back to society, and not just in tax dollars—though even there, their contribution is substantial. Having women in the workplace changes the culture. Today, 43 percent of representatives in the Swedish Parliament and half of all State Ministers are women. In the long run, that will have an effect on the tone of the government as well as the laws that are passed.

CHILDREN ARE PEOPLE, TOO

Children in Sweden are not considered merely a lifestyle choice. They're members of society in their own right. Flexibility and support for families means that parents are better able to meet the needs of their children, something the children deserve. This approach offers myriad benefits to children, both emotionally and physically. Recent studies have suggested that "parental leave has favorable and possibly cost-effective impacts on pediatric health."[3] The same studies also indicate that with longer parental leaves, child and infant mortality rates go down.[4]

Respect for children is an important aspect of Swedish culture. Sweden has a Children's Ombudsman who represents children and young people in public debates, the ultimate goal being that young people can make their voices heard and gain respect for their views. In line with this, corporal punishment of any kind is illegal. Though controversial when it was first proposed, a Parliamentary Minister put the issue into context: "In a free democracy like our own, we use words as arguments, not blows....If we can't convince our children with words, we will never convince them with violence."[5]

Children in Sweden are people, not property. Family policy is very much about creating a better situation for men and women who choose to have families, but at its core, family policy is all about children. A society that cherishes and respects children must make it possible for every child to be raised with certain minimal standards. Ensuring healthcare coverage, making sure children have enough to eat, and keeping children free of the risks that inevitably accompany poverty are a few modest goals. In Sweden, every child is entitled to be home with his or her parents for the first year of life. That is the minimum standard the society has chosen.

What that means is that any child you see on the street had access to her parents for the most important time in her development, and has access to free, high-quality medical and dental care. You know that she has enough food to eat, and that she likely attends a well-run preschool. That child has advocates in government and the support of society. Who will that child become? Right now it doesn't matter. The bottom line is that she lives in a society that values her just the way she is.

CRITICAL THINKING QUESTIONS

Reread to following passage from this article:

> Children in Sweden are people, not property. Family policy is very much about creating a better situation for men and women who choose to have families, but at its core, family policy is all about children. A society that cherishes and respects children must make it possible for every child to be raised with certain minimal standards. Ensuring healthcare coverage, making sure children have enough to eat, and keeping children free of the risks that inevitably accompany poverty are a few modest goals. In Sweden, every child is entitled to be home with his or her parents for the first year of life. That is the minimum standard the society has chosen.

Is there anything in this passage that you find particularly compelling? Anything you particularly disagree with?

Which of the Swedish family policies described in this article do you think would garner the most political support in the United States? Which would attract the least support?

NOTES

1. Kristina Hultman, "A Step Away from a Childless Society?" *New Life: A Gender Equality Magazine for New Parents* (Stockholm: Swedish Government Division for Gender Equality, 2001): 10.
2. "What Is JämO?," a brochure published by the Equal Opportunity Ombudsman's office; see www.jamombud.se.
3. C. J. Ruhm, "Parental Leave and Child Health," *NBER Working Paper* no. W6554 (Cambridge, MA: National Bureau of Economic Research, 1998): 27.
4. Sheila Kamerman, "Parental Leave Policies: An Essential Ingredient in Early Childhood Education and Care Policies," *Social Policy Report 14*, no. 2 (2000): 10.
5. Louise Sylwander, "The Swedish Corporal Punishment Ban—More Than Twenty Years of Experience," Barnombudsmannen website, www.bo.se (choose the British flag for English).

CHAPTER 17

Life without Children

David Popenoe and Barbara Defoe Whitehead

INTRODUCTION

For most of the nation's history, Americans expected to devote much of their adult lives to the nurture and rearing of children. Life with children has been central to norms of adulthood, marriage and the experience of family life. Today, however, this historic pattern is changing. Life *without* children is becoming the more common social experience for a growing percentage of the adult population.

This is not to suggest that Americans are anti-child. On the contrary, the vast majority of Americans want, and expect to have, children. Parents love and enjoy their children. Some—famously tagged "helicopter parents"—are investing huge amounts of time, money and anxiety in sponsoring their children's careers from birth to age thirty—and even beyond. Nor is it to suggest that Americans are having too few babies. Largely due to the flood of recent immigrants, the U.S. birth rate remains at replacement level—well above the declining rates of European nations like Italy and Germany.

But what key indicators do suggest is that American society is changing in ways that make children less central to our common lives, shared goals and public commitments. This report looks at the social indicators and cultural trends that are contributing to this large, if largely unacknowledged, transformation in American life and considers what the loss of child-centeredness means for the future prospects of children...

CHILD-CENTEREDNESS IN THE UNITED STATES: WHAT IS IT AND HOW IS IT MEASURED?

Broadly speaking, all human societies are child-centered, because the successful rearing of children is essential to human survival. But in a narrower sense, societies vary in the breadth, location, duration and intensity of child-centeredness. In most societies, the responsibility for child rearing is highly communal. It is widely shared among families, kin networks, and the larger adult community. In the United States, to a greater degree than almost any other place in the world, social responsibility for child rearing—and thus the primary source of child-centeredness—is highly individualistic. It rests with lone couples and increasingly with lone parents.

Further, in other societies, child-centeredness is rooted in ethnic identity, national heritage or common culture. The French have a stake in children because they want their children to be French in their blood, bones, and consumption of Brie. In the United States, on the other hand, such cultural traditions don't matter nearly as much. Here, child-centeredness is mainly driven by the demographic dominance and political influence of the child-rearing population....

THE DECLINE OF CHILD-CENTERED MARRIAGE

Throughout our history and in much of the world today, marriage is first and foremost an institution for bearing and rearing children. For our grandparents, as for generations before them, it would have been ridiculous to ask the question: What does marriage have to do with children? What *else* is marriage for, they might have replied, but for the purpose of having and raising children?

But today, marriage is undergoing profound change, and much of that change is shifting the focus away from children. This is happening on two levels. First of all, there is a weakening link between marriage and child-bearing. More couples are having children outside of marriage and, increasingly, without ever marrying each other. Births to unwed women rose from 5.3 percent in 1960 to a record high of 38 percent in 2006. More than half of all births to women under thirty are now outside of marriage.

In addition, cohabitation among opposite-sex couples has soared in recent decades, and this trend contributes to high rates of unwed births, especially among young adults. More than forty percent of cohabiting couples have children,

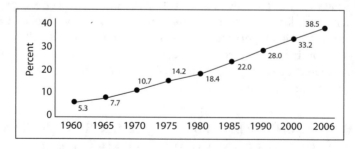

Figure 17.1 Percentage of Live Births to Unmarried Women, by Year, United States
SOURCE: *Statistical Abstract of the United States, 1995*, page 77, Table 94; *Statistical Abstract of the United States, 1999*, page 79, Table 99; *Statistical Abstract of the United States, 2000*, page 69, Table 85; and *Statistical Abstract of the United States, 2001*, page 63, Table 76; National Vital Statistics Reports, Vol. 50, 5. Hamilton, B., et al. *Births: Preliminary Data for 2006*, National Vital Statistics Report, 56:7, Dec. 5, 2007, Table 1.

and these unions are much more likely to break up than marital unions—one study estimates the risk as five times greater for cohabiting parents compared to married parents.[1] The high rate of breakup places children in cohabiting households at greater risk of the hardships associated with family fragmentation. Significantly too, the experience of motherhood for cohabiting women is uniformly and dramatically poorer compared to married new mothers—an indication that the quality of mothering might be lower for children born to cohabiting couples.[2]

And finally, the persistence of high rates of divorces involving children has contributed to the weakening of the connection between marriage and parenthood. Today, most Americans believe that it is better to leave an unhappy marriage than to stay together "for the sake of the children"—a popular view that both reflects and contributes to the incidence of parental divorce.

At a second level, child-centeredness *within* marriage is fading. Americans today are less likely to see children as central to a successful marriage. As recently as 1990, a clear majority—65 percent—of the public said that "children are very important to a successful marriage." By 2007, according to a recent Pew survey, only slightly more than forty percent of respondents agreed with the statement. Indeed, as measures of marital success, children ranked below other couple activities, such as sharing household chores, sexual fulfillment, and mutual interests.[3]

The retreat from child-centeredness within marriage is part of a larger transformation in the meaning and purpose of marriage. In recent decades, marriage has been deinstitutionalized—that is, it has lost much of its influence as a social institution governing sex, procreation and parenthood. Legally, socially, and culturally, marriage is now defined primarily as a couple relationship dedicated to the fulfillment of each individual's innermost needs and desires.

To be sure, the emphasis on the couple relationship is not new. The ideal of companionship in marriage is a distinctive part of a long-standing tradition in Anglo-American societies.[4] What is new is that today's couples are ratcheting up their expectations from companionship to the even harder-to-achieve ideal of a emotionally satisfying "best friends" relationship—what some call a "soul-mate" marriage.

Young adults, in particular, are looking to marriage as a source of personal and emotional rewards. Asked to rank the most important characteristics in a spouse, college students placed companionship, personality development and emotional security high on the list while "healthy and happy children," "moral and religious unity" and "maintenance of the home" fell much lower.[5]

It is easy to understand why the soul-mate ideal holds such appeal. Americans live in a "bowling alone" society. Given the frazzling pace and fractured relationships of a mobile society and a boom-and-bust economy, people are less involved in social relationships and community ties that provide occasions for friendship and acceptance. Consequently, many turn to marriage for the warmth, intimacy, and emotional security that is missing in other domains of adult life.

However, isolated from other social ties and institutions, this new marital ideal is fragile. It takes lavish investments of time, attention and vigilance for lone couples to sustain high levels of mutual happiness. If such personal investments are absent or insufficient, spouses can feel neglected and estranged. They may wonder if they have made a bad mistake in their choice of a mate. And given the high expectations for happiness and growth, unhappy couples may have reason—some might even say a personal obligation—to find a new and better soul mate.

Further, such high maintenance marriages may contribute to greater dissatisfaction during the child-rearing years. Like babies, soul-mate marriages have to be nurtured and coddled in order to thrive. When a real baby comes along, much of that nurture has to be devoted to the child. This can be especially threatening to parents who expect the same level of time and attention in their relationship to continue after the baby arrives. This is not to say that couples should neglect each other during the child-rearing years but it is to suggest that their expectations for sustained intimacy may be disappointed—leading some new parents to feel lonely, resentful and uncared for.

Thus, although this new kind of American marriage is potentially more rewarding for adults, it is demonstrably less secure for children. The high expectations for personal satisfaction in marriage, though a good thing to pursue and even better to achieve, have also made such marriages harder to sustain. The greater liabilities and costs associated with the fragile, couple-centered marital ideal fall heavily on children. It is children who are exposed to the risks of parental breakups, residential instability, and the likelihood of spending part of their childhood in households with a lone parent, stepparents, and half or step-siblings. In short, soul-mate marriage is more oriented to meeting adults' emotional needs for intimacy than to ensuring children's emotional needs for secure and long-lasting attachments....

CRITICAL THINKING QUESTIONS

One argument being made in this reading is that the new generation of marriages is becoming more couple-centered than child-centered. Do you agree? If so, what are the implications of this trend for future social problems? If not, why not?

Does this article assume the preexistence of a "golden age" of family, which Stephanie Coontz (Chapter 14) warns us not to do in an earlier reading?

NOTES

1. Georgina Binstock and A. Thornton, "Separations, Reconciliations and Living Apart in Cohabiting and Marital Unions," *Journal of Marriage and Family* 65 (2003): 432–443.

2. Hyeyoung Woo and R. Kelly Raley, "A Small Extension to 'Costs and Rewards of Children: The Effects of Becoming a Parent on Adults' Lives,'" *Journal of Marriage and Family* 67 (2005), 216.

3. "As Marriage and Parenthood Drift Apart, Public Is Concerned about Social Impact: A Social and Demographic Trends Report," Pew Research Center, July 1, 2007. http://pewresearch.org.

4. Visiting England in 1784, Duc de La Rochefoucauld noted that three out of four marriages are based on affection and most are perfectly happy. And once married, he wrote: "husband and wife are always together and share the same society. It is the rarest to meet one without the other.... It would be more ridiculous to do otherwise in England than to go everywhere with your wife in Paris." Cited in Randolph Trumbach, *The Rise of the Egalitarian Family: Aristocratic Kinship and Domestic Relations in Eighteenth Century England* (New York: Academic Press, 1978), 112–113.

5. Paul R. Amato, Alan Booth, David R. Johnson, and Stacy J. Rogers, *Alone Together: How Marriage in America Is Changing* (Cambridge: Harvard University Press, 2007), 16.

PART V

Crime and Drugs

Why is it that the vast majority of inmates in the nation's prison system were poor and unemployed before they got there? Why is it that African Americans and Hispanics are vastly overrepresented in the prison population compared to their representation in the general population? How is it that one can look at the numbers reflecting these trends and deny the influence of poverty, unemployment, and race on the likelihood of someone ending up in prison? These are factors with an undeniable influence on the likelihood of a person's incarceration. Whether these influence the likelihood of criminal behavior or the likelihood of arrest, prosecution, conviction, and incarceration is an important but difficult question. Unemployment, poverty, and race probably influence all of these processes. But in any case, the relationship between unemployment, poverty, race, and incarceration indicates that inequalities and lack of opportunities for certain segments of the population play a role in a person's likelihood of ending up behind bars.

The problem, says Jeffrey Reiman, is that our criminal justice system is set up to legitimize those inequalities, exonerate society for its responsibility, and, therefore, perpetuate the inequalities that lead to crime and incarceration. By focusing on the criminal and his or her misbehavior, the social factors that led that person to the courtroom are ignored. By being ignored, they are taken for granted and accepted as the status quo. Reiman states that "Justice is a two-way street—but criminal justice is a one-way street" because justice would consider both what society owes the individual and what the individual owes society; but criminal justice only considers the latter. In so doing, the criminal justice system plays an ideological role in sustaining a capitalist system that produces winners and losers and sends many of those who have lost to prison.

In the next article, Marc Mauer and Ryan King examine explanations for the large number of African Americans in the U.S. prison population. First it should be duly noted that there are larger numbers of virtually all groups in the prison population today than there were 30 years ago because there are far more people in prison today—both numerically and as a percentage of the population. The expansion in the prison population is best explained by the fact that the criminal justice system has become far more punitive than it was 30 years ago. More prison sentences are handed out today and the sentences have become longer. But minorities are more likely to be targeted by "get tough" policies than whites, especially when sentenced for drug offenses in the nation's decades-long "war on drugs." While the data show that African Americans and Hispanics are no more likely to be doing illegal drugs than their white counterparts, they are much more likely to be incarcerated for drug offenses.

As the next article demonstrates, many of the same trends occurring in the U.S. prison system can be seen in the Dutch system. In the 1970s, the Netherlands had one of the lowest incarceration rates in the world. In the decades since, they have seen their rates increase many times over. As in the United States, this increase can be explained by an exaggerated public fear of crime, the politicization of crime, a crackdown on drugs, and poor majority/minority relations. The disproportionate representation of minorities in Dutch prisons mirrors the racial composition of American inmate populations and reflects an intolerance for immigrants of color prevalent in many Western societies.

There is a certain contradiction between philosophy and practice when it comes to drug control policy in the United States. On the one hand, we see habitual drug use as stemming from addiction, which many or most of us consider a disease. On the other hand, we treat illegal drug use quite punitively. The last two articles in this part describe programs designed to deal with illegal drug users that avoid this contradiction. One of these programs is in England and the other in Canada; both are considered methods of "harm minimization." Harm minimization programs treat drug use as a public health concern rather than a criminal matter, recognizing that no matter how harsh the criminal penalties for drug use, many people are going to use them habitually anyway. The object of these programs is to avoid the obvious pitfalls of criminalization—black market violence, dirty drugs, and prison expansion—and keep drug offenders as healthy as possible. Though quite sensible in the eyes of their supporters, such programs would face enormous political opposition in the United States.

CHAPTER 18

The Implicit Ideology of Criminal Justice

Jeffrey Reiman

Any criminal justice system like ours conveys a subtle yet powerful message in support of established institutions. It does this for two interconnected reasons. First, it concentrates on *individual* wrongdoers. This means that *it diverts our attention away from our institutions, away from consideration of whether our institutions themselves are wrong or unjust or indeed "criminal."*

Second, the criminal law is put forth as the *minimum neutral ground rules* for any social living. We are taught that no society can exist without rules against theft and violence, and thus the criminal law seems to be politically neutral: the minimum requirements for *any* society, the minimum obligations that any individual owes his or her fellows to make social life of any decent sort possible. Thus, the criminal law not only diverts our attention away from the possible injustice of our social institutions, but also bestows upon those institutions the mantle of its own neutrality.

Because the criminal law protects the established institutions (the prevailing economic arrangements are protected by laws against theft, and so on), attacks on those established institutions become equivalent to violations of the minimum requirements for any social life at all. In effect, the criminal law enshrines the established institutions as equivalent to the minimum requirements for *any* decent social existence—and it brands the individual who attacks those institutions as one who has declared war on *all* organized society and who must therefore be met with the weapons of war.

This is the powerful magic of criminal justice. By virtue of its focus on *individual* criminals, it diverts us from the evils of the social order. By virtue of its presumed neutrality, it transforms the established social (and economic) order from being merely *one* form of society open to critical comparison with others into *the* conditions of *any* social order and thus immune from criticism. Let us look more closely at this process.

What is the effect of focusing on individual guilt? Not only does this divert our attention from the possible evils in our institutions, but it also puts forth half the problem of justice as if it were the *whole* problem. To focus on individual guilt is to ask whether the individual citizen has fulfilled his or her obligations to his or her fellow citizens. It *is to look away from the issue of whether the fellow citizens have fulfilled their obligations to him or her.* To look only at individual responsibility is to look away from social responsibility. Writing about her stint as a "story analyst" for a prime-time TV "real crime" show based on videotapes of actual police busts, Debra Seagal describes the way focus on individual criminals deflects attention away from the social context of crime and how television reproduces this effect in millions of homes daily:

> By the time our 9 million viewers flip on their tubes, we've reduced fifty or sixty hours of mundane and compromising video into short, action-packed segments of tantalizing, crack-filled, dope-dealing, junkie-busting cop culture. How easily we downplay the pathos of the suspect; how cleverly we breeze past the complexities that cast doubt on the very system that has produced the criminal activity in the first place.[1]

Seagal's description illustrates as well how a television program that shows nothing but videos of actual events, that uses no reenactments whatsoever, can distort reality by selecting and recombining pieces of real events.

A study of 69 TV law and crime dramas finds that fictional presentations of homicide focus on individual motivations and ignore social conditions:

> Television crime dramas portray these events as specific psychological episodes in the characters' lives and little, if any, effort is made to connect them to basic social institutions or the nature of society within which they occur.[2]

To look only at individual criminality is to close one's eyes to social injustice and to close one's ears to the question of whether our social institutions have exploited or violated the individual. *Justice is a two-way street—but criminal justice is a one-way street.* Individuals owe obligations to their fellow citizens because their fellow citizens owe obligations to them. Criminal justice focuses on the first and looks away from the second. *Thus, by focusing on individual responsibility for crime, the criminal justice system effectively acquits the existing social order of any charge of injustice!*

This is an extremely important bit of ideological alchemy. It stems from the fact that the same act can be criminal or not, unjust or just, depending on the circumstances in which it takes place. Killing someone is ordinarily a crime, but if it is in self-defense or to stop a deadly crime, it is not. Taking property by force is usually a crime, but if the taking is retrieving what has been stolen, then no crime has been committed. Acts of violence are ordinarily crimes, but if the violence is provoked by the threat of violence or by oppressive conditions, then, like the Boston Tea Party, what might ordinarily be called criminal is celebrated as just. This means that when we call an act a crime, *we are also making an implicit judgment about the conditions in response to which it takes place.* When we call an act a crime, we are saying that the conditions in which it occurs are not themselves criminal or deadly or oppressive or so unjust as to make an extreme response reasonable or justified or non-criminal. This means that when the system holds an individual responsible for a crime, *it implicitly conveys the message that the social conditions in which the crime occurred are not responsible for the crime,* that they are not so unjust as to make a violent response to them excusable.

Judges are prone to hold that an individual's responsibility for a violent crime is diminished if it was provoked by something that might lead a "reasonable man" to respond violently and that criminal responsibility is eliminated if the act was in response to conditions so intolerable that any "reasonable man" would have been likely to respond in the same way. In this vein, the law acquits those who kill or injure in self-defense and treats leniently those who commit a crime when confronted with extreme provocation. The law treats understandingly the man who kills his wife's lover, and the woman who kills her brutal husband even when she has not acted directly in self-defense. By this logic, when we hold an individual completely responsible for a crime, we are saying that the conditions in which it occurred are such that a "reasonable man" should find them tolerable. In other words, by focusing on individual responsibility for crimes, *the criminal justice system broadcasts the message that the social order itself is reasonable and not intolerably unjust.*

Thus, the criminal justice system focuses moral condemnation on individuals and deflects it away from the social order that may have either violated the individual's rights or dignity or pushed him or her to the brink of the crime. This not only serves to carry the message that our social institutions are not in need of fundamental questioning, but further suggests that the justice of our institutions is obvious, not to be doubted. Indeed, because it is deviations from these institutions that are crimes, the established institutions become the implicit standard of justice from which criminal deviations are measured.

This leads to the second way in which a criminal justice system always conveys an implicit ideology. It arises from the presumption that the criminal law is nothing but the politically neutral minimum requirements of any decent social life. What is the consequence of this? As already suggested, this presumption transforms the prevailing social order into justice incarnate and all violations of the prevailing order into injustice incarnate. This process is so obvious that it may be easily missed.

Consider, for example, the law against theft. It does seem to be one of the minimum requirements of social living. As long as there is scarcity, any society— capitalist or socialist—will need rules to deter individuals from taking what does not belong to them. The law against theft, however, is more: It is a law against stealing what individuals *presently own.* Such a law has the effect of making the present distribution of property a part of the criminal law.

Because stealing is a violation of the law, this means that the present distribution of property becomes the implicit standard of justice against which criminal deviations are measured. Because criminal law is thought of as the minimum requirements of any social life, this means that the present distribution of property is treated as the equivalent of the minimum requirements of *any* social life. The criminal who would alter the present distribution of property becomes someone who is declaring war on all organized society. The question of whether this "war" is provoked by the injustice or brutality of the society is swept aside. Indeed, this suggests yet another way in which the criminal justice system conveys an ideological message in support of the established society.

Not only does the criminal justice system acquit the social order of any charge of injustice; it also specifically cloaks the society's own crime-producing tendencies. I have already observed that by blaming the individual for a crime, the society is acquitted of the charge of injustice. I would like to go further now and argue that by blaming the individual for a crime, the society is acquitted of the charge of *complicity* in that crime. This is a point worth developing, because many observers have maintained that modern competitive societies such as our own have structural features that tend to generate crime. Thus, holding the individual responsible for his or her crime serves the function of taking the rest of society off the hook for their role in sustaining and benefiting from social arrangements that produce crime. Let us take a brief detour to look more closely at this process.

Cloward and Ohlin argued in their book *Delinquency and Opportunity*[3] that much crime is the result of the discrepancy between social goals and the legitimate opportunities available for achieving them. The same point is basic to "strain theory" including recent variations like Messner and Rosenfeld's *Crime and the American Dream*.[4] Simply put, in our society everyone is encouraged to be a success, but the avenues to success are open only to some. The conventional wisdom of our free-enterprise democracy is that anyone can be a success if he or she has the talent and the ambition. Thus, if one is not a success, it is because of one's own shortcomings: laziness, lack of ability, or both. On the other hand, opportunities to achieve success are not equally open to all. Access to the best schools and the best jobs is effectively closed to all but a few of the poor and becomes more available only as one goes up the economic ladder. The result is that many are called but few are chosen. Many who have taken the bait and accepted the belief in the importance of success and the belief that achieving success is a result of individual ability must cope with feelings of frustration and failure that result when they find the avenues to success closed. Cloward and Ohlin argue that one method of coping with these stresses is to develop alternative avenues to success. Crime is such an alternative avenue.

Crime is a means by which people who believe in the American dream pursue it when they find the traditional routes barred. Indeed, it is plain to see that the goals pursued by most criminals are as American as apple pie. One of the reasons that American moviegoers enjoy gangster films—movies in which gangsters such as Al Capone, Bonnie and Clyde, or Butch Cassidy and the Sundance Kid are the heroes, as distinct from police and detective films, whose heroes are defenders of the law—is that even when we deplore the hero's methods, we identify with his or her notion of success, because it is ours as well, and we admire the courage and cunning displayed in achieving that success.

It is important to note that the discrepancy between success goals and legitimate opportunities in America is not an aberration. It is a structural feature of modern competitive industrialized society, a feature from which many benefits flow. Cloward and Ohlin write that

> a crucial problem in the industrial world is to locate and train the most talented persons in every generation, irrespective of the vicissitudes of birth, to occupy technical work roles. Since we cannot know in advance who can best fulfill the requirements of the various occupational roles, the matter is presumably settled through the process of competition. But how can men throughout the social order be motivated to participate in this competition?
>
> One of the ways in which the industrial society attempts to solve this problem is by defining success-goals as potentially accessible to all, regardless of race, creed, or socioeconomic position.[5]

Because these universal goals are urged to encourage a competition to select the best, there are necessarily fewer openings than seekers. Also, because those who achieve success are in a particularly good position to exploit their success to make access for their own children easier, the competition is rigged to work in favor of the middle and upper classes. As a result, "many lower-class persons are the victims of a contradiction between the goals toward which they have been led to orient themselves and socially structured means of striving for these goals."[6]

> [The poor] experience desperation born of the certainty that their position in the economic structure is relatively fixed and immutable—a desperation made all the more poignant by their exposure to a cultural ideology in which failure to orient oneself upward is regarded as a moral defect and failure to become mobile as a proof of it.[7]

The outcome is predictable. "Under these conditions, there is an acute pressure to depart from institutional norms and to adopt illegitimate alternatives."[8]

This means that the very way in which our society is structured to draw out the talents and energies that go into producing our high standard of living has a costly side effect: It produces crime. By holding individuals responsible for this crime, those who enjoy that high standard of living can have their cake and eat it too. They can reap the benefits of the competition for success and escape the responsibility of paying for the costs of the competition. By holding the poor crook legally and morally guilty, the rest of society not only passes the costs of competition on to the poor, but also effectively denies that it (meaning primarily the affluent part of society) is the beneficiary of an economic system that exacts such a high toll in frustration and suffering.

William Bonger, the Dutch Marxist criminologist, maintained that competitive capitalism produces egotistic motives and undermines compassion for the misfortunes of others, and thus makes human beings literally *more capable of crime*—more capable of preying on their fellows without moral inhibition or remorse—than earlier cultures that emphasized cooperation rather than competition.[9] Here again, the criminal justice system relieves those who benefit from the American economic system of the costs of that system. By holding criminals morally and individually responsible for their crimes, we can forget that the motives that lead to crime—the drive for success, linked with the beliefs that success means outdoing others and that violence is an acceptable way of achieving one's goals—are the *same motives* that powered the drive across the American continent and that continue to fuel the engine of America's prosperity.

David Gordon, a contemporary political economist, maintains "that nearly all crimes in capitalist societies represent perfectly *rational* responses to the structure of institutions upon which capitalist societies are based."[10] Like Bonger, Gordon believes that capitalism tends to provoke crime in all economic strata. This is so because most crime is motivated by a desire for property or money and is an understandable way of coping with the pressures of inequality, competition, and insecurity, all of which are essential ingredients of capitalism. Capitalism depends, Gordon writes,

> on basically competitive forms of social and economic interaction and upon substantial inequalities in the allocation of social resources. Without inequalities, it would be much more difficult to induce workers to work in alienating environments. Without competition and a competitive ideology, workers might not be inclined to struggle to improve their relative income and status in society by working harder. Finally, although rights of property are protected, capitalist societies do not guarantee economic security to most of their individual members. Individuals must fend for themselves, finding the best available opportunities to provide for themselves and their families. Driven by the fear of economic insecurity and by a competitive desire to gain some of the goods unequally distributed throughout the society, many individuals will eventually become "criminals."[11]

To the extent that a society makes crime a reasonable alternative for a large number of its members from all classes, that society is itself not very reasonably or humanely organized and bears some degree of responsibility for the crime it encourages. Because the criminal law is put forth as the minimum requirements that can be expected of any "reasonable man," its enforcement amounts to a denial of the real nature of the social order to which Gordon and the others point. Here again, by blaming the individual criminal, the criminal justice system serves implicitly but dramatically to acquit the society of its criminality.

THE BONUS OF BIAS

We now consider the additional ideological bonus derived from the criminal justice system's bias against the poor. This bonus is a product of the association of crime and poverty in the popular mind. This association, the merging of the "criminal classes" and the "lower classes" into the "dangerous classes," was not invented in America. The word *villain* is derived from the Latin *villanus,* which means a farm servant. The term *villein* was used in feudal England to refer to a serf who farmed the land of a great lord and who was wholly subject to that lord.[12] In this respect, our present criminal justice system is heir to a long tradition....

It is quite obvious that throughout the great mass of Middle America, far more fear and hostility are directed toward the predatory acts of the poor than toward the acts of the rich. Compare the fate of politicians in recent history who call for tax reform, income redistribution, prosecution of corporate crime, and any sort of regulation of business that would make it better serve American social goals with that of politicians who erect their platform on a call for "law and order," more police, fewer limits on police power, and stiffer prison sentences for criminals—and consider this in light of what we have already seen about the real dangers posed by corporate crime and "business as usual."

It seems clear that Americans have been effectively deceived as to what are the greatest dangers to their lives, limbs, and possessions. The very persistence with which the system functions to apprehend and punish poor crooks and ignore or slap on the wrist equally or more dangerous individuals is testimony to the sticking power of this deception. That Americans continue to tolerate the comparatively gentle treatment meted out to white-collar criminals, corporate price fixers, industrial polluters, and political-influence peddlers while voting in droves to lock up more poor people faster and for longer sentences indicates the degree to which they harbor illusions as to who most threatens them. It is perhaps also part of the explanation for the continued dismal failure of class-based politics in America. American workers rarely seem able to forget their differences and unite to defend their shared interests against the rich whose wealth they produce. Ethnic divisions serve this divisive function well, but undoubtedly the vivid portrayal of the poor—and, of course, blacks—as hovering birds of prey waiting for the opportunity to snatch away the workers' meager gains serves also to deflect opposition away from the upper classes. A politician who promises to keep working-class communities free of blacks and the prisons full of them can get votes even if the major portion of his or her policies amount to continuation of the favored treatment of the rich at their expense. The sensationalistic use, in the 1988 presidential election, of photos of Willie Horton (a convicted black criminal who committed a brutal rape while out of prison on a furlough) suggests that such tactics are effective politics. Recent studies suggest that the identification of race and violent crime continues, albeit in subtler form.[13]

The most important "bonus" derived from the identification of crime and poverty is that it paints the picture that the threat to decent Middle Americans comes from those below them on the economic ladder, not from those above. For this to happen, the system must not only identify crime and poverty, *but also fail enough in the fight to reduce crime that crime remains a real threat.* By doing this, it deflects the fear and discontent of Middle Americans, and their possible opposition, away from the wealthy.

There are other bonuses as well. For instance, if the criminal justice system sends out a message that bestows legitimacy on the present distribution of property, the dramatic impact is greatly enhanced if the violator of the present arrangements is without property. In other words, the crimes of the well-to-do "redistribute" property among the haves. In that sense, they do not pose a symbolic challenge to the larger system in which some have much and many have little or nothing. If the criminal threat can be portrayed as coming from the poor, then the punishment of the poor criminal becomes a morality play in which the sanctity and legitimacy of the system in which some have plenty and others have little or nothing are dramatically affirmed. It matters little whom the poor criminals really victimize. What counts is that Middle Americans come to fear that those poor criminals are out to steal what they own.

There is yet another bonus for the powerful in America, produced by the identification of crime and poverty. It might be thought that the identification of crime and poverty would produce sympathy for the criminals. My suspicion is that it produces or at least reinforces the reverse: *hostility toward the poor.*

There is little evidence that Americans are very sympathetic to poor criminals. Very few Americans believe poverty to be a cause of crime (6 percent of those questioned in a 1981 survey, although 21 percent thought unemployment was a cause—in keeping with our general blindness to class, these questions are not even to be found in recent surveys). Other surveys find that most Americans believe that courts do not deal harshly enough with criminals (67 percent of those questioned in 2002), and that the death penalty should be used for convicted murderers (66 percent of those questioned in 2002).[14]

Indeed, the experience with white-collar crime...suggests that sympathy for criminals begins to flower only when we approach the higher reaches of the ladder of wealth and power. For some poor ghetto youth who robs a liquor store, five years in a penitentiary is our idea of tempering justice with mercy. When corporate crooks rob millions, incarceration is rare. A fine is usually thought sufficient punishment.

My view is that, because the criminal justice system, in fact and fiction, deals with *individual legal and moral guilt,* the association of crime with poverty does not mitigate the image of individual moral responsibility for crime, the image that crime is the result of an individual's poor character. It does the reverse: It generates the association of poverty and individual moral failing and thus *the belief that poverty itself is a sign of poor or weak character.* The clearest evidence that Americans hold this belief is to be found in the fact that attempts to aid the poor are regarded as acts of charity rather than as acts of justice. Our welfare system has all the demeaning attributes of an institution designed to give handouts to the undeserving and none of the dignity of an institution designed to make good on our responsibilities to our fellow human beings. If we acknowledged the degree to which our economic and social institutions themselves breed poverty, we would have to recognize our own responsibilities toward the poor. If we can convince ourselves that the poor are poor because of their own shortcomings, particularly moral shortcomings such as incontinence and indolence, then we need acknowledge no such responsibility to the poor. Indeed, we can go further and pat ourselves on the back for our generosity in handing out the little that we do, and, of course, we can make our recipients go through all the indignities that mark them as the undeserving objects of our benevolence. By and large, this has been the way in which Americans have dealt with their poor.[15] It is a way that enables us to avoid asking the question of why the richest nation in the world continues to produce massive poverty. It is my view that this conception of the poor is subtly conveyed by how our criminal justice system functions.

Obviously, no ideological message could be more supportive of the present social and economic order than this. It suggests that poverty is a sign of individual failing, not a symptom of social or economic injustice. It tells us loud and clear that massive poverty in the midst of abundance is not a sign pointing toward the need for fundamental changes in our social and economic institutions. It suggests that the poor are poor because they deserve to be poor or at least because they lack the strength of character to overcome poverty. When the poor are seen to be poor in character, then economic poverty coincides with moral poverty and the economic order coincides with the moral order. As if a divine hand guided its workings, capitalism leads to everyone getting what he or she morally deserves!

If this association takes root, then when the poor individual is found guilty of a crime, the criminal justice system acquits the society of its responsibility not only for crime *but for poverty as well.*

With this, the ideological message of criminal justice is complete. The poor rather than the rich are seen as the enemies of the majority of decent Americans. Our social and economic institutions are held to be responsible for neither crime nor poverty, and thus are in need of no fundamental questioning or reform. The poor are poor because they are poor of character. The economic order and the moral order are one. To the extent that this message sinks in, the wealthy can rest easily—even if they cannot sleep the sleep of the just.

We can understand why the criminal justice system is allowed to create the image of crime as the work of the poor and fails to reduce it so that the threat of crime remains real and credible. The result is ideological alchemy of the highest order. The poor are seen as the real threat to decent society. The ultimate sanctions of criminal justice dramatically sanctify the present social and economic order, and *the poverty of criminals makes poverty itself an individual moral crime!*

Such are the ideological fruits of a losing war against crime whose distorted image is reflected in the criminal justice carnival mirror and widely broadcast to reach the minds and imaginations of America.

CRITICAL THINKING QUESTIONS

What, according to this article, is the connection between crime and capitalism? What role does the criminal justice system play in maintaining capitalism in our society?

NOTES

1. Debra Seagal, "Tales from the Cutting-Room Floor: The Reality of 'Reality-Based' Television," *Harper's Magazine*, November 1993, p. 52.
2. David Fabianic, "Television Dramas and Homicide Causation," *Journal of Criminal Justice* 25, no. 3: p. 201.
3. Richard A. Cloward and Lloyd E. Ohlin, *Delinquency and Opportunity: A Theory of Delinquent Gangs* (New York: Free Press, 1960), esp. pp. 77–107.
4. Steven Messner and Richard Rosenfeld, *Crime and the American Dream*, 3rd ed. (Belmont, Calif.: Wadsworth), 2000.
5. Ibid., p. 81.
6. Ibid., p. 10.
7. Ibid., p. 107.
8. Ibid., p. 10.
9. Willem Bonger, *Criminality and Economic Conditions*, abridged and with an intro. by Austin T. Turk (Bloomington: Indiana University Press, 1969), pp. 7–12, 40–47. Willem Adriaan Bonger was born in Holland in 1876 and died by his own hand in 1940 rather than submit to the Nazis. His *Criminalité et conditions économiques* first appeared in 1905. It was translated into English and published in the United States in 1916. Ibid., pp. 3–4.
10. David M. Gordon, "Capitalism, Class and Crime in America," *Crime and Delinquency* (April 1973): p. 174.
11. Ibid.
12. William and Mary Morris, *Dictionary of Word and Phrase Origins*, vol. 2 (New York: Harper & Row, 1967), p. 282.
13. See, for example, Jon Hurwitz and Mark Peffley, "Playing the Race Card in the Post–Willie Horton Era: The Impact of Racialized Code Words on Support for Punitive Crime Policy," *Public Opinion Quarterly* 69, no. 1 (2005): pp. 99–113.
14. *Sourcebook—1981*, pp. 192, 205, 210–11; and *Sourcebook—2003*, p. 126, Table 2.27; p. 141, Table 2.47; and p. 145, Table 2.50.
15. Historical documentation of this can be found in David J. Rothman, *The Discovery of the Asylum: Social Order and Disorder in the New Republic* (Boston: Little, Brown, 1971); and in Frances Fox Piven and Richard A. Cloward, *Regulating the Poor: The Functions of Public Welfare* (New York: Pantheon, 1971), which brings the analysis up to recent times.

CHAPTER 19

Schools and Prisons: How Far Have We Come since *Brown v. Board of Education*?

Marc Mauer and Ryan S. King[1]

OVERVIEW

It has been more than a half-century since the United States Supreme Court, in the landmark case of *Brown v. Board of Education*, put the weight of the U.S. Constitution behind the ongoing struggle to desegregate public education. The decision in many ways marked the beginnings of the modern day civil rights movement and in its wake has followed significant social and economic progress for African Americans. Access to educational and economic opportunity has been expanded and many governmental institutions were established for the purpose of enforcing principles of racial equality. But, despite progress in the judicial and legislative arenas toward eradicating explicit forms of racial discrimination, there can be little argument that race still plays a major role in such critical areas as school admissions, employment, health care, and, perhaps most glaringly, the criminal justice system.

No institution has changed more in the last half-century than the criminal justice system, and in ways that have had profound effects on the African American community. The unprecedented growth in the prison system has produced record numbers of Americans in prison and jail, and has had a disproportionate effect on African Americans. As seen in Figure 19.1, there were more than nine times as many African Americans in prison or jail in 2004 as on the day of the *Brown* decision.[2] An estimated 98,000 blacks were incarcerated in 1954, a figure that rose to 910,200 by 2004.[3]

These absolute numbers translate into dramatic rates of incarceration for black men in particular. One of every 20 adult black men is imprisoned on any given day.[4] For black men in their late twenties, the figure is one in eight.[5] There are now far more incarcerated black men in this age group (155,600) than the total number of *all* incarcerated African Americans in 1954 (98,000).[6] Given current trends, one of every three (32%) black males born today can expect to go to prison in his lifetime.[7]

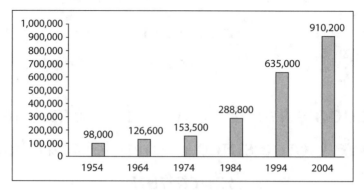

Figure 19.1 African Americans in Prison or Jail

The intersection between education and criminal justice is profound as well. In 1954, Chief Justice Warren noted, "In these days, it is doubtful that any child may reasonably be expected to succeed in life if he is denied the opportunity of an education."[8] In an era dominated by information technology where success is measured by one's specialized training, the fact that more than half (59%) of black men in their early 30s who are high school dropouts have a prison record underscores the nation's failure to heed Chief Justice Warren's warning.[9]

While the incarceration rates for women are lower overall than for men, the racial disparities are equally dramatic. One of every 18 black females born today can expect to go to prison if current trends continue, or six times the rate for white women.[10] These odds have increased dramatically in recent decades. Black women born today are five times more likely to go to prison in their lifetimes than black women born in 1974.[11]

CAUSAL FACTORS

The factors contributing to the dramatic increase in the number of African Americans in prison and jail are complex, and involve dynamics both within and outside the criminal justice system. Overall, they represent a social policy that has emphasized a punitive response to the problem of crime at the expense of alternative approaches that focus on strengthening families and communities. These include the following:

Crime Rates—Higher rates of involvement in some crimes explain part of the high rate of black imprisonment. For property offenses, blacks constituted 29% of arrests in 2006 and for violent offenses, 39%; these compare to the 12% black proportion of the total population.[12] (Note that an arrest may not always be an accurate indicator of involvement in crime, but it often remains the only means of approximating this measure.) However, criminologist Alfred Blumstein, in a study on race and imprisonment, noted that higher arrest rates for drug crimes in particular were not correlated with higher rates of use in the general population. In fact, differential law enforcement practices and tactical decisions regarding where the "war on drugs" is pursued play a substantial contributing role in shaping the demographics of arrestees. Blumstein was particularly wary of placing too much faith in patterns of drug arrests because the discretion that is intrinsic to drug enforcement "also offers the opportunity for the introduction of racial discrimination."[13]

What appears to be a race-based relationship for some offenses is in many respects one of social class. Youth surveys document that a significant proportion of teenage males of all races have engaged in serious crime. These rates drop much more sharply by the early 20s for whites than blacks, due to more ready access to adult roles—employment, college education, and stable relationships. Further, researchers have identified not just poverty, but *concentrated* poverty, as a significant contributor to crime rates due to the socioeconomic disadvantages that accrue. Housing patterns in the U.S. often result in low-income African Americans living in concentrated poverty, while poor whites and other groups are found in such situations less frequently.

Rising Imprisonment—Much of the rising incarceration of African Americans mirrors the dramatic increases in imprisonment overall since 1970. From a combined prison and jail population of about 330,000, the nation's incarcerated population has now increased to 2.2 million.[14] This increase is largely attributable to the adoption of "get tough" policies that emphasize harsher sentencing practices, rather than any significant increases in crime rates.[15] An examination of the growth of the prison population from 1992 to 2001 found that the entire increase was explained not by crime rates, but by an increased likelihood that convicted offenders would be sentenced to prison and with longer sentences.[16]

War on Drugs—Two overlapping trends since 1980 have contributed to a substantial increase in the number of African Americans in prison. First, the inception of the war on drugs has resulted in a dramatic surge in the number of incarcerated persons, rising from about 40,000 persons awaiting trial or serving a sentence for a drug charge in 1980 to nearly 500,000 in 2003.[17] The current figure is only slightly less than the total number of incarcerated persons for *all* offenses in 1980.

Second, the prosecution of the drug war has disproportionately affected communities of color. Surveys conducted by the Department of Health and Human Services estimate that blacks constitute 14% of monthly drug users,[18] yet blacks represent 35% of persons arrested for drug offenses.[19] Of all persons in state prison for a drug offense, 79% are black or Latino.[20] These disparities result in large part through a two-tiered application of the drug war. In communities with substantial resources, drug abuse is primarily addressed as a public health problem utilizing prevention and treatment approaches. In low-income communities those resources are in short supply and drug problems are more likely to be addressed through the criminal justice system.

Crack/Cocaine Sentencing—Federal legislation adopted in 1986 and 1988 provides for far harsher punishment of crack cocaine offenders than powder cocaine offenders, even though crack is a derivative of powder cocaine. Persons convicted of selling 500 grams of powder cocaine are subject to a mandatory five-year prison term; for crack cocaine, the same penalty is triggered by possession of just five grams of the drug. Differential patterns of enforcement of these laws have resulted in African Americans constituting more than 80% of crack defendants,[21] despite the fact that currently 60% of users in the general population are white or Latino.[22] This represents a policy decision by agencies in the criminal justice system to pursue the "war on drugs" primarily in low-income communities of color. In addition, 13 states also maintain disparities in their sentencing differentials between crack and powder cocaine.[23]

Widespread concern about these disparities led the U.S. Sentencing Commission ("Commission") to recommend the elimination of the sentencing differential in 1995. This recommendation was overwhelmingly rejected by Congress and the Clinton Administration. A subsequent effort to revise the penalty structure in 2002 was opposed by the Bush Administration's Department of Justice. Despite these setbacks, advocates, practitioners, and many policymakers continued to speak out about the injustices resulting from federal cocaine sentencing laws. In 2006, the confluence of renewed attention to the issue by some members of Congress and continued calls by the Commission for reform renewed optimism that progress might be made addressing this contentious law. In the Senate, three bills were introduced in 2006 and 2007 to reduce or eliminate the sentencing disparity between powder and crack cocaine. In addition, in May 2007, the Commission issued a report to Congress outlining their conclusions coming out of a November 2006 public hearing. Leading national sentencing and drug policy experts testified about the current penalty structure and many called for reforming the mandatory sentencing laws to ensure that federal resources target serious and major drug traffickers. The Commission went on record for the fourth time in 12 years, echoing their past recommendations for reform to the federal cocaine sentencing laws. In addition, the Commission offered an amendment, effective November 2007, which adjusts the penalty structure of the Guidelines, effectively reducing the average sentence for an eligible crack cocaine defendant by 16 months.

"Drug-Free Zone" Laws—In recent years many states have adopted "drug-free zone" laws that increase penalties for drug crimes committed near schools, parks, churches, and other areas where children are known to congregate. For persons convicted of a drug offense within these zones, the penalty is enhanced. These laws, intended to deter drug-selling either directly to or in close proximity to young children, have in practice contributed to extreme racial/ethnic disparities. This is the result of concentrated settlement patterns in urban areas. For example, in New Jersey, persons caught possessing or selling drugs within 1,000 feet of a school or 500 feet of public parks, public housing, or other public structures face

enhanced punishment. In urban areas, large proportions of most cities are within the typical 1,000 foot range of these sanctions, whereas in suburban or rural communities, far fewer locations fall within this limit. Since African Americans disproportionately live in urban areas, any such crime (even a drug sale between consenting adults at 3 a.m. near a school) will produce these enhanced penalties. In one recent year, 99% of the juveniles automatically prosecuted as adults in Cook County (Chicago), Illinois, under the school zone law were black and Latino.[24] A recent study by the New Jersey Commission to Review Criminal Sentencing found that 96% of persons convicted under that state's drug-free zone laws were African American or Latino.[25] The Commission concluded that "the unintended, but profoundly discriminatory, impact of the laws is the direct result of the size of the zones" and called for a reduction in the size of the zone to 200 feet, while also recommending the repeal of associated mandatory minimum sentences.[26]

"Three Strikes" and Habitual Offender Policies—Sentencing legislation that imposes harsher prison terms on offenders with prior convictions exerts a disproportionate effect on African Americans. Judges have always had the ability to impose lengthier terms on repeat offenders, but this effect has been magnified through policies such as habitual offender laws and "three strikes and you're out" legislation. Whether one believes that African Americans are more likely to engage in crime or are subject to racial profiling and other discriminatory forms of decisionmaking, the result is that African Americans are more likely to have a prior criminal record than other groups. Therefore, policies that impose harsher penalties based on criminal history will have a disproportionate effect on African Americans. In California, for example, blacks constitute 28.7%[27] of the prison population, but 44.9%[28] of the persons serving a "three strikes" sentence. These disparities take on added significance due to the extreme disparities created by such policies. A non-violent offense in California that might otherwise lead to no more than a few years in prison becomes a sentence of 25 years to life when treated as a third strike offense.

Inadequate Defense Resources—Forty years after the historic *Gideon* decision guaranteeing right to counsel in criminal cases, the state of indigent defense remains highly inadequate in many areas of the country. An estimated 80% of criminal defendants are indigent and a 2000 report by the Department of Justice declared that public defense was in a "chronic state of crisis."[29] A lack of adequate funding is the most significant problem most public defense systems face. In Virginia, for example, the maximum payment for attorneys representing a defendant in a felony case that can result in a life sentence is $1,096. In Illinois, the rate of compensation for a contract defender is $1,250 for a defendant facing a felony charge.[30] This rate has not changed in more than 25 years.

Insufficient funding for public defense results in irresponsibly high caseloads. The National Advisory Commission on Criminal Justice Standards recommends a caseload limit of 150 felony cases per attorney per year. A recent survey of Baltimore public defenders found attorneys handling 80 to 100 felony cases at one time.[31] The combination of inadequate funding and insufficient staffing leads to "assembly line" justice. A study in Alabama found no motions filed in 99.4% of cases where a defendant was represented by a contract defender.[32] In Mississippi, half of cases with a public defender resulted in a guilty plea on the day they were assigned to counsel.[33] In Clark County (Las Vegas), Nevada, less than 1% of cases handled by the public defender are taken to trial.[34] Because African Americans disproportionately rely upon the public provision of counsel, they are more likely to suffer the deficiencies produced by these dynamics.

Zero Tolerance Policies—In response to the perceived problem of school violence, many states and school districts have enacted "zero tolerance" policies for violations of school regulations. Such policies result in automatic suspension or expulsion of students for infractions that previously might have been handled by school officials. While ostensibly targeted at gun violence and other serious crimes, in practice these policies have led to disciplinary action for behaviors such as bringing Advil or water pistols to school. Zero tolerance policies contribute to higher rates of suspension and expulsion, and ultimately to increased numbers of school dropouts. Children of color have been disproportionately affected by these policies. According to the Department of Education, 35% of African American children in grades 7–12 had been suspended or expelled at some point in their school careers, compared to rates of 20% for Hispanics and 15% for whites.[35] These figures in turn result in increased risk of involvement in the juvenile and adult criminal justice system.

IMPLICATIONS

At current rates of incarceration, one of every three black males born today can expect to be imprisoned at some point in his lifetime. Whether or not one believes that current crime control policies are "working" to reduce crime, such an outcome should be shocking to all Americans. Imposing a crime policy with such profound racial dynamics calls into question the nation's commitment to a free and democratic society.

Current imprisonment policies affect not only the more than 900,000 African Americans in prison and jail, but increasingly, their families and communities as well. One of every 14 black children has a parent in prison on any given day; over the course of childhood, the figures would be much higher. Family formation, particularly in urban areas heavily affected by incarceration, is also affected by these trends. In the highest incarceration neighborhoods of Washington, D.C., the absence of black men has created a gender ratio of 62 men for every 100 women.[36]

Community power is affected by felony disenfranchisement laws as well, which restrict voting rights while serving a felony sentence or in some cases permanently, depending on the state in which one lives. One of every eight black males (13%) cannot vote as a result of a current or previous felony conviction. These laws affect the political influence not only of people with a felony conviction, but of their communities as well. People in these neighborhoods who do not have a felony conviction have their political voices diluted since fewer residents representing their interests are able to participate in the electoral process.

None of these issues suggests that crime is not a problem for all Americans, including African Americans. However, the approaches taken to address this problem over the past several decades have created a situation whereby imprisonment has come to be seen as a seemingly inevitable aspect of the maturing process for black men, and increasingly for black women. The social cost of these policies is substantial and growing larger each year. More than 50 years have passed since the *Brown* decision and it is time for the nation to reflect not only on progress in education, but also to assess how the overall status of the black community has been affected. The dynamics of criminal justice policy suggest that the nation has taken a giant step backward in this regard.

Despite this dire portrait, there is reason for optimism. Many of the problems identified here are simply the result of misguided policy, meaning that policymakers have the ability to change the current course by revisiting some of the most egregiously unfair practices. Repealing mandatory minimum sentencing, fighting racial profiling and other corrosive law enforcement practices linked with the "war on drugs," and investing in prevention strategies are good places to begin. In addition, ensuring that policymakers are aware of the racially disparate impact of new sentencing laws by requiring a "racial/ethnic impact statement" to attach to any new legislation that will affect sentencing or correctional populations is a simple way to assist lawmakers in being proactive about addressing this issue. As the civil rights movement extends into the 21st century, it is imperative that we close the book on the wrongheaded policies of recent decades and commit ourselves anew to equality and fairness for all Americans.

CRITICAL THINKING QUESTIONS

The authors outline many of the causes of minority overrepresentation in today's prison population. Where would you like to see policymakers start to remedy the problem? Or do you think the problem is not the result of or a matter of public policy?

NOTES

1. Marc Mauer and Ryan S. King are the Executive Director and Policy Analyst, respectively, of The Sentencing Project, www.sentencingproject.org.
2. Prison and jail custody data for Figure 19.1 were collected from various Bureau of Justice Statistics publications. Where possible, exact numbers were taken directly from Bureau of Justice Statistics' reports. In the case of years in which exact prison or jail data were not available, the numbers were interpolated based on available information for contiguous years. These estimates were most commonly produced by taking the difference between the two points in time and assuming an average annual increase based on the number of years.

3. Figure for 2004 taken from Paige M. Harrison and Allen J. Beck, *Prison and Jail Inmates at Midyear 2004*, Washington, DC, NCJ 208801, April 2005, at 11.

4. Ibid.

5. Ibid.

6. Ibid.

7. Thomas P. Bonczar, *Prevalence of Imprisonment in the U.S. Population, 1974–2001*, Washington, DC, NCJ 197976, August 2003, at 8.

8. *Brown vs. Board of Education of Topeka*, 347 U.S. 483, 493 (1954).

9. Bruce Western, Mary Pattillo, and David Weiman, "Introduction," in Mary Pattillo, David Weiman, and Bruce Western (Eds.), *Imprisoning America: The Social Effects of Mass Incarceration*, New York: Russell Sage Foundation, 2004, pp. 1–18, at 7.

10. Bonczar, supra note 7.

11. Ibid.

12. United States Department of Justice, Federal Bureau of Investigation, *Crime in the United States, 2006*, Washington, DC, September 2007, at Table 43.

13. Alfred Blumstein, "Racial Disproportionality of U.S. Prison Populations Revisited," *University of Colorado Law Review*, Vol. 64, 1993, 743–760, at 746.

14. William J. Sabol, Todd D. Minton, and Paige M. Harrison, *Prison and Jail Inmates at Midyear 2006*, Washington, DC, NCJ 217675, at 1.

15. Alfred Blumstein and Allen J. Beck, "Reentry as a Transient State between Liberty and Recommitment," in Jeremy Travis and Christy Visher (Eds.), *Prisoner Reentry and Crime in America*, New York: Cambridge University Press, 2005, at 50–79.

16. Jennifer C. Karberg and Allen J. Beck, "Trends in U.S. Correctional Populations: Findings from the Bureau of Justice Statistics." Presented at the National Committee on Community Corrections Meeting, Washington, DC, April 16, 2004.

17. Marc Mauer and Ryan S. King, *A 25-Year Quagmire: The War on Drugs and Its Impact on American Society*, Washington, DC: The Sentencing Project, September 2007, at 10.

18. Substance Abuse and Mental Health Services Administration, Office of Applied Studies, *National Survey on Drug Use and Health, 2006*, Washington, DC, 2007, at Table 1.19A.

19. United States Department of Justice, supra note 12, at Table 43.

20. Ryan S. King and Marc Mauer, *Distorted Priorities: Drug Offenders in State Prisons*, Washington, DC: The Sentencing Project, September 2002, at 11.

21. United States Sentencing Commission, Report to Congress: *Cocaine and Federal Sentencing Policy*, Washington, DC, May 2007, at 16.

22. Substance Abuse and Mental Health Services Administration, supra note 18, at Table 1.34A.

23. United States Sentencing Commission, supra note 21, at 98–104.

24. Marc Mauer and Steve Drizin, "Transfer Laws Victimize Fairness," *Chicago Sun-Times*, December 27, 2000.

25. The New Jersey Commission to Review Criminal Sentencing, *Report on New Jersey's Drug-Free Zone Crimes and Proposal for Reform*, December 2005, at 5.

26. Ibid at 6.

27. California Department of Corrections and Rehabilitation, *California Prisoners and Parolees 2005*, Sacramento, CA, Data Analysis Unit, 2006, at 23.

28. California Department of Corrections and Rehabilitation, *Second and Third Strikers in the Adult Institution Population*, Sacramento, CA, Data Analysis Unit, March 2007, at 94.

29. Caroline Wolf Harlow, *Defense Counsel in Criminal Cases*, Washington, DC: Bureau of Justice Statistics, November 2000.

30. American Bar Association, Indigent Defense Briefing Sheet: Illinois, 2005.

31. American Bar Association, Indigent Defense Briefing Sheet: Maryland, 2005.

32. American Bar Association, Indigent Defense Briefing Sheet: Alabama, 2005.

33. American Bar Association, Indigent Defense Briefing Sheet: Mississippi, 2005.

34. American Bar Association, Indigent Defense Briefing Sheet: Nevada, 2005.

35. National Center for Education Statistics, Status and Trends in the Education of Blacks, U.S. Department of Education, September 2003, at 38.

36. Donald Braman, "Families and Incarceration," in Marc Mauer and Meda Chesney-Lind (Eds.), *Invisible Punishment: The Collateral Consequences of Mass Imprisonment*, New York: The New Press, 2002, at 128.

CHAPTER 20

The Growth of Incarceration in the Netherlands

Robert Heiner

INTRODUCTION

In the 1970s, the Netherlands and the Scandinavian countries were distinguished for their relatively low incarcerations rates. In the last two decades of the twentieth century, as we all know, U.S. incarceration rates have skyrocketed; the rates in the Scandinavian countries have, for the most part, seen slight but steady increases; and the Dutch incarceration rate has quintupled, surpassing even the growth rate of the U.S. (though, of course, the Dutch rate remains only a fraction of the U.S. rate). In 1974, the Dutch incarceration rate was the lowest in Europe, with 22 people in prison per 100,000 population; by 2000, this rate had climbed to 90 per 100,000 population. Most of this surge in the Dutch incarceration rate took place between the mid-1980s and the mid-1990s. Between 1985 and 1995, the Dutch had, by far, the fastest growing incarceration rate in Europe.

Three decades ago, the Netherlands was held up to the world as a model of tolerance and progressive criminal justice. Experts came from all over the world to see what they were doing right. Today, their incarceration rate is most unremarkable, neither well above, nor well below those of her European neighbors. Once progressive criminologists *hoped* the Netherlands symbolized the future; now they *fear* that what happened in the Netherlands may symbolize the future. What happened to precipitate the surge in the Dutch incarceration rate and what is the significance of this surge for European and American criminologists?

METHODS

With financial support from the Marion and Jasper Whiting Foundation, I spent a week interviewing Dutch criminologists, asking them for their interpretation of this surge. This is a relatively "soft" method in the social sciences, but it approximates the method used by the British criminologist David Downes in his often cited book, *Contrasts in Tolerance: Post-War Penal Policy in The Netherlands and*

England and Wales. This method is, of course, not without its flaws. Downes has been criticized for his inability to speak the native language and for interviewing criminologists who shared his biases and for relying too heavily on interpretations of criminologists employed by the government, who want to cast Dutch criminal justice policies in the best possible light.[1] These are possible limitations in my study as well (except for the latter criticism, as I interviewed only academic criminologists, not government criminologists).

HISTORICAL TRENDS

Incarceration Rates

In the 1970s the Netherlands was famous for its toleration of drug use, prostitution, and youthful dissent. The famous Dutch tolerance was manifested in a number of other social policies as well; most notably for criminologists, the Dutch were known for their leniency in criminal sentencing. Remarkably, for example, in 1970, while sixty-three people were convicted of homicide, only fourteen were sentenced to three or more years in prison (with the understanding that they would be automatically granted parole before the end of their sentences).[2] Throughout most of the 1970s, the Dutch incarceration rate remained below thirty people per 100,000 population. The first half of the 1980s saw only slight increases, with the incarceration rate reaching 33 by 1987. But the next ten years saw incredible growth, with the rate reaching 85 by 1997 and 90 by the year 2000.[3]

In the midst of this growth in their prison population, the Dutch have maintained their policy of one prisoner to a cell. Thus, the Dutch have embarked on a program of prison expansion, building new prisons at a rate probably unprecedented in modern European history. Prison capacity rose from 3,900 cells in 1980 to almost 12,000 in 1995.[4] Early in their crackdown on crime, the Dutch courts were finding that they had to put convicted offenders on waiting lists before they could enter prison and serve their sentences. Meanwhile, the prisons were releasing convicts from the "back door" in order to accommodate the onslaught of new convicts. The waiting lists still continue today as does the prison expansion program.

Prison Conditions

While there have been enormous increases in their incarceration rate, it started from a very small base, and stands today at about the European average. Hence, it would be unfair to call the recent crackdown "draconian." The same can be said of the conditions in the Dutch prisons. Like other symbols of Dutch tolerance, the prisons used to be held up to the world as models of humanity. In fact, Dutch houses of correction were praised by the British prison reformer, John Howard, as far back as 1777. Prisons are kept small, usually holding less than 200 inmates each. There are committees, made up of members of the community, visiting the prisons regularly to ensure a certain degree of transparency and community oversight. And the rights of prisoners compare very favorably to those of prisoners in most countries around the world.

Philosophical Underpinnings

In the wake of World War II, the Dutch began putting their society back together again, strongly influenced by their experiences during the war. The new society was to be governed by a philosophy of "humane paternalism" and this philosophy would be particularly exemplified in the Dutch prison system. Many well-renowned Dutch citizens and leaders had themselves been confined in Nazi prisons and they were shocked by the experiences and determined to bring an end to prison atrocities. "After the war, prison experts were immediately struck with an almost revolutionary urge to reform," writes Downes.[5] This reform spirit was philosophically and intellectually reinforced by a number of faculty at Utrecht University who would come to have a powerful influence on Dutch criminology and criminal justice. This group of intellectuals came to be known as "the Utrecht School" and "[w]hat bound the group together...was their deep aversion to imprisonment, particularly long-term imprisonment." The reform spirit of the Utrecht School was reflected in the 1951 Prison Act which "substituted resocialization for retribution as the governing principle for prison life."[6]

Four decades later, in the midst of the Dutch crackdown on crime, a radical departure from the Utrecht School's philosophy was reflected in the government's 1990 *Law in Motion* report which was highly critical of modern criminology and its influence on criminal justice policy. The report provided some indication the government's inclination to give more weight to public demands for crime control and less weight to the advice of the experts. And, then, the 1994 report *Effective Detention* called for the extraction of more productivity from prison labor, shifting emphasis away from work as a means of rehabilitation to work as a means of cost containment. Together, these two reports represented a radical departure from the philosophy that had for so long distinguished Dutch criminal justice. Heretofore, the Dutch government had given much credence to the advice of progressive intellectuals and it had placed a high priority on the rehabilitation of prison inmates. The 1990s saw the government becoming much more attuned to the politics of criminal justice.

EXPLAINING THE GROWTH OF INCARCERATION

Some of the increase in the Dutch incarceration rate has less to do with changes in their tolerance levels than with increases in their crime rate. Much of Europe has experienced a similar trend.

A Changing Europe

"Globalization" is a vague, sweeping, and amorphous concept, but we all know that it is producing profound changes in all societies around the world; and some of these changes have or will have an impact on crime and criminal justice in different parts of the world. Those changes that seem most significant for our discussion are those that deal with cultural and economic integration. Capital flows more freely across national boundaries than it ever has before. In order to compete in an increasingly international free market economy, European countries have been virtually forced to join the European Union and, for member states, national and cultural boundaries are becoming less and less relevant. As people can cross national boundaries with increasing ease, countries are having to deal with more immigration issues, and with the import of contraband, and consequently with organized crime. Occupying a, more or less, central location in Europe, the Netherlands may be dealing with more than its fair share of these problems.

Many of the countries in Europe have opened their borders to immigrants from their former colonies. In the past, the United States was distinguished from most other countries in the degree to which it opened its borders to immigration. During the 1980s and 1990s, many European countries were accepting higher rates of immigrant flow than the U.S. Dispossessed aliens were immigrating in such large numbers that it has been difficult for them to be integrated into the economy; that is, it has often been difficult for them to find employment. A large proportion of these immigrants are poor and most come from racial or ethnic backgrounds that distinguish them from the majority populations in their host countries. Their presence is often resented by many from the majority group. These are, of course, key ingredients for a crime problem: poverty, unemployment, and discrimination. In 1998, 53 percent of detainees in the Dutch prison system were born outside of the Netherlands and this number has been steadily increasing.[7]

Europe's permeable borders also facilitate the smuggling of contraband, especially illegal drugs. As noted earlier, the Netherlands was once renowned for their toleration of narcotics use. The Dutch toleration of this behavior made it difficult for neighboring countries to enforce their narcotics statutes. Leaders of other European countries feared that the Dutch toleration of drug use compromised their moral authority for enforcement and it increased the likelihood of drug flow in and around Europe. As Holland's reputation for the toleration of drug use grew, so too did pressure from neighboring European countries to crack down. In response, the Netherlands did little to tighten up on drug use, but they did crack down on drug trafficking.

Drug trafficking was just one of the offenses of recent concern to many European countries. "The drug scene seems to have been growing in all European countries," writes Finnish criminologist Kauko Aromaa, "accompanied by organized crime developments that have a growing influence on other illegal activities, from smuggling of profitable commodities and even people to trade in a variety of other opportunity-dictated commodities."[8] Indeed organized transnational crime is receiving increasing levels of attention from law enforcement agencies throughout Europe.

Finally, free market economics is another aspect of globalization that may be impacting crime and criminal justice in many European countries. The United States has managed to maintain its dominance over such a large share of world markets by providing little in the way of security for its citizens and its labor force. Compared to its Western European counterparts and many other countries around the world, unemployment benefits, retirement benefits, healthcare benefits, and other benefits in the U.S. are quite paltry. By minimizing these costs, the United States is able to market commodities and services at often much lower costs than its European competitors. Already strained by immigration trends and a graying population, many European countries are finding it necessary to cut back on some of their welfare benefits and market controls in order to survive in the fiercely capitalistic market driven by the United States. The result is that, in most European countries, the rich are getting richer and the poor are getting poorer, more closely approximating the situation in the United States. It is the lack of a safety net for the poor that has frequently been used to explain the high rates of crime in the United States relative to Europe. Following this logic, as European safety nets dwindle, rising crime rates are likely to follow.

Increasing Levels of Punitiveness

Earlier it was stated that much of the growth in Dutch incarceration rates may be the result of increasing crime rates rather than diminishing tolerance among the Dutch. This was an oversimplification. Criminological research has, at best, found only a tenuous relationship between crime rates and incarceration rates. In fact, much of the expansion of the Dutch prison population in the 1990s was not due to an increased number of offenders receiving prison sentences, but to a doubling in the length of prison sentences. This is, in part, explained by the fact that there were increases not only in the number of crimes being committed, but also in the severity of crimes committed in the 1990s.[9] But, concurrently, certain types of crimes came to be punished more severely than they had in the past. Tak reports, "For drug, violent, and property crimes, the likelihood of imprisonment increased significantly and the number of sentences longer than one year nearly tripled."[10] Many European countries saw increases in the severity of sentences for certain types of crimes, but these increases were of a lower magnitude. Thus, it appears that the increasing incarceration rates in the Netherlands are in part due to a changing, more serious, crime picture, but also, in part, due to decreasing levels of tolerance, inasmuch as the two can be separated.

FACTORS UNRELATED (OR LESS RELATED) TO RISING CRIME RATES

With often exaggerated reports of rising crime rates and increasing levels of seriousness of crime, many criminologists attributed the Dutch crackdown to a moral panic which followed these reports. The International Crime Survey of 1989 showed the Netherlands to have the highest crime rate among fourteen countries (including the United States). Even though criminologists were quick to point out that the extraordinarily high rates of bicycle theft in the Netherlands accounted, in large part, for their being ranked number one, the Dutch were shocked by their ranking and felt overwhelmed by crime. Indeed, the Netherlands remained a relatively safe society, but government officials realized that what mattered were people's *perceptions* of crime growing out of hand. In this sense, the move to more stringent measures can be seen as an effort to placate a growing sense of insecurity rather than as a means to control crime. Surely this strategy is not unfamiliar to American policy-makers and accounts, perhaps in large degree, to the extraordinarily high incarceration rate in the United States.

Aside from the "moral panic," other changes in Dutch society over the last several decades help to explain their decreasing levels of tolerance. Dutch society has become more industrialized and urbanized and, along with these changes, as Emile Durkheim would have predicted, the Dutch people have become more individualized. The traditional sense of community is breaking down in Holland as it is (or has) throughout most of the industrialized world. But it was this solid sense of community that many held to be one of the strongest explanations for the famous Dutch tolerance. The philosophy of humane paternalism weakens considerably when people start thinking more as individuals than as members of the community. When many of those associated with the "crime problem" are people of color coming from places like Surinam and Morocco, the majority group is even less likely to think of them as members of the community and deal with them with even less tolerance.

Along with increased industrialization and urbanization, Dutch policy-making institutions and the Dutch criminal justice system are becoming more bureaucratized and more "managerialist" in their approach to social problems. Kelk puts it eloquently, writing,

> The bastion of Justice has not remained unaffected by all this. There, too, people have come to think in terms of "business," emphasizing "output" and "product-management," of being organized according to the requirements of efficiency.... We must conclude that an impersonal society is producing an increasingly impersonal system of penal law.... All of this boils down to a process of diminishing tolerance in the traditional Dutch sense. It can be seen in our attitude towards ethnic minorities, people on social security, and other weak groups in society. We take less care of the weak.... In criminal law this means that the traditionally good things about penitentiary law, the guarantees of criminal procedure and sentencing, the things that form, as it were, the conscience of criminal law, are overshadowed by identification with a purely instrumental way of thinking that, in the end, constitutes pure deterioration of fundamental values.[11]

Modernization, bureaucratization, and increased managerialism certainly do not distinguish the Netherlands from most other European countries; but nor does its incarceration rate (as noted, it is roughly at the European average). These trends, however, likely represent a more radical break from the recent past in the Netherlands than in other European countries and, therefore, may, in part explain the recent and extraordinary growth in the Dutch incarceration rate.

THE FUTURE

It is, of course, difficult to predict the future of incarceration trends in the Netherlands because it depends on the future of so many factors already mentioned here and many other factors not mentioned here. Much depends upon the future of global financial integration. If it continues on its present trajectory, so too might the Dutch incarceration rate as well as rates in most other countries. This could happen for a number of reasons. First as "free markets" expand their influence and as financial interests become increasingly competitive, social welfare provisions are often first on the chopping block as governments strive to make their economies "leaner and meaner." European states have already cut back on their social welfare provisions, providing less and less in the way of a safety net for those being left behind; consequently, further cutbacks could exacerbate problems of crime. Second, as governments, economies, and industries become leaner and meaner, it may well be that this attitude will influence people in their social relations; the Dutch sense of community may be further compromised and, thus, people may become increasingly less tolerant of criminal offenders. And finally, with capitalism ascendant, more power will concentrate in the hands of a few. History has shown that, in times of crises, those in power can very effectively shift blame for society's problems from themselves onto those with the least power in society, resulting in elevated, and sometimes horrific, levels of punitiveness. All of these trends have to do with the intensification of capitalism around the world. There needs to be more research examining the relationship between capitalism, globalization, crime and incarceration.

Two recent high-profile murders have put what was left of the famous Dutch tolerance to a further test. The first was the assassination of Pim Fortuyn in May of 2002, and the second was the murder of Theo van Gogh in November 2004. Both of these murders brought the issues of tolerance and immigration to the forefront of political discourse in the Netherlands. Fortuyn was a popular right-wing politician who campaigned on an anti-immigrant platform and van Gogh was a film-maker who had made a documentary critical of radical Islam's treatment of women. The latter was brutally murdered by a member of a radical Islamic group. These murders have stoked anti-immigrant sentiments in the Netherlands, and it would not be surprising to find that they have solidified support for increasing punitiveness in the Dutch criminal justice system.

Another pull in the direction of continuing growth rates may be the growth of U.S. incarceration rates. The U.S. incarceration rate now tops 700 inmates per 100,000, a rate which many believe to be the highest in the world and a rate that is roughly eight times higher than the Dutch rate. Nils Christie argues that the very high rate of incarceration in the United States (and in Russia) may influence debates in other countries.

> When the USA breaks away from all earlier standards by what she does against parts of her population, and when Russia regresses to her former standards, then a threat is created against what is usually seen as an acceptable number of prisoners across the industrialized world. A new frame of reference is established. As a result, Western Europe might have increasing difficulty in preserving its relatively humane penal policies.[12]

And as David Downes writes, "The chiché that what happened in California yesterday is happening in the rest of America today, and will happen in Europe tomorrow, cannot be lightly dismissed."[13]

CRITICAL THINKING QUESTIONS

What are the similarities between U.S. and Dutch incarceration trends? Do these trends have similar explanations? Do you think these trends are likely to occur in other parts of the world? Why or why not?

NOTES

1. Franke, H., "Dutch Tolerance: Facts and Fables." *British Journal of Criminology*, 1990, vol. 30, no. 1, pp. 81–93.
2. Christie, N., *Crime Control as Industry: Toward Gulags Western Style*, 3rd edition. London: Routledge, 2000.
3. Tak, P., "Sentencing and Punishment in The Netherlands." In M. Tonry and R. Frase (Eds.), *Sentencing and Sanctions in Western Countries*. New York: Oxford, 2001, pp. 151–187.
4. Tak, P., "Sentencing and Punishment in The Netherlands." In M. Tonry and R. Frase (Eds.), *Sentencing and Sanctions in Western Countries*. New York: Oxford, 2001, p. 179.
5. Downes, D., "The Buckling of the Shields: Dutch Penal Policy: 1985–1995." In R. Weiss and N. South (Eds.), *Comparing Prison Systems: Toward a Comparative and International Penology*. Amsterdam: Gordon Breach Publishers, 1998, p. 147.
6. Downes, D., "The Buckling of the Shields: Dutch Penal Policy: 1985–1995." In R. Weiss and N. South (Eds.), *Comparing Prison Systems: Toward a Comparative and International Penology*. Amsterdam: Gordon Breach Publishers, 1998, p. 147.
7. *Statistical Yearbook of the Netherlands*. 2000. Voorburg: Statistics Netherlands.
8. Aromaa, K., "Trends in Criminality." In *Crime and Criminal Justice in Europe*. Strasbourg: Council of Europe, 2000, p. 30.
9. Tak, P., "Sentencing and Punishment in The Netherlands." In M. Tonry and R. Frase (Eds.), *Sentencing and Sanctions in Western Countries*. New York: Oxford, 2001, 151–187.

10. Tak, P., "Sentencing and Punishment in The Netherlands." In M. Tonry and R. Frase (Eds.), *Sentencing and Sanctions in Western Countries*. New York: Oxford, 2001, p. 179.

11. Kelk, C., "Criminal Justice in the Netherlands." In P. Fennell, C. Harding, and N. Jorg (Eds.), *Criminal Justice in Europe: A Comparative Study*. Oxford: Clarendon Press, 1995, pp. 5–7.

12. Christie, N., *Crime Control as Industry: Toward Gulags Western Style*, 3rd edition. London: Routledge, 2001, p. 110.

13. Downes, D., "The Macho Penal Economy: Mass Incarceration in the United States—A European Perspective." In D. Garland (Ed.), *Mass Imprisonment: Social Causes and Consequences*. London: Sage Publications, 2001, p. 56.

CHAPTER 21

First, Reduce Harm

Vince Beiser

On a chilly, overcast morning in downtown Vancouver, British Columbia, a steady trickle of sallow-faced drug addicts shambles up to a storefront painted with flowers and the words "Welcome to Insite." One by one, they ring the doorbell and are buzzed into a tidy reception area staffed by smiling volunteers.

The junkies come here almost around the clock, seven days a week. Some just grab a fistful of clean syringes from one of the buckets by the door and head out again. But about 600 times a day, others walk in with pocketfuls of heroin, cocaine or speed that they've scored out on the street; sign in; go to a clean, well-lit room lined with stainless steel booths; and, under the protective watch of two nurses, shoot their drugs into their veins.

Welcome to North America's only officially sanctioned "supervised injection site." The facility sits in the heart of Vancouver's Downtown East Side, 10 square blocks that compose one of the poorest neighborhoods in all of Canada. The area is home to an estimated 4,700 intravenous drug users and thousands of crack addicts. For years, it's been a world-class health disaster, not to mention a public relations nightmare for a town that is famous for its beautiful mountains and beaches (and is gearing up to host the 2010 Winter Olympics). Nearly a third of the Downtown East Side's inhabitants are estimated to be HIV-positive, according to the United Nations Population Fund, a rate on par with Botswana's. Twice that number have hepatitis C. Dozens die of drug overdoses every year.

Largely in response to this nightmare neighborhood, Canada's third largest city has embarked on a radical experiment: Over the last several years, it has overhauled its police and social services practices to re-frame drug use as primarily a public health issue, not a criminal one. In the process, it has become by far the continent's most drug-tolerant city, launching an experiment dramatically at odds with the U.S. War on Drugs.

Smoking weed has been effectively decriminalized. The famous "B.C. bud," rivaled in potency only by California's finest, is puffed so widely and openly that the city has earned the nickname "Vansterdam." A single block in the Downtown

East Side hosts several pot seed wholesalers, the headquarters of the British Columbia Marijuana Party and the toking-allowed New Amsterdam Café.

But that's nothing next to the city's approach to drugs like heroin and crack. Impelled by the horror show of the Downtown East Side, prodded by activists and convinced by reams of academic studies, the police and city government have agreed to provide hard drug users with their paraphernalia, a place to use it and even, for a few, the drugs themselves.

More than 2 million syringes are handed out free every year. Clean mouthpieces for crack pipes are provided at taxpayers' expense. Around 4,000 opiate addicts get prescription methadone. Thousands come to the injection site every year.

On top of that, health officials just wrapped up a pilot program in which addicts were given prescription heroin. And it doesn't stop there. The mayor is pushing for a "stimulant maintenance" program to provide prescription alternatives for cocaine and methamphetamine addicts. Emboldened advocates for drug users are even calling for a "supervised inhalation site" for crack smokers.

Vancouver has essentially become a gigantic field test, a 2 million-person laboratory for a set of tactics derived from a school of thought known as "harm reduction." It's based on a simple premise: No matter how many scare tactics are tried, laws passed or punishments imposed, people are going to get high. From winemaking monks to coca-leaf-chewing Bolivian peasants to peyote-chomping Navajos to caffeine-fueled office workers to the junkies of Vansterdam, human beings have never been willing to settle for our inherently limited palette of states of consciousness.

If you accept the notion that people aren't going to stop abusing drugs, it makes sense to try to minimize the damage they inflict on themselves and the rest of us while they're at it. Harm reduction is less about compassion than it is about enlightened self-interest. The idea is to give addicts clean needles and mouthpieces not to be nice but so they don't get HIV or pneumonia from sharing equipment and then become a burden on the public health system. Give them a medically supervised place to shoot up so they don't overdose and clog up emergency rooms, leaving their infected needles behind on the sidewalk. Give them methadone—or even heroin—for free so they don't break into cars and homes to get money for the next fix.

These aren't just theoretical notions. Some harm reduction tactics have been researched extensively—and the findings are often impressive. In recent years, no fewer than eight major studies in the U.S. on needle-exchange programs— probably the best-known and most widespread harm reduction technique—have concluded that they work. As then–Assistant Surgeon General David Satcher summed up in a 2000 report, "There is conclusive scientific evidence that syringe exchange programs...are an effective public health intervention that reduces the transmission of HIV and does not encourage the use of illegal drugs."

Methadone maintenance, first introduced in the 1960s, has been the subject of hundreds of scientific studies. "The findings...have been consistent," according to a recent article in the Mount Sinai Journal of Medicine. "Methadone maintenance reduces and/or eliminates the use of heroin, reduces the death rates and criminality associated with heroin use and allows patients to improve their health and social productivity. In addition, enrollment in methadone maintenance has the potential to reduce the transmission of infectious diseases associated with heroin injection, such as hepatitis and HIV."

In Vancouver, harm reduction seems to be delivering. Since the city began seriously supporting needle exchanges and other such tactics in the 1990s, HIV infections have fallen by half, and hepatitis C rates have plunged by two-thirds, according to city and provincial health authorities. The annual number of drug-induced deaths has dropped from a peak of 191 in 1998 to 46 in 2005, the most recent year for which statistics are available.

Nonetheless, harm reduction remains controversial, even in relatively liberal Vancouver. "People are always going to beat each other up, too—so should we be handing out boxing gloves to reduce the harm they do?" asks Al Arsenault, a recently retired Vancouver cop who spent much of his 27-year career in the Downtown East Side and now makes documentaries about the area. "That's just normalizing the behavior. The whole premise is nonsense."

It took a careful, sustained campaign to convince politicians and a critical mass of voters that such critics were misguided. Philip Owen, who as Vancouver's mayor from 1993 to 2002 was one of the key forces pushing the city to embrace harm reduction, was convinced by the research on the subject, some of which was brought to his attention by the U.S.-based Drug Policy Alliance Network and other advocacy groups.

Once on board, Owen set about building support. "You need to walk slowly before you can run," he says. Owen organized dozens of public meetings with community groups and cultivated provincial and federal officials. He even took the then-federal Minister of Health on an undercover tour, both of them wearing blue jeans and old hats, of the Downtown East Side to see the problem firsthand.

Owen's groundwork helped Vancouver secure a special exception to federal drug laws that allowed Insite to open. The heroin maintenance program won approval on a trial basis. "If you set something like that up as a scientific experiment rather than a policy change, it's easier to sell," says Ethan Nadelmann, executive director of the Drug Policy Alliance Network. Meanwhile, a local activist group, the Vancouver Area Network of Drug Users, kept up the pressure with noisy street demonstrations.

A quick visit to the Downtown East Side is enough to convince anyone that the city had to do something. The area was always sketchy, but Vancouver's booming economy and rapid growth have combined to gentrify most of downtown, pushing the dope fiends and crackheads and mentally ill homeless into an ever smaller, more densely concentrated island of cheap housing, where their addictions and pathologies and sundry bad behaviors feed on each other.

Today, the Downtown East Side protrudes like a gangrenous limb from the city's sleek core. Literally from one block to the next, a world of chic clothing boutiques, jewelry shops and high-rise luxury condos suddenly gives way to Planet Junkie. Haggard, prematurely aged men and women with sunken cheeks, missing teeth and feral expressions drift along trash-strewn sidewalks lined with abandoned buildings. The only legitimate businesses are check-cashing operations, pawn shops, bars, squalid residential hotels and 24-hour convenience stores with barred doors and windows. It's a bit like an unsupervised, open-air hospice where the patients have been left to find their own medications and get them into their bodies however they see fit, a dark carnival of misery smack in the middle of what *The Economist* recently dubbed "the most livable city in the world."

In just an hour of randomly walking around one recent morning, I passed at least a dozen people smoking crack in plain view, stepped over countless discarded needles and turned down muttered offers of a whole pharmacopeia of substances. The worst that police are likely to do to street-level users is take away their drugs. That evening, I accompanied a couple of constables walking the beat who passed a grizzled man with long, greasy hair smoking crack at a bus stop on busy Hastings Street. Sighing at his stupidity—couldn't he have at least gone around the corner into an alley?—the cops made him drop his pipe, crushed it underfoot, gave him a warning and walked away without even searching him.

That's more or less official policy. "If you look at an addicted drug user, who likely has a mental illness, you have to ask, 'What's the best bang for our buck?'" says Inspector Scott Thompson, the Vancouver Police Department's drug policy coordinator. "If we lock them up, it costs between $75,000 and $90,000 per year. By dealing with it as a health issue, we'll save a lot of money and hopefully solve more problems." The department focuses instead on traffickers and producers, he says.

Efforts to keep drug use as healthy as possible are everywhere in the Downtown East Side. Free needles, tourniquets and clean crack-pipe mouthpieces are available in soup kitchens and clinics on practically every block. Blue metal syringe disposal boxes are installed at alley entrances.

The supervised injection site is the most visible and controversial of these measures. Opened in late 2003, it's a newer and much-less-tested tactic than needle exchange. So far, a flock of peer-reviewed studies has found the program has not led to increased crime or drug use in the area. Last March, a report commissioned by the Canadian federal government concluded that "(t)here was no evidence of increases in drug-related loitering, drug dealing or petty crime in areas around Insite...(and) police data for the (Downtown East Side) and surrounding areas showed no changes in rates of crime." Moreover, the report noted, "(T)here is no evidence that (supervised injection sites) influence rates of drug use in the community or increase relapse rates among injection drug users."

In short, Insite is not making things worse. But is it making anything better? Studies indicate that Insite has reduced needle sharing, one of the major transmission routes for HIV. But Colin Mangham, a researcher with the Drug Prevention Network of Canada, points out that much of the data is based on injection drug users' reporting of their own behavior—not exactly the gold standard of credibility.

The facility is, however, clearly saving at least some lives. Its staff has intervened in more than 336 potential overdoses. Rico Machado, a surprisingly healthy-looking heroin addict whom I met in Insite's check-in area, was one of those cases. "I did my normal dose, but this stuff was too strong," he says. "I hit the ground. But they gave me Narcan (a drug that reverses opiate overdoses) and resuscitated me. Before this place was open, I would have been in an alley. I would have been dead."

Moreover, Insite has provided a gateway into detox programs for a number of addicts and served as an immunization center during a recent pneumonia outbreak. The site has even added a small residential rehab facility.

A couple of blocks away, a small clinic is stashed behind papered-over windows on the ground floor of an unmarked, 1930s-era building. Here, every day for three years, nurses behind bulletproof glass handed dozens of addicts a tourniquet, a needle, an alcohol swab and a carefully measured dose of pure heroin.

The theory being tested in this program, which wound up its pilot phase in August, was that it would keep junkies from having to steal or prostitute themselves for their fixes. As a side benefit, they would have more time and energy to take advantage of the program's treatment component.

Official results were slated to be released in October, after this story was published. Dr. David Marsh, the program's medical director, says he's already seen its participants benefit. "They're eating better, getting their health problems dealt with, getting into better housing," he says. "Some are even going back to work. One guy started out homeless, got clean and now runs a business with 15 employees."

Much of what Vancouver is doing is already long-standing policy in many countries, especially in Europe. Methadone and needle-exchange programs are commonplace in many nations. Six European countries and Australia are home to dozens of supervised injection sites. Holland, Denmark, Switzerland, Germany and Spain have experimented with heroin maintenance. Even Iran, of all places, recently launched a pilot program to distribute clean needles through vending machines.

In the United States, however, conservative politics and "Drug-Free America" rhetoric keep punishment as the primary response to drug use. Mandatory minimum sentencing and "three strikes" laws have sent the number of drug offenders in America's prisons skyrocketing. There are more than half a million inmates currently locked up on narcotics charges—more than the total of all prisoners in 1980. Each of those prisoners costs taxpayers on average more than $22,000 per year, according to the federal Bureau of Justice Statistics—several times the price of providing them with treatment.

The U.S. doesn't seem to be gaining much from the billions of dollars it invests in incarcerating drug offenders. Perhaps the decades-long "War on Drugs" has kept illicit substance use from growing, but it certainly hasn't done anything to reduce it. The most recent annual survey of drug use by the University of Michigan found that about 85 percent of 12th-graders in America say marijuana is easy to get. Almost 1 in 3 of those teenagers has smoked up in the past year, a number that has not changed much over the last 30 years.

All told, some 8 percent of Americans over age 12—about 20 million people—use illicit drugs, according to the most recent estimates from the U.S. Department of Health. That's a higher rate than the same agency found in the early 1990s. More than 1 in 3 Americans—including, by their own admissions, Sarah Palin and Barack Obama—have tried some kind of illicit substance at least once.

Meanwhile, tens of thousands of people in the U.S. are infected with HIV or hepatitis C every year thanks to shared needles. And according to the Centers for Disease Control and Prevention, nearly 20,000 people died of drug overdoses in 2004—the most recent year for which statistics are available—way up from the 12,000 reported fatal ODs in 1999.

No surprise, then, that there is a small movement pushing for more harm-reduction-based policies. Voters in California, Arizona and Maryland have passed initiatives in recent years mandating treatment instead of incarceration for first-time drug offenders. Not long ago, needle-exchange programs were banned everywhere; now there are nearly 200 such programs in 38 states.

The liberal, forward-operating base of San Francisco is at the vanguard of these efforts. Surging overdose deaths among the city's estimated 16,000 intravenous drug users spurred the city to officially embrace harm reduction in 2000. "We've tried to take drug addiction from being seen as a moral issue to being seen instead as a chronic disease," says Barbara Garcia, deputy director of the San Francisco Department of Public Health.

Today, a welter of programs hands out more than 2 million clean syringes every year, more than in any other city. At one storefront needle exchange in the notoriously skivey Tenderloin district, for instance, visitors can choose from three different sizes of syringes; speed shooters and junkies with narrow veins prefer smaller hardware. They can also pick up little metal cups and tubes of sterile water to cook the drugs in, hand wipes and alcohol swabs to clean their skin before stabbing it and other handy accessories, including tourniquets and crack-pipe mouthpieces.

One recent evening, Ian Johnson, a veteran local drug user dressed in pin-striped slacks, a soiled white shirt with a neatly knotted tie and a stained double-breasted jacket two shades darker than his pants, came in for another service: overdose prevention training. A friend had recently died from a too-big shot of heroin, he explained, and he didn't want to see that again. A volunteer trainer sat Johnson down with a torso-and-head CPR mannequin and showed him how to inject a dose of Narcan into someone's shoulder. Satisfied that Johnson had the simple procedure down, the trainer passed him along to a nurse who wrote a prescription making it legal for Johnson to walk out with a little black plastic box containing two needles and a vial of Narcan.

More than 1,200 people have been trained to administer Narcan this way, and trainees have used it at least 260 times to intervene in potentially fatal overdoses, according to the Harm Reduction Coalition, a nonprofit group that runs the trainings for the city. San Francisco also puts up the money to give methadone to about 5,000 people a year and to train dozens of "peer counselors"—current and former speed users—to advise their drug buddies on basics like remembering to eat while on multiday meth binges. There's even talk of opening a supervised injection site.

Outside of New York, Baltimore, Chicago and a few other places, though, harm reduction is a tough sell in the United States. Congress forbids federal dollars from funding needle exchanges. In many jurisdictions, it's illegal to possess a syringe without a prescription, making widespread needle distribution impossible, no matter who funds it. Federal drug czar John Walters has denounced Vancouver's Insite program as "state-sponsored suicide" and harm reduction in general as a Trojan horse for the goal of legalizing drugs outright.

Even in Canada, the Vancouver experiment is under pressure. The country's ruling Conservative Party has denounced the safe injection site and is pushing for a tougher line against drugs nationwide. "Allowing and/or encouraging people to inject heroin into their veins is not harm reduction," said Health Minister Tony Clement at a recent AIDS conference. "We believe it is a form of harm addition."

At first blush, the proposition that making drug use easier for addicts will benefit everyone does seem a bit far-fetched. As many critics have pointed out, it seems to send the message that hard drug use is all right, as long as you're careful about it. It's a message that, critics insist, could lead more people to experiment with narcotics and leave fewer addicts inclined to seek treatment.

Though the "wrong message" idea makes intuitive sense, the overwhelming preponderance of research on the subject does not bear it out. Over and over again, studies find that measures like needle exchange and even supervised injection sites do not promote drug use and do help curb some of the damage it causes.

The critique of harm reduction best supported by actual evidence is that it doesn't do enough.

"The harm reduction approach within the UK appears to have had only modest success in reducing the breadth of drug-related harms," University of Glasgow researcher Neil McKeganey wrote in a recent overview published in the journal Addiction Research & Theory. "Despite a plethora of initiatives aimed at increasing drug (injectors') awareness of the risks of needle and syringe sharing, and of providing drug users with access to sterile injecting equipment, around a third of injectors are still sharing injecting equipment."

That's a weighty objection to Insite, considering the facility costs $3 million a year to operate. On a typical day, only about 5 percent of all injections in the Downtown East Side are done in the facility's relative safety, according to the federal government's study. I found discarded syringes in the alley right behind Insite.

Creating a safe place to shoot up may make good sense, but that's not necessarily relevant to people whose cravings regularly trump their judgment. Watching Liane Gladue, a longtime junkie, searching for a vein under a streetlight in a Downtown East Side alley, I asked why she didn't go instead to the injection site just a few blocks away. "It's too crowded in there," she answered. "I didn't want to wait."

Though Vancouver is cutting the collateral damage caused by hard drugs, the city is making far less progress in reducing the number of users. Surveys report that drug use is higher in British Columbia than in the rest of Canada. A recent poll found that almost half of all Vancouverites consider drugs a major problem in their communities—a figure double that for residents of Canada's biggest cities, Toronto and Montreal.

With serious drug users come rip-offs, break-ins and holdups for fix money. So it's no surprise that Vancouver's property crime and bank robbery rates are higher than most of Canada's. The city also has more gun-related crimes per capita than any other in the nation, a fact at least one criminologist has linked to the number of substance abusers.

All of this underscores why widespread drug addiction is ultimately everybody's problem. Obviously, getting street addicts to clean up takes more than free needles. It takes affordable housing, mental health services, counseling and treatment, all of which are in short supply, even in Vancouver. For some addicts, it might also take the threat of jail.

But it doesn't have to be an either/or choice. As the American Medical Association states in its official position on the issue, "Harm reduction...can coexist, and is not incompatible, with a goal of abstinence for a drug-dependent person, or a policy of 'zero-tolerance' for society."

Advocating anything that sounds "soft on drugs" is generally considered political suicide for elected officials in most parts of the U.S. But as Vancouver has proved, a coalition of health care officials, activists and courageous politicians armed with solid data can change that equation. "No one in the U.S. wants to touch this stuff because they're afraid they won't get elected if they do," says Philip Owen, Vancouver's former mayor. "Well, I was re-elected three times."

CRITICAL THINKING QUESTIONS

What do you think of the services offered by Insite? The author indicates that a program such as the one at Insite is not likely to be politically feasible in the United States today. Do you think such programs might become feasible when the next generation of political leaders take the reins of government?

CHAPTER 22

Rx Drugs

60 Minutes

TRANSCRIPT

ED BRADLEY: Can Britain teach us anything about dealing with drug addicts? That remains to be seen, but one thing seems certain, there's little or nothing we can teach them. They tried our hard-line methods back in the '70s and '80s and all they got for their trouble was more drugs, more crime and more addicts. So they went back to their way, letting doctors prescribe whatever drug a particular addict was hooked on. Does it work? If they're ever going to know, Liverpool, where drugs are out of control, is the place to find out.

This is a gram of 100 percent pure heroin. It's pharmaceutically prepared. On the streets, it would be cut 10 to 15 times and sell for about $2,000. But take it away from the black market, make it legal and heroin's a pretty cheap drug. The British National Health Service pays about $10 for this gram of heroin and for an addict with a prescription, it's free.

(Footage of Dr. John Marks sitting at his desk)

BRADLEY: *(Voiceover)* In Britain, doctors who hold a special license from the government are allowed to prescribe hard drugs to addicts. Dr. John Marks, a psychiatrist who runs an addiction clinic just outside Liverpool, has been prescribing heroin for years.

DR. JOHN MARKS *(Runs Addiction Clinic in Liverpool)*: If they're drug takers determined to continue their drug use, treating them is an expensive waste of time. And really the choice that I'm being offered and society is being offered is drugs from the clinic or drugs from the Mafia.

(Footage of a woman dispensing a drug and a patient talking to Dr. Marks, a nurse and a social worker)

BRADLEY: *(Voiceover)* To get drugs from the clinic rather than from the Mafia, addicts have to take a urine test to prove they're taking the drugs they say they are. And unlike most other addiction clinics, where you have to say you want to kick the habit before they'll take you in, addicts here have to convince Dr. Marks, a nurse, and a social worker that they intend to stay on drugs come what may. But doesn't Dr. Marks try to cure people?

DR. MARKS: Cure people? No. Nobody can. Regardless of whether you stick them in prison, put them in mental hospitals and give them electric shocks—we've done all these things—put them in a nice rehab center away in the country; give them a social worker; pat them on the head. Give them drugs; give them no drugs. Doesn't matter what you do. Five percent per annum, one in 20 per year, get off spontaneously. Compound interested up, that reaches about 50 percent. Fifty-fifty after 10 years are off. They seem to mature out of addiction regardless of any intervention in the interim. But you can keep them alive and healthy and legal during that 10 years if you so wish to.

BRADLEY: By giving them drugs?

DR. MARKS: It doesn't get them off drugs. It doesn't prolong their addiction either. But it stops them offending; it keeps them healthy and it keeps them alive.

(Footage of Julia pushing her daughter on a swing)

BRADLEY: *(Voiceover)* That's exactly what happened to Julia. Although she doesn't look it, Julia is a heroin addict. For the last three years, the heroin she injects every day comes through a prescription. Before she had to feed her habit by working as a prostitute, a vicious circle that led her to use more heroin to cope with that life.

JULIA *(Heroin Addict)*: And once you get in that circle, you can't get out. And I didn't think I was ever going to get out.

BRADLEY: But once you got the prescription…

JULIA: I stopped straight away.

BRADLEY: Never went back?

JULIA: No, I've never. I went back once just to see, and I was almost physically sick just to see these girls doing what I used to do.

(Footage of Julia talking to her daughter)

BRADLEY: *(Voiceover)* Julia says she's now able to have normal relationships, to hold down a job as a waitress and to care for her three-year-old daughter.

Without that prescription, where do you think you'd be today?

JULIA: I'd probably be dead by now.

DR. MARKS: OK.

UNIDENTIFIED MAN: OK.

DR. MARKS: One sixty then…

MAN: If I can, yes.

DR. MARKS: …of heroin.

(Footage of a man sitting in Dr. Marks' office)

BRADLEY: *(Voiceover)* Once they've got their prescriptions, addicts must show up for regular meetings to show they're staying healthy and free from crime. But how can anyone be healthy if they're taking a drug like heroin?

MR. ALLAN PARRY *(Former Drug Information Officer)*: Pure heroin is not dangerous. We have people on massive doses of heroin.

(Footage of Parry talking to Bradley)

BRADLEY: *(Voiceover)* Allan Parry is a former drug information officer for the local health authority and now a counselor at the clinic. So how come we see so much damage caused by heroin?

MR. PARRY: The heroin that is causing that damage is not causing damage because of the heroin in it. It's causing the damage because of brick dust in it, coffee, crushed bleach crystals, anything. That causes the harm. And if heroin is 90 percent adulterated, that means only 10 percent is heroin; the rest is rubbish. Now you inject cement into your veins, and you don't have to be a medical expert to work out that's going to cause harm.

OK, George, let's put your leg up. Let's have a look.

(Footage of George having his leg looked at)

BRADLEY: *(Voiceover)* Many at the clinic, like George, still suffer from the damage caused by street drugs. Allan Parry believes you can't prescribe clean drugs and needles to addicts without teaching them how to use them.

(Footage of George in the office)

MR. PARRY: *(Voiceover)* The other major cause of ill health to drug injectors is not even the dirty drugs they take; it's their bad technique, not knowing how to do it.

I've seen drug users in the States with missing legs and arms, and that is through bad technique.

Can I have a look at your arms. Have you been...

(Footage of George in the office)

BRADLEY: *(Voiceover)* George's legs have ulcerated and the veins in his arms have collapsed. To inject, he must use a vein in his groin which is dangerously close to an artery.

MR. PARRY: Now when you go in there, you getting any sharp pains?

GEORGE *(Addict)*: No.

MR. PARRY: If you hit the artery, how would you recognize it?

GEORGE: If I hit the artery?

MR. PARRY: Yeah.

GEORGE: By me head hitting the ceiling.

MR. PARRY: So we show people how to—not how to inject safely, but how to inject less dangerously. We have to be clear about that. You know, stoned people sticking needles into themselves is a dangerous activity, but the strategy is called "harm minimization."

(Footage of a billboard with the words: Heroin screws you up; police entering a building and a man under arrest)

BRADLEY: *(Voiceover)* In the '70s, the British weren't content with minimizing the harm of drug abuse. They adopted the American policy of trying to stamp it out altogether. Prescription drugs were no longer widely available, and addicts who couldn't kick the habit had to find illegal sources. The result? By the end of the '80s, drug addiction in Britain had tripled. In Liverpool, there was so much heroin around it was known as smack city. And then came a greater threat.

More than anything else, it's been the threat of AIDS that has persuaded the British to return to their old policy of maintaining addicts on their drug of choice. In New York, it's estimated that more than half of those who inject drugs have contracted the AIDS virus through swapping contaminated needles. Here in Liverpool, the comparable number—the number of known addicts infected—is less than 1 percent.

(Footage of a pharmacist Jeremy Clitherow dispensing cigarettes containing heroin)

BRADLEY: *(Voiceover)* In an effort to get addicts away from injecting, Liverpool pharmacist Jeremy Clitherow has developed what he calls "heroin reefers." They're regular cigarettes with heroin in them. Whatever you feel about smoking, he says, these cigarettes hold fewer risks than needles for both the addicts and the community.

MR. JEREMY CLITHEROW *(Pharmacist)*: So we then use this to put in a known volume of pharmaceutical heroin into the patient's cigarette. And there we are, one heroin reefer containing exactly 60 milligrams of pharmaceutical heroin.

BRADLEY: So the National Health Service will pay for the heroin, but not for the cigarettes.

MR. CLITHEROW: Oh yes. Yes, of course. It's the patient's own cigarette, but with the National Health prescription put into it.

(Footage of the outside of Clitherow's pharmacy and people waiting in line inside the store)

BRADLEY: *(Voiceover)* Addicts pick up their prescriptions twice a week from his neighborhood pharmacy. And how does this affect his other customers?

MR. CLITHEROW: *(Voiceover)* The patient who comes in to pick up a prescription of heroin in the form of reefers would be indistinguishable from a patient who picks up any other medication.

PAUL *(Heroin Addict)*: Good morning.

MR. CLITHEROW: Hello, Paul. How are you doing?

PAUL: Fine.

MR. CLITHEROW: All right.

PAUL: Cigarettes next—next week?

MR. CLITHEROW: That's my sheet. Anything else we can do for you?

PAUL: No, that's fine...

MR. CLITHEROW: The prescription is ready and waiting, and they pick it up just as they would pick up their Paracetamol, aspirin or bandages.

BRADLEY: But with all of these drugs available to—to—to most people, plus the hard drugs which you have here, what's your security like?

MR. CLITHEROW: Like Fort Knox. But we keep minimal stocks. We buy the stuff in—regularly, frequently. It comes in, goes out.

(Footage of Clitherow filling a prescription)

BRADLEY: *(Voiceover)* And heroin isn't the only stuff to come in and out of here. Clitherow also fills prescriptions for cocaine, and that's 100 percent pure freebase cocaine—in other words, crack.

So in fact when you're putting cocaine in here...

MR. CLITHEROW: Yes.

BRADLEY:...you're actually making crack cigarettes?

MR. CLITHEROW: Yes.

BRADLEY: In America that has a very negative connotation...

MR. CLITHEROW: Mm-hmm.

BRADLEY:...but not for you?

MR. CLITHEROW: It depends which way you look at it. If they continue to buy on the street, whether it's heroin, methadone, crack or whatever, sooner or later they will suffer from the—the merchandise that they are buying. I want to bring them into contact with the system. And let's give them their drug of choice—if the physician agrees and prescribes it—in a form which won't cause their health such awful deterioration.

BRADLEY: And you don't have any problems giving people injectable cocaine or cocaine cigarettes.

DR. MARKS: No, not in principle. I mean, there are—there are patients to whom I've prescribed cocaine and to whom I've then stopped prescribing the cocaine because their lives do not stabilize. They continue to be thieves or whatever. But there are equally many more to whom we prescribe cocaine who've then settled to regular, sensible lives.

(Footage of Mike)

BRADLEY: *(Voiceover)* Mike is one of those who has settled into a regular, sensible life on cocaine. He has a prescription from Dr. Marks for both the cocaine spray and the cocaine cigarettes. Before he got that prescription, the cocaine he bought on the street cost him $1,000 a week, which at first he managed to take from his own business. But it wasn't long before it cost him much more than that.

So you lost your business.

MIKE *(Cocaine Addict)*: Yeah.

BRADLEY: You lost your—your wife.

MIKE: Yeah.

BRADLEY: You lost the kids.

MIKE: Yeah.

BRADLEY: And the house.

MIKE: Yeah.

BRADLEY: But you kept going after the cocaine.

MIKE: Yeah. That's what addiction is. That's the whole—the very nature of addiction is the fact that one is virtually—chemically and physically—forced to continue that way.

(Footage of Mike sitting in a chair writing)

BRADLEY: *(Voiceover)* Now after two years of controlled use on prescription cocaine, Mike has voluntarily reduced his dose. He's got himself a regular job with a trucking company and is slowly putting his life back together again.

Where do you think you would be now if—if Dr. Marks had not given you a—a prescription for cocaine?

MIKE: I wouldn't be here now talking to you, and you probably wouldn't be interested in talking to me, either. I'd be on the street.

BRADLEY: Dr. Marks, how would you reply to critics who would say that you're nothing more than a legalized dealer, a pusher?

DR. MARKS: I'd agree. That's what the state of England arranges, that there's a legal, controlled supply of drugs. The whole concept behind this is control.

(Footage of Bradley talking to Parry while they're walking outside)

BRADLEY: *(Voiceover)* And there are signs that control is working. Within the area of the clinic, Allan Parry says the police have reported a significant drop in drug-related crime. And since addicts don't have to deal anymore to support their habit, they're not recruiting new customers. So far fewer new people are being turned on to drugs.

What do the dealers around the area of the clinic think about it all?

MR. PARRY: *(Voiceover)* Well, there aren't any around the clinic.

BRADLEY: *(Voiceover)* You—you've taken away their business.

MR. PARRY: Exactly. There's no business there. The scene is disappearing. So if you want to get rid of your drug problem, which presumably all societies do, there are ways of doing it, but you have to counter your own moral and political prejudice.

BRADLEY: What would you say to people who would ask, "Why give addicts what they want? Why give them drugs?"

JULIA: So they can live. So they have a chance to live like everyone else does. No one would hesitate to give other sorts of maintaining drugs to diabetics. Diabetics have insulin. In my mind it's no different. It's the same. I need heroin to live.

(Show motif)
(Announcements)

CRITICAL THINKING QUESTION

The two addicts who describe their lives before entering the program describe lifestyles that closely fit popular stereotypes of the drug addict. Once they gain regular access to the drug of their choice, their lifestyles seem to normalize. What are popular stereotypes of drug addicts, and why would these addicts' lifestyles begin to depart from those stereotypes once they acquired regular access to their drugs?

PART VI

Problems of the Environment

This part begins with writer-environmentalist Bill McKibben explaining how different the present is from the past and how different the future will be from the present—in terms of our material expectations and our impact on the environment. If the former does not change significantly, he argues, then the latter will change radically. Put in other terms, if we in the wealthy and the getting-wealthy countries do not temper our appetites moderately, environmental exigencies will force us to do so drastically. The capitalist model calling for continual economic growth, which has served many societies well for centuries, has become environmentally untenable. Perhaps, as McKibben suggests, the capitalist model served us so well because it provided so many with the basic necessities; once it started providing more than the basics, however, it became less correlated with happiness and more with excess and environmental degradation. McKibben finds hope in the new economic field of hedonics, which finds that, beyond the basics threshold, happiness is more likely to be found in things without economic value, which do not strain the environment.

Watching or reading the mainstream news media today, it is pretty clear that climate change is a fact and that human activities are contributing to the problem. But this was not the impression conveyed by the media just a few years ago. Despite the fact that almost all of the climate experts in the world agreed that the world was getting warmer, largely because of industrial and CO_2 emissions, the media gave equal credence to industry's claim that there was no problem—equal credence to the very industries responsible for CO_2 emissions. The next article, "The Establishment vs. the Environment," discusses tactics used by industry to sway the public and the failure of the media to critically examine the evidence—effectively delaying a more timely response, allowing industry to reap more profits, and discrediting the United States in the global community.

Many or most of the poor countries today were once rich in natural resources. Then European colonization spread throughout the world and began extracting these resources and sending them to Europe and, later, to the United States.

Though these countries have been "liberated" of their colonial status, chances are that their most valuable resources are still being extracted and sent to the wealthier countries. The poor have to struggle to survive on what little natural resources are left. As the article from the World Resources Institute indicates, the poor are much more vulnerable to any fluctuations in the supply of environmental resources. Temporary fluctuations in rainfall, for example, can lead to widespread starvation, disease, and death. (Climate change poses a much more real and immediate threat to the poor in the developing world than to those of us living in the First World.) With so many of their resources being exported and with their survival so dependent on what is left, the lives of the poor will become increasingly dependent on good resource management. Wise resource management, argue the authors, will not only help them to survive but may help to pull them out of poverty.

In the United States, the recognition of the connection between environmental problems, poverty, and race gave rise to the environmental justice movement. In the last reading in this part, renowned environmental sociologist Robert Bullard provides an example of environmental injustice by documenting a connection between race and governmental responses to (un)natural disasters. Given the inevitability of hurricanes, floods, and other environmental threats, it is often striking how poorly governmental responses are planned in advance and executed in the aftermath—especially for those areas known to be at greatest risk (e.g., New Orleans)—especially in a society as wealthy as the United States. Many observers suspect that the U.S. government's inadequate response to Hurricane Katrina in 2005—particularly after investing immense resources into homeland security and disaster preparedness—had something to do with the racial composition of the population at risk. Indeed, Bullard finds this interpretation entirely consistent with the history of governmental responses to other "unnatural" disasters in the United States.

While most people may consider the death and destruction following a hurricane a "natural" disaster or an act of God, the fact that these consequences could have been avoided had there been the political will or would have been greatly reduced had the population at risk been white makes them unnatural disasters. While the environmental justice movement has traditionally been concerned with the disproportionate effects of pollution on the poor and minority groups, as weather-related disasters are increasing in both frequency and intensity, the concern of the movement could well shift to focus increasingly on the disproportionate effects of climate change on the poor and minorities. This article, in fact, reveals that minorities and the poor are exposed to disproportionate risk of weather-related disasters *and* to the spread of dangerous environmental contaminants that are frequently released in their aftermath.

CHAPTER 23

Reversal of Fortune

Bill McKibben

The formula for human well-being used to be simple: Make money, get happy. So why is the old axiom suddenly turning on us?

For most of human history, the two birds More and Better roosted on the same branch. You could toss one stone and hope to hit them both. That's why the centuries since Adam Smith launched modern economics with his book *The Wealth of Nations* have been so single-mindedly devoted to the dogged pursuit of maximum economic production. Smith's core ideas—that individuals pursuing their own interests in a market society end up making each other richer; and that increasing efficiency, usually by increasing scale, is the key to increasing wealth—have indisputably worked. They've produced more More than he could ever have imagined. They've built the unprecedented prosperity and ease that distinguish the lives of most of the people reading these words. It is no wonder and no accident that Smith's ideas still dominate our politics, our outlook, even our personalities.

But the distinguishing feature of our moment is this: Better has flown a few trees over to make her nest. And that changes everything. Now, with the stone of your life or your society gripped in your hand, you have to choose. It's More or Better.

Which means, according to new research emerging from many quarters, that our continued devotion to growth above all is, on balance, making our lives worse, both collectively and individually. Growth no longer makes most people wealthier, but instead generates inequality and insecurity. Growth is bumping up against physical limits so profound—like climate change and peak oil—that trying to keep expanding the economy may be not just impossible but also dangerous. And perhaps most surprisingly, growth no longer makes us happier. Given our current dogma, that's as bizarre an idea as proposing that gravity pushes apples skyward. But then, even Newtonian physics eventually shifted to acknowledge Einstein's more complicated universe.

"WE CAN DO IT IF WE BELIEVE IT": FDR, LBJ, AND THE INVENTION OF GROWTH

It was the great economist John Maynard Keynes who pointed out that until very recently, "there was no very great change in the standard of life of the average man living in the civilized centers of the earth." At the utmost, Keynes calculated, the standard of living roughly doubled between 2000 B.C. and the dawn of the 18th century—four millennia during which we basically didn't learn to do much of anything new. Before history began, we had already figured out fire, language, cattle, the wheel, the plow, the sail, the pot. We had banks and governments and mathematics and religion.

And then, something new finally did happen. In 1712, a British inventor named Thomas Newcomen created the first practical steam engine. Over the centuries that followed, fossil fuels helped create everything we consider normal and obvious about the modern world, from electricity to steel to fertilizer; now, a 100 percent jump in the standard of living could suddenly be accomplished in a few decades, not a few millennia.

In some ways, the invention of the idea of economic growth was almost as significant as the invention of fossil-fuel power. But it took a little longer to take hold. During the Depression, even FDR routinely spoke of America's economy as mature, with no further expansion anticipated. Then came World War II and the postwar boom—by the time Lyndon Johnson moved into the White House in 1963, he said things like: "I'm sick of all the people who talk about the things we can't do. Hell, we're the richest country in the world, the most powerful. We can do it all....We can do it if we believe it." He wasn't alone in thinking this way. From Moscow, Nikita Khrushchev thundered, "Growth of industrial and agricultural production is the battering ram with which we shall smash the capitalist system."

Yet the bad news was already apparent, if you cared to look. Burning rivers and smoggy cities demonstrated the dark side of industrial expansion. In 1972, a trio of MIT researchers released a series of computer forecasts they called "limits to growth," which showed that unbridled expansion would eventually deplete our resource base. A year later the British economist E.F. Schumacher wrote the best-selling *Small Is Beautiful*....By 1979, the sociologist Amitai Etzioni reported to President Carter that only 30 percent of Americans were "progrowth," 31 percent were "anti-growth," and 39 percent were "highly uncertain."

Such ambivalence, Etzioni predicted, "is too stressful for societies to endure," and Ronald Reagan proved his point. He convinced us it was "Morning in America"—out with limits, in with Trump. Today, mainstream liberals and conservatives compete mainly on the question of who can flog the economy harder. Larry Summers, who served as Bill Clinton's secretary of the treasury, at one point declared that the Clinton administration "cannot and will not accept any 'speed limit' on American economic growth. It is the task of economic policy to grow the economy as rapidly, sustainably, and inclusively as possible." It's the economy, stupid.

OIL BINGEING, CHINESE CARS, AND THE END
OF THE EASY FIX

Except there are three small things. The first I'll mention mostly in passing: Even though the economy continues to grow, most of us are no longer getting wealthier. The average wage in the United States is less now, in real dollars, than it was 30 years ago. Even for those with college degrees, and although productivity was growing faster than it had for decades, between 2000 and 2004 earnings fell 5.2 percent when adjusted for inflation, according to the most recent data from White House economists. Much the same thing has happened across most of the globe. More than 60 countries around the world, in fact, have seen incomes per capita fall in the past decade.

For the second point, it's useful to remember what Thomas Newcomen was up to when he helped launch the Industrial Revolution—burning coal to pump water out of a coal mine. This revolution both depended on, and revolved around, fossil fuels. "Before coal," writes the economist Jeffrey Sachs, "economic production was limited by energy inputs, almost all of which depended on the production of biomass: food for humans and farm animals, and fuel wood for heating and certain industrial processes." That is, energy depended on how much you could grow. But fossil energy depended on how much had grown eons before—all those billions of tons of ancient biology squashed by the weight of time till they'd turned into strata and pools and seams of hydrocarbons, waiting for us to discover them.

To understand how valuable, and irreplaceable, that lake of fuel was, consider a few other forms of creating usable energy. Ethanol can perfectly well replace gasoline in a tank; like petroleum, it's a way of using biology to create energy, and right now it's a hot commodity, backed with billions of dollars of government subsidies. But ethanol relies on plants that grow anew each year, most often corn; by the time you've driven your tractor to tend the fields, and your truck to carry the crop to the refinery, and powered your refinery, the best-case "energy output-to-input ratio" is something like 1.34-to-1. You've spent 100 Btu of fossil energy to get 134 Btu. Perhaps that's worth doing, but as Kamyar Enshayan of the University of Northern Iowa points out, "it's not impressive" compared to the ratio for oil, which ranges from 30-to-1 to 200-to-1, depending on where you drill it. To go from our fossil-fuel world to a biomass world would be a little like leaving the Garden of Eden for the land where bread must be earned by "the sweat of your brow."

And east of Eden is precisely where we may be headed. As everyone knows, the past three years have seen a spate of reports and books and documentaries suggesting that humanity may have neared or passed its oil peak—that is, the point at which those pools of primeval plankton are half used up, where each new year brings us closer to the bottom of the barrel. The major oil companies report that they can't find enough new wells most years to offset the depletion in the old ones; rumors circulate that the giant Saudi fields are dwindling faster than expected; and, of course, all this is reflected in the cost of oil.

The doctrinaire economist's answer is that no particular commodity matters all that much, because if we run short of something, it will pay for someone to develop a substitute. In general this has proved true in the past: Run short of nice big sawlogs and someone invents plywood. But it's far from clear that the same precept applies to coal, oil, and natural gas. This time, there is no easy substitute: I like the solar panels on my roof, but they're collecting diffuse daily energy, not using up eons of accumulated power. Fossil fuel was an exception to the rule, a one-time gift that underwrote a one-time binge of growth.

This brings us to the third point: If we do try to keep going, with the entire world aiming for an economy structured like America's, it won't be just oil that we'll run short of. Here are the numbers we have to contend with: Given current rates of growth in the Chinese economy, the 1.3 billion residents of that nation alone will, by 2031, be about as rich as we are. If they then eat meat, milk, and eggs at the rate that we do, calculates ecostatistician Lester Brown, they will consume 1,352 million tons of grain each year—equal to two-thirds of the world's entire 2004 grain harvest. They will use 99 million barrels of oil a day, 15 million more than the entire world consumes at present. They will use more steel than all the West combined, double the world's production of paper, and drive 1.1 billion cars—1.5 times as many as the current world total. And that's just China; by then, India will have a bigger population, and its economy is growing almost as fast. And then there's the rest of the world.

Trying to meet that kind of demand will stress the earth past its breaking point in an almost endless number of ways, but let's take just one. When Thomas Newcomen fired up his pump on that morning in 1712, the atmosphere contained 275 parts per million of carbon dioxide. We're now up to 380 parts per million, a level higher than the earth has seen for many millions of years, and climate change has only just begun. The median predictions of the world's climatologists—by no means the worst-case scenario—show that unless we take truly enormous steps to rein in our use of fossil fuels, we can expect average temperatures to rise another four or five degrees before the century is out, making the globe warmer than it's been since long before primates appeared. We might as well stop calling it earth and have a contest to pick some new name, because it will be a different planet. Humans have never done anything more profound, not even when we invented nuclear weapons.

How does this tie in with economic growth? Clearly, getting rich means getting dirty—that's why, when I was in Beijing recently, I could stare straight at the sun (once I actually figured out where in the smoggy sky it was). But eventually, getting rich also means wanting the "luxury" of clean air and finding the technological means to achieve it. Which is why you can once again see the mountains around Los Angeles, why more of our rivers are swimmable every year. And economists have figured out clever ways to speed this renewal: Creating markets for trading pollution credits, for instance, helped cut those sulfur and nitrogen clouds more rapidly and cheaply than almost anyone had imagined.

But getting richer doesn't lead to producing less carbon dioxide in the same way that it does to less smog—in fact, so far it's mostly the reverse. Environmental destruction of the old-fashioned kind—dirty air, dirty water—results from something going wrong. You haven't bothered to stick the necessary filter on your pipes, and so the crud washes into the stream; a little regulation, and a little money, and the problem disappears. But the second, deeper form of environmental degradation comes from things operating exactly as they're supposed to, just too much so. Carbon dioxide is an inevitable byproduct of burning coal or gas or oil—not something going wrong. Researchers are struggling to figure out costly and complicated methods to trap some CO_2 and inject it into underground mines—but for all practical purposes, the vast majority of the world's cars and factories and furnaces will keep belching more and more of it into the atmosphere as long as we burn more and more fossil fuels.

True, as companies and countries get richer, they can afford more efficient machinery that makes better use of fossil fuel, like the hybrid Honda Civic I drive. But if your appliances have gotten more efficient, there are also far more of them: The furnace is better than it used to be, but the average size of the house it heats has doubled since 1950. The 60-inch TV? The always-on cable modem? No need for you to do the math—the electric company does it for you, every month. Between 1990 and 2003, precisely the years in which we learned about the peril presented by global warming, the United States' annual carbon dioxide emissions increased by 16 percent. And the momentum to keep going in that direction is enormous. For most of us, growth has become synonymous with the economy's "health," which in turn seems far more palpable than the health of the planet. Think of the terms we use—the economy, whose temperature we take at every newscast via the Dow Jones average, is "ailing" or it's "on the mend." It's "slumping" or it's "in recovery." We cosset and succor its every sniffle with enormous devotion, even as we more or less ignore the increasingly urgent fever that the globe is now running. The ecological economists have an enormous task ahead of them—a nearly insurmountable task, if it were "merely" the environment that is in peril. But here is where things get really interesting. It turns out that the economics of environmental destruction are closely linked to another set of leading indicators—ones that most humans happen to care a great deal about.

"IT SEEMS THAT WELL-BEING IS A REAL PHENOMENON": ECONOMISTS DISCOVER HEDONICS

Traditionally, happiness and satisfaction are the sort of notions that economists wave aside as poetic irrelevance, the kind of questions that occupy people with no head for numbers who had to major in liberal arts. An orthodox economist has a simple happiness formula: If you buy a Ford Expedition, then ipso facto a Ford Expedition is what makes you happy. That's all we need to know. The economist would call this idea "utility maximization," and in the words of the economic historian Gordon Bigelow, "the theory holds that every time a person buys something, sells something, quits a job, or invests, he is making a rational decision about what will…provide him 'maximum utility.' If you bought a Ginsu knife at 3 a.m. a neoclassical economist will tell you that, at that time, you calculated that this purchase would optimize your resources." The beauty of this principle lies in its simplicity. It is perhaps the central assumption of the world we live in: You can tell who I really am by what I buy.

Yet economists have long known that people's brains don't work quite the way the model suggests. When Bob Costanza, one of the fathers of ecological economics and now head of the Gund Institute at the University of Vermont, was first edging into economics in the early 1980s, he had a fellowship to study "social traps"—the nuclear arms race, say—in which "short-term behavior can get out of kilter with longer broad-term goals."

It didn't take long for Costanza to demonstrate, as others had before him, that, if you set up an auction in a certain way, people will end up bidding $1.50 to take home a dollar. Other economists have shown that people give too much weight to "sunk costs"—that they're too willing to throw good money after bad, or that they value items more highly if they already own them than if they are considering acquiring them. Building on such insights, a school of "behavioral economics" has emerged in recent years and begun plumbing how we really behave.

The wonder is that it took so long. We all know in our own lives how irrationally we are capable of acting, and how unconnected those actions are to any real sense of joy. (I mean, there you are at 3 a.m. thinking about the Ginsu knife.) But until fairly recently, we had no alternatives to relying on Ginsu knife and Ford Expedition purchases as the sole measures of our satisfaction. How else would we know what made people happy?

That's where things are now changing dramatically: Researchers from a wide variety of disciplines have started to figure out how to assess satisfaction, and economists have begun to explore the implications. In 2002 Princeton's Daniel Kahneman won the Nobel Prize in economics even though he is trained as a psychologist. In the book *Well-Being*, he and a pair of coauthors announce a new field called "hedonics," defined as "the study of what makes experiences and life pleasant or unpleasant.…It is also concerned with the whole range of circumstances, from the biological to the societal, that occasion suffering and enjoyment." If you are worried that there might be something altogether too airy about this, be reassured—Kahneman thinks like an economist. In the book's very first chapter, "Objective Happiness," he describes an experiment that compares "records of the pain reported by two patients undergoing colonoscopy," wherein every 60 seconds he insists they rate their pain on a scale of 1 to 10 and eventually forces them to make "a hypothetical choice between a repeat colonoscopy and a barium enema." Dismal science indeed.

As more scientists have turned their attention to the field, researchers have studied everything from "biases in recall of menstrual symptoms" to "fearlessness and courage in novice paratroopers." Subjects have had to choose between getting an "attractive candy bar" and learning the answers to geography questions; they've been made to wear devices that measured their blood pressure at regular intervals; their brains have been scanned. And by now that's been enough to convince most observers that saying "I'm happy" is more than just a subjective statement. In the words of the economist Richard Layard, "We now know that what people say about how they feel corresponds closely to the actual levels of activity in different parts of the brain, which can be measured in standard scientific ways." Indeed, people who call themselves happy, or who have relatively high levels of electrical activity in the left prefrontal region of the brain, are also "more likely to be rated as happy by friends," "more likely to respond to requests for help," "less likely to be involved in disputes at work," and even "less likely to die prematurely." In other words, conceded one economist, "it seems that what the psychologists call subjective well-being is a real phenomenon. The various empirical measures of it have high consistency, reliability, and validity."

The idea that there is a state called happiness, and that we can dependably figure out what it feels like and how to measure it, is extremely subversive. It allows economists to start thinking about life in richer (indeed) terms, to stop asking "What did you buy?" and to start asking "Is your life good?" And if you can ask someone "Is your life good?" and count on the answer to mean something, then you'll be able to move to the real heart of the matter, the question haunting our moment on the earth: Is more better?

IF WE'RE SO RICH, HOW COME WE'RE SO DAMN MISERABLE?

In some sense, you could say that the years since World War II in America have been a loosely controlled experiment designed to answer this very question. The environmentalist Alan Durning found that in 1991 the average American family owned twice as many cars as it did in 1950, drove 2.5 times as far, used 21 times as much plastic, and traveled 25 times farther by air. Gross national product per capita tripled during that period. Our houses are bigger than ever and stuffed to the rafters with belongings (which is why the storage-locker industry has doubled in size in the past decade). We have all sorts of other new delights and powers—we can send email from our cars, watch 200 channels, consume food from every corner of the world. Some people have taken much more than their share, but on average, all of us in the West are living lives materially more abundant than most people a generation ago.

What's odd is, none of it appears to have made us happier. Throughout the postwar years, even as the GNP curve has steadily climbed, the "life satisfaction" index has stayed exactly the same. Since 1972, the National Opinion Research Center has surveyed Americans on the question: "Taking all things together, how would you say things are these days—would you say that you are very happy, pretty happy, or not too happy?" (This must be a somewhat unsettling interview.) The "very happy" number peaked at 38 percent in the 1974 poll, amid oil shock and economic malaise; it now hovers right around 33 percent.

And it's not that we're simply recalibrating our sense of what happiness means—we are actively experiencing life as grimmer. In the winter of 2006 the National Opinion Research Center published data about "negative life events" comparing 1991 and 2004, two data points bracketing an economic boom. "The anticipation would have been that problems would have been down," the study's author said. Instead it showed a rise in problems—for instance, the percentage who reported breaking up with a steady partner almost doubled. As one reporter summarized the findings, "There's more misery in people's lives today."

This decline in the happiness index is not confined to the United States; as other nations have followed us into mass affluence, their experiences have begun to yield similar results. In the United Kingdom, real gross domestic product per capita grew two-thirds between 1973 and 2001, but people's satisfaction with their lives changed not one whit. Japan saw a fourfold increase in real income per capita between 1958 and 1986 without any reported increase in satisfaction. In one place after another, rates of alcoholism, suicide, and depression have gone up dramatically, even as we keep accumulating more stuff. Indeed, one report in 2000 found that the average American child reported higher levels of anxiety than the average child under psychiatric care in the 1950s—our new normal is the old disturbed.

If happiness was our goal, then the unbelievable amount of effort and resources expended in its pursuit since 1950 has been largely a waste. One study of life satisfaction and mental health by Emory University professor Corey Keyes found just 17 percent of Americans "flourishing," in mental health terms, and 26 percent either "languishing" or out-and-out depressed.

DANES (AND MEXICANS, THE AMISH, AND THE MASAI) JUST WANT TO HAVE FUN

How is it, then, that we became so totally, and apparently wrongly, fixated on the idea that our main goal, as individuals and as nations, should be the accumulation of more wealth? The answer is interesting for what it says about human nature. Up to a certain point, more really does equal better. Imagine briefly your life as a poor person in a poor society—say, a peasant farmer in China. (China has one-fourth of the world's farmers, but one-fourteenth of its arable land; the average farm in the southern part of the country is about half an acre, or barely more than the standard lot for a new American home.) You likely have the benefits of a close and connected family, and a village environment where your place is clear. But you lack any modicum of security for when you get sick or old or your back simply gives out. Your diet is unvaried and nutritionally lacking; you're almost always cold in winter.

In a world like that, a boost in income delivers tangible benefits. In general, researchers report that money consistently buys happiness right up to about

$10,000 income per capita. That's a useful number to keep in the back of your head—it's like the freezing point of water, one of those random figures that just happens to define a crucial phenomenon on our planet. "As poor countries like India, Mexico, the Philippines, Brazil, and South Korea have experienced economic growth, there is some evidence that their average happiness has risen," the economist Layard reports. Past $10,000 (per capita, mind you—that is, the average for each man, woman, and child), there's a complete scattering: When the Irish were making two-thirds as much as Americans they were reporting higher levels of satisfaction, as were the Swedes, the Danes, the Dutch. Mexicans score higher than the Japanese; the French are about as satisfied with their lives as the Venezuelans. In fact, once basic needs are met, the "satisfaction" data scrambles in mind-bending ways. A sampling of *Forbes* magazine's "richest Americans" have identical happiness scores with Pennsylvania Amish, and are only a whisker above Swedes taken as a whole, not to mention the Masai. The "life satisfaction" of pavement dwellers—homeless people—in Calcutta is among the lowest recorded, but it almost doubles when they move into a slum, at which point they are basically as satisfied with their lives as a sample of college students drawn from 47 nations. And so on.

On the list of major mistakes we've made as a species, this one seems pretty high up. Our single-minded focus on increasing wealth has succeeded in driving the planet's ecological systems to the brink of failure, even as it's failed to make us happier. How did we screw up?

The answer is pretty obvious—we kept doing something past the point that it worked. Since happiness had increased with income in the past, we assumed it would inevitably do so in the future. We make these kinds of mistakes regularly: Two beers made me feel good, so ten will make me feel five times better. But this case was particularly extreme—in part because as a species, we've spent so much time simply trying to survive. As the researchers Ed Diener and Martin Seligman—both psychologists—observe, "At the time of Adam Smith, a concern with economic issues was understandably primary. Meeting simple human needs for food, shelter and clothing was not assured, and satisfying these needs moved in lockstep with better economics." Freeing people to build a more dynamic economy was radical and altruistic.

Consider Americans in 1820, two generations after Adam Smith. The average citizen earned, in current dollars, less than $1,500 a year, which is somewhere near the current average for all of Africa. As the economist Deirdre McCloskey explains in a 2004 article in the magazine *Christian Century*, "Your great-great-great-grandmother had one dress for church and one for the week, if she were not in rags. Her children did not attend school, and probably could not read. She and her husband worked eighty hours a week for a diet of bread and milk—they were four inches shorter than you." Even in 1900, the average American lived in a house the size of today's typical garage. Is it any wonder that we built up considerable velocity trying to escape the gravitational pull of that kind of poverty? An object in motion stays in motion, and our economy—with the built-up individual expectations that drive it—is a mighty object indeed.

You could call it, I think, the Laura Ingalls Wilder effect. I grew up reading her books—*Little House on the Prairie, Little House in the Big Woods*—and my daughter grew up listening to me read them to her, and no doubt she will read them to her children. They are the ur-American story. And what do they tell? Of a life rich in family, rich in connection to the natural world, rich in adventure—but materially deprived. That one dress, that same bland dinner. At Christmastime, a penny—a penny! And a stick of candy, and the awful deliberation about whether to stretch it out with tiny licks or devour it in an orgy of happy greed. A rag doll was the zenith of aspiration. My daughter likes dolls too, but her bedroom boasts a density of Beanie Babies that mimics the manic biodiversity of the deep rainforest. Another one? Really, so what? Its marginal utility, as an economist might say, is low. And so it is with all of us. We just haven't figured that out because the momentum of the past is still with us—we still imagine we're in that little house on the big prairie.

THIS YEAR'S MODEL HOME: "GOOD FOR THE DYSFUNCTIONAL FAMILY"

That great momentum has carried us away from something valuable, something priceless: It has allowed us to become (very nearly forced us to become) more thoroughly individualistic than we really wanted to be. We left behind hundreds of thousands of years of human community for the excitement, and the isolation, of "making something of ourselves," an idea that would not have made sense for 99.9 percent of human history. Adam Smith's insight was that the interests of each of our individual selves could add up, almost in spite of themselves, to social good—to longer lives, fuller tables, warmer houses. Suddenly the community was no longer necessary to provide these things; they would happen as if by magic. And they did happen. And in many ways it was good.

But this process of liberation seems to have come close to running its course. Study after study shows Americans spending less time with friends and family, either working longer hours, or hunched over their computers at night. And each year, as our population grows by 1 percent we manage to spread ourselves out over 6 to 8 percent more land. Simple mathematics says that we're less and less likely to bump into the other inhabitants of our neighborhood, or indeed of our own homes. As the *Wall Street Journal* reported recently, "Major builders and top architects are walling people off. They're touting one-person 'Internet alcoves,' locked-door 'away rooms,' and his-and-her offices on opposite ends of the house. The new floor plans offer so much seclusion, they're 'good for the dysfunctional family,' says Gopal Ahluwahlia, director of research for the National Association of Home Builders." At the building industry's annual Las Vegas trade show, the "showcase 'Ultimate Family Home' hardly had a family room," noted the *Journal*. Instead, the boy's personal playroom had its own 42-inch plasma TV, and the girl's bedroom had a secret mirrored door leading to a "hideaway karaoke room." "We call this the ultimate home for families who don't want anything to do with one another," said Mike McGee, chief executive of Pardee Homes of Los Angeles, builder of the model.

This transition from individualism to hyper-individualism also made its presence felt in politics. In the 1980s, British prime minister Margaret Thatcher asked, "Who is society? There is no such thing. There are individual men and women, and there are families." Talk about everything solid melting into air— Thatcher's maxim would have spooked Adam Smith himself. The "public realm"—things like parks and schools and Social Security, the last reminders of the communities from which we came—is under steady and increasing attack. Instead of contributing to the shared risk of health insurance, Americans are encouraged to go it alone with "health savings accounts." Hell, even the nation's most collectivist institution, the U.S. military, until recently recruited under the slogan an "Army of One." No wonder the show that changed television more than any other in the past decade was *Survivor,* where the goal is to end up alone on the island, to manipulate and scheme until everyone is banished and leaves you by yourself with your money.

It's not so hard, then, to figure out why happiness has declined here even as wealth has grown. During the same decades when our lives grew busier and more isolated, we've gone from having three confidants on average to only two, and the number of people saying they have no one to discuss important matters with has nearly tripled. Between 1974 and 1994, the percentage of Americans who said they visited with their neighbors at least once a month fell from almost two-thirds to less than half, a number that has continued to fall in the past decade. We simply worked too many hours earning, we commuted too far to our too-isolated homes, and there was always the blue glow of the tube shining through the curtains.

NEW FRIEND OR NEW COFFEEMAKER? PICK ONE

Because traditional economists think of human beings primarily as individuals and not as members of a community, they miss out on a major part of the satisfaction index. Economists lay it out almost as a mathematical equation: Overall, "evidence shows that companionship...contributes more to well-being than does income," writes Robert E. Lane, a Yale political science professor who is the author of *The Loss of Happiness in Market Democracies.* But there is a notable difference between poor and wealthy countries; When people have lots of companionship but not much money, income "makes more of a contribution to subjective well-being." By contrast, "where money is relatively plentiful and companionship relatively scarce, companionship will add more to subjective well-being." If you are a poor person in China, you have plenty of friends and family around all the time—perhaps there are four other people living in your room. Adding a sixth doesn't make you happier. But adding enough money so that all five of you can eat some meat from time to time pleases you greatly. By contrast, if you live in a suburban American home, buying another coffeemaker adds very little to your quantity of happiness—trying to figure out where to store it, or wondering if you picked the perfect model, may in fact decrease your total pleasure. But a new friend, a new connection, is a big deal. We have a surplus of individualism and a deficit of companionship, and so the second becomes more valuable.

Indeed, we seem to be genetically wired for community. As biologist Edward O. Wilson found, most primates live in groups and get sad when they're separated—"an isolated individual will repeatedly pull a lever with no reward other than the glimpse of another monkey." Why do people so often look back on their college days as the best years of their lives? Because their classes were so fascinating? Or because in college, we live more closely and intensely with a community than most of us ever do before or after? Every measure of psychological health points to the same conclusion: People who "are married, who have good friends, and who are close to their families are happier than those who do not," says Swarthmore psychologist Barry Schwartz. "People who participate in religious communities are happier than those who are not." Which is striking, Schwartz adds, because social ties "actually decrease freedom of choice"—being a good friend involves sacrifice.

Do we just *think* we're happier in communities? Is it merely some sentimental good-night-John-Boy affectation? No—our bodies react in measurable ways. According to research cited by Harvard professor Robert Putnam in his classic book *Bowling Alone*, if you do not belong to any group at present, joining a club or a society of some kind cuts in half the risk that you will die in the next year. Check this out: When researchers at Carnegie Mellon (somewhat disgustingly) dropped samples of cold virus directly into subjects' nostrils, those with rich social networks were four times less likely to get sick. An economy that produces only individualism undermines us in the most basic ways.

Here's another statistic worth keeping in mind: Consumers have 10 times as many conversations at farmers' markets as they do at supermarkets—an order of magnitude difference. By itself, that's hardly life-changing, but it points at something that could be: living in an economy where you are participant as well as consumer, where you have a sense of who's in your universe and how it fits together. At the same time, some studies show local agriculture using less energy (also by an order of magnitude) than the "it's always summer somewhere" system we operate on now. Those are big numbers, and it's worth thinking about what they suggest—especially since, between peak oil and climate change, there's no longer really a question that we'll have to wean ourselves of the current model.

So as a mental experiment, imagine how we might shift to a more sustainable kind of economy. You could use government policy to nudge the change—remove subsidies from agribusiness and use them instead to promote farmer-entrepreneurs; underwrite the cost of windmills with even a fraction of the money that's now going to protect oil flows. You could put tariffs on goods that travel long distances, shift highway spending to projects that make it easier to live near where you work (and, by cutting down on commutes, leave some time to see the kids). And, of course, you can exploit the Net to connect a lot of this highly localized stuff into something larger. By way of example, a few of us are coordinating the first nationwide global warming demonstration—but instead of marching on Washington, we're rallying in our local areas, and then fusing our efforts, via the website stepitup07.org, into a national message.

It's easy to dismiss such ideas as sentimental or nostalgic. In fact, economies can be localized as easily in cities and suburbs as rural villages (maybe more easily), and in ways that look as much to the future as the past, that rely more on the solar panel and the Internet than the white picket fence. In fact, given the trendlines for phenomena such as global warming and oil supply, what's nostalgic and sentimental is to keep doing what we're doing simply because it's familiar.

THE OIL-FOR-PEOPLE PARADOX: WHY SMALL FARMS PRODUCE MORE FOOD

To understand the importance of this last point, consider the book *American Mania* by the neuroscientist Peter Whybrow. Whybrow argues that many of us in this country are predisposed to a kind of dynamic individualism—our gene pool includes an inordinate number of people who risked everything to start over. This served us well in settling a continent and building our prosperity. But it never got completely out of control, says Whybrow, because "the marketplace has always had its natural constraints. For the first two centuries of the nation's existence, even the most insatiable American citizen was significantly leashed by the checks and balances inherent in a closely knit community, by geography, by the elements of weather, or, in some cases, by religious practice." You lived in a society—a habitat—that kept your impulses in some kind of check. But that changed in the past few decades as the economy nationalized and then globalized. As we met fewer actual neighbors in the course of a day, those checks and balances fell away. "Operating in a world of instant communication with minimal social tethers," Whybrow observes, "America's engines of commerce and desire became turbocharged."

Adam Smith himself had worried that too much envy and avarice would destroy "the empathic feeling and neighborly concerns that are essential to his economic model," says Whybrow, but he "took comfort in the fellowship and social constraint that he considered inherent in the tightly knit communities characteristic of the 18th century." Businesses were built on local capital investment, and "to be solicitous of one's neighbor was prudent insurance against future personal need." For the most part, people felt a little constrained about showing off wealth; indeed, until fairly recently in American history, someone who was making tons of money was often viewed with mixed emotions, at least if he wasn't giving back to the community. "For the rich," Whybrow notes, "the reward system would be balanced between the pleasure of self-gain and the civic pride of serving others. By these mechanisms the most powerful citizens would be limited in their greed."

Once economies grow past a certain point, however, "the behavioral contingencies essential to promoting social stability in a market-regulated society—close personal relationships, tightly knit communities, local capital investment, and so on—are quickly eroded." So re-localizing economies offers one possible way around the gross inequalities that have come to mark our societies. Instead of aiming for growth at all costs and hoping it will trickle down, we may be better off living in enough contact with each other for the affluent to once again feel some sense of responsibility for their neighbors. This doesn't mean relying on noblesse oblige; it means taking seriously the idea that people, and their politics, can be changed by their experiences. It's a hopeful sign that more and more local and state governments across the country have enacted "living wage" laws. It's harder to pretend that the people you see around you every day should live and die by the dictates of the market.

Right around this time, an obvious question is doubtless occurring to you. Is it foolish to propose that a modern global economy of 6 (soon to be 9) billion people should rely on more localized economies? To put it more bluntly, since for most people "the economy" is just a fancy way of saying "What's for dinner?" and "Am I having any?," doesn't our survival depend on economies that function on a massive scale—such as highly industrialized agriculture? Turns out the answer is no—and the reasons why offer a template for rethinking the rest of the economy as well.

We assume, because it makes a certain kind of intuitive sense, that industrialized farming is the most productive farming. A vast Midwestern field filled with high-tech equipment ought to produce more food than someone with a hoe in a small garden. Yet the opposite is true. If you are after getting the greatest yield from the land, then smaller farms in fact produce more food.

If you are one guy on a tractor responsible for thousands of acres, you grow your corn and that's all you can do—make pass after pass with the gargantuan machine across a sea of crop. But if you're working 10 acres, then you have time to really know the land, and to make it work harder. You can intercrop all kinds of plants—their roots will go to different depths, or they'll thrive in each other's shade, or they'll make use of different nutrients in the soil. You can also walk your fields, over and over, noticing. According to the government's most recent agricultural census, smaller farms produce far more food per acre, whether you measure in tons, calories, or dollars. In the process, they use land, water, and oil much more efficiently; if they have animals, the manure is a gift, not a threat to public health. To feed the world, we may actually need lots more small farms.

But if this is true, then why do we have large farms? Why the relentless consolidation? There are many reasons, including the way farm subsidies have been structured, the easier access to bank loans (and politicians) for the big guys, and the convenience for food-processing companies of dealing with a few big suppliers. But the basic reason is this: We substituted oil for people. Tractors and synthetic fertilizer instead of farmers and animals. Could we take away the fossil fuel, put people back on the land in larger numbers, and have enough to eat?

The best data to answer that question come from an English agronomist named Jules Pretty, who has studied nearly 300 sustainable agriculture projects in 57 countries around the world. They might not pass the U.S. standards for organic certification, but they're all what he calls "low-input." Pretty found that over the past decade, almost 12 million farmers had begun using sustainable practices on about 90 million acres. Even more remarkably, sustainable agriculture increased food production by 79 percent per acre. These were not tiny isolated demonstration farms—Pretty studied 14 projects where 146,000 farmers across a broad swath of the developing world were raising potatoes, sweet potatoes, and cassava, and he found that practices such as cover-cropping and fighting pests with natural adversaries had increased production 150 percent—17 tons per household. With 4.5 million small Asian grain farmers, average yields rose 73 percent. When Indonesian rice farmers got rid of pesticides, their yields stayed the same but their costs fell sharply.

"I acknowledge," says Pretty, "that all this may sound too good to be true for those who would disbelieve these advances. Many still believe that food production and nature must be separated, that 'agroecological' approaches offer only marginal opportunities to increase food production, and that industrialized approaches represent the best, and perhaps only, way forward. However, prevailing views have changed substantially in just the last decade."

And they will change just as profoundly in the decades to come across a wide range of other commodities. Already I've seen dozens of people and communities working on regional-scale sustainable timber projects, on building energy networks that work like the Internet by connecting solar rooftops and backyard windmills in robust mini-grids. That such things can begin to emerge even in the face of the political power of our reigning economic model is remarkable; as we confront significant change in the climate, they could speed along the same kind of learning curve as Pretty's rice farmers and wheat growers. And they would not only use less energy; they'd create more community. They'd start to reverse the very trends I've been describing, and in so doing rebuild the kind of scale at which Adam Smith's economics would help instead of hurt.

In the 20th century, two completely different models of how to run an economy battled for supremacy. Ours won, and not only because it produced more goods than socialized state economies. It also produced far more freedom, far less horror. But now that victory is starting to look Pyrrhic; in our overheated and under happy state, we need some new ideas.

We've gone too far down the road we're traveling. The time has come to search the map, to strike off in new directions. Inertia is a powerful force; marriages and corporations and nations continue in motion until something big diverts them. But in our new world we have much to fear, and also much to desire, and together they can set us on a new, more promising course.

CRITICAL THINKING QUESTIONS

Do you agree with McKibben's argument? Do material expectations and capitalist growth need to be moderated? Will such moderation enhance personal happiness?

Do you think the most recent economic downturn has made his argument more relevant or less relevant?

CHAPTER 24

The Establishment vs. the Environment

Robert Heiner

Environmentalists generally seek government regulation, and corporations, preferring to operate in the so-called free market, are almost always opposed to regulation. In the 1970s, the environmental movement was at its peak, enjoying a great deal of public and political support throughout North America and Western Europe. In the United States, by the mid-1970s, "5.5 million people contributed financially to nineteen leading national organizations, and perhaps another 20 million to over 40,000 local groups. Environmentalism," write Daniel Faber and James O'Connor, "had arrived as a mass-based movement."[1] Environmentalists were winning significant political victories, and the corporate world was rocked by the passage of legislation such as the Clean Air Act, the Clean Water Act, and the establishment of the Environmental Protection Agency. In their "near-hysterical determination" to "put the environmental lobby out of business," according to Sharon Beder, corporations formed coalitions and alliances, established "public affairs" departments or increased the status of existing departments, and diverted increasing resources to lobbying Congress. In 1971, there were 175 firms represented by lobbyists in Washington; by 1982, the number had climbed to 2,445.[2] Since college graduates were among those most supportive of the environmental movement, many corporations and conservative foundations pumped millions of dollars each year into establishing endowed chairs of "free enterprise"; establishing the Institute of Educational Affairs, "which was conceived," writes Beder, "...to coordinate the flow of money from corporations into the production of conservative ideas"; and funding scholars "whose views were compatible with the corporate view."[3] According to Beder, in her book *Global Spin: The Corporate Assault on Environmentalism*,

> In the late 1970s U.S. business was spending a billion dollars each year on propaganda of various sorts "aimed at persuading the American public that their interests were the same as business's interests." The result of all this expenditure showed in the polls when the percentage of people who thought there was too

much regulation soared from twenty-two percent in 1975 to sixty percent in 1980.[4]

The corporate world succeeded throughout most of the 1980s in its battle against the environmentalists, and many environmental regulations were repealed or went unenforced during the Reagan administration. Ozone depletion, global warming, and other environmental concerns attracted a great deal of public attention in the mid- to late 1980s; but this time the corporate world was ready for battle with the techniques they had learned earlier.

Exploiting Uncertainty

One of the corporate world's principal weapons in the battle against scientific findings that are unfavorable to its interests is to exploit the presence of scientific uncertainty. According to environmental sociologists Frederick Buttell and Peter Taylor, "Scientific uncertainty can be an enormously powerful tool and it is one that is often wielded against environmentalists with particular effectiveness."[5] As long as there is a shred of scientific uncertainty (and there almost always is), it can be exploited by skeptics. Most of us are familiar with this tactic as it was used by the tobacco companies. Despite the endless number of scientific studies linking cancer and cigarette smoking, the tobacco companies could always claim that it had not been proven that smoking causes cancer. Theoretically, they had a point; the link between smoking and cancer, after all, could be due to the possibility that people who are prone to cancer are more likely to smoke rather than smokers being more likely to contract cancer. Virtually the only scientific study that could determine which is the cause and which is the effect would require taking a random sample of newborn babies, randomly dividing them into two groups, later forcing one group to smoke incessantly, never allowing the other group near a cigarette, and then later examining which group developed higher rates of lung cancer. Obviously, such a study could never take place. The problem then with this type of research is one of methodology, and all scientific research encounters some sort of methodological difficulty. Few of us today, however, doubt there is a causative link between smoking and cancer.

One of the principal tactics for exploiting uncertainty is for industry and its defenders to claim that more research is needed (often, while, at the same time, they are covering up research findings that are detrimental to their interests). Gerald Markowitz and David Rosner, authors of *Deceit and Denial: The Deadly Politics of Industrial Pollution*, write of the "political value of scientific ambiguity."

> The call for more scientific evidence is often a stalling tactic. The inability of science in the 1920s to prove that lead in gasoline, for example, was dangerous resulted in severe damage to children a half a century later. The inability of science to agree about whether or not there is a problem with the use and disposal of plastics and the willingness of industries to use new chemicals before they are proved safe may also have terrible consequences for society.[6]

While calling for more research into these matters, industry is fully aware that government and private foundations have limited resources and often cannot afford to conduct costly scientific research. More often than not, such research is conducted or funded by the industries themselves. Just as much of the research that once found tobacco to be a harmless substance was funded by tobacco companies themselves, much of the research that fails to find a link between various pollutants and environmental harm is funded by corporations. The corporation, of course, has an interest in producing findings that minimize the harm caused by its product or its emissions; therefore, it is reasonable to suspect that corporate-funded research is significantly biased. As with the tobacco companies, beyond using methodologies that are likely to produce desirable findings, corporations have been discovered on a number of occasions to have covered up findings that may lead to an increase in their production costs and/or a reduction in their profits.

Defenders of industry say that we should trust industry to look after the public interest and that, when there is uncertainty about a product's safety, government regulation is rarely in the public interest. History has shown this stance to be very problematic. The tobacco industry did all that it could to cover up the dangers of tobacco; the asbestos industry did all that it could to cover up the dangers of asbestos; and the lead industry did all that it could to cover up the dangers of lead. Just these three products alone have been responsible for the deaths of millions of people and for the impairments of millions more.

Environmental law requires that chemical companies have to turn over any research findings that indicate a substance may be harmful to people's health or to the environment. In 1991 and 1992, the Environmental Protection Agency offered an amnesty, allowing corporations who had not yet done so (who had been covering up) to turn such scientific documents over with impunity. Chemical manufacturers produced documents from over 10,000 studies indicating that their products produced substantial risks. "Until the amnesty was offered, until it was clear that they wouldn't be sanctioned, the manufacturers simply kept those studies to themselves, even though they were obligated by law to turn over the information."[7] In the name of profit, they had kept these documents secret, breaking the law, violating the ethical tenets of scientific discovery, and putting the environment and the public at risk. It is likely many damaging documents were not turned over because the products were still turning profits.

Public Relations

Corporations have also been very successful at fending off regulation by hiring public relations (PR) firms to fight their battles against environmentalists. The PR industry is steadily becoming an increasingly powerful force in business and industry today. "Rather than substantially change business practices so as to earn a better reputation," writes Beder, "many firms are turning to PR professionals to create one for them. After all 'It is easier and less costly to change the way people think about reality than it is to change reality.'"[8]

Of course, one of the tactics employed by PR firms to protect their clients is to exploit the uncertainty surrounding so many environmental issues. For instance, when CFCs were implicated in ozone depletion, the $3 billion aerosol industry engaged the services of PR firms. The PR firms issued press releases emphasizing that the CFC link was theoretical, and they produced a handbook for their clients instructing them how to testify in hearings and respond to news journalists. When asked if aerosols should be banned, for example, the handbook suggested an appropriate response might be "There is slight risk that thousands of different products could be modifying the atmosphere to one degree or another. I do not think it is reasonable or proper to ban products at random to eliminate a threat that many qualified people doubt even exists."[9] U.S. Gypsum, which was being sued for installing asbestos in public buildings, was reportedly advised by its PR firm that by

> enlisting "independent experts," the issue of asbestos, instead of being a public health problem, could be redefined as "a side issue that is being seized on by special interests and those out to further their own causes...." The media and other audiences important to US Gypsum should ideally say, "Why is all this furor being raised about this product? We have a non-story here.'"[10]

The best PR is that which is not recognized as such. In fact, a good deal of PR output today passes as "news." To put it another way, much of today's newspaper and television news is generated by PR firms. It is estimated that "40 percent of all 'news' flows virtually unedited from public relations offices."[11] A former editor of the *Wall Street Journal* admitted that approximately half of their news stories were generated by press releases but added, "In every case we try to go beyond the press release." The *Columbia Journalism Review*, however, upon examining the *Wall Street Journal*, found that more than half of its news stories were "based solely on press releases" often "almost verbatim or in paraphrase" even though those articles usually carried the byline "By a *Wall Street Journal* Staff Reporter."[12] As mentioned earlier, the PR campaign for the aerosol industry involved sending out press releases emphasizing "knowledge gaps" rather than ozone holes, and its releases were often reprinted as news.[13]

A sophisticated and attractive alternative to the press release is the production and distribution of the video news release (VNR). PR firms are now producing video segments that are indistinguishable from—often better than—the segments produced in-house by television news staffs. Martin Lee and Norman Solomon, authors of the book *Unreliable Sources: A Guide to Detecting Bias in News Media*, report, "Every week, hundreds of local TV stations, beset by budget and staff cutbacks, air these free, ready-made news releases, which look increasingly realistic. Even veteran media observers often fail to distinguish between video PR spots and station-produced news."[14] One survey found that "eighty percent of U.S. news directors use VNRs a few times each month."[15] Together, the traditional press release and the VNR "ensure that much of the news people read or watch on television is manufactured by PR firms rather than discovered by journalists."[16] Thus, corporations, in addition to those actually owning the news agencies, are involved in the business of news production.

Another tactic used by PR firms is to advise their corporate clients to establish or work through what are sometimes called "front groups." Front groups are organizations that are supported by corporate interests and are made up of citizens and/or "experts," which are mobilized to achieve particular political ends. Corporations that are often accused of environmental destruction frequently fund, what many consider, antienvironmental organizations such as the Wise Use Movement. If an organization that suits its cause does not already exist, the corporation can hire a PR firm to organize one. Lawyers for electric companies opposed to the Endangered Species Act reportedly advised their clients to "[i]ncorporate as a nonprofit, develop easy-to-read information packets for Congress and the news media and woo members from virtually all walks of life. Members should include Native American entities, county and local governments, universities, school boards."[17] According to an article in *Consumer Reports*, PR firms organizing such groups often recruit with financial incentives, paying as much as $500 "for every citizen they mobilize for a corporate client's cause."[18]

Referring to the deceptive nature of industry front groups, the same article in *Consumer Reports*, entitled "Public Interest Pretenders," observes,

> There was a time when one usually could tell what an advocacy group stood for—and who stood behind it—simply by its name. Today, "councils," "coalitions," "alliances," and groups with "citizens" and "consumers" in their names could as likely be fronts for corporations and trade associations as representatives of "citizens" or "consumers."... [Many industry front groups] use names that make them sound as if they represent the public interest, not a business interest.... Someone looking at the logo of the National Wetlands Coalition, which features a duck flying over a marsh, would have no clue that the coalition is made up mainly of oil drillers, developers, and natural gas companies that want national policy on wetlands use and development shaped for their industries' benefit.[19]

One might think the Global Climate Coalition (GCC) was an organization concerned with the prevention of global warming; instead, it was a coalition of "fifty U.S. trade associations and private companies representing oil, gas, coal, automobile, and chemical interests" whose aims were likely altogether different.[20] As the GCC was increasingly exposed as a front group for industry intent on obstructing measures to prevent climate change, many of its prominent corporate members began withdrawing from the group (including DuPont, British Petroleum, Texaco, and General Motors).[21] Consumers for Responsible Solutions was a front group allegedly funded by Philip Morris to defeat antismoking statutes in Florida. The group was disbanded when its connection to Philip Morris became public.[22]

PR firms have developed a vast array of tactics in addition to press releases, VNRs, and front groups. In the 1990s, the PR firm representing the California raisin industry reportedly undertook a campaign to discredit David Steinman's book *Diet for a Poisoned Planet* even before it was published. In his book, Steinman recommended that people eat no fruits and vegetables other than those grown without pesticides. Ketchum, one of the largest PR firms in the country, specializes in "crisis management"; and apparently it was perceived that the publication of the Steinman book would precipitate a crisis for their clients. John Stauber and Sheldon Rampton detail Ketchum's campaign against the book in their exposé of the PR industry, entitled *Toxic Sludge Is Good for You*. The campaign was carried out in the utmost secrecy. A memo from a senior vice president at Ketchum warned, "All documents…are confidential.…Make sure that everything—even notes to yourself—are so stamped.…Remember that we all have a shredder.…All conversations are confidential, too. Please be careful talking in the halls, in elevators, in restaurants, etc."[23] Using an informant at Steinman's publishing company, Ketchum reportedly managed to get an itinerary of his publicity tour, according to the vice president's memo, "so that we can 'shadow' Steinman's appearances; best scenario: we will have our spokesman in town prior to or in conjunction with Steinman's appearances."[24] Then, according to Stauber and Rampton, Ketchum employees contacted newspapers and television shows, describing him as an "off-the-wall extremist without credibility" and/or demanding equal time to present opposing arguments.

The vice president's memo also mentioned other "external ambassadors" who might be recruited in their campaign against the book. One such apparent "ambassador" was Elizabeth M. Whelan, a "prominent antienvironmentalist" and head of the American Council on Science and Health (ACSH). ACSH is funded largely by the chemical industry and happened also to have been a client at Ketchum. Stauber and Rampton report that Whelan sent a letter to John Sununu, chief of staff at the White House, warning that Steinman and others "who specialize in terrifying consumers" and who "were threatening the U.S. standard of living and, indeed, may pose a future threat to national security."[25] The introduction to Steinman's book had been written by Dr. William Marcus, senior science advisor to the U.S. Environmental Protection Agency. According to Stauber and Rampton, Marcus was pressured to have his introduction removed; he refused and was later fired. Since then, government policy was changed to prohibit officials from writing book forewords.

Stauber and Rampton also detail PR firms sabotaging other environmental books. In one case, the PR firm "hired an infiltrator to pose as a volunteer"[26] in the author's office. After they obtained a copy of his publicity tour itinerary, the producers of the radio and television shows on which the author was to appear received phone calls from a woman falsely claiming to be the author's publicist and canceling his appearances.

While some of the techniques employed by PR firms are certainly legal and ethical, others might be legal and unethical, and others are certainly illegal. Further, there is no denying that environmental groups have sometimes resorted to similar tactics, some legal and some illegal. However, the financial resources that industry can use to sway popular constructions far outweigh those that are available to environmental groups. The PR firms might claim that they are just trying to expose the public to the truth or even to the uncertainty of environmental issues, and they are reasonable in their claim that both sides to an issue should be presented. Yet, we should keep in mind that the PR firm is merely representing a paying client and has no interest in getting at the truth regarding their client's product or emissions that may cause harm. By using sometimes underhanded methods and by exploiting the uncertainty involved, PR firms are often very effective at preventing environmentalists' messages from ever reaching the public. Stauber and Rampton write,

> Neither Ketchum Public Relations nor the White House has any right to interfere with your access to good food or good reading materials.... You have never voted for a politician who campaigned on a pledge that he would work to limit your access to information about the food you eat. You have never voted for Ketchum PR, and, if you are like most people, you've never even *heard* of them. You never gave consent for them to be involved in your life, and in return, they have never bothered to ask for your consent. After all, they're not working for *you*. They are working for the California Raisin Board.[27]

SLAPPs

Another weapon in the corporate arsenal is the lawsuit. Oftentimes environmentalists and other activists are sued for defamation, nuisance, interference with contract, or a similar charge by the industry that feels threatened. The party initiating such a suit often has no intention of winning but is instead attempting to tie the issue up in court, drain the financial resources of the activists, and intimidate others who might be thinking of publicly criticizing their operations. Such lawsuits are called *SLAPPs*, or "strategic lawsuits against public participation." There have been thousands of such cases filed in the courts, with the plaintiffs often seeking millions of dollars in damages. One woman in Texas, for example, was sued for $5 million for simply calling a landfill a "dump." The case dragged on for 3 years, costing the defendant thousands of dollars in legal fees. Finally, the case was dropped; and following an investigation, the Environmental Protection Agency ordered that the site be cleaned up.[28]

Critics, of course, argue that SLAPPs are a threat to activists' freedom of speech. Beder writes,

> Multi-million dollar lawsuits are being filed against individual citizens and groups for circulating petitions, writing to public officials, speaking at, or even just attending, public meetings, organizing a boycott and engaging in peaceful demonstrations. Such activities are supposed to be protected by the First Amendment of the U.S. Constitution, but this has not stopped powerful organizations who want to silence their opponents.[29]

University of Denver professors George Pring and Penelope Canan were among the first to study this phenomenon, and they were the ones who coined the term *SLAPP*. They found in their research that two-thirds of SLAPPs are dismissed before trial and, of those that are decided in favor of the plaintiff, most are overturned or dismissed on appeal.[30] Nonetheless, SLAPPs can be a traumatic ordeal for defendants, and they can be very effective at chilling the speech of those who might otherwise engage in protest. Pring and Canan write, "[T]ens of thousands have been SLAPPed, and still more have been muted or silenced by the threat."[31]

THE MEDIA

The media play a critical role in shaping popular constructions of social problems. The media are themselves run by corporations, and they are dependent upon the advertising revenue of other corporations. Consequently, corporate interests are highly influential in shaping the content of what we read in newspapers and see on television. In the early days of network television, presenting the news was seen largely as a public service and news programs were not expected to bring in big profits. Small newspapers might be considered a success by their owners if they could simply produce enough revenue to pay the costs of overhead and salaries. Today, however, more and more media are being bought out by huge corporations. As this book is being written, ABC belongs to Disney, CNN belongs to Time Warner, and NBC belongs to General Electric. These are all multibillion-dollar, transnational corporations that are heavily invested in a number of other businesses and industries. Meanwhile, both large and small newspapers are being bought up in a frenzy of corporate media acquisitions. "Gone is the owner–editor who purchased a press because, for better or worse, he had something to say."[32] Like their television counterparts, newspaper owners have one overriding goal—the same goal of almost all other corporate executives—profit. Relates Calvin Exoo, author of *The Politics of the Mass Media*,

> Indeed, when GE took over NBC and installed one of its corporate lawyers as its president, he firmly declared that the network's overriding responsibility was to "shareholders." At that point, a member of the news division asked whether the network had another responsibility, whether the news was a "public trust." "It isn't a public trust," replied the boss. "I can't understand that concept."[33]

Americans cherish the notion of a "free press" and loathe the notion of "censorship." The press, as it is popularly construed today, is considered to be free of censorship; but this construction considers only government censorship. Indeed, there is relatively little government censorship of U.S. media. *Corporate censorship*, on the other hand, guides so much of media content that it is hardly recognized as such. Beder writes, "Commercial television and radio [and newspapers] receive most if not all of their income from advertisers. Tens of billions of dollars are spent every year just on television advertising, and the media does its best to create a product that suits those advertisers."[34] The goal of both a news program and an entertainment program is to hold the audience's attention long enough to get them to the commercial, to "deliver the audience to the commercial." It is overwhelmingly in the media's best interest to present a pro-corporate bias in its program content. To do otherwise would compromise their ability to maximize their profits.

A survey of news editors found that 33 percent admitted they would not "feel free" to air a program that might harm the interests of their parent company.[35] (That is only the proportion who admitted that they might violate the ethics of news journalism in favor of corporate interests.) In the 1970s, *New York Times* editors were reportedly instructed to downplay the role played by the auto industry in air pollution because the auto industry was one of the paper's major advertisers.[36] Lee and Solomon write,

> These days, no commercial TV executive in his right mind would produce a program without considering whether it will fly with the sponsors. Prospective shows are often discussed with major advertisers, who review script treatments and suggest changes when necessary.... Procter and Gamble, which spends over a billion dollars a year on advertising, once decreed in a memo on broadcast policy "There will be no material that will give offense, either directly or indirectly to any commercial organization of any sort." Ditto for Prudential Insurance: "A positive image of business and finance is important to sustain on the air."[37]

Lee and Solomon discuss in some detail a documentary aired by NBC about nuclear power plants in France, which "could have passed for an hour-long nuclear power commercial." The correspondent stated, "Looking at a foreign country where nuclear power is a fact of life may restore some reason to the discussion at home.... In most countries, especially the U.S., emotions drive the nuclear debate and that makes rational dialogue very difficult." The implication is that opposition to nuclear power in the United States is emotional, not rational. No mention was made that NBC's parent company, General Electric, was a major supplier of nuclear power, with 39 nuclear reactors in the United States. Nor was there mention of contentious debate among the French about nuclear power. Nor did NBC later report the accidents injuring seven people in French nuclear power plants only one month after the airing of the special, accidents that received a good deal of coverage in the French media and some coverage in U.S. newspapers.[38]

When the major media outlets are owned by transnational corporations and dependent upon advertising revenue from corporations, they do not constitute a "free press." In the strictest sense, there probably is no such thing as a free press. Government-controlled media are, of course, not free either. Both government-controlled media and commercially controlled media are inherently inclined to bias. However, of interest to the critical constructionist is the popular perception of corporate control as representing the opposite of government control and, therefore, representing the "free" alternative. This construction enables corporate interests to have immeasurable influence on social problem construction. According to David Edwards,

> [T]he mass media system is not a medium for the "free" discussion of ideas and viewpoints, but is deeply embedded in, and dependent on, the wider corporate

status quo, and on the related capacity of corporate communications to boost facts, ideas, and political choices that are conducive to profit maximization, and to stifle those that are not.[39]

Irrespective of their ties to the corporate world, the status quo receives further nourishment from news journalists by their ostensible obsession with "impartiality." Though, as described earlier, their interests are aligned with corporate interests, news journalists are very careful not to appear to be taking sides. News journalists frequently boast about their objectivity, claiming to be impartial in obsessively covering "both" sides of the issues—even when there might be more than two sides to an issue or when one of the two sides to an issue happens to represent a minority opinion or the lunatic fringe. The British tend to take the issue of global warming much more seriously than do Americans. Fiona Harvey, environment correspondent for the *Financial Times*, explains, "In the United States, you have lots of news stories that, in the name of balance, give equal credence to the skeptics. We don't do that here—not because we're not balanced—but because we think it's unbalanced to give equal validity to a fringe few with no science behind them."[40]

In the realm of politics, one can be either for maintaining the status quo or for change. If one is not in favor of change, then, in effect, one supports the status quo. In striving to maintain the appearance of objectivity, in failing to take sides, news journalists are thus supporting the status quo by default. Those advocating change face an uphill battle trying to influence problem construction when the media can always be expected to give the opposing side "equal time." Environmental sociologist John Hannigan writes,

> [R]eporters may turn to the "equal time" technique whereby both environmental claims-makers and their opponents are quoted with no attempt to resolve who is right. In this case it becomes difficult for environmentalists to convince the public that an "issue" is in fact a "problem."[41]

The principle of impartiality in news journalism makes it very easy for corporations (and often their paid skeptics) to exploit the scientific uncertainty surrounding global warming. According to Paul Rauber,

> In the pursuit of "impartiality" the U.S. news media reflexively seek out the Two Sides to Every Question....It happens more so when the topic is the least bit technical; most reporters don't know much about science, and are unable to distinguish legitimate scientific dispute from bogus posturing. Which is why there is still a "debate" about global warming.[42]

Though it is likely that many of the scientists who are skeptical of global warming are sincere and not just "posturing," the skeptics do make up a very small minority in the scientific community, and the tendency of news journalism to present both sides "equally" obscures their minority status, thereby weakening the argument of the majority. The public is left with the impression that "nobody knows what they are talking about" and, therefore, there is no need for more regulations on industry.

Since James Hansen, director of NASA's Institute for Space Studies, alerted the public to the potential devastation of global warming in 1988—even if U.S. policymakers took up the mantle today—the denial, obstructionism, and foot-dragging that has taken place over the past 20 years is not likely to have been without consequence. Mark Hertsgaard writes in a 2006 *Vanity Fair* article,

> But if the deniers appear to have lost the scientific argument, they prolonged the policy battle, delaying actions to reduce emissions when such cuts mattered the most. "For 25 years people have been warning that we have a window of opportunity to take action, and if we waited until the effects were obvious it would be too late to avoid major consequences," says Oppenheimer [a professor of geosciences and international affairs at Princeton]. Had some individual countries, especially the United States, begun to act in the early to mid-1990s, we might have made it. But we didn't, and now the impacts are here."[43]

CRITICAL THINKING QUESTIONS

It is often said that all is fair in love and war. Does that go as well for the war between industry and environmentalism? Or, can you cite cases, either given in this reading or found elsewhere, when either side has, in your opinion, stepped over the line?

NOTES

1. Daniel Faber and James O'Connor, "Capitalism and the Crisis of Environmentalism," in R. Hofrichter (ed.), *Toxic Struggles: The Theory and Practice of Environmental Justice*. Philadelphia: New Society, 1993, 14.
2. Sharon Beder, *Global Spin: The Corporate Assault on Environmentalism*. White River Junction, VT: Chelsea Green, 1997, 17.
3. Ibid., 19.
4. Ibid., 21.
5. Frederick H. Buttell and Peter J. Taylor, "Environmental Sociology and Global Environmental Change: A Critical Assessment," *Society and Natural Resources*, vol. 5, 1992, 223.
6. Gerald Markowitz and David Rosner, *Deceit and Denial: The Deadly Politics of Industrial Pollution*. Berkeley: University of California Press, 2002, 10.
7. "Toxic Deception: An Interview with Dan Fagin," *Multinational Monitor*, vol. 20, no. 3, March 1999, 3.
8. Beder, *Global Spin*, 109.
9. Ibid., 114.
10. Ibid., 115.
11. John Stauber and Sheldon Rampton, *Toxic Sludge Is Good for You: Lies, Damn Lies and the Public Relations Industry*. Monroe, ME: Common Courage Press, 1995, 2.
12. Martin A. Lee and Norman Solomon, *Unreliable Sources: A Guide to Detecting Bias in News Media*. New York: Carol, 1992, 66.
13. Ibid.
14. Ibid., 65.

15. Beder, *Global Spin*, 116.
16. Ibid., 112.
17. Ibid., 32.
18. "Public Interest Pretenders," *Consumer Reports*, vol. 59, no. 5, 1994, 318.
19. Ibid., 316.
20. Beder, *Global Spin*, 29.
21. Sharon Beder, *Global Spin: The Corporate Assault on Environmentalism*, revised edition. White River Junction, VT: Chelsea Green, 2002.
22. Arianna Huffington, *Pigs at the Trough: How Corporate Greed and Political Corruption Are Undermining America*. New York: Crown, 2003.
23. Quoted in Stauber and Rampton, *Toxic Sludge*, 5.
24. Ibid., 8.
25. Ibid., 9.
26. Ibid., 12.
27. Ibid., 10.
28. Beder, *Global Spin*, 1997, 63.
29. Ibid.
30. George Pring and Penelope Canan, *SLAPPs: Getting Sued for Speaking Out*. Philadelphia: Temple University Press, 1996.
31. Ibid., xi.
32. Calvin Exoo, *The Politics of the Mass Media*. St. Paul, MN: West, 1994, 88.
33. Ibid.
34. Beder, *Global Spin*, 1997, 180.
35. Exoo, *The Politics of the Mass Media*.
36. Michael Parenti, *Inventing Reality: The Politics of News Media*, 2nd ed. New York: St Martin's Press, 1993.
37. Lee and Solomon, *Unreliable Sources*, 60.
38. Ibid., 78.
39. Edwards, Foreword, in Beder, *Global Spin*, 1997, 9.
40. Quoted in Mark Hertsgaard, "While Washington Slept," *Vanity Fair*, May 2006. Retrieved online July 11, 2008.
41. John Hannigan, *Environmental Sociology: A Social Constructionist Perspective*. London: Routledge, 1995, 68.
42. Paul Rauber, "The Uncertainty Principle," *Sierra*, vol. 81, September–October 1996, 20.
43. Hertsgaard, "While Washington Slept."

CHAPTER 25

The Wealth of the Poor: Managing Ecosystems to Fight Poverty

World Resources Institute

NATURAL RESOURCES PLAY A VITAL ROLE IN THE LIVELIHOODS OF THE POOR

Poor rural families make use of a variety of sources of income and subsistence activities to make their livings. Many of these are directly based on nature—like small-scale farming and livestock-rearing, fishing, hunting, and collecting of firewood, herbs, or other natural products. These may be sold for cash or used directly for food, heat, building materials, or innumerable other household needs. This "environmental income" is added to other income sources such as wage labor and remittances sent from family members who have emigrated. The decline of natural systems through soil depletion, deforestation, overexploitation, and pollution represents a direct threat to nature-based income and is a contributor to increasing poverty....

Common Pool Natural Resources Are a Key Source of Subsistence

The poor make extensive use of goods collected from lands or waters over which no one individual has exclusive rights—resources known generally as common pool resources (CPRs) or simply the "commons" (Jodha 1986:1169; Ostrom 1990:30). Common pool resources exist in many different ecosystems and under a variety of public or community ownership regimes. Typical examples include village pastures, state or community forests, waste lands, coastal waters, rivers, lakes, village ponds, and the like (Jodha 1986:1169).

Materials gleaned from CPRs consist of a wide range of items for personal use and sale including food, fodder, fuel, fiber, small timber, manure, bamboos, medicinal plants, oils, and building materials for houses and furniture. Fish, shellfish, seaweed, and other items harvested from coastal waters, rivers, and other aquatic environments are also of major importance to the poor. Nearly all rural families—both rich and poor—benefit from CPR income, but it is particularly important to landless households, for whom it provides a major fraction of total income. Researchers estimate that common pool resources provide about 12 percent of household income to poor households in India—worth about $5 billion a year, or double the amount of development aid that India receives (Beck and Nesmith 2001:119).

When access to common pool resources is unrestricted, as it is often is, it is difficult to keep them from being overexploited. Degradation of open access resources in the form of overfishing, deforestation, and overgrazing is an increasing burden on the poor—a trend that leads away from wealth.

Natural Resources Are Vital Social Safety Nets during Lean Times

Natural resources play a key role as a subsistence source of last resort in times of economic decline and when other food supplies are constrained. In southeastern Ghana, for example, recession and drought in 1982 and 1983 coincided with the normal lean season—the time before harvest when food supplies are naturally low. During this lean season, the poorest households depended on the "bush" for 20 percent of their food intake, compared to the highest income bracket, for which the bush provided only 2 percent of the household food intake. Women and children in particular relied on wild products such as roots, fibers, leaves, bark, fruit, seeds, nuts, insects, and sap. Men also hunted and trapped small mammals, reptiles, and birds (Dei 1992:67).

Environmental Factors Add to the Health Burden of the Poor

Environmental risks such as unclean water, exposure to indoor air pollution, insect-borne diseases, and pesticides account for almost a quarter of the global burden of disease, and an even greater proportion of the health burden of the poor (Cairncross et al. 2003:2; Lvovsky 2001:1). The poor are far more likely to be exposed to environmental health risks than the rich by virtue of where they live. They also have much less access to good health care, making their exposure more damaging. In turn, poor health is an important obstacle to greater income and a contributor to diminished well-being in every dimension of life.

Climate Change Adds to the Vulnerability of the Poor

The adverse impacts of climate change will be most striking in developing nations—and particularly among the poor—both because of their high dependence on natural resources and their limited capacity to adapt to a changing climate. Water scarcity is already a major problem for the world's poor, and changes in rainfall and temperature associated with climate change will likely make this worse. Even without climate change, the number of people impacted by water scarcity is projected to increase from 1.7 billion today to 5 billion by 2025 (IPCC 2001:9).

In addition, crop yields are expected to decline in most tropical and subtropical regions as rainfall and temperature patterns change with a changing climate (IPCC 2001:84). A recent report by the Food and Agriculture Organization estimates that developing nations may experience an 11 percent decrease in lands suitable for rain fed agriculture by 2080 due to climate change (FAO 2005:2). There is also some evidence that disease vectors such as malaria-bearing mosquitoes will spread more widely (IPCC 2001:455). At the same time, global warming may bring an increase in severe weather events like cyclones and torrential rains. The inadequate construction and exposed locations of poor people's dwellings often makes them the most likely victims of such natural disasters.

NATURE AS AN ECONOMIC STEPPING STONE

Nature has always been a route to wealth, at least for a few. Profit from harvesting timber and fish stocks, from converting grasslands to farm fields, and from exploiting oil, gas, and mineral reserves has created personal fortunes, inspired stock markets, and powered the growth trajectories of nations for centuries. But this scale of natural resource wealth has been amassed mostly through unsustainable means, and the benefits have largely accrued to the powerful. It is the powerful who generally control resource access through land ownership or concessions for logging, fishing, or mining on state lands; who command the capital to make investments; and who can negotiate the government regulatory regimes that direct the use of natural resources. The poor, by contrast, have reaped precious little of the total wealth extracted from nature. But that can change.

Natural Resources Are a Key Determinant of Rural Wealth

Even though they do not currently capture most of the wealth created by natural systems, the livelihoods of the poor are built around these systems. Indeed, natural resources are the fundamental building block of most rural livelihoods in developing nations, and not just during lean times....

The ability to efficiently tap the productivity of ecosystems is often one of the most significant determinates of household income. For example, studies show that the key variable explaining income levels for rural households in Uganda is access to land and livestock. In Ugandan villages near Lake Victoria, the key variable explaining wealth is access to fishing boats and gear. Income-wise, these are found to be even more important than other wealth-associated factors such as access to education (Ellis and Bahiigwa 2003:1003).

Beyond Subsistence: Natural Endowments as Capital for the Poor

Ecosystem goods and services—the natural products and processes that ecosystems generate—are often the only significant assets the poor have access to. These natural endowments, if managed efficiently, can provide a capital base—a foundation for greater economic viability, and a stepping stone beyond mere subsistence. Yet the potential of these assets is often overlooked.

Typical commercial evaluation of natural resources tends to undervalue the total array of ecosystem goods and services, which includes not just the crops, lumber, fish, and forage that are the usual focus of exploitation, but also a wide variety of other collectibles, agroforestry products, small-scale aquaculture products, as well as services such as maintenance of soil fertility, flood control, and recreation (Lampietti and Dixon 1995:1–3; Pagiola et al. 2004:15–19). One of the consequences of the difficulty of assigning a monetary value to ecosystem benefits is that it has led to the systematic undervaluation of the assets of the poor and the underestimation of the potential benefits of improved environmental management.

But the potential for strategic management of ecosystems to raise the incomes of the poor is real. In fact, good ecosystem management can become one of the engines of rural economic growth more generally. Experience shows that the poor use several strategies to make their ecosystem assets a stepping-stone out of poverty.

Restoring Productivity

Where ecosystems are degraded, it limits their potential as a source of environmental income. Many communities have found that restoring the productivity of local forests, pastures, or fisheries has the opposite effect, raising local incomes substantially. Often this entails a community effort to more carefully control the use of common property areas and even private lands. For example, the village of Sukhomajri in Haryana, India, has gained widespread recognition for its success in raising village incomes through community efforts to restore and maintain the productivity of local forests and farmland. Careful land management and rainwater harvesting produced large gains in agricultural production, tree density, and available water, increasing annual household incomes by 50 percent in five years (Agarwal and Narain 1999:16).

Many other watershed management projects in India have also reported benefits to village residents, including poor families who do not own land. In the Adgaon watershed in Maharashtra, annual days of employment (wage labor) per worker increased from 75 days at the project's inception to over 200 days after restoration was complete. In Mendhwan Village, laborers found eight months of agricultural work per year after four years of watershed management, compared with only three months before the community began its restoration and management project (Kerr et al. 2002:56).

Marketing Niche Products and Services

One common way to translate ecosystem assets into economic gain is to create or take advantage of niche markets for nontimber forest products, such as bamboo, mushrooms, herbs, and other collectibles. In Nam Pheng village in northwestern Laos, villagers began a cooperative effort in 1996 to expand the market for bitter bamboo and cardamom. They created a coordinated management plan for sustainable harvest of these traditional products, improved the harvest technology, and established a marketing group to both increase sales and obtain higher prices for their wares. By 2001 a day's harvest of bitter bamboo brought ten times the wages of slash-and-burn cultivation, which had been the villagers' main livelihood activity (Morris 2002:10–24).

By 2002, harvesting bitter bamboo and cardamom provided the main source of income for most villagers and the community had made considerable progress toward higher incomes and more secure livelihoods. The village poverty rate had fallen by more than half, food security had increased, and the mortality rate for children under five had fallen to zero. In addition, enough community funds from the joint marketing group had been raised to build a school, prompting school enrollment to double, with more than half of the students being girls. While the income potential from bamboo and cardamom is not unlimited, it has clearly provided a stepping stone to larger capital investments, such as livestock, and allowed villagers to diversify their income sources. It has also brought villagers an appreciation of the forest as an economic asset, providing an incentive for long-term care of the forest ecosystem (Morris 2002:10–24).

In addition to marketing forest products like bamboo, poor households can find substantial income marketing ecosystem services, such as recreation. In Namibia, communities have successfully tapped the ecotourism trade built around viewing and hunting the area's springbok, wildebeest, elephants, giraffes, and other animal populations. To accomplish this, the communities have formed legally constituted "conservancies" to regulate the hunting, sightseeing, camping, and other activities that affect local wildlife. The conservancies have generated direct benefits ranging from jobs and training to cash and meat payouts to community members. In 2004, total community benefits reached N$14.1 million (US$2.5 million) in value. Studies have documented that, over the course of 10 years, the conservancies have enhanced the livelihood security of local people while spurring major recoveries in wildlife populations (WWF and Rossing Foundation 2004:v–vi; Vaughan et al. 2003:18–19).

Capturing a Greater Share of the Natural Resource Value

Maximizing environmental income involves not only improved resource management or creation of new markets for nontraditional or underexploited products. It also requires greater attention to marketing traditional products such as fish, so that more of the revenue generated is captured by the fishers themselves in the form of higher prices for their harvests. In Kayar, a community along the coast of Senegal, local fishers worked together to regulate their fish catch, with the idea of stabilizing the catch and insuring a good price at market (Lenselink 2002:43). By limiting the quantity of fish each boat owner could deliver to market each day, they successfully raised fish prices to the point that fishers had surplus income to save. At the same time, fish stocks were better managed by limiting the number of fishers allowed in a given area, the number of fishing trips allowed per day, and the kinds of permissible fishing gear (Lenselink 2002:43; Siegel and Diouf 2004:4, 6). The Kayar fishers made economics and ecosystem management work hand in hand. The examples described above involved a different understanding of nature's wealth from the conventional view of large-scale extraction—a different view of what natural wealth is, how it can best be tapped, and who is to benefit from it.

ECOSYSTEM MANAGEMENT AS A BASIS FOR AGRICULTURE GROWTH, RURAL DIVERSIFICATION, AND GENERAL ECONOMIC GROWTH

Making ecosystems work as an economic asset for the poor should be seen not as an isolated goal but part of a larger strategy for rural development. Utilizing the natural assets of the poor is not a "silver bullet" for poverty reduction that can single-handedly bring wealth to poor families. It is rather part of a general transition of rural economies from subsistence to wealth accumulation, working first to support a more profitable small scale agriculture and natural resource economy—the current mainstays of rural livelihoods—and eventually to build a complementary rural industrial and service economy (World Bank 2003:xix–xxvi).

Agriculture is a particularly important piece of the rural poverty equation. There is a well-established connection between improvements in small-scale agriculture and poverty reduction. One study in Africa found that a 10 percent increase in crop yields led to a 9 percent decrease in the number of people living on $1 per day (Irz et al. 2001 in World Bank 2003:xix). Indeed, rapid agricultural growth is considered a primary avenue for poverty alleviation (Smith and Urey 2002:71). From the 1960s to the 1980s, the Green Revolution's use of modern seeds and fertilizers, irrigation, better credit, roads, and technical assistance helped bring this kind of rapid agricultural growth to many rural areas, with a corresponding reduction in poverty. For example, from 1965 to 1991—the period of greatest Green Revolution gains—rural poverty rates in India declined from 54 percent of the population to 37 percent (Smith and Urey 2002:17).

But spreading the Green Revolution's success to the poor families and the marginal lands it has by-passed will require something more than the technocratic approach of those earlier decades. It will also require good ecosystem management by the poor that helps build and retain soil fertility and allows small farmers to harvest and efficiently use water resources. Failure to take this approach has resulted in fertility loss, salinization, and overdrafting of groundwater on many of the Green Revolution farms—environmental problems that have begun to erode productivity gains in many areas (Smith and Urey 2002:10).

Sustained agricultural growth, augmented by other forms of environmental income, from forest products to forage to aquaculture, can help many poor rural families to create an asset base that allows them to begin the transition away from sole dependence on farming and nature-based activities. Research shows that as growth proceeds, agriculture eventually begins to play a less crucial role in the overall development process and subsequently declines as a share of economic output (Timmer 1988:276, 279). Rural residents begin to depend more on rural industry and so-called "off-farm" income, which provide an additional and quicker route out of poverty to complement agriculture.

But even as rural economies slowly diversify, nature will still play an important role. Many rural industries—such as local processing of agriculture or fishing products, crafts production, and ecotourism—will themselves be indirectly dependent on natural resources. They will thus benefit from a sound approach to ecosystem management. For example, when the shrimp processing company Aqualma was established in 2000 in a remote corner of Madagascar, it brought permanent jobs to 1,200 rural workers, most of whom had never held a wage paying job. But Aqualma's future relies entirely on sound fishing practices that insure a continuing shrimp supply. In other words, a good relationship to ecosystems and environmental income supports many dimensions of rural growth and is beneficial at several points in the economic evolution of the rural poor from subsistence to wealth (World Bank 2003:xxii).

BETTER GOVERNANCE IS VITAL FOR HIGHER INCOMES

Maximizing environmental income for the poor requires changes in the governance of natural resources. The need for such changes is pressing because the poor are at a great disadvantage when it comes to controlling natural resources or the decisions surrounding them. They often lack legal ownership or tenure over land and resources, which restricts their access and makes their homes and livelihoods insecure. They also suffer from a lack of voice in decision-making processes, cutting them out of the decision-making loop. Natural-resource corruption falls harder on the poor as well, who may be the victims of bribe-demanding bureaucrats or illegal logging and fishing facilitated by corrupt officials who look the other way. The poor are also subject to a variety of policies—such as taxes and various regulations—that are effectively anti-poor.

These governance burdens make it hard for poor families to plan effectively, to make investments that might allow them to profit from their assets or skills, or to work together effectively to manage common areas or create markets for their products. In other words, governance burdens quickly translate to economic obstacles.

Tenure Security Is a Primary Obstacle

Ownership and access are the most fundamental keys to the wealth of nature. Unfortunately, many poor people do not own the land or fishing grounds they rely on for environmental income. This lack of secure tenure makes them vulnerable to being dispossessed of their homes and livelihoods, or, if they rent homes or land, subject to sometimes exorbitant rent payments. The importance of tenure—or the lack of it—to the ability to tap nature's wealth can't be stressed too much. The rights to exploit, sell, or bar others from using a resource—the bundle of rights associated with tenure or ownership—are essential to legal commerce. Ownership also provides an incentive to manage ecosystems sustainably by assuring that an owner will be able to capture the benefits of long-term investments like soil improvements, tree planting, or restricting fishing seasons to keep fish stocks viable.

Tenure issues affecting the poor involve not only private ownership of land, but also the use of common lands. Many areas under state ownership provide the resource base for poor communities, but these communities often have no legal basis for their use of common pool resources. In many instances, these resources—whether they are forests, grazing areas, or fishing grounds—have been governed locally for centuries under traditional forms of "communal tenure," in which resources are owned in common by a group of individuals, such as a village or tribe.

Unfortunately, such customary arrangements are often not legally recognized, and conflicts between communal tenure and modern state-recognized ownership frequently threaten rural livelihoods. State recognition of such traditional ownership arrangements or new power-sharing agreements between local communities and the state that grant specific rights to use and profit from the state commons are often important ingredients in successful efforts to tap the wealth of natural systems (Meinzen-Dick and Di Gregorio 2004:1–2).

LACK OF VOICE, PARTICIPATION, AND REPRESENTATION

When important decisions about local resources are made, the poor are rarely heard or their interests represented. Often these decisions, such as the awarding of a timber concession on state forest land that may be occupied by poor households, are made in the state capitol or in venues far removed from rural life. Even if they could make it to these decision-making venues, the poor—and other rural residents as well—would still be unlikely to find a seat at the table. The right for local resource users to participate in resource decisions is still a relatively new concept in most areas and often not embodied in law. Language barriers, ignorance of their legal rights, and a lack of full information about how resource decisions are likely to affect them are also potent obstacles to the participation of the poor. Lack of money, of political connections, and of lawyers or other advocates that can articulate their needs are all sources of political isolation and marginalization (WRI et al. 2003:44–64).

THE WEALTHY DOMINATE THE ECONOMIC MACHINERY

Wealthier landowners and traders tend to dominate the resources and economic tools necessary to turn natural resources to wealth. In addition to owning more and better land, livestock, farm machinery, boats, or other assets directly relevant to profiting from ecosystems, the rich also tend to have greater access to resources like irrigation water, seed, fertilizers, pest control, and labor (Narayan and Petesch 2002:58–59, 188; Narayan et al. 2000:49–50; Kerr et al. 2002:61). The wealthy also have easier access to credit, which is a key constraint for the poor wishing to improve their ecosystem assets by planting trees, undertaking soil or water conservation projects, or developing new products or markets.

These advantages are often magnified by the dense and interlinked social networks in rural areas, which tend to reinforce the near-monopoly position enjoyed by some wealthier families, leaving poorer families with fewer options and sometimes all-or-nothing choices (Bardhan 1991:240). For instance, surveys from West Bengal, India, found that laborers tied to their landlords through credit were less likely to take part in group bargaining and agitation for raising rural wages. These indentured workers felt it was a choice between a low wage or no job at all—a cycle of dependence that can be self-perpetuating (Bardhan 1991:240).

Capture of State-Owned Natural Resources by the Elite—Facilitated by Corruption

In many cases, state-owned resources like forests and fisheries are opened to exploitation by granting individuals or companies concessional leases or harvest licenses. The wealthy are much more likely to be able to take advantage of these. In Bangladesh, the government leases rights to fish in state-owned water bodies for a period of one to three years through a public auctioning system that generates considerable revenue for the state. Unfortunately, poor fishermen can rarely afford to bid, so the licenses are purchased by rich investors known as "waterlords." These entrepreneurs hire fishermen as daily laborers at low wages, keeping most of the profits for themselves. This has led, in effect, to the institutionalized exploitation of the fishermen by a small rural elite (Béné 2003:964). In other instances, lease holders will exclude the poor altogether from their concession, even though they may have traditionally lived on and collected from these lands.

This problem of the capture of state resources by the elite is worsened by corruption, political patronage, and sweetheart deals for insiders. Such corruption and favoritism often focuses on natural resource concessions in remote areas far from official concern and public scrutiny—precisely those areas inhabited by the poor. In 2001, Bob Hasan, Indonesia's former Minister of Industry and Trade, was sentenced to prison for forest-related graft worth $75 million. For years, the timber magnate and close associate of former President Suharto dominated Indonesia's lucrative plywood trade, at one point controlling nearly 60 percent of world tropical plywood exports (Borsuk 2003:1; Barr 1998:2, 30).

Apart from its role in enabling the elite capture of state resources, corruption also stands as a fundamental obstacle to the sustainable management of resources and thus another way in which the natural assets of the poor are diminished. Illegal logging and fishing are prime causes of the depletion of common pool resources that the poor depend on, short-circuiting effective state management of ecosystems and undermining customary management arrangements at the village or tribal level as well (WRI et al. 2003:36–38). Demands by local officials for bribes or other considerations for access to resources place a special burden on the poor and encourage low income families to themselves engage in illegal logging, fishing, and other unsustainable resource uses. At a national level, corruption acts as a drag on the economy, behaving essentially as a tax on legitimate businesses. Research shows that corruption suppresses national economic growth—one of the main requirements for effective and widespread poverty reduction (Thomas et al. 2000:144–150).

Anti-Poor Taxes and Regulations Work against Economic Empowerment

In many countries, natural resource-related activities such as timber extraction, fishing, grazing, small-scale agriculture, and water use are subject to controls and taxes that are regressive with respect to the poor. In China, grain farmers—many of whom are poor—until recently were obliged to sell the government a fixed quota of their production at below market prices, essentially lowering their potential income (Ravallion and Chen 2004:21–22). In Uganda, households face a confusing array of resource-related taxes, which often appear arbitrary to rural families. These include taxes on activities as diverse as smoking fish, growing maize, and slaughtering cows or goats (Ellis and Bahiigwa 2003:1008–1009). Around Lake Chad in central Africa, fishery fees are levied by three distinct groups: by traditional authorities, by the central government, and by soldiers (Béné 2003:970). Such overlapping fees discourage low-income families from engaging in market transactions that would help them generate returns from their access to natural resources.

In addition, well-intentioned environmental regulations are sometimes introduced in a draconian way that hurts the poor. For example, there is evidence that China's 1998 ban on tree felling in the upper watersheds of the Yangtze and Yellow River Basins has had very negative impacts on some poor households. The ban was meant to restore the health of the watersheds and avoid repeating the disastrous floods on the Yangtze that had occurred earlier that year. However, expansion of the logging ban beyond state-owned forests into private and collectively owned land has cost numerous jobs and restricted local communities' access to forest products in these areas (Xu et al. 2002:6, 8). In Mali, a 1986 forest law banned bush fires, made felling of certain species illegal without Forest Department permission, and made wood-saving stoves compulsory. In response, the wood trade was forced underground, and poor people unable to pay fines levied against them had their livestock confiscated (Benjaminsen 2000:97, 99–100).

THE ENVIRONMENT AS A ROUTE TO DEMOCRATIC GOVERNANCE

The environment provides a powerful tool to promote democratic reform. Particularly among the poor, it offers a unique opening for localizing and building demand for democratic practices because of its connection with livelihoods. In turn, good environmental governance is essential to developing, strengthening, and consolidating democracy in the world's poorest nations because it is a prerequisite for the poor to realize greater income from the environment.

Counteracting the bias against the poor that is embedded in government policies, institutions, and laws will require significant political change. That in turn demands greater access by the poor to true participation, accurate information, and fair representation. The environment itself provides one effective route for this needed transition to democratic decision-making. In countless communities in Africa, Asia, and Latin America, control over and use of natural resources are matters of everyday survival. These are governance issues with immediate bearing. The prospect of more equitable decisions about land and resources gives the ideals of democracy personal relevance to the poor. And it provides a motive for the kind of public activism that brings political change.

There are many examples of poor people organizing around environmental issues to prompt government action, gain rights, or call attention to gross inequities. The 1980s saw poor fishermen in the Indian state of Kerala organize to demand a seasonal ban on industrial trawlers that directly competed with local fishers and reduced their catch. Using tactics such as public fasts, road blocks, and marches against the government, the fishers became a political force that eventually coaxed fisheries managers to adopt a three-month seasonal ban on trawlers (Kurien 1992:238, 242–243). In Brazil's Amazon region, rubber tappers joined forces with the Indigenous People's Union to form the Alliance of Forest Peoples in the mid-1980s, demanding greater recognition of their resource rights. By 1995, their efforts had gained widespread support and the government designated some 900,000 hectares of rainforest as Extractive Reserves (Brown and Rosendo 2000:216).

Civil society in general has used the environment to great effect to push the process of democratization in regimes where civil liberties had been restricted. During the turn towards democracy in Chile and East Asia in the 1980s, and Eastern Europe in the 1990s, protests led by environment-focused civil society groups played an important role (McNeill 2000:347–348; WRI et al. 2003:67). For example, WAHLI, a prominent Indonesian environmental group, was one of the few NGOs tolerated by the Suharto government in the 1980s (Steele 2005).

The power of the environment as a stage for social action arose for two reasons. First, environmental problems were serious and were widely known, and second, environmental protests were seen—at least initially—as less overtly "political" and hence were more tolerated by government authorities. This ability for the environmental movement to maneuver where other civil society groups have not been given as much latitude is now manifesting in China, where activity by environmental NGOs is increasing (Economy 2005:1).

LINKING ENVIRONMENT AND GOVERNANCE IN THE GLOBAL POVERTY FIGHT

More than ever, national governments, international institutions, and donors are focused on poverty reduction. But their efforts have often given limited attention to the role of healthy ecosystems in providing sustainable livelihoods, and equally limited attention to the importance of environmental governance in empowering the poor. The models of economic growth that nations continue to rely on for poverty reduction—job creation through increased industrialization, intensified large-scale agriculture, industrial fishing fleets, and so on—do not fully appreciate the realities of rural livelihoods.

For example, these strategies miss the fundamental fact that if ecosystems decline through poor governance, the assets of the poor decline with them. Findings from the recently concluded Millennium Ecosystem Assessment—a five-year effort to survey the condition of global ecosystems—confirm that the burden of environmental decline already falls heaviest on the poor (MA 2005:2). This often results in an immediate drop in living standards—a descent into greater poverty. This in turn precipitates migration from rural areas to urban slums or a resort to unsustainable environmental practices—overfishing, deforestation, or depletion of soil nutrients—for bare survival's sake. For this reason alone—simply to prevent an *increase* in poverty—greater attention to ecosystem management and governance practices that serve the poor is vital. The promise that environment can be one of the engines of rural growth is all the more reason to keep environment as a focal point in poverty reduction efforts.

CRITICAL THINKING QUESTIONS

What are the obstacles to better resource management in poor countries? How do the interests and activities of the elite impede improved resource management?

REFERENCES

Agarwal, A., and S. Narain. 1999. "Community and Household Water Management: The Key to Environmental Regeneration and Poverty Alleviation." Presented at EU-UNDP Conference, Brussels, February 1999. Online at http://www.undp.org/seed/pei/publication/water.pdf.

Bardhan, P. 1991. "A Note on Interlinked Rural Economic Arrangements." In *The Economic Theory of Agrarian Institutions*, ed. P. Bardhan, 237–242. Oxford, UK: Clarendon Press.

Barr, C. 1998. "Bob Hasan, the Rise of Akpindo and the Shifting Dynamics of Control in Indonesia's Forestry Sector." *Indonesia* 65:1–36. Online at http://epublishing.library.cornell.edu/Dienst/Repository/1.0/Disseminate/seap.indo/1106953918/body/pdf?userid=&password=.

Beck, T., and C. Nesmith. 2001. "Building on Poor People's Capacities: The Case of Common Property Resources in India and West Africa." *World Development* 29(1): 119–133.

Benjaminsen, T. 2000. "Conservation Policies in the Sahel, Policies and People in Mali, 1990–1998." In *Producing Nature and Poverty in Africa*, eds. V. Broch-Due and R. Schroeder, 94–108. Uppsala: Nordiska Afrikainstitutet.

Béné, C. 2003. "When Fishery Rhymes with Poverty: A First Step Beyond the Old Paradigm in Small-Scale Fisheries." *World Development* 31(6):949–975.

Borsuk, R. 2003. "Suharto Crony Stays Busy Behind Bars: 'Bob' Hasan Starts Business, Pulls Strings at Olympics." *The Wall Street Journal* (August 13).

Brown, K., and S. Rosendo. 2000. "Environmentalists, Rubber-Tappers and Empowerment: The Politics of Extractive Reserves." *Development and Change* 31:201–227.

Cairncross, S., D. O'Neill, A. McCoy, and D. Sethi. 2003. "Health, Environment and the Burden of Disease; A Guidance Note." London: United Kingdom Department for International Development.

Dei, G. 1992. "A Ghanian Rural Community: Indigenous Responses to Seasonal Food Supply Cycles and the Socio-Economic Stresses of the 1990s." In *Development from Within: Survival in Rural Africa,* eds. D. Fraser Taylor and F. Mackenzie, 58–81. London: Routledge.

Economy, E. 2005. "China's Environmental Movement." Testimony before the Congressional Executive Commission on China, Roundtable on Environmental NGOs in China, February 7, 2005. Washington, DC: Council on Foreign Relations. Online at http://www.cfr.org/pub7770/elizabeth_c_economy/chinas_environmental_movement.php#.

Ellis, F., and G. Bahiigwa. 2003. "Livelihoods and Rural Poverty Reduction in Uganda." *World Development* 31(6):997–1013.

Food and Agriculture Organization of the United Nations (FAO). 2005. "Special Event on Impact of Climate Change, Pests and Diseases on Food Security and Poverty Reduction: Background Document." Paper presented to the 31st Session of the Committee on World Food Security. Rome: FAO.

Irz, X., L. Lin, C. Thirtle, and S. Wiggins. 2001. "Agricultural Productivity Growth and Poverty Alleviation." *Development Policy Review* 19(4):449–466.

Intergovernmental Panel on Climate Change (IPCC). 2001. "Climate Change 2001: Impacts, Adaptation and Vulnerability." *Contribution of Working Group I to the Third Assessment Report of the Intergovernmental Panel on Climate Change,* eds. J. McCarthy, O. Canziani, N. Leary, D. Dokken and K. White. Cambridge: Cambridge University Press.

Jodha, N. 1986. "Common Property Resources and Rural Poor in Dry Regions of India." *Economic and Political Weekly* 21(27):1169–1181.

Kerr, J., G. Pangare, and V. Pangare. 2002. "Watershed Development Projects in India: An Evaluation." Research Report 127. Washington, DC: International Food Policy Research Institute. Online at http://www.ifpri.org/pubs/abstract/127/rr127.pdf.

Kurien, J. 1992. "Ruining the Commons and Responses of the Commoners: Coastal Over-Fishing and Fishworkers' Actions in Kerala State, India." In *Grassroots Environmental Action,* eds. G. and J. Vivian, 221–258. London, UK: Routledge.

Lampietti, J., and J. Dixon. 1995. *To See the Forest for the Trees: A Guide to Non-Timber Forest Benefits.* Environmental Economics Series, Paper No. 013. Washington, DC: World Bank.

Lenselink, N. 2002. "Participation in Artisanal Fisheries Management for Improved Livelihoods in West Africa: A Synthesis of Interviews and Cases from Mauritania, Senegal, Guinea and Ghana." FAO Fisheries Technical Paper No. 432. Rome: Food and Agriculture Organization of the United Nations. Online at http://www.fao.org/DOCREP/005/Y4281E/Y4281E00.HTM.

Lvovsky, K. 2001. "Health and Environment." Environment Strategy Paper No. 1. Washington, DC: World Bank. Online at http://www-wds.worldbank.org/servlet/WDS_IBank_Servlet?pcont=details&eid=000094946_0205040403117.

McNeill, J. 2000. *Something New Under the Sun—An Environmental History of the Twentieth Century.* New York: W.W. Norton & Co.

Meinzen-Dick, R., and M. Di Gregorio. 2004. "Collective Action and Property Rights for Sustainable Development: Overview." In *Collective Action and Property Rights for Sustainable Development,* eds. R. Meinzen-Dick and M. DiGregorio, 3–4. 2020 Vision for Food, Agriculture and the Environment, Focus 11, Policy Brief No. 1. Washington, DC: International Food Policy Research Institute. Online at http://www.ifpri.org/2020/focus/focus11/focus11.pdf.

Morris, J. 2002. *Bitter Bamboo and Sweet Living: Impacts of NTFP Conservation Activities on Poverty Alleviation and Sustainable Livelihoods.* Prepared for IUCN's 31-C Project on Poverty Alleviation, Livelihood Improvement and Ecosystem Management. IUCN The World Conservation Union. Online at http://www.iucn.org/themes/fcp/publications/files/3ic_cs_lao.pdf.

Narayan, D., and P. Petesch. 2002. *Voices of the Poor: From Many Lands.* New York: Oxford University Press for the World Bank.

Ostrom, E. 1990. "Governing the Commons. The Evolution of Institutions for Collective Action." In *The Political Economy of Institutions and Decisions,* eds. J. Alt and D. North. Cambridge, UK: Cambridge University Press.

Pagiola, S., K. von Ritter, and J. Bishop. 2004. *Assessing the Economic Value of Conservation.* Environment Department Paper No. 101. Washington, DC: World Bank, IUCN World Conservation Union, and Nature Conservancy.

Ravallion, M., and S. Chen. 2004. "China's (Uneven) Progress Against Poverty." Policy Research Working Paper 3408. Washington, DC: World Bank. Online at http://econ.worldbank.org/files/38741_wps3408.pdf.

Siegel, P., and P. Diouf. 2004. "New Approaches to Shared Objectives." PowerPoint presentation. Dakar, Senegal: World Wildlife Fund West African Marine Ecoregion.

Smith, L., and I. Urey. 2002. *Agricultural Growth and Poverty Reduction: A Review of Lessons from the Post-Independence and Green Revolution Experience in India.* United Kingdom Department for International Development. Online at http://www.imperial.ac.uk/agriculturalsciences/research/sections/aebm/projects/poor_ag_downloads/indiaback.pdf.

Steele, P. 2005. Personal Communication. E-mail. June 7, 2005.

Timmer, P. 1988. "Agricultural Transformation." In *Handbook of Development Economics,* Volume 1, eds. H. Chenery and T. Srinivasan, 275–332. Elsevier Science.

Vaughan, K., S. Mulonga, J. Katjiuna, and N. Branston. 2003. "Cash from Conservation. Torra Community Tastes the Benefits: A Short Survey and Review of the Torra Conservancy Cash Payout to Individual Members." Wildlife Integration for Livelihood Diversification Project (WILD) Working Paper 15. Windhoek, Namibia: Namibia Directorate of Environmental Affairs and United Kingdom Department for International Development.

World Bank. 2003. *Reaching the Rural Poor: A Renewed Strategy for Rural Development.* Washington, DC: World Bank.

World Resources Institute (WRI), United Nations Development Programme, United Nations Environment Programme, and World Bank. 2000. *World Resources 2000–2001: People and Ecosystems—The Fraying Web of Life.* Washington, DC: WRI.

World Resources Institute (WRI), United Nations Development Programme, United Nations Environment Programme, and World Bank. 2003. *World Resources 2002–2004: Decisions for the Earth—Balance, Voice, and Power.* Washington, DC: WRI.

World Wildlife Fund, and Rossing Foundation. 2004. "Living in a Finite Environment Project. End of Project Report for Phase II: August 12, 1999 September 30, 2004." Draft Report, October 2004. Washington, DC: United States Agency for International Development.

Xu, J., E. Katsigris, and T. White, eds. 2002. *Implementing the Natural Forest Protection Program and the Sloping Land Conversion Program: Lessons and Policy Recommendations.* China Council for International Cooperation on Environment and Development.

CHAPTER 26

Differential Vulnerabilities: Environmental and Economic Inequality and Government Response to Unnatural Disasters

Robert D. Bullard

On August 29, 2005, Hurricane Katrina made landfall near New Orleans, leaving death and destruction across the Louisiana, Mississippi, and Alabama Gulf coast counties. Katrina was the most destructive hurricane in US history, costing over $70 billion in insured damage. Katrina was also one of the deadliest storms in decades, with a death toll of 1,836, and still counting. Katrina's death toll is surpassed only by the 1928 hurricane in Florida (estimates vary from 2,500 to 3,000 deaths) and the 8,000 who perished in the 1900 Galveston hurricane (Kleinberg, 2003; Pastor et al., 2006).

After some two and a half years, reconstruction continues to move at a slow pace in New Orleans and the Louisiana, Mississippi, and Alabama Gulf coast region. The lethargic recovery is now beginning to overshadow the deadly storm itself (Kromm and Sturgis, 2007). Questions linger: What went wrong? Can it happen again? Is government equipped to plan for, mitigate, respond to, and recover from natural and man-made disasters? Can the public trust government response to be fair? Does race matter when it comes to disaster relief?

WHY FOCUS ON THE SOUTH?

This paper uses the events that unfolded in New Orleans, the Gulf coast region, and the southern United States as the sociohistorical backdrop for examining social vulnerability and government response to unnatural disasters. The case studies of disparate treatment date back more than eight decades. The South is unique because of the legacy of slavery, Jim Crow segregation, and entrenched white supremacy. The region has a history of black business ownership, black home ownership, and black land ownership. Most black farmers are located in the South. It is no accident that the South gave birth to the modern civil rights movement and the environmental justice movement. And the vast majority (over 95 percent) of the 105 historically black colleges and universities are located in the South.

The 2000 census showed that African Americans ended the century by returning "home" to the South—the same region they spent most of the century escaping. Since the mid-seventies, reverse migration patterns indicate that more blacks are entering the South than leaving for other regions. Today, over 54 percent of the nation's blacks live in the South (McKinnon, 2000). In the 620 counties that make up the southern "blackbelt," stretching from Delaware to Texas, African Americans comprise a larger percentage of the total population than they do in the country as a whole—about 12 percent. In the 15 southern states (excluding Texas and Florida), blacks make up 22.8 percent of the population, compared with 3.5 percent for Hispanics.

Transportation serves as a key component in addressing poverty, unemployment, and equal opportunity goals, ensuring access to education, health care, and other public services. American society is largely divided between individuals with cars and those without cars (Bullard and Johnson, 1997). The private automobile is still the dominant travel mode of every segment of the American population, including the poor and people of color.

Nationally, only 7 percent of white households do not own a car, compared with 24 percent of African-American households, 17 percent of Latino households, and 13 percent of Asian-American households. Cars are an essential part of emergency evacuation plans. Disaster evacuation plans across the nation assume that people own a car. Nearly 11 million households in the United States lack vehicles, or more than 28 million Americans who would have difficulty evacuating their area in an emergency.

In 1997, to encourage better disaster planning, the Federal Emergency Management Agency (FEMA) launched Project Impact, a pilot program that provided funding for communities to assess their vulnerable populations and make arrangements to get people without transportation to safety (Elliston, 2004). The program reached 250 communities and proved quite effective. However, the Bush administration ended the program in 2001, and funds once earmarked for disaster preparation were shifted away.

For many individuals who do no own a car or drive, public transit is the primary mode of travel. However, transit does not always get you where you need to go. More important, many of the nation's regional transportation systems are "regional" in name only—with a good number of "separate and unequal" urban and suburban transit systems built along race and class lines. Too often race has literally stopped regional transit in its tracks.

New Orleans and Jefferson Parish, Louisiana, for example, run separate bus systems. Passengers on the New Orleans Rapid Transit Authority (NORTA) and Jefferson Transit are forced to switch buses at the parish line. Even Hurricane

Katrina floodwaters did not wash away the stubborn cultural divide that separates New Orleans from its suburbs. In November 2006, New Orleans and Jefferson Parish councils met to try to end the longtime regional transportation roadblock and bring the fractured city and suburban bus system in sync (Moran, 2006). The two jurisdictions had a chance to combine forces a year after Katrina, when Jefferson Parish awarded a three-year contract for management of its bus system. NORTA made a bid for the job, but Jefferson Parish chose a private Illinois company that offered a better deal.

On August 28, 2005, Mayor Ray Nagin ordered New Orleans' first ever mandatory evacuation since the city was founded in 1718. Hurricane Katrina demonstrated to the world the race and class disparities that mark who can escape a disaster by car. Emergency plans were particularly insufficient with regard to evacuation for the car-less and "special needs" populations—individuals who cannot simply jump into their cars and drive away (Department of Homeland Security, 2006). At least 100,000 New Orleans residents—and more than one-third of New Orleans' African-American residents—did not have cars to evacuate in case of a major storm (City of New Orleans, 2005). Over 15 percent of the city's residents relied on public transportation as their primary mode of travel (State of Louisiana, 2000; Bourne, 2004; City of New Orleans, 2005).

New Orleans had only one-quarter the number of buses that would have been needed to evacuate all car-less residents. Katrina's evacuation plan worked relatively well for people with cars, but failed to serve people who depend on public transit (Liftman, 2005).

After more than 80 percent of New Orleans flooded after the levee breach, most of the city's 500 transit and school buses were without drivers. About 190 NORTA buses were lost to flooding. Most of the NORTA employees were dispersed across the country and many were made homeless (Eggler, 2005). Disaster planners failed the weakest and most vulnerable in New Orleans—individuals without cars, nondrivers, children, the disabled, the homeless, the sick, and the elderly (Riccardi, 2005). Katrina exposed a major weakness in mass evacuation plans and for a moment focused the national spotlight on the heightened vulnerability of people without cars—a population that faces transportation challenges in everyday life (Dyson, 2006).

GOVERNMENT RESPONSE TO
WEATHER-RELATED DISASTERS

In the real world, all communities are not created equal. Some are more equal than others. If a community happens to be poor, black, or located on the "wrong side of the tracks," it receives less protection than communities inhabited largely by affluent whites in the suburbs. Generally, rich people tend to take the higher ground, leaving the poor and working class more vulnerable to flooding and environmental pestilence. Race maps closely with social vulnerability and the geography of environmental risks (Pastor et al., 2006).

Much of the death and destruction attributed to "natural" disasters is in fact unnatural and man-made. Humans prefer to make Mother Nature or God the villain in catastrophic losses from tsunamis, earthquakes, droughts, floods, and hurricanes, rather than placing responsibility squarely on social and political forces (Steinberg, 2003). What many people often call "natural" disasters are in fact acts of social injustice perpetuated by government and business on the poor, people of color, the disabled, the elderly, the homeless, those who are transit dependent and non-drivers—groups least able to withstand such disasters.

Quite often the scale of a disaster's impact has more to do with the political economy of the country, region, and state than with the hurricane's category strength (Jackson, 2005). Similarly, measures to prevent or contain the effects of disaster vulnerability are not equally provided to all. Typically, flood-control investments provide location specific benefits—with the greatest benefits going to populations who live or own assets in the protected area.

Weather-related disasters, including hurricanes, floods, droughts, and windstorms, are growing in frequency and intensity. Since 1980, 10,867 weather-related disasters have caused more than 575,000 deaths and have forced millions to flee their homes. Since 1980, the cost of weather-related disasters amount to more than $1 trillion (Worldwatch Institute, 2003). In 2004 alone, weather-related disasters caused $104 billion in economic losses, almost twice the total in 2003.

Each year communities along the Atlantic and Gulf coast are hit with tropical storms and hurricanes, forcing millions to flee to higher ground. Hurricanes Dennis, Katrina, and Rita displaced hundreds of thousands of people, destroyed tens of thousands of homes, and disrupted oil rigs and refineries. Historically, the Atlantic hurricane season produces on average ten storms, of which about six become hurricanes and two to three become major hurricanes.

The 2005 hurricane season produced a record of 27 named storms, topping the previous record of 21 storms set in 1933. It also saw 13 hurricanes—besting the old record of 12 hurricanes set in 1969 (Tanneeru, 2005). Twelve was the most hurricanes in one season since record keeping began in 1851. Three of the hurricanes in the 2005 season reached Category 5 status, meaning they had wind speeds greater than 155 mph at some point during the storm. Katrina's death toll (1,836) made it the third most deadly hurricane in the U.S.—surpassed, as was noted earlier, only by the 1928 hurricane in Florida (2,500 to 3,000) and the 1900 Galveston hurricane (8,000). The past events will show how marginalized populations are at risk to the built and natural environment. It will also show how various levels of government have responded differently to black and white disaster victims.

Mississippi River Flood (1927)

In his 1997 book, *Rising Tides: The Great Mississippi Rood of 1927 and How It Changed America*, John M. Barry details one of the most destructive natural disasters in American history (Barry, 1998). The 1927 flood was the worst flood to strike the country until the flooding caused by Hurricane Katrina in 2005. In the spring of 1927, incessant rains pushed the Mississippi River to over 30 feet in height and began eroding the levees from Cairo, Illinois, to Greenville, Mississippi. More than 27,000 square miles were inundated, and thousands of farms and hundreds of towns were wiped away by floodwater. Estimates of the damage ranged from $246 million to $1 billion (roughly $2 billion to $7.8 billion in modern dollars). The official death toll reached 246 with perhaps thousands more African-American deaths uncounted.

Nearly a million people in the Mississippi Delta were made homeless. White racism and Jim Crow added to the disaster. Government response to the flood is a classic case of environmental racism. Whites were evacuated, while 330,000 African Americans were interned in 154 relief "concentration camps." Over 13,000 flood victims near Greenville, Mississippi, were taken from area farms and evacuated to the crest of an unbroken levee, and stranded there for days without food or clean water, while boats arrived to evacuate white women and children. Many blacks were detained and forced to work on the levee at gunpoint during flood relief efforts.

Black work gangs and their families were held as virtual prisoners in dreadfully squalid concentration camps set up along miles of the Greenville levee (Barry, 1998). Thousands of displaced residents, black and white, left the land and never returned—accelerating black migration to the North and thus changing the political landscape of the country.

Florida Okeechobee Hurricane (1928)

In September 1928, the Okeechobee hurricane struck Florida with devastating force. It was the first Category 5 hurricane ever officially recorded in the Atlantic. The eye of the storm passed ashore in Palm Beach County with 140 mph winds, then struck a populated area on the southern edge of Lake Okeechobee (Brochu, 2003). The only bulwark between the low-lying communities and the massive lake was a 5-foot mud dike constructed to hold back the Lake Okeechobee during summer rains.

In his book, *Black Cloud: The Deadly Hurricane of 1928*, Eliot Kleinberg provides a graphic account of Florida's deadliest storm (Kleinberg, 2003). When the hurricane had passed, the dike broke and 2,500 to 3,000 people drowned, making it the second-deadliest hurricane in US history, behind the Galveston, Texas, hurricane of 1900 that killed 8,000 people.

Nobody really knows how many people died in the storm. For years, the Red Cross set the death toll at 1,836. In the summer of 2003, the National Hurricane Center increased the death toll from 1,836 to 2,500, with an asterisk suggesting the total could be as high as 3,000. Some accounts put the deaths closer to 3,500 (Barnes, 1998). Half of the 6,000 people living in the farming communities between Clewiston and Canal Point perished. More than 75 percent of the recorded deaths were black migrant workers, segregated in life and abandoned in death.

Palm Beach County in the 1920s was, as today, home to one of the world's great wealth enclaves with its glittering ocean drawing tourists from around the world. But just a 30-minute drive to the west takes you into a world of dirt roads, farm fields, poverty, and shantytowns inhabited largely by black migrant workers from the Deep South and the impoverished islands of the Caribbean. The 1928 Okeechobee hurricane "killed more people than the 1906 San Francisco earthquake (about 700), more than sinking of the *Titanic* (1,505), and probably more than the estimated 3,000 who died on September 11, 2001" (Kleinberg, 1998: xiv).

Devastation was complete. Although the storm destroyed everything in its path with impartiality, it hit the poor low-lying black areas around the lake the hardest. Belle Glade, Pahokee, and South Bay were virtually wiped off the map (Klinkenberg, 1992). Bodies, livestock, and lumber floated everywhere. Some survivors used bloated cows as rafts and splintered lumber as paddles. The bodies of the dead overwhelmed officials. The few caskets available were used to bury the bodies of whites. Other bodies were either burned or buried in mass graves. Burials were segregated and the only mass gravesite to receive a memorial contained only white bodies.

The savage storm was even immortalized in African-American writer Zora Neal Hurston's classic novel, *Their Eyes Were Watching God* (Hurston, 1998). However, no amount of public relations and government cover-up could hide the horror left by the floodwaters—especially damage the storm inflicted on the black population and the racism by whites that followed.

Hurricane Betsy, New Orleans (1965)

Hurricane Betsy struck the state of Louisiana and the city of New Orleans in 1965. Before Hurricane Katrina, Betsy was the most destructive hurricane on record to strike the Louisiana coast. The damage and flooding throughout the state covered 4,800 square miles, killed 81 people, caused about 250,000 to be evacuated, and disrupted transportation, communication, and utilities service throughout the eastern coastal area of Louisiana for weeks.

Betsy hit the mostly black and poor New Orleans Lower Ninth Ward especially hard. Betsy accelerated the decline of the neighborhood and out-migration of many of its longtime residents. This is the same neighborhood that was inundated by floodwaters from Katrina. Over 98 percent of the Lower Ninth Ward residents are black and a third live below the poverty level.

Many black New Orleans residents still believe that white officials intentionally broke the levee and flooded the Lower Ninth Ward to save mostly white neighborhoods and white business district. Many older blacks are still bitter about being trapped in attics after rising floodwaters from Hurricane Betsy in 1965. Blacks from diverse socioeconomic backgrounds believe the flooding of the Lower Ninth Ward and other black areas after Betsy was a deliberate act stemming from New Orleans Mayor Victor Schiro, who was not known for his progressive views on race, ordering the levees breached and floodwaters pumped out of his well-to-do white subdivision, Lake Vista, and into the Lower Ninth Ward (Remnick, 2005). Whether a conspiracy rumor or fact, the "Betsy experience" is the primary reason many Lower Ninth Ward residents keep hatchets in their attics. This mistrust of government probably saved thousands of lives after the levee breach four decades later when Katrina struck in 2005.

Debris from Betsy was dumped at the Agriculture Street landfill. Two mostly black New Orleans subdivisions, Gordon Plaza and Press Park, were later built on a portion of land that was used as a municipal landfill. The landfill was classified as a solid waste site but hazardous waste ended up at the site (Lyttle, 2004).

In 1969, the federal government created a home ownership program to encourage lower income families to purchase their first home. Press Park was the first subsidized housing project on this program in New Orleans. The federal program allowed tenants to apply 30 percent of their monthly rental payments toward the purchase of a family home. In 1987, 17 years later, the first sale was completed. In 1977, construction began on a second subdivision, Gordon Plaza. This development was planned, controlled, and constructed by the US Department of Housing and Urban Development (HUD) and the Housing Authority of New Orleans (HANO). Gordon Plaza consists of approximately 67 single-family homes.

In 1983, the Orleans Parish School Board purchased a portion of the Agriculture Street landfill site for a school. That this site had previously been used as a municipal dump prompted concerns about the suitability of the site for a school. The board contracted engineering firms to survey the site and assess it for contamination of hazardous materials. Heavy metals and organics were detected at the site.

Despite the warnings, Moton Elementary School, an $8 million "state of the art" public school opened with 421 students in 1989. In May 1986, the Environmental Protection Agency (EPA) performed a site inspection at the Agriculture Street landfill community. Although lead, zinc, mercury, cadmium, and arsenic were found at the site, based on the Hazard Ranking System (HRS) model used at that time, the score of 3 was not high enough to place them on the National Priorities List (the National Priorities List, or NPL, is the list of hazardous waste sites eligible for long-term remedial action financed under the EPA's federal Superfund program. The EPA regulations outline a formal process for assessing hazardous waste sites and placing them on the NPL).

On December 14, 1990, the EPA published a revised HRS model in response to the Superfund Amendment and Reauthorization Act (SARA) of 1986. On the request of community leaders, in September 1993, an Expanded Site Inspection (ESI) was conducted. On December 16, 1994, the Agriculture Street landfill community was placed on the National Priorities List (NPL) with a new score of 50.

The Agriculture Street landfill community is home to approximately 900 African-American residents. The average family income is $25,000 and the educational level is high school graduate and above. The community pushed for a buyout of their property and to be relocated. However, this was not the EPA's resolution of choice. A cleanup was ordered at a cost of $20 million; the community buyout would have cost only $14 million. The actual cleanup began in 1998 and was completed in 2001 (Lyttle, 2004).

The Concerned Citizens of Agriculture Street landfill filed a class-action suit against the city of New Orleans for damages and cost of relocation (Bullard, 2005). The residents filed the suit in order to force a relocation from the contaminated neighborhood. They were in the end forcibly relocated by Katrina. In January 2006, after 13 years of litigation, Seventh District Court Judge Nadine Ramsey ruled in favor of the residents—describing them as poor minority citizens who were "promised the American dream of first-time home ownership," though the dream "turned out to be a nightmare" (Finch, 2006). Her ruling could end up costing the city, the Housing Authority of New Orleans, and Orleans Parish School Board tens of millions of dollars.

Hurricane Hugo, South Carolina (1989)

In September 1989, Hurricane Hugo made its way to shore in South Carolina. Hugo caused 49 deaths, widespread damages and losses estimated to exceed $9 billion, temporary displacement of hundreds of thousands of people, and disruption of the lives of about 2 million people. Twenty-six of South Carolina's 46 counties, covering two-thirds of the state, were declared federal disaster areas. Following Hugo, African-Americans and less-educated victims received less help than similarly affected victims who were white or more educated (Kaniasty and Norris, 1995).

Bureaucratic blindness and biased relief assistance in South Carolina following Hugo further marginalized an already economically marginalized African American population, leaving behind many blacks who lacked insurance and other support systems. These practices deepened the existing economic divide between blacks and whites (Cannon et al., 2004).

Hurricane Andrew, Miami-Dade and South Florida (1992)

Hurricane Andrew struck southern Florida in 1992 and forced an estimated 700,000 residents from their homes (Pittman, 2002). Over 250,000 people were left homeless, 15 were killed, and 1.5 million were left without water, electricity, and telephones. At least 75,000 homes were destroyed and 108 schools were damaged (3 were destroyed).

An estimated 100,000 South Dade residents moved away from the area and this migration changed the area's racial makeup. In studying race and social vulnerability in Hurricane Andrew, disaster researchers at Florida International University found that:

> some neighborhoods are located on the wrong side of the tracks, the bad side of town, or in slums and urban war zones. Others are on the right side of the tracks, uptown, upscale, or on the good side of town. Minorities, particularly black households, are disproportionately located in poor quality housing

segregated into low-valued neighborhoods. This segregation creates communities of fate that can take on added salience in a disaster context. Race and
ethnicity linked to housing quality—not because of ethnically based cultural
variations in housing preferences as is true in some societies—but because
race and ethnicity are still important determinants of the economic resources,
such as income and credit, critical for obtaining housing. (Peacock et al.,
1992:173)

Blacks were more vulnerable to hurricane damage due to residential segregation, location of their neighborhoods, and the conditions of their housing.
Andrew marginalized the already marginalized. Recovery was also problematic
for black Miami neighborhoods, where poorer quality building construction
and insufficient insurance made these neighborhoods more vulnerable. Post-
hurricane relocation was impeded for blacks. For example, "blacks were less
likely than Anglos to relocate after the hurricane not only because of possible
economic constraints, but because of barriers created by residential segregation"
(Peacock et al., 1992: 201).

Tropical Storm Alberto (1994)

In July 1994, Tropical Storm Alberto dumped at least 17 inches of rain on parts
of Georgia, flooding the basins of the Flint and Ocmulgee Rivers. The floods
were responsible for 30 deaths. Albany got the worst of Alberto. The flood displaced more than 22,000 residents in Albany and damaged 6,500 buildings,
having an estimated $1 billion impact in the state overall, including $500 million in damage to uninsured property and $200 million in agricultural losses
(Harrison, 1994).

Albany's nearly 80,000 residents make up most of the population of
Dougherty County. African Americans compose 65 percent of Albany's population. On average, Albany education level is lower than the state, and poverty is
greater than at the national level. Over 27 percent of the city's population is below
the poverty level. Medical facilities and transportation are also lacking.

The flood devastation in south-central Albany was so widespread that local
leaders feared many residents would not resettle there, thereby weakening black
voting strength in a city where blacks make up a majority of the population but
only in 1994 had won a majority of the seats on the city commission. Floodwaters
from the Flint River consumed nearly two-thirds of the 204-acre campus of historically black Albany State University, founded in 1903. Located on the banks
of the Flint River, the campus required a $112 million extensive construction
and renovation as the result of a devastating flood in 1994. The construction
created a new campus for Albany State students and the Albany community.

Seven weeks after floods ravaged southwest Georgia, the hardest hit sec-
tions of mostly black Albany had hardly begun (Harrison, 1994). The legacy of
racial separation and distrust tore people apart and delayed help from getting
to the most needy storm victims. Racial tension, which is generally high, was
heightened by the way disaster relief, rebuilding, and recovery were handled.

Black Farmers and USDA Disaster Relief (1997)

Black farmers have suffered severe damage from natural disasters such as floods, droughts, tornados, and hurricanes. They, like other farmers, suffer in the aftermath of the natural disasters with losses of crops, livestock, supplies, equipment, barns, and storage areas. These losses result in reduced family income, delayed production, stunted business growth, and for some, a total loss of their livelihood.

Unlike black farmers, white farmers get results from the United States Department of Agriculture (USDA) when they apply for disaster relief, emergency loans, and operating loans. Black farmers get the runaround. Melvin Bishop, a black farmer testifying at the Eatonton, Georgia stop of the Economic Human Rights Bus Tour along with several other black farmers, summarized the problem: "Even more devastating than the tornado was being denied USDA funds appropriated for emergency disaster and relief purposes. The process involved in waiting and standing in long lines to shuffle paper, completing forms and applications, was physically, mentally, and emotionally draining" (Mittal and Powell, 2000).

Melvin Bishop is among hundreds of black farmers who filed administrative complaints or lawsuits charging that for decades USDA loan officials have discouraged, delayed, or rejected loan applications because of their race. Federal officials have upheld these charges. The farmers say that such discrimination is a major reason that the nation's already tiny corps of black farmers is dwindling at three times the rate of farmers nationwide.

In 1997, African-American farmers brought a lawsuit against the USDA, charging it with discrimination in denying them access to loans and subsidies mandated by law. The lawsuit was filed in August 1997 on behalf of 4,000 of the nation's 17,000 black farmers and former farmers. A consent decree was signed in January 1999. The estimated cost of the settlement ranges from $400 million to more than $2 billion (Estes, 2001).

Hurricane Floyd, Eastern North Carolina (1999)

Hurricane Floyd pounded more than 30 North Carolina counties on September 1999 and dropped an estimated 15 to 20 inches of rain. Floyd left 17,000 homes uninhabitable, 56,000 damaged, and 47,000 people in temporary shelters in eastern North Carolina (Wing et al., 2002). Eastern North Carolina is a poor rural area with large concentration of African Americans.

Hurricane Floyd flooded the banks of the Tar River, drowning Princeville, the nation's first town chartered by blacks in the United States. Princeville is located in Edgecombe County, which was 57.5 percent black according to the 2000 census. Much of the town was lost when flooding from back to back hurricanes hit the all-black town. Before the flood struck, Princeville was a town of 2,100 residents, 850 homes, 30 businesses, and 3 churches. The town covers 40 streets spread over 1.3 square miles.

Hurricane Floyd's floodwater exposed the people to contaminants from a variety of sources, including municipal solid waste facilities, sewage treatment

facilities, hazardous waste facilities, underground storage tanks containing petroleum products, and thousands of dead hogs. More than six years after Hurricane
Floyd, many black families were still suffering from respiratory infections, skin
irritations, moldy homes, and unmet home repair needs that leave them vulnerable to future storms (Solow, 2004).

Hurricane Katrina, New Orleans (2005)

On August 29, 2005, Hurricane Katrina laid waste New Orleans, an American city
built below sea level in 1718 on the banks of the Mississippi River. New Orleans,
like most major urban centers, was in peril long before Katrina floodwaters
devastated the city (Pastor et al., 2006). Katrina was complete in its devastation
of homes, neighborhoods, institutions, and community. Flooding in the New
Orleans metropolitan area largely resulted from breached levees and flood walls
(Gabe et al., 2005). The city's coastal wetlands, which normally serve as a natural
buffer against storm surges, had been destroyed by offshore drilling, Mississippi
River levees, canals for navigation, pipelines, highway projects, agricultural and
urban development.

Over the past century more than 2,000 of the original 7,000 square miles of
coastal marsh and swamp forests that formed the coastal delta of the Mississippi
River have vanished. An average of 34 square miles of south Louisiana land,
mostly marsh, has disappeared each year for the past five decades. More than 80
percent of the nation's coastal wetland loss in this time occurred in Louisiana.
From 1932 to 2000, the state lost 1,900 square miles of land to the Gulf of Mexico
(Tibbetts, 2006). Hurricane Katrina pushed New Orleans closer to the coast
because of extensive erosion at the coastal edge. This is a national problem. A
range of groups, including researchers, policymakers, and environmentalists,
are calling for restoration of wetlands and barrier islands to help protect New
Orleans the next time a hurricane strikes.

Emergency planners at FEMA have known for decades which populations
are most vulnerable and what types of people are most likely to be left behind
in disasters—individuals who are poor, sick, elderly, young, or of color. In 2001,
FEMA experts ranked a hurricane striking New Orleans, a terrorist attack on
New York City, and a strong earthquake in San Francisco as the top three catastrophic disasters most likely to occur in the country (Berger, 2001).

A 2004 FEMA Hurricane Pam simulation foretold the Katrina disaster
(Federal Emergency Management Agency, 2004). The exercise was held at the
State Emergency Operations Center in Baton Rouge using realistic weather and
damage information developed by the National Weather Service, the US Army
Corps of Engineers, the Louisiana State University Hurricane Center, and other
state and federal agencies to help develop joint response plans for a catastrophic
hurricane in Louisiana.

The disaster response team developed action plans in critical areas such as
search and rescue, medical care, sheltering, temporary housing, school restoration, and debris management. Few of Hurricane Pam's simulation action plan

preparedness tasks had been implemented prior to Hurricane Katrina. Writer Joel K. Bourne, Jr. (2004) also predicted with eerie accuracy the disaster that would follow if a powerful hurricane would strike New Orleans.

Cleaning up after Katrina

Katrina has been described as one of the worst environmental disasters in American history. Some commentators predicted that it would take the "mother of all toxic cleanups" to handle the untold tons of "lethal goop" left by the storm and flooding ("The Mother," 2005). However, the billion-dollar question facing New Orleans is which neighborhoods will get cleaned up, which ones will be left contaminated, and which ones will be targeted as new sites to dump storm debris and waste from flooded homes.

Hurricane Katrina left debris across a 90,000-square-mile disaster area in Louisiana, Mississippi, and Alabama, compared with a 16-acre tract in New York on September 11, 2001 (Luther, 2006). Louisiana parishes had 25 times more debris than was collected after the 9/11 terrorist attack in 2001. More than 110,000 of New Orleans' 180,000 homes were flooded, and half sat for days or weeks in more than six feet of water (Nossiter, 2005). An additional 350,000 automobiles had to be drained of oil and gasoline and then recycled; 60,000 boats were destroyed; and 300,000 underground fuel tanks and 42,000 tons of hazardous waste must be cleaned up and properly disposed at licensed facilities. Government officials peg the numbers of cars lost in New Orleans alone at 145,000 (Dart, 2006).

The Politics of Waste Disposal

What has been cleaned up, what gets left behind, and where the waste is disposed of appears to be linked more to political science and sociology than to toxicology, epidemiology, and hydrology. Weeks after Katrina struck, the Louisiana Department of Environmental Quality (LDEQ) allowed New Orleans to open the 200-acre Old Gentilly landfill to dump construction and demolition waste from the storm (Burdeau, 2005). Federal regulators ordered the unlined landfill closed in the 1980s. In December 2005, more than 2,000 truckloads of debris were entering the landfill in east New Orleans every day (O'Driscoll, 2006).

Just four months after the storm, the Old Gentilly landfill grew about 100 feet high. LDEQ officials insist that the old landfill, which is still operating, meets all standards. But residents and environmentalists disagree. Even some high ranking elected officials expressed fear that reopening of the Old Gentilly landfill could create an ecological nightmare (Russell, 2005). In November 2005, four days after environmentalists filed a lawsuit to block the dumping, the landfill caught fire.

In April 2006, the Army Corps of Engineers and the Louisiana Department of Environmental Quality issued permits that allowed Waste Management Inc. to open and operate a construction and demolition-related material landfill in New Orleans East. The new landfill is located on Chef Menteur Highway, which runs through much of New Orleans East, where the majority of the population is

African American. Waste Management pledged to give the city 22 percent of all revenue derived from the site.

Every week, Waste Management picks up an average of 45 pounds of trash from each home, 20 more pounds per home than pre-Katrina. The new landfill could accept as much as 6.5 million cubic yards of vegetation and other debris generated by Katrina, including roofing materials, wallboard, and demolition debris, which are considered less harmful than other types of waste.

But after Katrina, the state LDEQ expanded its definition of what is considered construction debris to include potentially contaminated material (Luther, 2005). Yet, regulators acknowledge the potential toxic contamination threat from storm-related wastes. Much of the disaster debris from flooded neighborhoods in New Orleans has been mixed to the point that separation is either very difficult or essentially impossible.

Government officials assert that the risk of hazardous materials being dumped at the new Chef Menteur landfill is insignificant and that current sorting practices are adequate to keep hazardous waste out of the landfill. They also insist protective liners are not needed for construction and demolition landfills because demolition debris is cleaner than other rubbish (Eaton, 2006). Construction and demolition landfills are not required under federal law to have the protective liners required for municipal landfills, which are expected to receive a certain amount of hazardous household waste. LDEQ provided a permit for the landfill.

Landfill opponents think otherwise. Many fear the government's willingness to waive regulations will mean motor oil, batteries, electronics, ink toner, chlorine bleach, drain cleaners, and other noxious material will almost certainly wind up at the unlined landfills (Russell, 2006). The Chef Highway landfill is about four miles west of the Old Gentilly landfill and just 0.8 miles from the nearest apartments in a mostly Vietnamese-American community. More than a thousand Vietnamese-American families live less than two miles from the edge of the new landfill. Residents view the landfill as a roadblock to community recovery and rebuilding. After mounting public pressure, the Chef Menteur landfill was shut down by Mayor Nagin in August 2006.

A "Safe" Road Home

Two years after Katrina, one-third of New Orleans' residents had not made it back home (Liu and Plyer, 2007). New Orleans' population stood at 223,388 in July 2007—or about 68 percent of its pre-Katrina July 2005 population. The road home for many Katrina survivors has been a bumpy one, largely due to slow government actions to distribute the $116 billion in federal aid to help residents rebuild. Only about $35 billion has been appropriated for long-term rebuilding. Most of the Katrina money coming from Washington has not gone to those most in need—and the funding squeeze is stopping much of the Gulf coast from coming back (Kromm and Sturgis, 2007).

As of August 6, 2007, only 22 percent of the applicants to Louisiana's Road Home program had gone to closing. More than 180,424 Road Home applications had been received—far higher than the 123,000 the program was originally designed to handle (the Road Home program was designed to provide compensation to Louisiana homeowners affected by Hurricanes Katrina or Rita for the damage to their homes. The program afforded eligible homeowners up to $150,000 in compensation for their losses to get back into their homes) (LOCD). From January 2007 to August 2007, the average benefit per applicant had fallen by more than $12,000—from a high of $81,000 to $68,734.

In March 2006, seven months after the storm slammed ashore, organizers of "A Safe Way Back Home" initiative, the Deep South Center for Environmental Justice at Dillard University (DSCEJ), and the United Steel Workers (USW), undertook a proactive pilot neighborhood cleanup project—the first of its kind in New Orleans (Wright, 2006). The cleanup project, located in the 8100 block of Aberdeen Road in New Orleans East, removed several inches of tainted soil from front and backyards, replacing the soil with new sod, and disposing of the contaminated dirt in a safe manner.

Residents who choose to remove the top soil from their yards—which contains sediments left by flooding—find themselves in a Catch-22 situation, with the LDEQ, and EPA insisting the soil in their yards is not contaminated and the local landfill operators refusing to dispose of the soil because they suspect it is contaminated. This bottleneck of what to do with the topsoil was unresolved a year and a half after the devastating flood.

Although government officials insist the dirt in residents' yards is safe, Church Hill Downs, Inc., the owners of New Orleans' fairgrounds, felt it was not safe for its million-dollar thoroughbred horses to race on. (The fairgrounds is the nation's third-oldest track; only Saratoga and Pimlico have been racing longer.) The owners hauled off soil tainted by Hurricane Katrina's floodwaters and rebuilt a grandstand roof ripped off by the storm's wind (Martell, 2006). The fairgrounds opened on Thanksgiving Day, 2006. Surely, if tainted soil is not safe for horses, it is not safe for people—especially children who play and dig in the dirt.

The Safe Way Back Home demonstration project serves as a catalyst for a series of activities that will attempt to reclaim the New Orleans East community following the devastation caused by Hurricane Katrina. It is the government's responsibility to provide the resources required to address areas of environmental concern and to assure that the workforce is protected. However, residents are not waiting for the government to ride in on a white horse to rescue them and clean up their neighborhoods.

The DSCEJ/USW coalition received dozens of requests and inquiries from New Orleans East homeowners associations to help clean up their neighborhoods block-by-block. State and federal officials labeled the voluntary "A Safe Way Back Home" neighborhood cleanup efforts as "scaremongering" (Simmons, 2006). Despite barriers and red tape, thousands of Katrina evacuees are slowly moving back into New Orleans' damaged homes or setting up travel trailers in their yards. Homeowners are gutting their houses, treating the mold, fixing roofs and siding, and slowly getting their lives back in order. One of the main questions returning residents have: "Is this place safe?"

Residents are getting mixed signals from government agencies. The Louisiana Department of Environmental Quality announced that there is no unacceptable long-term health risk directly attributable to environmental contamination resulting from the storm. Yet, these same officials warn residents to keep children from playing in bare dirt, and advise them to cover bare dirt with grass, bushes, or 4 to 6 inches of lead-free wood chips, mulch, soil, or sand. EPA and LDEQ officials tested soil samples from the neighborhood in December 2005 and claim there was no immediate cause for concern. Although lead, arsenic, and other toxic chemicals turned up in samples, state toxicologists describe the soil in New Orleans as consistent with what they saw before Katrina (Williams, 2006).

In sharp contrast, Natural Resources Defense Council (NRDC) scientists arrived at different conclusions (Solomon and Rotkin-Ellman, 2005). NRDC's analyses of soil and air quality after Hurricane Katrina revealed dangerously high levels of diesel fuel, lead, and other contaminants in Gentilly, Bywater, Orleans Parish, and other New Orleans neighborhoods.

In August 2006, nearly a year after Katrina struck, the federal EPA gave New Orleans and surrounding communities a clean bill of health, while pledging to monitor a handful of toxic hot spots (Brown, 2006). EPA and LDEQ officials concluded that Katrina did not cause any appreciable contamination that was not already there. Although EPA tests confirmed widespread lead in the soil—a prestorm problem in 40 percent of New Orleans—the EPA dismissed residents' calls to address this problem as outside the agency's mission.

In June 2007, the US General Accounting Office (GAO) issued a report criticizing EPA's handling of contamination in post-Katrina New Orleans and the Gulf Coast (GAO, 2007). The GAO found inadequate monitoring for asbestos around demolition and renovation sites. Additionally, the GAO investigation uncovered that "key" information released to the public about environmental contamination was neither timely nor adequate, and in some cases, easily misinterpreted to the public's detriment.

The GAO (2007) also found that the EPA did not state until August 2006 that its 2005 report, which said that the great majority of the data showed that adverse health effects would not be expected from exposure to sediments from previously flooded areas—applied to short-term visits, such as to view damage to homes.

In March 2007, a coalition of community and environmental groups collected over 130 soil samples in Orleans Parish. Testing was conducted by Natural Resources Defense Council (Fields et al., 2007). Sampling was done at 65 sites in residential neighborhoods where post-Katrina EPA testing had previously shown elevated concentrations of arsenic in soils. Sampling was also done at 15 playgrounds and 19 schools. Six school sites had levels of arsenic in excess of the LDEQ's soil screening value for arsenic. The LDEQ soil screening value of 12 milligrams per kilogram (mg/kg) normally requires additional sampling, further investigation, and a site-specific risk assessment. It is clear that the levels of arsenic in the sediment are unacceptably high for residential neighborhoods.

Toxic FEMA Trailers

Shortly after Katrina, FEMA purchased about 102,000 travel trailers for $2.6 billion or roughly $15,000 each (Spake, 2007). Surprisingly, there were reports of residents becoming ill in these trailers due to the release of potentially dangerous levels of formaldehyde. In fact, formaldehyde is the industrial chemical (found in glues, plastics, building materials, composite wood, plywood panels, and particle board) that was used to manufacture the travel trailers.

In Mississippi, FEMA received 46 complaints of individuals who indicated that they had symptoms of formaldehyde exposure, which include eye, nose, and throat irritation, nausea, skin rashes, sinus infections, depression, asthma attacks, headaches, insomnia, intestinal problems, memory-impairment, and breathing difficulties. The Sierra Club conducted tests of 31 trailers and found that 29 of them had unsafe levels of formaldehyde. According to the Sierra Club, 83 percent of the trailers tested in Alabama, Louisiana, and Mississippi had formaldehyde levels above the EPA limit of 0.10 parts per million.

Even though FEMA received numerous complaints about toxic trailers, the agency only tested one occupied trailer to determine the levels of formaldehyde in it (Committee on Oversight and Government Reform, 2007). The test confirmed that the levels of formaldehyde were extraordinarily high and presented an immediate health risk to the displaced occupants. The monitored levels were 75 times higher than what the National Institute of Occupational Safety and Health recommend for adult exposure in industrial workplaces. Unfortunately, FEMA did not test any more occupied trailers and released a public statement discounting any risk associated with formaldehyde exposure (Babington, 2007).

FEMA deliberately neglected to investigate any reports of high levels of formaldehyde in trailers so as to bolster FEMA's litigation position just in case individuals affected by their negligence decided to sue them. More than 500 hurricane survivors and evacuees in Louisiana are pursuing legal action against the trailer manufacturers for being exposed to the toxic chemical formaldehyde. Two years after Katrina hit, 46,700 families who lost their homes to Hurricane Katrina lived in government-issued trailers—roughly 33,000 of those families were in Louisiana and about 13,000 were in Mississippi.

In July 2007, FEMA stopped buying and selling disaster relief trailers because of the formaldehyde contamination. FEMA administrator R. David Paulison admitted that the trailers used by displaced Katrina residents were toxic and concluded that the agency should have moved faster in addressing the health concerns of residents (Cruz, 2007). In August 2007, FEMA began moving families out of the toxic trailers and finding them new rental housing. On November 2007, a federal judge in New Orleans ordered FEMA and Paulison, its top administrator, to submit a "detailed plan" for testing the trailers for formaldehyde levels. The Centers for Disease Control and Prevention, the lead agency in developing parameters for testing the travel trailers, was scheduled to test 500 randomly selected travel trailers and mobile homes for the toxin, starting December 21, 2007 (Kim, 2007).

Post-Katrina Levee Protection

An Army Corps of Engineers flood risk report published in 2007 shows a disproportionately large swath of black New Orleans once again is left vulnerable to future flooding (Army Corps of Engineers Interagency Performance Evaluations Task Force, 2007). After three years and $7 billion of levee repairs, the Army Corps of Engineers has estimated that there is a 1 in 100 annual chance that about one-third of the city will be flooded with as much as six feet of water (Schwartz, 2007).

The mainly African-American parts of New Orleans are still likely to be flooded in a major storm. Increased levee protection correlates closely with race of neighborhoods; black neighborhoods such as the Ninth Ward, Gentilly, and New Orleans East receive little if any increased flood protection. These disparities could lead insurers and investors to think twice about supporting the rebuilding efforts in vulnerable black areas.

The Lakeview area resident can expect 5.5 feet of increased levee protection. This translates into 5.5 feet less water than they received from Katrina. Lakeview is mostly white and affluent; New Orleans East is mostly black and middle class. This same scenario holds true for the mostly black Lower Ninth Ward, Upper Ninth Ward, and Gentilly neighborhoods. There is a racial component to the post-Katrina levee protection. Whether you are rich, poor, or middle class, if you are a black resident of New Orleans, you are less protected and you have received less increased flood protection from the federal government than the more white and affluent community of Lakeview.

THE RACIAL DIVIDE IN DISASTER RELIEF

Using case studies dating back some 70 years, this paper uses New Orleans, the Gulf coast region, and the southern United States as a historical backdrop to answer the research questions of emergency response and race. Clearly, there is a racial divide in the way the US government responds to various types of emergencies in black and white communities. Government response to weather-related (natural disasters), epidemics, industrial accidents, toxic contamination, and bioterrorism threats points to clear preferences given to whites over blacks.

Differential response is linked to "white privilege" that provides preferences for whites while at the same time disadvantaging blacks, and making them more vulnerable to disasters and public health threats. Hurricane Katrina exposed the systematic weakness of the nation's emergency preparedness and homeland security. There can be no homeland security if people do not have homes to go to and if they lose trust in government to respond to an emergency in an effective, fair, and just manner.

What gets cleaned up and where the waste is disposed are key environmental justice and equity issues. Pollution from chemical plants located in populated areas poses a health threat to nearby residents. The plants themselves also pose a threat as possible targets for terrorism. Although both black and white hurricane survivors find themselves in similar circumstances (displacement from their homes), blacks, because of institutional discrimination, may face different experiences and challenges than whites in rebuilding their lives, homes, businesses, institutions, and communities. Thousands of Gulf Coast Louisiana, Mississippi, and Alabama residents also lost their homes in the hurricane. The relief and recovery efforts are not adequately meeting the needs of many African-American survivors in the disaster zone. Many of these same individuals and communities were "invisible" before Katrina struck. At every class level, racial discrimination artificially limits opportunities and choices for African Americans. Unfortunately, this sad fact of American life was not washed away by the floodwaters of Katrina.

Clearly, race skews government response to emergencies, whether natural or man-made, such as weather-related disasters, toxic contamination, public health threats, industrial accidents, and terrorism threats, with whites seeing faster action and better results than blacks and other people of color. No Americans, black or white, rich or poor, young or old, sick or healthy, should have to endure needless suffering from unnatural disasters.

Research contained in this paper was supported by a grant from the Ford Foundation. The views expressed are those of the author and do not reflect those of the foundation.

CRITICAL THINKING QUESTIONS

In this reading, Bullard describes examples of what he calls "environmental racism" and "unnatural disasters." What features characterize these examples as racist and unnatural? Can you think of other examples of environmental injustice that are not related to the weather?

REFERENCES

Army Corps of Engineers Interagency Performance Evaluations Task Force (IPEI). *Risk and Reliability Report* (June 20, 2007) <nolarisk.usace.army.mil>.
Babington, Charles. "FEMA Slow to Test Toxicity of Trailers." *USA Today*, July 19, 2007.
Baker, Earl J. *Hurricane Hugo, Puerto Rico, the Virgin Islands, and Charleston, South Carolina, September 17–22, 1989.* Washington, D.C.: National Academies Press, 1994 <www.nap.edu/books/0309044758/html/166.html>.
Barnes, Jay. *Florida's Hurricane History.* Chapel Hill: University of North Carolina Press, 1998.
Barry, John M *Rising Tide: The Great Mississippi Flood of 1927 and How It Changed America.* New York: Simon and Schuster, 1998.
Berger, Eric. "Keeping Its Head above Water." *Houston Chronicle*, December 1, 2001: A29.
Bourne, Joel K. Jr. "Gone with the Water." *National Geographic* (October 2004): 92.

Brochu, Nicole Sterghos. "Florida's Forgotten Storm: The Hurricane of 1928." *The Sun-Sentinel*, September 14, 2003.

Brown, Matthew. "Final EPA Report Deems N.O. Safe." *The Times Picayune*, August 19, 2006.

Bullard, Robert D. *The Quest for Environmental Justice: Human Rights and the Politics of Pollution.* San Francisco: Sierra Club Books, 2005.

Bullard, Robert D., and Glenn S. Johnson. *Just Transportation: Dismantling Race and Class Barriers to Mobility.* Gabriola Island, B.C.: New Society Publishers, 1997.

Burdeau, Cain. "New Orleans Area Becoming a Dumping Ground." *Associated Press*, October 31, 2005. Cannon, Terry, Ian Davis, Piers Blaikie, Ben Wisner, eds. *At Risk: National Hazards, People's Vulnerability, and Disasters.* New York: Routledge, 2004.

City of New Orleans. *City of New Orleans Comprehensive Emergency Management Plan.* City of New Orleans, 2005. Available at <www.cityofno.com>.

Cruz, Gilbert. 2007. "Grilling FEMA over Its Toxic Trailers." Time.com. July 19, 2007 <http://www.time.com/time/nation/article/0,8599,1645312,00.html>.

Dart, Bob, "Junk Cars, Boats Slow Recovery in Big Easy." *The Atlanta Journal-Constitution*, July 5, 2006:A1.

Department of Homeland Security (DHS). *National Plan Review, Phase 2 Report.* Washington, D.C.: DHS, 16 June 2006 <www.emforum.org/news/06061601.htm>.

Dyson, Michael Eric. *Come Hell or High Water. Hurricane Katrina and the Color of Disaster.* New York: Basic Books, 2006.

Eaton, Leslie. "A New Landfill in New Orleans Sets Off a Battle." *The New York Times*, May 8, 2006:A1.

Eggler, Bruce. "RTA Back on Track Slowly, Surely." *The Times Picayune*, October 14, 2005: B1.

Elliston, Jon. "Disaster in the Making." *The Orlando Weekly,* October 21, 2004.

Estes, Carol. "Second Chance for Black Farmers." *Yes! Magazine* (Summer 2001).

Fields, Leslie, Albert Huang, Gina Solomon, Miriam Rotkin-Ellman, and Patirce Simms, *Katrina's Wake: Arsenic-Laced Schools and Playgrounds Put New Orleans Children at Risk.* New York: NRDC, August 2007.

Federal Emergency Management Agency (FEMA). "Hurricane Pam Exercise Concludes." Press Release. July 23, 2004 <www.fema.gov/news/newsrelease.fema?id=13051>.

Finch, Susan. "Ag Street Landfill Case Gets Ruling: City Ordered to Pay Residents of Toxic Site." *The Times-Picayune,* January 27, 2006: A1.

Gabe, Thomas, Gene Falk, Maggie McCarthy, and Virginia W. Mason. *Hurricane Katrina: Social-Demographic Characteristics of Impacted Areas.* Congressional Research Service. Report no. RL33141. Washington, D.C.: Congressional Research Service, November 2005.

General Accounting Office. *Hurricane Katrina: EPA's Current and Future Environmental Protection Efforts Could Be Enhanced by Addressing Issues and Challenges Faced on the Gulf Coast.* Washington, D.C.: GAO Report to congressional Committees, June 2007.

Harrison, Eric. "Legacy if Racism Dams Up Post-Flood Effort in Georgia." *The Los Angeles Times,* August 26, 1994.

Hurston, Zora Neal. *Their Eyes Were Watching God.* New York: Harper Perennial Classics, 1998.

Jackson, Stephen "Un/natural Disasters, Here and There." Understanding Katrina: Perspectives from the Social Sciences. Social Science Research Council <http://understandingkatrina.ssrc.org/Jackson/>.

Kaniasty. K., and F. H. Norris. "In Search of Altruistic Community: Patterns of Social Support Mobilization Following Hurricane Hugo." *American Journal of Community Psychology* 4 (August 23, 1995): 447–477.

Kim, Eun Kyung. "Air Testing in FEMA Trailers Begins Next Week." *USA Today,* December 13, 2007.

Kleinberg, Eliot, *Black Cloud: The Deadly Hurricane of 1928.* New York: Carroll and Graf Publishers, 2003.

Klinkenberg, Jeff. "A Storm of Memories." *The St. Petersburg Times,* July 12, 1992: 1F.

Kromm, Chris, and Sue Sturgis. *Blueprint for Gulf Renewal: The Katrina Crisis and a community Agenda for Action.* Durham, N.C.: Institute for Southern Studies, August/September 2007.

Liu, Amy, and Allison Plyer. *The New Orleans Index: A Review of Key Indicators of Recovery Two Years after Katrina.* Washington, D.C.: Brookings Institution and Greater New Orleans Community Data Center, August 2007.

Litman, Todd. *Lesson from Katrina and Rita: What Major Disasters Can Teach Transportation Planners.* Victoria, B.C.: Victoria Transport Policy Institute, September 30, 2005.

LOCD. Disaster Recover Unit <http://www.doa.louisiana.gov/cdbg/DRhousing.htm>.

Lyttle, Alicia. "Agricultural Street Landfill Environmental Justice Case Study." University of Michigan School of Natural Resource and Environment <www/umich.edu/~, Desnre492/Jones/agstreet.htm>.

Luther, Linda. *Disaster Debris Removal after Hurricane Katrina: Status and Associated Issue.* Washington. D.C.: Congressional Research Service, June 16, 2006.

Martell, Brett. "Horse Racing Returns to New Orleans." *Associated Press,* November 23, 2006.

McKinnon, Jesse. *The Black Population: Census 2000 Brief.* Washington, D.C.: Department of Commerce, August 2001.

Mittal, Anuradha, and Joan Powell. "The Last Plantation." *Food First* (Winter 2000) <http://www.foodfirst.org/pubs/backgrdrs/2000/w00v6n1.html>.

Moran, Kate. "Public Transit on Agenda at Joint N.O., Jeff Session." *The Times Picayune,* November 6, 2006.

"The Mother of All Toxic Cleanups." *Business Week* (September 26, 2005).

Nossiter, Adam. "Thousands of Demolitions Are Likely in New Orleans." *The New York Times* October 2, 2005.

O'Driscoll, Patrick. "Cleanup Crews Tackle Katrina's Nasty Leftovers." *USA Today,* December 12, 2005.

Pastor, Manuel, Robert D. Bullard, James K. Boyce, Alice Fothergill, Rachel Morello Frosch, and Beverly Wright. *In the Wake of the Storm: Environment, Disaster, and Race after Katrina.* New York: Russell Sage Foundation, May 2006.

Peacock, Walter Gillis, Betty Hearn Morrow, and Hugh Gladwin. *Hurricane Andrew: Ethnicity, Gender, and the Sociology of Disasters.* Miami: Florida International University, Laboratory for Social and Behavioral Research, 1992.

Pittman, Craig. "Storm's Howl Fills the Ears of Survivors." *St. Petersburg Times* August 18, 2002.

Remnick, David. "High Water: How Presidents and Citizens React to Disaster." *The New Yorker* (October 3, 2005).

Riccardi, Nicholas. "Many of Louisiana Dead over 60." *The Atlanta Journal-Constitution,* November 6, 2005: A6.

Russell, Gordon. "Landfill Reopening Is Raising New Stink," *The Time-Picayune,* November 21, 2005.

———."Chef Menteur Landfill Testing Called a Farce: Critics Say Debris Proposal 'Would Be a Useless Waste of Time.'" *The Times-picayune,* May 29, 2006.

Sanchez. Thomas W. Rick Stolz, and Jacinta S. Ma. *Moving to Equity: Addressing Inequitable Effects of Transportation Policies on Minorities.* Cambridge: The Civil Rights Project, Harvard University, June 2003.

Schwartz, John. "Army Corps Details Flood Risks Facing New Orleans." *The New York Times,* June 20, 2007.

Simmons, Ann S. "New Orleans Activists Starting from the Ground Up." *The Los Angeles Times,* March 24, 2006.

Solomon, Gina M., and Miriam Rotkin-Ellman. *Contaminants in New Orleans Sediments: An Analysis of EPA Data.* New York: NRDC, February 2006.

Solow, Barbara. "Cracks in the System." *The Independent Weekly,* September 8, 2004 <indyweek.com/durham/2004-09-07/cover.html>.

Spake, Amanda. "Dying for a Home: Toxic Trailers Are Making Katrina Refugees III." *The Nation* (February 15, 2007).

State of Louisiana. *Southeast Louisiana Hurricane Evacuation and Sheltering Plan.* Baton Rouge: State of Louisiana, 2000 <www.ohsep.louisiana.gov/plans/EOPSupplementala. pdf>.

Steinberg, Ted. *Acts of God: The Unnatural History of Natural Disasters in America.* New York: Oxford University Press. 2003.

Tanneeru, Manav. "It's Official: 2005 Hurricanes Blew Records Away." CNN.com. December 30, 2005 <www.cnn.com/2005/WEATHER/12/19/hurricane.season.ender/>.

Tibbetts, John. "Louisiana's Wetlands: A Lesson in Nature Appreciation." *Environmental Health Perspective* 114 (January 2006): A40–A43.

U.S. House of Representatives, Committee on Oversight and Government Reform. "Committee Probes FEMA's Response to Reports of Toxic Trailers." July 19, 2007.

Williams, Leslie. "Groups Warn about Arsenic in Soil." *The Times Picayune,* March 24, 2006.

Wing, Steve, Stephanie Freedman, and Lawrence Band. "The Potential of Flooding on Confined Animal Feeding Operations in Eastern North Carolina." *Environmental Health Perspective* 110 (April 2002).

Worldwatch Institute. "Fact Sheet: The Impacts of Weather and Climate Change." September 23, 2003 <www.worldwatch.org/press/news/2003/09/15>.

Wright, Beverly. "A Safe Way Back Home." Deep South Center for Environmental Justice, Dillard University, March 29, 2007 <www.dscej.org/asafewayhome.htm>.

Credits

Chapter 1
Mills, C. Wright, *The Sociological Imagination*, New York: Oxford University Press, 2000 (orig. 1959), pp. 3–13. Reprinted by permission.

Chapter 2
Spector, Malcolm and John I. Kitsuse, *Constructing Social Problems*, New Brunswick, NJ: Transaction Publishers, 2008, (orig. 1977), pp. 74–81. Reprinted by permission.

Chapter 3
Heiner, Robert, *Social Problems: An Introduction to Critical Constructionism*, 2nd ed., New York: Oxford University Press, 2006, pp. 1–11. Reprinted by permission.

Chapter 4
McChesney, Robert W., *The Political Economy of Media: Enduring Issues, Emerging Dilemmas*, New York: Monthly Review Press, 2008, pp. 25–38 (edited). Copyright 2008 by MR Press. Reprinted by permission of Monthly Review Foundation.

Chapter 5
Faux, Jeff, *The Governing Class: How America's Bipartisan Elite Lost Our Future and What it Will Take to Win it Back*, Hoboken, NJ: John Wiley and Sons, pp. 59–75 (edited). Copyright 2006 by Jeff Faux. Reproduced with permission of John Wiley and Sons, Inc.

Chapter 6
Hacker, Jacob S., *The Great Risk Shift: The New Economic Insecurity and the Decline of the American Dream*, New York: Oxford University Press, 2006, pp. 11–34. Reprinted by permission.

Chapter 7
Kuttner, Robert, "The Copenhagen Consensus", Reprinted by permission of FOREIGN AFFAIRS (vol. 87, no. 2). Copyright 2008 by the Council of Foreign Relations, Inc. www.Foreign Affairs.org.

Chapter 8

Ferrante, Joan, "Global Inequality and the Challenges of Reducing Extreme Poverty," *Sociological Viewpoints*, Volume 22, Spring 2006. Reprinted with permission of the author and Pennsylvania Sociological Society.

Chapter 9

Gluckman, Amy, "Women and Wealth: A Primer," from *The Wealth Inequality Reader, 2nd ed.*, edited by Doallrs and Sense and United for a Fair Economy, Boston: Dollars and Sense—Economic Affairs Bureau, 2008, pp. 67–73. Reprinted by permission of *Dollars and Sense*, a progressive economics magazine <www.dollarsand sense.org>.

Chapter 10

Coleman, Isobel, "The Payoff from Women's Rights," Reprinted by permission of FOREIGN AFFAIRS (vol. 83, no. 3). Copyright 2004 by the Council of Foreign Relations, Inc. www.Foreign Affairs.org.

Chapter 11

Liu, Meizhu, "Doubly Divided: The Racial Wealth Gap," from *The Wealth Inequality Reader, 2nd ed.*, edited by Dollars and Sense and United for a Fair Economy, Boston: Dollars and Sense—Economic Affairs Bureau, 2008, pp. 44–51. Reprinted by permission of *Dollars and Sense*, a progressive economics magazine <www.dollarsand sense.org>.

Chapter 12

Engel, Michael, "School Finance: Inequality Persists," from *The Wealth Inequality Reader, 2nd ed.*, edited by Dollars and Sense and United for a Fair Economy, Boston: Dollars and Sense—Economic Affairs Bureau, 2008, pp. 92–99. Reprinted by permission of *Dollars and Sense*, a progressive economics magazine <www.dollarsand sense.org>.

Chapter 13

Russell, James W., *Double Standard: Social Policy in Europe and the United States*, Lanham, MD: Rowman and Littlefield Publishing, 2006, pp. 123–131. Reprinted by permission.

Chapter 14

Coontz, Stephanie, *The Way We Never Were: American Families and the Nostalgia Trap*, New York: Basic Books, 1992, pp. 8–22 (edited). Reprinted by permission of Basic Books, a member of Perseus Book Group.

Chapter 15

Drago, Robert W., *Striking a Balance: Work, Family, Life*, Boston: Dollars and Sense, 2007, pp. 23–40. Reprinted by permission of *Dollars and Sense*, a progressive economics magazine <www.dollarsand sense.org>.

Chapter 16

Shahmehri, Brittany, "More than Welcome: Families Come First in Sweden," originally published in *Mothering Magazine*, vol. 109, 2001. Reprinted by permission of the author.

Chapter 17

Popenoe, David and Barbara Defoe Whitehead. Life Without Children. Copyright 2008 by the National Marriage Project at Rutgers University. Reprinted by permission of the National Marriage Project.

Chapter 18

Reiman, Jeffrey, *The Rich Get Richer and the Poor Get Prison: Ideology, Class and Criminal Justice*. Boston: Pearson/Allyn and Bacon, 2007. Reiman, RICH GET RICHER AND THE POOR GET POORER, 2007 Reproduced by permission of Pearson Education, Inc.

Chapter 19

Mauer, Marc and Ryan S. King, "Schools and Prisons: How Far Have We Come Since Brown V. Board of Education?" Washington, DC: The Sentencing Project, 2004 (updated). Reprinted by permission.

Chapter 20

Heiner, Robert, "The Growth of Incarceration in the Netherlands," *Federal Sentencing Reporter*, vol. 17, no. 3 (February 2005), pp. 227–230. © The Vera Institute of Justice. Published by the University of California Press. Reprinted with permission.

Chapter 21

Beiser, Vince, "First, Reduce Harm," *Miller-McCune Magazine*, November/December 2008, pp. 61–71. Reprinted by permission of Miller-McCune Magazine.

Chapter 22

60 Minutes, "Rx Drugs," © 1992 CBS Worldwide, Inc., All rights reserved, Originally broadcast on 60 MINUTES on December 27, 1992 over the CBS Television Network. Reproduced by permission.

Chapter 23

McKibben, Bill, "Reversal of Fortune," *Mother Jones*, vol. 32, no. 2. © 2007, Foundation for National Progress. Reprinted by permission.

Chapter 24

Heiner, Robert, *Social Problems: An Introduction to Critical Constructionism*, 3rd ed., New York: Oxford University Press, 2010, pp. 163–173. Reprinted by permission.

Chapter 25

World Resources Institute, United Nations Development Programme, United Nations Environment Programme, The World Bank, World Resources Institute, *World Resources 2005: The Wealth of the Poor: Managing Ecosystems to Fight Poverty*, Washington, DC: World Resources Institute, 2005, pp. 13–26 (edited). Reprinted by permission.

Chapter 26

Bullard, Robert, "Differential Vulnerabilities: Environmental and Economic Inequality and Government Response to Unnatural Disasters," *Social Research*, vol. 75, no. 3, Fall 2008. Reprinted by permission.